The Focus on the Family
Parents' Guide to the Spiritual Growth of Children

PARENTS' GUIDE TO THE

Spiritual Growth of Children

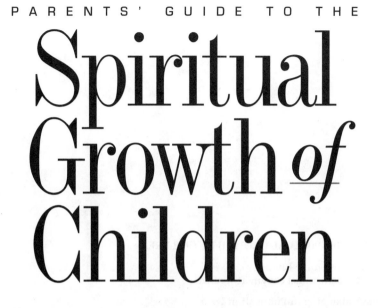

GENERAL EDITORS

John Trent, Ph.D.

Rick Osborne

Kurt Bruner

Tyndale House Publishers,
WHEATON, ILLINOIS

Heritage Builders

PARENTS' GUIDE TO THE SPIRITUAL GROWTH OF CHILDREN

Copyright © 2000 by Focus on the Family.
    All rights reserved. International copyright secured.

Library of Congress Cataloging-in-Publication Data

Focus on the Family's parents' guide to the spiritual growth of children /
general editors John Trent, Rick Osborne, Kurt Bruner.
            p. cm.
    ISBN 1-56179-791-X
    1. Christian education of children. 2. Parenting—Religious
aspects—Christianity. I. Title: Parents' guide to the spiritual growth
of children. II. Trent, John. III. Osborne, Rick. IV. Bruner, Kurt D.
V. Focus on the Family (Organization)

BV1475.2 .F59 2000
248.8'45—dc21

                                                            00-037788

A Focus on the Family book published by
    Tyndale House Publishers, Wheaton, Illinois.

Unless otherwise noted, scripture quotations are taken from the HOLY
    BIBLE, NEW INTERNATIONAL VERSION®. NIV®. Copyright © 1973,
    1978, 1984 by International Bible Society. Used by permission of
    Zondervan Publishing House. All rights reserved.

Scripture quotations marked (NIrV) are taken from the HOLY BIBLE,
    NEW INTERNATIONAL READER'S VERSION™. Copyright © 1995,
    1996, 1998 by International Bible Society. Used by permission of
    Zondervan Publishing House. All rights reserved.

Printed in the United States of America

00 01 02 03 04 05/10 9 8 7 6 5 4 3 2 1

Acknowledgements

This project has been a partnership in the fullest sense of the word, involving Focus on the Family, Lightwave Publishing, Encouraging Words, and Tyndale House Publishers. We wish to thank the following individuals for their help:

FOCUS ON THE FAMILY

Kurt Bruner
For his passion and vision for this project, his valuable insight, his leadership, and his writing.

Jim Mhoon
For managing the project and keeping everyone and everything on track (perhaps the hardest job of all!).

Larry Weeden
For reviewing content early on and giving valuable input.

Lissa Johnson
For writing many of the stories that give this book life.

John Duckworth
For his invaluable work editing and rewriting Part 3, "The Content of Your Spiritual Legacy."

Al Janssen
For leading the Focus editorial team and his work on Parts 1 and 2.

Edie Hutchinson and Jennifer Hurrell
For guiding the packaging and launch of the Guide and Heritage Builders tools.

Ken Janzen and John Perrodin
For review of the completed manuscript.

Jim Weidmann
For important input on the outline and content.

ENCOURAGING WORDS

John Trent
For his leadership, enthusiasm, and passionate writing.

Marty Kertesz
For her valuable and timely assistance.

LIGHTWAVE

Rick Osborne
For his passion and vision for the spiritual training of children, and for his leadership and writing.

Elaine Osborne
For scheduling and organizing this book and the team.

K. Christie Bowler
For her countless hours combing over, compiling, and organizing every word and punctuation mark; and for her great contribution in writing portions of this book.

Terry Van Roon
For his wonderful ability to make a large book look inviting, enjoyable, and easy to use.

Ken Save
For his whimsical drawings.

Ed van der Maas (Open Range Editorial)
For his theological and editorial input and for his great work on the charts and forms.

Andrew Jaster
For his many hours on the computer bringing all these ideas together.

Kevin Miller
For his assistance in writing and research on Parts 2 and 4.

Mikal Clarke and Ed Strauss
For their editorial assistance.

TYNDALE HOUSE

Doug Knox
For sharing the vision.

Jan Long Harris
For editorial support and input.

Thanks to all of you for a job well done!
Focus on the Family

Table of Contents

Introduction 1

PART I The Single Most Important Task for Christian Parents

Chapter 1: There Is a Better Way! 7

Chapter 2: Little Pictures Make the Big Picture 15

Chapter 3: Spiritual Training 101 25

Chapter 4: But What If . . . ? 37

Chapter 5: Making a Commitment You Can Keep 51

PART II How to Pass On Your Spiritual Legacy

Introduction 61

SECTION A Your Family's Portrait 65

Chapter 6: What Is Your Family's "History of Faith"? 67

Chapter 7: What Pace Does Your Family Live At? 73

Chapter 8: What Are Your Family's Interests? 79

Chapter 9: Identifying Your Family's Unique Personal
Strengths 87

Chapter 10: Your Family Portrait: Putting It All Together 97

SECTION B Your Children's Ages and Stages 101

Introduction 103

Chapter 11: Ages 0–4: Laying the Foundation 107

Chapter 12: Ages 5–6: Establishing and Teaching About
Relationships 115

Chapter 13: Ages 7–9: Giving Them the Reasons for
Their Faith 121

Chapter 14: Ages 10–12: Helping Them Make the Right
Choices 129

SECTION C Ideas and Methods You Can Choose From 137

Introduction 139

Church-Related Spiritual Training

Chapter 15: Church 143

"On-the-Spot" Spiritual Training

Chapter 16: Mealtime 149

Chapter 17: Drive Time 155

Chapter 18: Bedtime 161

Chapter 19: Fun Time 167

Chapter 20: Teachable Moments 173

Ideas, Methods, and Tools for the Family

Chapter 21: Family Nights 177

Chapter 22: Family Devotions 185

Chapter 23: Meaningful Memories 189

Special Times and Events

Chapter 24: Blessing Ceremonies 197

Chapter 25: Holidays 203

Ideas, Methods, and Tools for Individual Growth

Chapter 26: Quiet Time 213

Chapter 27: Exploration Time 221

Section D Designing Your Family Spiritual Growth Plan 229

Chapter 28: Putting It All Together in a Plan 231

Part III The Content of Your Spiritual Legacy

Introduction 271

Chapter 29: From Hugs to Hosannahs:
What Your 0–4-Year-Old Can Learn 277

Chapter 30: From Friendships to Faith:
What Your 5–6-Year-Old Can Learn 291

Chapter 31: From Bikes to Bibles:
What Your 7–9-Year-Old Can Learn 319

Chapter 32: From Wrestling to Worship:
What Your 10–12-Year-Old Can Learn 357

Part IV Practical Questions and Resources

Appendix I: Topical Questions and Answers 387

Appendix II: Resource List 401

Appendix III: Memory Verses 425

Index 435

Parents' Guide to the Spiritual Growth of Children

Several years ago, on a rainy August day, two young adventurers decided to scale the highest summit wholly within Switzerland—Mount Dom, near Zermatt, Switzerland[1]. At 14,942 feet, it's higher even than the Matterhorn.

Even though they were young and relatively inexperienced, they felt confident in their mountain climbing abilities. Too confident, it turned out. For at noon, despite deteriorating weather, they boldly strode forth from the tiny village of Randa at the base of the Dom. Their goal was a house halfway up the mountain where they would spend the night before tackling the icy summit the next morning.

The two moved quickly up the forested trail as the rain continued to fall and even intensify. The sky darkened as they climbed upward, and the temperature dropped significantly. Because their goal was the "high hut" staffed by the Swiss Alpine Club, not the summit, they hadn't bothered to bring cold-weather gear. They soon regretted that fact as the constant rain soaked through their inadequate clothing.

At six o'clock P.M. they were still climbing when the rain suddenly turned to snow. They had long since crossed the timberline, and the trail before them was increasingly difficult to follow. By eight o'clock P.M. darkness had fallen, and they both knew they weren't just lost—they were in life-threatening trouble. They were soaked, shivering, and at risk of hypothermia. In the pitch-black darkness they had no way of knowing whether they were still headed toward the "high hut." Their

It's our calling and privilege to set before each of our children the "Light of the World"—Jesus.

path had disappeared, and they carried no tent or sleeping bags to shelter them from the storm or help them escape the cold.

Suddenly, just when their situation was most desperate, something miraculous happened. From a great distance away, a tiny light began to flicker. Even at a distance the faint glow looked as bright as a lighthouse beacon to those two shivering, frightened young men.

Where did it come from? Before retiring for the night, the keeper of the Dom's "high hut" decided to step outside and place a kerosene lamp next to the door—just in case a beacon might be needed by anyone caught in the worsening storm. Encouraged, the boys pressed forward and in a few minutes found shelter that saved their lives.

In many ways, that story captures the essence of this book.

Our children begin the journey of life with high aspirations, naive to the fact that they are walking right into the gathering darkness of a fallen world. On their own, even with loads of self-confidence and the vitality of youth, they will face a world growing darker and colder with sin, and like each of us, one day they will face death itself.

Those two climbers couldn't find their own way that night; they needed a light to guide them to life and safety . . . and someone willing to put that light where it could be seen.

That is our role as Christian parents. It's our calling and privilege to set before each of our children the "Light of the World"—Jesus—the One who alone can save them, guide them, and keep them safe and warm, both now and forever.

But the same question confronts each of us— how do we do it?

A Helping Hand

For more than two decades, millions of parents have turned to Focus on the Family for advice and resources as they attempt to successfully navigate the often turbulent waters of parenthood. In a recent survey, the number one appeal from those parents was for Focus on the Family to help them with the spiritual growth of their children. This guide is a major step in responding to that request. As part of the Heritage

Builders ministry, this and other tools are designed to help parents build a family of faith by equipping those with children 12 and under to make an active, intentional plan for directing their children's spiritual growth. In short, we seek to lend a helping hand as parents, grandparents, and others shine the light of Christ for the next generation.

Let's face it, all of us want to be more intentional about passing the Christian faith on to our children, but few of us feel qualified for such an important and often intimidating assignment. In this context, this guide has been designed to serve two primary purposes: first, to help you create an easy-to-use, effective plan for guiding the spiritual growth of your children; and second, to serve as a "safety net" as you head into what may be uncharted water.

Here's a quick overview of what's ahead. This guide is broken into three primary sections, each designed to provide a different level of support.

◆ *Level One:* Part I gives you an overview of the "what," "why," and "how" of spiritual training in the home. It also helps you get started with a basic plan for starting the Heritage Builder process in your home. This section is relatively short (53 pages) and is intended to be read straight through to give you confidence and direction as you get started.

◆ *Level Two:* Part II is designed to help you develop a more detailed plan that is specific to the unique needs and characteristics of your family. It answers questions about the various ages and stages of your children's spiritual development. It helps you profile the particular interests, pace, and personality of your family so that you can make these realities work *for* you rather than against you. It also summarizes the many methods of spiritual training available to parents—allowing you to craft a customized plan that seems to fit your family best.

◆ *Level Three:* Parts III and IV are primarily reference sections, designed to provide a "safety net" as you launch into uncharted water. Part III gives you the biblical and theological content you can pass on to your children as they go through the various developmental stages from ages 0 to 12. It also gives you some practical tips, hints, and ideas for teaching your kids these concepts. Part IV provides you with answers to some practical questions and contains a list of additional resources and memory verses. These two sections are not intended to be read straight through, but rather to be read and used as needed.

This guide is intended to be a general resource for Christians of every background and denomination. We have tried to cover the basics of the Christian faith—those beliefs that Christians through the ages have held—in such a way that the majority of Christian denominations would agree. If we have presented any concepts in a manner that differs from the teachings of your particular denomination, we hope that you will nevertheless use this guide to set up a plan adapted to your needs and perspective. Also, since we have only covered the basics, each family will want to add more to their program and teaching to help their children understand their family's individual church, worship style, approach, traditions, and doctrinal emphasis.

The team of parents and experts who have assembled this resource offer their collective encouragement and counsel in saying, "You can do it!"—you *can* become intentional about passing your faith on to your children, no matter where you find yourself, and no matter how much or how little confidence you may have in your own abilities. We pray that this book will be a practical help to you along the way.

It's our fervent prayer that thousands of young lives will be changed, churches strengthened, and God's name will be lifted up across our world as parents take an active role in helping their children come to know and love Jesus.

General Editors
John Trent, Ph.D.
Rick Osborne
Kurt Bruner

NOTES
1. Michael Useem, *The Leadership Moment* (Random House, 1998), 6.

PART I

The Single Most Important Task for Christian Parents

There Is a Better Way!

Little Pictures Make the Big Picture

Spiritual Training 101

But What If . . .?

Making a Commitment You Can Keep

CHAPTER 1

There Is a Better Way!

Little Kurt sits between his siblings, gathered together by Mom and Dad for a ritual that always results in Kurt being bored and scolded. He hates this part of the day. He's been told it is for his own good, but to this seven-year-old squirming ball of energy the supposed benefits haven't shown themselves. Given the option, he would choose a visit to the dentist over the routine of sanctimonious torment known in this household as family devotions. Besides enduring Sunday morning sermons at church, there are few experiences less exciting in life.

If they were honest, Kurt's parents would have to agree. Dad would much rather watch the ball game. But guilt and Mom's nudge have compelled him to force the kids to sit through his awkward presentation of a Bible lesson and prayer. He feels inadequate, ill-equipped, and embarrassed as he fumbles his way through yet another chapter in the little book billed as containing "meaningful family reflections" on the faith. From the looks on the faces of his kids, the meaning is getting missed. Little Kurt is staring out the window, yearning to join the neighbor kids as they play hide-and-seek, and the older kids are sneaking glances at the clock, wondering when this is going to end. "Yes, sir," Dad muses, "another highly rewarding investment of time."

Mom, though pleased her husband is finally "taking spiritual leadership" in the home, wonders whether she made a mistake by pushing daily devotions onto her family. The moments of lively, scriptural discussion and resulting spiritual growth she expected have yet to occur. In fact, each episode seems to reinforce her children's perception that Christianity is boring. She worries but would never say anything to discourage Dad in his effort at spiritual training.

Sound familiar? Is it any wonder that so many kids who grow up in Christian homes consider the faith boring and irrelevant by the time they reach adulthood? It is unlikely that this is what the Lord had in mind when He instructed us to "teach [my commands] to your children" (Deuteronomy 4:9; 11:19).

There must be a better way.

Fast-forward twenty-five years. Kurt's seven-year-old son Kyle is laughing as he watches his younger brother attempt to navigate his way through an obstacle course of balloons while blindfolded. Kyle already had his turn and did no better than five-year-old Shaun is doing now. Both did much better before they were blindfolded. Dad has created this activity to teach his boys how sin impacts mankind—darkening our eyes to the dangerous pitfalls of life.

Tonight's activity is part of a weekly routine in which Dad creates opportunities for spiritual training. "Family Night," as they call it, is the highlight of the week for these two young guys. Mom and Dad both enjoy these moments with the kids.

Incidently, spiritual training is taking place. But we won't mention that—it might spoil the fun!

Train Up a Child—and Have Fun Doing It

For better or worse, you are responsible for much more than you bargained for back when you decided to start a family. With the esteemed title "Mommy" or "Daddy" comes a tremendous responsibility. Now that you have been thrust into the most important role of your life, your routine, everyday choices suddenly have long-term implications for your children. Like it or not, you are faced with the realization that, for good or bad, parents influence the lives of future generations in ways they can't even imagine. No pressure—it's all part of the job!

Throughout the progression from diapers to diplomas, there is one overarching issue that confronts every Christian parent: the spiritual growth of our children. We read in Proverbs 22:6, "Train a child in the way he should go, and when he is old he will not turn from it," and we realize that we're not all that clear on what it means. We have promised ourselves that we won't make the same mistakes our parents made with us, but beyond that we're most likely hard-pressed to come up with a clear, coherent, biblical statement of what is involved in training up a child in the way he should go.

At this point you may think, *What about the church? Isn't the spiritual training of our kids the church's responsibility? After all, that's what pastors are trained for, right?*

It's true that pastors across our country are effectively teaching and preaching God's Word and lighting up many lives as a result. But they'd be the first to tell you that the spiritual training of children was never meant to be relegated to a single hour on Sunday morning. Alongside gathering together at church, spiritual training was meant to be lived out every day before children by loving parents and grandparents.

The urgency of pastors' warnings that spiritual training should not be left up to the church is borne out by the results. Some studies have shown that as high as 70 percent of young people raised in church have not embraced the faith as their own by the time they graduate from high school[1]. Think for a moment what the attendance figures at our churches across North America would be if every person who grew up in the church came back next Sunday morning. The current church buildings wouldn't come close to holding the crowds. That's what attendance at church would be like if we were successfully reaching our own kids, never mind any other outreach.

In Deuteronomy 6 we read how communicating our love for God to our children is supposed to happen in the home during the course of everyday life: "Love the LORD your God with all your heart and with all your soul and with all your strength. These commandments that I give you

Josh McDowell Ministry, in preparation for the Right from Wrong campaign, conducted a survey in 1994 through the Barna Research Group. They surveyed 3,795 youth from 13 denominations. All the respondents were churched youth and involved to some degree in the youth programs of their churches. The survey examined four categories: Love and Sex, Marriage and Family, Faith and Religion, and Attitudes and Lifestyles. Here are some of the results:

- Only one in 11 youth shows that he or she has a consistent, cohesive belief in absolute truth.
- By age 18, 27 percent of churched youth have experienced sexual intercourse.
- Twenty percent see sexual intercourse outside of marriage as moral.
- Nearly 50 percent hold that love, not marriage, makes sexual intercourse right.
- Kids favor divorce by two to one for parents who don't love each other.
- Forty percent think no one can prove which religion is absolutely true.
- One in five thinks Christianity is nothing special— it's not more true, correct in its teachings, or central to salvation than any other religion.
- Two in five say lying is sometimes necessary.
- One in six says the measure of right and wrong is if it "works."
- Nearly 50 percent base their choice in moral matters on feelings and emotions.*

For the most part, the children growing up in our churches know very little about their faith.

* For more information on this, read Josh McDowell's book *Right from Wrong* (Dallas: Word Publishing, 1994).

today are to be upon your hearts. Impress them on your children. Talk about them when you sit at home and when you walk along the road, when you lie down and when you get up" (vv. 5–7).

But how am I supposed to be a spiritual trainer for my children? you ask. *I've never been to seminary or taught a Bible class. How do I "train a child in the way he should go" when no one modeled how to do that for me?*

Questions like these motivated the book you hold in your hands. The plain truth is that it is our responsibility as parents to be the primary spiritual trainers of our own children. That task isn't reserved for seminary graduates or meant only for those from a long line of faith. It is meant for every person wearing the label "Mommy" or "Daddy."

To train up a child to know Jesus, to love Him, and to serve Him, doesn't take the knowledge of a professional theologian. It just requires the commitment to start the process and become intentional. In fact, if you know how to blow up a balloon you've got what it takes to teach your children life-changing truths about the love and character of God!

When his sons were five and three years old, Kurt asked them this question: "How could God be real if we can't see Him?"

The kids stared at their dad for a few moments before the five-year-old said, "That's a good question, Dad!"

"Well, is there anything else we know is real but we can't see?" asked Kurt.

The boys pondered that for a moment before Mom chimed in: "How about air?"

Kurt then pulled some balloons out of his pocket and gave everyone a couple of them. Kurt and his wife blew up their balloons and held the opening shut. "Air is real enough to expand these balloons," Kurt announced to the boys. "Now, here's another question. Does this air have any power?" With that Kurt released his balloon and it shot across the table as the air escaped. "Cool!" said the boys.

For the next 10 minutes, there was intense competition to see who could make his balloon fly the farthest. As they did this, Kurt introduced a slogan for the evening's activity: "Just like air, God is there!"

That fun activity made a lasting impression. Several years from that night, if you ask either boy about how God can be real even though we can't see Him, he will immediately respond, "Just like air, God is there!" Ask the boys what that means, and they'll explain, "God is real and has power, even though we can't see Him."

As children get older, there are opportunities to build on this kind of knowledge. For example, you could take them on a hike in a nearby mountain or forest, or for a walk in a park, and explore the beauty and creativity of God firsthand. We can't see God, but we see evidence of Him through His creation. At a particularly impressive vista, take out your Bible and read Psalm 148 together.

Young Life ministry founder Jim Rayburn was fond of saying, "It's a sin to bore a kid with the gospel." Teaching spiritual truth to your children—teaching them to know, love, and serve Jesus—can be fun, exciting, and most of all, life-changing and meaningful. The psalmist prays, "You will fill me with joy in your presence" (Psalm 16:11), and our Lord Himself tells us, "I have come that [you] may have life, and have it to the full" (John 10:10).

That's what the Heritage Builders ministry is all about. It's about helping your children fall in love with Jesus and experience His abundant life. It's about helping you become equipped and successful in fulfilling your God-given role as the spiritual trainer in your home.

So don't wait to become intentional about passing down your faith. Spiritual training isn't going to happen by accident. It will happen because you've decided to begin the process in your own home, to help your children grow up loving the Lord and eventually pass down their faith to their children, your grandchildren.

Why Don't You Try It?

Are you ready to give it a try?

If one or more of your children are under the age of eight, why don't you take a few minutes some evening this week and do the following activity (adapted from John Trent's book *Bedtime Blessings* [Wheaton, Ill.: Tyndale House Publishers, 2000]). It's all mapped out for you.

Remember, you can do it!

Let's Pretend
Scary Shadows

What you'll need ahead of time:
A flashlight, some construction paper, and scissors.

What to say and do:
[Say the following statements to your child. Actions to take are in italics.]

"Let's close our eyes. Imagine we're walking in the woods." *[Take your child's hand, but stay on the bed.]* "I'm pretending that I see a deer in the woods. What do you see?" *[Let your child share some imaginary sights.]* "I think I hear a woodpecker going rat-a-tat-tat on a tree. What sounds do you hear?"

"Now open your eyes. Why don't you draw some of the animals we might see on a walk in the woods? I'll cut them out for you." *[When you've finished, turn off the lights and turn on the flashlight.]*

"Let's go walking through the woods again, this time with our eyes open. Oh, look! What's that?" *[Shine the flashlight on the figure of one of the animals, projecting its shadow onto the wall. After you've done a few, let your child use the flashlight.]*

"If we were really in the woods at night, do you think any of these shadows would be a little scary? Which ones?" *[After your child responds, gently squeeze his or her hand.]* "You know that if we were *really* in the woods at night, I'd hold your hand tight and keep you safe."

"What are some of the things that sometimes seem scary to you?" *[Listen to your child's fears without trying to explain them away.]* "Did you know that God stays right with you to keep you safe when you are scared? Listen to what David wrote in the Bible about being scared: 'Even though I walk through the darkest valley, I will not be afraid. You [God] are with me'" (Psalm 23:4a, NIrV).

What to pray:
Say this prayer over your child.

"Dear God, thank You that I can hold _____'s *[your child's name]* hand and keep him/her safe. And thank You that You love _____ *[your child's name]* so much that You stay with him/her no matter how scary things get. Next time _____ *[your child's name]* gets scared about _____ *[list some of the fears your child mentioned]*, help him/her to remember that You are taking care of him/her. Amen."

So, did you try it? What did your kids think? Did they enjoy it? Not only are there many more ideas just as simple and effective for you to use with your kids, but hopefully you will be able to add your own ideas.

You *can* change your children's views of God and give them a solid foundation with Him. Through prayer, patience, and a positive plan designed for your unique family, you can take on the role of spiritual trainer in your home. You can provide a whole series of positive "snapshots" of moments, events, words, and attitudes that will stay with your children throughout their lives. You can reframe, restore, or replace any negative pictures they might have with positive pictures of faith—positive moments captured in memory forever.

And in the process, beginning one family at a time, one precious life at a time, the larger picture of the nation and world will change as well.

NOTES
1. Greg Johnson and Mike Yorkey, *Faithful Parents, Faithful Kids* (Wheaton, Ill.: Tyndale House Publishers, 1993).

CHAPTER 2

Little Pictures Make the Big Picture

You've undoubtedly seen one of those pictures that at first glance looks like a photograph of someone but upon closer inspection is in fact composed of many hundreds or thousands of little pictures. All the little pictures make up the big picture. Imagine looking at a very large picture of yourself that, as you look more closely, you discover is made up of smaller pictures of all the significant moments in your life. From your birth till now, every experience of your life, every snapshot, has had an impact on you for good or for bad—birthdays, school years, experiences with friends and family. All of those little pictures join together to make up the big picture of who you are today.

Now, consider this admonition from Proverbs: "Train a child in the way he should go, and when he is old he will not turn from it" (Proverbs 22:6). Those words strike fear into our hearts. We wonder what we should do, if we're training our children right, if our efforts will really pay off in a healthy adult who loves the Lord.

We tend to worry when we think about the big picture. However, Proverbs 22:6,

15

We just need to concentrate on one little picture at a time and God Himself will take care of the big picture.

as a principle, is simply saying that when you bring your child up with each little picture placed in their lives God's way, the big picture will look as it should.

The real encouragement for us as parents is that we don't need to spend time worrying about the big picture and how we are going to accomplish this huge task. We just need to concentrate on one little picture at a time and God Himself will take care of the big picture.

How can you intentionally create those individual snapshots in your child's life? Very simply, we need to give our children three things: an unshakable foundation, an internal line, and the big picture.

Give Them an Unshakable Foundation

Focus on the Family began in southern California—land of endless summers, eleven o'clock P.M. traffic jams, and from time to time, unnerving earthquakes. If you've ever lived through an earthquake, you know that even a "mild" one can be unforgettable and frightening. A common response for those in an earthquake is to feel helpless when it hits. Suddenly, the world that seemed so solid underfoot only moments before shakes and sways.

What would you think if you moved to California and your real estate agent told you he had a house for you with a foundation *guaranteed* to "never be shaken"? No matter what size earthquake hit your neighborhood, *your* foundation would never move, never shake. If you happened to be moving near a known fault line, you'd have every right to be skeptical, right? In fact, if the agent put his claim of an unshakable foundation in writing, you'd have legal grounds for a lawsuit. No person can make that kind of unfounded promise.

But almighty God can and did put such a promise in writing.

If you'll take the time to read the five verses that make up Psalm 15, you'll see that it's like shooting light through a prism. Those five verses illuminate 10 character traits of a godly person . . . and end with an incredible promise.

"Lord," the psalm begins, "who may dwell in your sanctuary? Who may live on your holy hill?"(v. 1). The answer reads like a character development course. The one who dwells with the Lord is one "whose walk is blameless," "who does what is righteous," and "who speaks the truth from his heart" (v. 2). This person "has no slander on his tongue" and "does his neighbor no wrong" (v. 3). Such a person helps and doesn't hurt the poor, and gives honor to those whom God honors.

And what's the reward for someone who seeks to live out such a godly life or pass such a life down to their children? It's the promise of an unshakable foundation for his or her life. In King David's words, "He who does these things will never be shaken" (v. 5b).

When you take the time to introduce your children to Jesus and He becomes their personal Lord and Savior, you're laying an unshakable foundation for their lives. King David wrote about having an "unshakable life" even though he faced incredible trials and temptations and even people who threatened to take his life. Yet through it all his love for almighty God gave him an unshakable inner foundation—the same foundation your children need in these turbulent times.

Your children need Jesus to be the foundation of their lives. How you build on that foundation through teaching them to know and love Jesus can help them today and in their future. In 1 Corinthians 3 the apostle Paul writes, "By the grace God has given me, I laid a foundation as an expert builder, and someone else is building on it. But each one should be careful how he builds. For no one can lay any foundation other than the one already laid, which is Jesus Christ" (vv. 10–11).

The sure foundation for your children's lives is Jesus Christ—just like the old hymn says, "All other ground is sinking sand." And those who actively build up their faith, 1 Timothy 6:19 says, "lay up treasure for themselves as a firm foundation for the coming age, so that they may take hold of the life that is truly life."

The only sure, unshakable foundation for our children's lives—and for their future—is Jesus. That's true if you live near the ocean or in the mountains or anywhere in between.

Give Them an Internal Line

Generations of moviegoers would have lost a hero if it weren't for an unsung hero named William Bachrach. Bachrach had a profound

What We Potentially Give Our Children Through Spiritual Training

- Eternal life through Jesus' death.
- A personal, loving relationship with God.
- God's guidance, wisdom, and direction for their lives, as well as His discipline, correction, and forgiveness for when they make mistakes.
- A working knowledge of God's principles so that they understand the practical rules that govern life—and the resulting wisdom for life and life's complex situations.
- God's love in their hearts and an understanding of the principles that govern interpersonal relations so they can have healthy relationships with others.
- God's strength and help for and through difficult times.
- Purpose and a sense of value through knowing that God made them unique, loves them, and has a special plan for their lives.
- Strong character through openness to the working of the Holy Spirit.
- A strong understanding of right and wrong.
- Thankful hearts, teachable spirits, strong morals, and a desire for personal growth.

impact on a young man named Johnny Weissmuller—who was to become Hollywood's first Tarzan. It happened while Bachrach was at the Illinois Athletic Club serving as the head swimming coach.

Bachrach had taken a special interest in the tall, lanky, 15-year-old Johnny. The coach worked daily with this young man, developing his stroke, helping him improve his breathing, starts, and turns. He would tell him, "Swim *over* the water, not through it," giving his star pupil a mental picture of what he wanted his stroke to feel like.

But there was a real problem with Johnny's swimming.

When Johnny swam at his "home" pool, he was unbeatable. In fact, in the I.A.C. pool he was clocked at an amazing 52 seconds in the 100-yard freestyle *at age 14*. The I.A.C. pool was one of the finest indoor pools in the country at the time, with thick black tile stripes marking out the lanes that guided the swimmers in competition. While coach and swimmer didn't know it then, those lines were the reason Johnny kept losing at away meets.

Subconsciously, Johnny had come to depend on those clearly marked lines to keep him on a straight course. So when he competed in an unmarked pool (which was the norm for the away-meet pools), his times dropped dramatically.

It was during an away meet, after Johnny lost yet another winnable race, that his coach recognized the problem. He waited until after the meet and made Johnny get back into the pool. He had him swim one length against the stop watch—and then another.

Then he exploded. "Johnny!" he roared. "You aren't swimming straight! You don't have that black guideline and so you're wobbling all over the pool!"

To solve the problem, Coach Bachrach slammed his hat down on a kickboard at one end of the pool and sent Johnny to the other.

"All right now," he ordered, "that hat is your goal. Fix it in your mind, draw a mental line to it, and swim for it." Johnny did, and his times were as fast as ever. From that point on, Johnny Weissmuller would carry his own "lines" when we went to an unmarked pool. And by staying within those lines he ended up swimming in two Olympic Games and winning five Olympic medals! And all that before he was Tarzan!

Our children face a problem similar to the one Johnny Weissmueller faced long ago. As Christian parents, we do our best to give our children guidelines to follow. In fact, the word for "righteousness" in the Bible means "to stay within the lines."

Yet there's a problem. Our children may thrive when they're in the security of our home where the lines are clear, but outside, when they start swimming in the world, they quickly discover that there are no bold, well-marked lines of behavior or commitment! There's nothing to steer children away from problems, stop them from drifting out of bounds, or keep them focused on winning the race when it comes to a godly life.

Fifty years ago, that wasn't the case. You could send your child to school or out into society and there were still "lines" of bib-

The Line

One day Janae was invited to see a movie with two of her friends. I dropped her off at the movie theater and continued on to the car repair shop to complete an errand. While I was there, my cell phone rang. I answered and it was Janae.

"Hi, Dad," she said. "I need you to come pick me up."

I glanced at my watch. "Sweetheart, where are you?" I asked, confused.

"I'm still at the movie, Dad. I walked out early."

"Why did you do that?"

"They used God's name in vain in the movie."

She paused while I thought back to the conversation we had had just weeks before. We had discussed choosing the line where an action honors God or it dishonors God. Specifically we had discussed movies, videos, and television. I had shared that using God's name in vain was my line. If I heard it, I left the movie. And now my daughter had done the same thing.

"Uh, Dad," she said, her voice quiet, "I want to let you know that I feel real bad, because they had to use it twice before I walked out."

I chuckled. "Oh, sweetheart," I reassured her, "God's smiling because you're getting the message."

J. W.

Water and Ice

To teach the principle of looking beyond current hardships to the reward set before us, I brought my four children into the room, asking them to sit and remove their shoes. I brought out a dishpan filled with snow, water, and ice. An assortment of marbles lay in the bottom.

I put this pan in front of my elder daughter and said, "Janae, sweetheart, I will pay you 50 cents for every marble you can pull out of there with your toes."

She said, "Okay, Daddy," and plunged her bare foot into the freezing water. After removing one marble, she burst into tears. "Oh Daddy, it's so cold."

I said, "It's okay; you don't have to do it."

Then I put the water in front of little Joy-Joy. She poked her toe in and said, "Daddy, I ain't playin'."

And I said, "Okay, sweetheart."

It was Josh's turn next. Josh was getting excited. "Fifty cents a marble? What's my limit?"

When I told him it was five minutes, he said, "Start the clock." In five minutes he pulled out 14 marbles.

Well, his brother Jake looked at him and said, "He just got seven bucks."

"That's right."

He said, "Start the clock."

So I started the clock and he pulled 14 marbles out in four minutes, quitting when he tied with his brother.

By now Janae had changed her mind. She wanted to try again. This time she endured the agony of the cold to pull out 12 marbles.

As I looked at the row of brilliant blue feet, I asked, "Why did you put your feet in the water? I didn't make you."

They said, "We wanted the money."

"Oh, you wanted the money," I said. "You looked through the pain of the ice and snow to get to your reward, which was the money."

Josh popped up and said, "Dad, Dad, I understand. Look through the pain of persecution to the reward which is yours in heaven."

"Absolutely, Josh," I said. "Absolutely."

J. W.

lically based standards painted on the bottom of every "pool." Today, not only is the swimming water muddied by smut and sin presented as normalcy on television, but even if children *could* see through all the societal grunge, the American Civil Liberties Union and special interest groups have spent billions of dollars in court—and in the court of public opinion—trying to scrub any lines off the bottom of the pool!

The post-Christian age we live in, in fact, *demands* that there be no absolute lines. There are only situational ethics and standards. And if anyone dares think there *are* enduring standards (or, heaven forbid, *eternal* standards), they're dismissed as narrow-minded, uneducated, bigoted, archaic, right-wing religious wakos—and those are the positive descriptions!

But every parent knows intuitively that our children need moral and ethical boundaries. They need lines of behavior that don't waver or change based on opinion polls. They need godly character standards that can guide and direct them away from sin and toward God's best. Lines of righteousness add meaning and purpose to a child's life.

Those moral and ethical lines haven't vanished! They're still there! Despite the best efforts of a post-Christian culture to take the Ten Commandments and prayer out of our schools and culture, God's Word endures. As a Christian parent, you can teach your children to stay between the lines of righteous living and to know right from wrong, and in so doing, you can keep them pointed toward the positive future God has for them.

Give Them the Big Picture

When we spiritually train our children, we are preparing them for life, not just for guilt-free church attendance. This point is further illustrated in Ephesians 6:4: "Fathers, do not exasperate your children; instead, bring them up in the training and instruction of the Lord."

In this one verse Paul sums up or defines what Christian parenting—raising Christian children to adulthood—is.

First of all, we are to "bring them up" in the training and instruction of the Lord. If we are not careful, we may read this as meaning that we should *add* things—like going to church and learning about God, Jesus, and Bible stories—to the overall mix of our children's lives. We then might say something like "My kids are going to school to get an education, to music lessons to develop their artistic side, and to Sunday school to learn about their faith."

But that is emphatically *not* what Paul is saying here. He is saying, "In every part of bringing them up, in every part of their lives, use the training and instruction of the Lord, teaching them about who they are, what life is about, and how to live according to God's principles and His Word."

Spiritual training is not an add-on; it forms the core of your children's being and life.

The spiritual training of our children should be the foundation of our parenting, handing over to our children the truths and principles that explain and govern life itself. If we imagine our children's large pictures as adults made up of all those little pictures, their spiritual training should not be a small section of those pictures but rather the foundation of, and the reason for, the orderly placement of every one of those pictures.

That sounds like a tall order until we remember that it's one little picture at a time. It is actually easier to teach your children one step at a time in the context of everyday life than to sit down and try to effectively communicate a systematic theology to them (although they need the theology, too). Spiritual training is much more practical than theoretical.

Ephesians 6:4 shows us two key methods for spiritual training that will help us keep it practical and real. "Bring them up in the *training and instruction* of the Lord" (Ephesians 6:4b, emphasis added). Any learning process requires theory (instruction) and practical training. You can learn the rules and details of how to play baseball from a book or have someone explain them to you—but until you have someone physically and practically show you how to play the game and then start practicing, everything you know is just theory. The apostle Paul is instructing us as parents to not only teach our children about God and the Christian life but to also, by example and training, show them how to live it out.

That's the point of the instructions in Deuteronomy 6:5–7 that we reviewed in chapter 1. Moses and Paul taught the same thing—that spiritual instruction and training are the foundations for everything our children learn in life. Therefore, both instruction and training need to happen on the appropriate training field—right in the midst of everyday life, where the little pictures are constantly being shot and placed into the bigger picture of who our children will become.

Helping your children know and love Jesus gives them an unshakable foundation, unchanging "lines" to follow to God's best, and solid preparation to live the life that God has given them. It also causes you to live out your calling as a parent, which strengthens your own faith.

In the Midst

One night when Ryan was six, he broke from our usual pattern of bedtime prayer and said from his heart, "God, can I please go over to Daniel's house tomorrow? I really want to!"

I praised him for talking to God about the things he really wanted and hugged him goodnight. The next day when I arrived home from work, I asked where Ryan was. The response got me excited. "Oh, Daniel's mom invited him over for dinner."

That night I reminded Ryan of his prayer and had him tell me what happened. When he remembered, he got very excited. "That's the first time God has really answered one of my prayers!" he said. That night he prayed with a new freedom and excitement.

Anonymous

The Importance of Training

Talkative Trevor was almost two years old. An adorable, blond-headed, sweet child, he was mild mannered and very obedient. At a friend's house, the families chatted while Trevor sat on the side of the pool, his chubby feet dangling in the cool, clear water. Mom watched him carefully, never taking her eyes off him while the adults laughed and told stories.

A belligerent bee flew into the group of adults, insisting on landing on people and being a nuisance. The adults stood, and Mom turned her back on Trevor to take a swat at the bee with a sandal. When she turned around, Trevor was floating facedown in the water.

Auntie leaped the two strides to the pool, reached in, and snagged Trevor's shirt, pulling him from the water. Mom cried as she held her little boy, knowing the tragedy that could have happened.

After much sputtering and coughing, Trevor told them he had been reaching for a ball that had fallen into the pool. He had reached too far and had simply and quietly slipped into the water. "I was calling you, Mommy," Trevor said. "But you didn't hear me. You didn't come get me."

Tremendous guilt and horror crashed in on Mom. It was only seconds that she had her back to the pool. Only seconds. And if she had not spun around when she did, if the adults' attention had been taken away from the pool for much longer, her precious child would have drowned.

With water-safety training, Trevor would have been able to at least paddle to the side of the pool until someone came to help him out.

As he grows, swimming lessons will become important to help him gradually become more and more water safe, until he is able to be in the water completely on his own. It will be a hassle for Mom or Dad to take the time out to drive him to the lessons, and it will be a financial sacrifice to pay for them. But the result will be worth the effort: Trevor will know how to swim.

And so it is with spiritual training. Without it, we do not toss our kids into the deep end of the pool of life and expect them to know how to swim through daily life or even how to reach the side safely during the difficulties bound to come their way. Spiritual training contains the lessons, the foundation, for all that our children will face in life.

CHAPTER 3

Spiritual Training 101

Beginning with Nothing

Jim thought he was a great spiritual leader. He took his kids to Sunday school every week and planned to send them to a Christian school when he could afford it. But then one Sunday as he was getting ready to go to church, he found three of his young children at the bottom of the stairs, crying.

"What's wrong?" he asked them.

"We don't want to go to church, Daddy," his daughter, Janae, said.

"It's *boring*," Jake said, wiping his tears with a fist.

"We've heard the Noah story so many times we don't want to go anymore," the eldest, Josh, added.

Jim looked at his children and realized he had no idea what they were being taught in church. He had no idea how the Bible was being presented.

"Not that I knew so much," Jim says. "I was raised in a church where I was told that I couldn't understand calculus without algebra, and therefore I could not understand scripture without years of theological training. I was told to leave the Bible reading and interpretation to those with training. But as I looked at my kids that day, I realized that I need-ed to assume the responsibility of teaching them biblical truth."

He didn't know where to begin. He didn't know what to do. At first he thought he should know everything about God and scripture before

he began. But he quickly knew that wouldn't happen.

"So I just dived right in. Whatever I learned, that's what I taught the kids. I'd start with a problem or what I learned in Bible study and pass that concept on to them. For understanding the scriptures, I found resources to help me like the *Life Application Bible*. When I wanted to dig deeper, I bought a *Nave's Topical Bible* and *Strong's Concordance*."

Jim also knew the typical reading from a family devotional wouldn't inspire him or the kids. "I wanted it to be *fun*," Jim said. "So I thought of having Family Nights." These would be times of fun for the family with a spiritual message blended in with the fun. "I could define a biblical principle and impress it upon my children as Deuteronomy says." He quickly discovered that Family Nights, although formal, set up the informal.

So whether the family is huddling in the bug-infested crawl space to discuss persecution, the children are climbing on Dad's back to experience how we cannot get to God without Him coming to help us, or they're using a dummy electrical situation to evoke worry, the family is having a great time while lessons are being taught.

For many, like Jim, the notion of becoming intentional about spiritual training at home creates a knot of tension in the stomach due to past failure or intimidation. Let's start with a clean sheet of paper. Erase all your preconceived notions about training your children in the Christian faith. For a moment forget all the guilt-driven, unpleasant attempts you've made in the past or any ideas you may have about this being boring and ineffective. There are a few principles that

Just Me and My Kid

"Dad, can we go to IHOP? Please? Please?"

"Yes, Kyle, we can go to IHOP," I say, smiling as I tousle his hair.

Kyle is excited about the chance to be alone with Dad. He looks forward to our Saturday breakfasts at the place of his choosing. Next week will be his brother Shaun's turn. For less than $10 and an hour a week, I get one of my boys all to myself. We talk about anything and everything. Sometimes it's nothing. Sometimes it's as important as the difference between religions. But it's always good for our relationship—building our casual times together so that when there's something important to convey, the boys are more willing to listen and absorb the faith lesson.

K. B.

comprise the core of our "Spiritual Training 101" course. Remembering four simple phrases, you can keep the process simple and your priorities clear: Relationship is your priority. The Bible is your handbook. Life is your classroom. Your methods should target your child.

Principle 1: Relationship Is Your Priority

Kathleen grew up in a Christian home. She attended church regularly with Mom, Dad, and her siblings. The family Bible was prominently displayed on the den coffee table. There was prayer before every meal, even in restaurants. From all appearances, you would describe Kathleen as living in the ideal Christian family. And in many ways, you would be right. But there was one problem—Kathleen and her father didn't get along.

During childhood, Kathleen barely got to know her dad. As a successful professional, long hours and business travel kept him away from home during the week. As an adult Sunday school teacher, study and church activities consumed his weekends. His heart was right, but his schedule was full. Consequently, little relationship was fostered between him and his daughter during Kathleen's critical childhood years.

During adolescence, Kathleen struggled with low self-worth. But since no foundation of trust had been built between them, she never shared these feelings with her father. Between acne, roller-coaster emotions, and boys, Kathleen could have used a daddy's hug. And he would have given it had she invited him into her world. But she didn't.

By the time Kathleen was a junior in high school, the tension between her and her father was thick. Whenever he led the family in prayer or tried to read a short devotion, her body stiffened. As the family marched

Always Take a Kid Along

"Hey, Jake. Put your shoes on. Let's get going."

"Okay, Dad."

It's Saturday: errand day for Dad. The van needs an oil change. A trip to the hardware store for screws and pipes and gadgets for the latest home improvement project: The perfect time for a one-on-one with one of the kids.

My dad taught me that. "Never go anywhere without a child," he told me. And he's right. By taking a kid away from the siblings, I get his or her full attention, and the child gets mine. I'm building the relationship while setting up the impromptu times. These are the moments when life presents the questions either from me or from the child, and the answers come from our faith view. The principle is that I must develop the relationship, for the relationship gives me the ability to share spiritual truth.

J. W.

dutifully into church behind her father, the deacon, Kathleen felt sick to her stomach. In those moments every fault in his life was magnified and profound disrespect burned in her heart. *What a hypocrite!* Kathleen thought behind her wooden stare. *If 'Mr. Holier-Than-Thou' thinks he can cram this religious garbage down my throat, he's got another think coming.*

When Kathleen left home as a young adult, she left the faith of her family as well. Despite her father's best intentions and diligent efforts to instill Christian values, they didn't take. She rejected the values—not because they were bad, but because they were his. You see, Kathleen needed more than mere knowledge of her father's faith—she needed a relationship with her father's heart. Without the latter, she wasn't interested in the former.

There are countless Kathleens in the world. Raised in Christian homes, they were given a solid spiritual legacy but rejected the values taught. Why? People reject the faith for many reasons. Quite often, it is because the relationship with Mom, Dad, or both was weak. Don't misunderstand: Kathleen is responsible for her own decision to reject the faith. Her father is not to blame for the choices she made. But one can't help wondering how

---

The Watch

One night I tucked our youngest daughter Laura into bed. She wiggled herself under the covers as I removed my multifunction watch. "Here, Laura," I said, placing it into her little hands. I showed her how some of the buttons worked, then let her push the ones that made it into a stopwatch or made the dial light up with a beautiful blue glow. She marveled at all the things the watch could do.

As the watch cast a blue glow onto her eager face, I asked, "Do you think this watch just happened to become a watch, or do you think someone made it?"

"Someone made it," she answered.

I opened our Bible to Psalm 139 and read the passage that says we didn't just happen to have the hair or nose or toes God gave us—we were "fearfully and wonderfully" made by Divine design.

J. T.

---

things might have been different if he had been as intentional about spending time playing with and getting to know Kathleen as he was about praying over meals and getting the family to church on time.

The old adage is true—people don't care how much you know until they know how much you care. Our children need more than a list of precepts and principles to embrace. If we want the values we teach them to stick, we must apply heavy amounts of the glue called love. We cannot have one without the other. Children perceive parental instruction through emotional lenses. Those lenses are framed by the quality of the parent-child relationship.

Real-Life Tip 1: Hold yourself accountable.

Bruce is the father of two. He has been spending time each week conducting activities designed to teach the faith to his children. He has also been busy at work and various other commitments. Concerned that he might not be spending the time necessary to maintain a strong relationship with the kids, he decided to take a risk. Bruce sat the kids down one evening and asked them to grade the job he was doing as a dad.

"Tonight, I want you to fill out a 'Report Card for Dad' to grade me on how I'm doing," Bruce explained. "There are several things the Lord expects me to do as your father, and I want your opinion on how well I'm doing."

The kids were surprised but more than willing to go along. So they spent the next few minutes grading Dad by completing the report card he had developed. Once it was completed, Bruce had an opportunity to discuss his grades with the kids. As expected, he received a different rating depending upon the child. His daughter, for example, graded him down on fair discipline but high on showing love. His son, on the other hand, thought the discipline was okay, but Dad didn't spend enough time with him. As promised, Bruce resisted the urge to defend himself. The goal was to discover how the kids perceived his efforts, regardless of what Bruce himself thought of them.

Bruce shared later that the exercise, though painful, was extremely helpful as he assessed the relationship with his kids. It created an opportunity to clarify expectations and to discover areas he might improve in as a father. The risk was more than worth it.

Bruce understands the power of relationship in the spiritual training process. He realizes that it is not enough to merely instruct his children; he must also foster a strong relationship with them in order to create a context for success. As must we all.

Principle 2: The Bible Is Your Handbook

God gave us an instruction manual for life—the Bible. It's funny how we sometimes take this awesome gift for granted and struggle along in life or in the teaching of our kids without consulting the handbook. It's like the do-it-yourselfer

who refuses to read the instruction manual when assembling his child's gift, stays up until two in the morning trying to figure it out, and then blames the manufacturer for making it wrong.

Asking, "Should I be teaching my children the Bible or should I wait until they're old enough to decide for themselves?" is like asking, "Should I make my children eat fruits and vegetables and have a proper diet now, or should I let them eat what they want until they're old enough to decide for themselves?"

The Bible is "useful for teaching, rebuking, correcting and training in righteousness" (2 Timothy 3:16). Teaching the Bible to our children is not an exercise in teaching religious ideas and ceremonies; it is teaching them how to live and have a good life. The Bible is their guidebook, their lifeline, their textbook, their help menu, their answer, their emergency first aid kit and, most importantly, their key to knowing God. If we believe the Bible is God's Word, we will not only teach our children that its contents should guide their lives, but we will also demonstrate our belief by using it as a guide for our own lives.

The Directions

One evening we turned a trip to McDonald's into a faith lesson. We piled into the van and I handed a simple map that I had created to seven-year-old Kyle.

"Okay, Kyle. It's up to you to make sure we get to McDonald's." I started the car and proceeded down our street. At the corner, I stopped and looked over my shoulder at him. "Where do I go now?"

Kyle looked at his map. "You turn left."

"Naw," I told him. "I think I know what I'm doing; I don't think I need to turn left." I turned right instead.

Kyle burst out in frustration, "It says you're supposed to turn left."

At the next point of decision, I did the same thing. Soon Kyle was really mad.

When we ended up at a dead end, I said, "I guess I didn't know where I was going, did I?"

"That's right, Dad, because you were supposed to follow the directions," Kyle shouted.

"Well, now what are we going to do?" I asked.

"Go back to the beginning and we'll follow the directions."

So that's what we did. We went back to the beginning. This time I followed the directions. During this second attempt at reaching McDonald's, we discussed what had occurred on our first trip.

"That's what happens when we don't obey the Bible," I told the children. "When we think we know what we're doing and we don't follow the directions, we lose our way. The scriptures are our directions for life."

An extra five minutes out of an already planned trip became a powerful faith lesson.

K. B.

Real-Life Tip 2: Use the Bible and what it says as the foundation for your own life first.

Where do we parents go when we need guidance and help? We need to live our own lives by the Bible's principles. We need to apply ourselves not only to learning the Bible but also to learning how to better learn from the Bible. There are lots of great books available on how to use and study the Bible. We need to allow our children to see our own commitment to learning God's Word and to allowing Him to speak to us and change us through it.

To help you increase your own knowledge of the Bible, the following may be useful: *How to Study the Bible for All It's Worth* by Gordon D. Fee and Douglas Stuart (Grand Rapids, Mich.: Zondervan, 1993) is a good place to start. *The NIV Study Bible* (Grand Rapids, Mich.: Zondervan, 1995) has lots of useful study notes, a commentary, and some study tools in the back (such as a concordance and maps). Also Lawrence O. Richards' *Zondervan Expository Dictionary of Bible Words* (Grand Rapids, Mich.: Zondervan, 1991) is a very useful tool. It explores the meaning of the Hebrew and Greek words behind the English words and gives the reader an understanding of the different shades of meaning and nuances that are important for a dynamic interpretation of the Word of God. You might also like to try one of the popular Bible-based daily devotionals that have proven their worth over decades, such as *My Utmost for His Highest* by Oswald Chambers, (Grand Rapids, Mich.: Discovery).

Principle 3: Life Is Your Classroom

When someone is learning how to fix a transmission, his practical training would probably take place in a garage. If the topic were football, the practical training would take place on the football field. In our case, the topic is the foundational principles and concepts that are to govern who we are, our behavior, our lives, and our relationships with God and others. Therefore, the practical training needs to take place in a relevant venue: moment by moment, day by day, in the hustle and bustle of everyday life.

The Bible has not been taught once a principle has been explained and a verse memorized. No one becomes a great quarterback through classroom instruction alone. Would you care how many books the surgeon who is about to take out your gall bladder has read if you knew that was the sum total of his training? On the other hand, you'd be

We need to allow our children to see our own commitment

equally scared of a surgeon who had never read any books about the human body or the techniques of surgery but was on his second operation and doing much better.

God has designed the world and us so that learning about the things of God and applying them in everyday life happen together. That's the idea behind Deuteronomy 6:6–9. We're to impress God's commands on our children daily. We're to talk about them when we sit at home, when we're on the road, when we lie down at night, and when we get up in the morning. This can't be accomplished merely by taking our children to church and reading them Bible stories. We need to demonstrate to our children—through our growth, by our example, and by when and what we teach— that our faith is about who we are, how we act, and what we do as well as about what we believe. When we teach our children about their faith in this way, connecting our teaching with our life, our teaching method matches our message and becomes instantly more effective.

Two important points need to be made in this context. First, our life is a major example to our kids. Practice-what-you-preach parenting is the only kind that works. However, *parenting by example does not demand that we be perfect.*

There is a right and a wrong way to deal with our own imperfections and shortcomings as people and as parents. The wrong way is denial. We simply refuse to accept that we are imperfect and pretend that we have no failings. This is what Jesus accused the Pharisees of doing when He said, "Be on your guard against the yeast of the Pharisees, which is hypocrisy. There is nothing concealed that will not be disclosed, or hidden that will not be made known. What you have said in the dark will be heard in the daylight, and what you have whispered in the ear in the inner rooms will be proclaimed from the roofs" (Luke 12:1b–3).

A hypocrite in Jesus' day was a professional stage actor, someone who put on a mask and pretended to be someone he wasn't. Thus a hypocrite is a person who pretends to be a certain thing by presenting one thing while living another. If we attempt to show our kids we are perfect when we aren't, we're acting and are hypocrites. But if we live out our growth in Christ, we're parenting by example. If we demand performance and perfection, our faults will appear as signs of hypocrisy. But if we encourage growth by grace, our faults will become signs of authenticity as we grow.

A second key point is that we are all fellow learners. Our children and we are both learning about God. This means discussing our growth in Christ in practical, everyday terms with them. It includes letting them see us apply our faith to our lives. Then they will get excited about joining in the process. It's easier to get kids in the water when you're swimming than when you're sitting warm and dry on the beach.

Real-Life Tip 3: Have fun with your kids.

When Dad spends time wrestling with the kids in the basement, he has done more to create a context for passing on the faith than when he reads them a Bible passage. Both are important, but the former makes the latter more meaningful.

When Mom plays a round of Go Fish with her six-year-old son, he learns to enjoy her as a person, not merely obey her as a parent. Again, both are important, but the former makes the latter easier to swallow.

When the family takes a "backward" walk and everyone wears their clothes backwards, it

It's in the Music

Our family loves music, so we often have some playing as we go about our chores and errands. One day I finally paid attention to the words of a song on our favorite tape. My daughter, Kelsie, came into the room.

"Hey, Kelsie, have you ever paid attention to this song?"

She paused and shook her head.

"Listen to it."

So we cuddled on the couch as she listened to the words. When it was over, she looked up at me. "That's a cool song, Dad."

"But do you know what it means?"

From there we launched into a discussion about storing up treasures in heaven, and how the song spoke of what we do on earth. Are we being selfish with our resources, ourselves, our time? Or are we doing things that have eternal value?

Even music afforded opportunities to pass along spiritual truths to my daughter—and we had fun doing it!

J. M.

builds relationships and shows that Mom and Dad are not always serious. They know how to have fun.

Everyone has the right to speak; we must earn the right to be listened to. As parents, we must realize that when we enjoy our kids today, we are earning the right to shape their values tomorrow. People are far more likely to embrace the values of someone they enjoy being with than those of someone they don't. So let's remember to have fun with our kids.

Principle 4: Your Methods Should Target Your Child

To the Jews I became like a Jew, to win the Jews. To those under the law I became like one under the law (though I myself am not under the law), so as to win those under the law. To those not having the law I became like one not having the law (though I am not free from God's law but am under Christ's law), so as to win those not having the law. To the weak I became weak, to win the weak. I have become all things to all men so that by all possible means I might save some. (1 Corinthians 9:20–22)

Paul adapted his approach for each audience. The message remained the same, but Paul would get in step with his audience, understanding their needs and viewpoints. Then he would alter his presentation accordingly.

This is a very, very important principle when it comes to teaching our children: *We can't expect children to rise to our level; we need to go to theirs.* When Jesus said, "Let the little children come to me" (Mark 10:14), He stopped doing what He was doing to communicate truth to adults and adapted His approach for a new audience. Mark

A Child's First Understanding of Prayer

When Ryan was just old enough to put a few words together, I really wanted him to understand the importance of prayer. I sat with him nightly, gently rocking him as he lay in my arms listening to me pray—or that was what I thought would happen. Actually, I tried my best to hang onto his squirming body while I prayed wonderfully spiritual prayers. It was difficult, but I was determined to stick with it!

One night, during an extra furious round of hold-and-squirm, I asked God for help and wisdom. Suddenly the lights came on. I stopped praying *my* prayers over him and prayed *his.*

"Dear God, thank You for making Ryan and please help him use the potty. Amen." His eyes widened and he seemed to understand prayer for the first time—and the war of grasp and escape was over.

Anonymous

10:16 says, "And he took the children in his arms, put his hands on them and blessed them." Jesus changed what He was doing in order to be effective with the children.

We need to be able to understand what the important issues are for our children—in their eyes, not ours—and communicate on their level. When we can at least imagine walking in their shoes, our teaching will be more effective and, certainly, more relevant.

Like Jim at the beginning of our chapter, many parents have questions, hesitations, and fears about training their children. But also like Jim, parents can become intentional about passing on their faith and values to their children—and have a great time doing it.

"But wait!" some of you are saying. "You don't understand. My situation is special. What if . . .?"

Our next chapter addresses many of these frequently asked questions. No matter what your situation is, you *can* do it! And we'll show you how.

Real Life Tip 4: Make it fun.

The fact that our children are growing up in an entertainment-drenched culture with new media technologies and high production values constitutes the need for us to learn to speak a different language and form a different approach. One of our children's primary interests at their stage of life and in our culture, is fun and play. We as parents should endeavor to work with this need in their lives while trying to teach them, seeking to achieve a balance between fun and serious intent.

Say you enjoy roughhousing with your kids. They enjoy it when you give them rides, flipping them over and onto a bed or gently onto the floor. Is there some lesson that could be taught in the context of roughhousing, for example, by telling the story of Jacob wrestling the angel?

CHAPTER 4

But
What
If . . . ?

By now, you no doubt have some questions. We tried to anticipate some of them, so read through this list and check the ones that apply to you:

What If . . .

____ I have no time?

____ I feel inadequate—or fail?

____ I'm doing it alone?

____ our children are all different ages and stages?

____ we're a blended family? (It just seems more difficult for us.)

____ I'm still hurting from a difficult past? Don't I need to get healed before I try and pass something down to my kids?

____ my own spiritual life is shaky?

____ I'm not a theologian? How can I make sure I teach them well and cover it all?

____ my child has a learning disability or other special need?

____ my spouse and I are from different church backgrounds?

____ I don't see the need for all the facts and doctrine? I just want my children to love God.

____ we've already tried something like this and it didn't work?

So how many did you check? If you're like most of the people we interact with, you checked at least five. Be encouraged; you aren't alone! We're here to help. Please feel free to skip ahead directly to your questions.

What If I Have No Time?

If you're struggling to find time to spiritually train your children, you're not alone. The modern equivalent of Israel fruitlessly marching in circles for 40 years has to be the way today's culture plays catch-up with the clock. This "lack" of time isn't a twenty-first century phenomenon. Plautus, a Roman playwright some 2,000 years ago, moaned about the stress the *sundial* brought: "The gods confound the man who first found out how to distinguish hours! Confound him who has cut and hacked my days so wretchedly into small pieces. Confound him who in this place set up . . . a sundial."[1]

Life is full of "progressive" changes aimed at helping you "save time": shoes (buttons to shoelaces to Velcro); writing (pens to typewriters to word processors); cooking (wood burning stoves to microwaves); banking (personal tellers to drive-up ATMs); mail (letters to e-mail).

Everything is faster and more "convenient" today—but there are costs. The greatest cost is that people work longer and harder to afford the conveniences. Across all professions in the United States, people are now on the job 163 hours more than they were in 1970. That's a month more of work per person per year! The increased hours and competitive acquisition of "things" (not to mention other pressures) have played havoc with families and family time. So first, let us say that if you don't have time to fulfill one of your greatest responsibilities, you may be letting the clock and other less important pursuits drive you around in wilderness circles.

But even with a good balance of priorities, we still have a lot on our plates. Don't despair, however. Spiritual training takes a lot less

Only 20 Minutes per Week!

If you spend 20 minutes per week intentionally teaching your children from the time they are 4 until they are 15, they will have received over 190 hours of biblical training.

time than you think. In fact, effective spiritual training can be done in as little as one hour a week with the whole family and a few minutes of one-on-one time with each child five days a week. Some of this time can be taken from things you are already doing. The family plan that we will help you develop will take into consideration your family's pace and show you how you can fit effective spiritual training into the busiest schedule.

- Do you drive your kids to the gym or school? You'll see how you can teach lessons of faith in the car.
- Do (could) you put your kids to bed with a story? That precious time can become a slam-dunk opportunity to teach them about God's love.
- Do you eat meals—even one a week—with the family? You can use that time.
- Does your family like to do active, fun-oriented things? Family Night activities show how blowing up balloons can help children understand why God is real even though He's "invisible," or squirting a tube of toothpaste in a family contest can teach why the Bible says not to slander others.

All of these and others can be easy-to-use times of spiritual training.

What If I Feel Inadequate— or Fail?

That's the best place to be. When you're weak, Christ can be your strength (Philippians 4:13). Only inadequate parents need apply— or need His adequacy.

To bolster your confidence, consider these things: First, you're not alone in making the decision to spend time passing your faith down to your children. You may *feel* like the only one serious about becoming a spiritual trainer, but there are thousands with no more experience or any fewer doubts than you already doing it, and thousands more are stepping up to this challenge right now.

Second, remember the concept of "grace parenting." The greatest gift we can receive as we raise our children is the profound sense of our own

Grace takes the pressure off and allows us to simply work at the task to the best of our ability, trusting God for strength, wisdom, and results.

lack of abilities and an even more profound awareness of God's grace and God's willingness to help us learn and grow, and to cover our shortcomings in the process. It is God's grace that makes us strong when we are weak (2 Corinthians 12:10). It is God's grace that gives us wisdom when we need it (James 1:5). And God's grace is enough (2 Corinthians 12:9).

God's grace is available to help us accomplish anything and everything He gives us to do, including spiritual training. So the first part of grace parenting is going to God and trusting Him for His aid and wisdom, trusting that He will change us, teach us, give us His wisdom, and help us be effective spiritual trainers.

The second part is that we need to trust Him to work in the hearts, minds, and lives of our children in the same way He worked in us. We need to trust God (and sometimes that means asking God to help us trust Him) that He's working with them and in them and that He will fulfill His promise in the life of each of them.

God has given us significant responsibilities in the process, but grace takes the pressure off and allows us to simply work at the task to the best of our ability, trusting Him for strength, wisdom, and results. God knows your limitations and strengths, He knows everything about you, and He knows how to work together with you from where you are.

In fact, the best place for you to be right now is asking the question "Can I do this?" This shows that you know your limitations and are ready to rely on God's grace to accomplish the task. Continually tell God your fears and doubts, then ask Him, by His grace, to teach you and give you wisdom and all you need to get the job done. Keep reading, prepare your plan as we'll show you, choose resources—looking to God every step of the way for help.

Third, remember the little picture: One snapshot at a time is all you need to focus on. As you provide positive snapshots day by day, you fill your children's lives with memorable moments of life, God, truth, and hope.

Every parent needs help and support. That's what this book is all about—equipping you for the task and making spiritual training accessible and easy for parents of all kinds. You're going to love the step-by-step system and the practical tools that support it.

What If I'm Doing It Alone?

You're not completely alone. God is working alongside you and the many others facing the same challenge.

Single and "spiritually single" parents face a daunting task with little support. You can feel like the suitors for Ulysses' wife in the ancient legend. Ulysses fought in the Trojan Wars and was gone so long that he was declared legally dead. Anxious suitors soon showed up to court his beautiful wife. She agreed to marry one of them when she finished her tapestry. They waited patiently for the work to be complete. But unfortunately for them, she wove all day and unraveled all night. It can sometimes seem like you work hard to set a godly example, making sure that the fabric of faith is being woven into your children's lives, only to see your spouse's indifference or the negative influence of the world unravel your work. But don't despair! God provides a spiritual safety stitch (a stitch running horizontally that stops threads from unraveling too far). "He who began a good work in you will carry it on to completion" (Philippians 1:6). God is working in you and your children.

Everyone who decides to spiritually train their children will face obstacles of one kind or another. And all of those hurdles can be cleared only one way: by trusting God to help you. When God calls you to do something, He wants to see you respond with obedience and faithfulness. When you do, He is faithful to multiply your efforts. The bigger your obstacles are, the more help you can count on. So keep on turning the pages, fill out your plan, get started, and let God show you how He can help as you trust Him—and how He can reward your obedience.

Going It Alone

I started out as a spiritually single mom and ended up a completely single mom. Throughout those years I thought there was little I could do to train my kids. After all, I had no emotional support from anyone. I certainly couldn't do after-dinner devotions. Nor could I take evenings for family activities with a spiritual emphasis. But there are more ways to impart faith lessons than just devotions, and more opportunities for activities than just the evening.

Each night I prayed with the children as they lay in their beds. I had printed a verse on a 3" x 5" card and read the same verse every night for a week. After the verse, I sang hymns to them. These times were precious as we discussed all sorts of things there in the darkness of their rooms. We talked about how God viewed friendships and how to pray for our enemies. We talked about hurts and God's presence with us at all times—even in the hard times.

Trips around town in the car afforded many opportunities to talk about how God views us, loves us, and wants us to act and care for others.

Our poverty provided faith lessons as we prayed for our needs and watched God miraculously answer those needs some of the time, and at others how He simply sustained us as we struggled.

Yes, such lessons took two of us—me and God.

L. H. J.

What If Our Children Are All Different Ages and Stages?

The spiritual training plan that we've laid out in the following pages involves both a do-it-all-together family plan and a spend-some-time-with-each-child plan. You will find that we talk about many different methods to spiritually train your children, and we encourage you to match the method to your family.

The methods and tools we recommend come with suggestions on how to make them work effectively for each different stage of growth and for a group of differing ages. Even with these helps, some families who, say, have preteens and very young children, may have difficulty making some of the methods work. If this is your situation, your older children can take more of a supportive mentoring role in the family activities, and then you can spend a little more time focusing on them in the individual time.

For Teens

Here are some resources that you can turn to for help with your teenagers.

Reality 101 by Wayne Rice and Dave Veerman (Wheaton, Ill.: Tyndale).

This book for teenagers answers 101 questions on a variety of topics like faith, friendships, family, finances, and the future. The questions came from today's teens and the answers are straightforward and honest. It includes humorous cartoon illustrations and scriptural help.

LifeTraining by Joe White (Wheaton, Ill.: Tyndale, 1998).

This book is a unique devotional, written for parents to share with their teens. With 260 devotions based upon the books of Matthew, Luke, John, Acts, James, and Revelation, *Life Training* is filled with practical tools to create and strengthen the faith of families.

LifeTraining 2 by Joe White (Wheaton, Ill.: Tyndale, 2000).

Like the first book, *Life Training 2* is filled with unique devotionals for parents to share with their teens. These devotions cover the books of Mark, Romans, 1 & 2 Corinthians, Galatians, Ephesians, Philippians, Colossians, 1 & 2 Thessalonians, 1 & 2 Timothy, Titus, Philemon, Hebrews, Peter (1, 2, 3), John (1, 2, 3), and Jude.

For those of you with teenagers, include them in the process of training the younger children, but also recognize that they have different needs. By the time your children reach the teen years, you are pretty much done forming their values. Now your role shifts to that of a mentor. There are many resources available to help you in this role.

What If We're a Blended Family? (It just seems more difficult for us.)

With a blended family (and any family) there are many "unwritten rules." Like invisible cables laying on the floor, it takes time to know where they are to stop tripping over them. Yet if a mom and dad will sit down as a team, these obstacles can become opportunities for growth. Blended families have more to draw on—different heritages, different backgrounds that, rather than being problems, can provide additional resources and wisdom. It's a matter of bringing your past, all your "little pictures" and those of your children, to God and asking for His wisdom, then sitting down together, going through this book, and talking with each other and your children to discover that wisdom.

Dr. Robert Barnes, one of the United States' leading experts on blended families, recommends that blended families do exactly what you'll be doing in this book: Get a clear, prayed over, talked through, written out parenting plan! Check out his book *You're Not My Daddy!* (Dallas: Word, 1992). By completing the exercises and tools that follow, you'll highlight where each person is in their growth, understand their strengths, and clarify goals and expectations for each one—wonderful tools for "blending" a family. And there is absolutely nothing more unifying than having everyone fall in love with God. The love that begins vertically, spreads horizontally.

What If I'm Still Hurting from a Difficult Past? (Don't I need to get healed before I try and pass something down to my kids?)

In short, no. None of us are completely healed until heaven. God can turn the ashes of broken dreams into beautiful pictures and replace negative snapshots with positive ones. It takes time, grace, and hard work—and you may need help from a pastor or Christian counselor. One book that

Get a clear, prayed over, talked through, written out parenting plan!

Healing Together

When I was six years old, my father died under tragic circumstances. Mom remarried a man who turned out to be an alcoholic.

For several years my family went through a period of turmoil that I could not understand since I was so young. Sometime after becoming a single mother the second time, Mom met Christ. It was then that the healing process in our family began, starting with my mother.

As a new, first-generation Christian, overwhelmed with emotional and spiritual grief, she was ill-prepared to spiritually train us. She was also only just beginning to become acquainted with God herself. Much of her malady was reflected in my siblings and me. However, as God began working in Mom's life, we kids observed how God enveloped her in love and gave her strength and the will to go on. Watching this changed us. We listened as she shared what she learned. We followed in her steps and found healing and spiritual growth for ourselves. Mom didn't need to be emotionally healthy to teach us; she just needed to follow God and lead us to Him. It was a journey we took as a family.

Anonymous

talks about overcoming this hurt is John Trent's *Pictures the Heart Remembers*, (Colorado Springs, Co: Waterbrook Press, 2000) based upon Deuteronomy 30:19 which says, "I have set before you life and death, blessings and curses. Now choose life."

Life involves choices. Choosing life often means choosing to forgive and turn away from the hurt, leaving it in God's hands. We realize this is not easy, nor is it necessarily the full solution, but your children need you. And in large measure, this method works. So choose to pursue your healing by getting busy loving and serving others—starting with your own children. Knowing God more and pouring positive times into your children can help you heal.

What If My Own Spiritual Life Is Shaky?

You don't have to have unshakable faith to train your children. Even giants of the faith like Moses, Elisha, Peter, and Paul had times of questioning, doubt, or disappointment. King David, that man of God, did too: "My God, my God, why have you forsaken me? . . . O my God, I cry out by day, but you do not answer, by night, and am not silent" (Psalm 22:1–2). A strong faith doesn't mean you never question or feel far from God.

David was secure enough to share his feelings, doubts, and hurts, but he always came back to reality. He followed those words of hurt and abandonment with what he knew to be true: "Yet you are enthroned as the Holy One; . . . In you our fathers put their trust; they trusted and you delivered them" (vv. 3–4).

In the middle of long-term doubts, serious questions about God, or times you just can't face things, the fact remains: God is, and He revealed Himself in the Bible saying He is love. Sometimes you just have to hold on to what the Bible says as if it were the only unshakable thing in the world. Feelings are not arbiters of truth; God is. Hang on to the basics: "For God so loved the world that he gave his one and only Son, that whoever believes in him shall not perish but have eternal life" (John 3:16).

If your doubts go even deeper and you're not sure you've ever received Jesus' gift of eternal life, it could be decision time. You *can* know for sure where you'll spend eternity. God is knocking at the door of your heart right now. "If you confess with your mouth, 'Jesus is Lord,' and believe in your heart that God raised him from the dead, you will be saved. For it is with your heart that you believe and are justified, and it is with your mouth that you confess and are saved" (Romans 10:9–10). If you're ready to open that door, pray this simple prayer:

"Dear God, I confess that You are Lord. Thank You so much for sending Jesus to die for me and pay the penalty for my sins. Please forgive me. Thank You for raising Him from the dead and defeating Satan. Thank You so much for saving me. Teach me to follow You. In Jesus' name, amen."

If you prayed that prayer for the first time, tell a loved one (or several) about it. And don't worry about being a new Christian when it comes to passing down your faith. Growing together with your children can be the most effective way to spiritually train them. (For information on salvation and Jesus' ministry and death, see Topic No. 22 in chapter 30.)

Rollerblade? I've Never Done It

"Kelsie, look what I bought!"

"Rollerblades! Thanks, Daddy!" Kelsie threw her arms around me and gave me a big hug. Then she looked closer. "Two pairs? Who are those for?"

"Me," I told her.

She looked at me quizzically. "But you don't know how to rollerblade."

"Nope," I said. "I thought we'd learn together."

Together we laced up those skates. We padded our elbows and knees. And then we wobbled and fell together. We laughed at Daddy's inadequacies. We laughed that Daddy didn't know everything or do everything well.

Kelsie saw firsthand that learning is not always easy, that all people learn and grow in new things. We can be shaky at first, but with practice and persistence, the shakiness becomes confidence.

It's the same when we learn new spiritual concepts. It doesn't matter if I'm wobbly or shaky on a spiritual truth. With prayer and practice and taking small steps at a time, my child and I can learn together.

J. M.

What If I'm Not a Theologian? (How can I make sure I teach them well and cover it all?)

Remember, your goal is to create positive snapshots, memorable moments, one picture at a time. To do that you don't need to be a theologian, have great fountains of knowledge, or have years of Christianity under your belt. You *do* need to be learning yourself and working on your own relationship with God so that you stay in step with your children, or perhaps one or two steps ahead. You'll be surprised how much you learn as you teach your children. If they ask questions you don't know the answer to, tell them you don't know for sure and look them up together. Growing together can be a great bonding time.

As for theology and covering it all, we've done most of the work for you. We've broken the job down into snapshot-sized pieces, providing the basics of what your children need to learn, with supporting scriptures and tips on how to teach it (see parts III and IV). Additional scriptures are also included if you want to do further study. These cover what children up to age 12 can understand about the Bible, God, and the Christian life, and are fairly comprehensive.

Look It Up

"Dad," Jake said in the kitchen one day after I came home from work, "they asked us this really weird question at school today."

"What was that?"

"The teacher asked all of us what we feared the most."

"What were the answers?" I asked. By now, Jake and I had the attention of his three siblings.

"Most of the kids said they fear their dad and they fear God."

"Fear God," I said. "Isn't that interesting? You hear that all the time in church, don't you?"

All the kids were caught up and I saw four heads nodding.

"What do you think that means?"

"I don't know," Janae said. "What does it mean, Dad?"

"I'll tell you what," I said, looking at each of them. "You have Bibles. I want you to go get your Bibles and look in the back for the phrase 'Fear God'." (We use the *Life Application Bible* which contains a concordance in the back.)

Within moments the kids had all snagged their Bibles and returned to the kitchen. The table soon had open Bibles spread out on it and eager eyes searching for the answer. Together we all went to the verse and discussed "fear"—meaning to have an incredible awe and reverence for. Our discussion continued for some time.

The important point I wanted to make to my kids wasn't so much to answer the question as to teach them to go get the Bible and open it up to find answers for life questions.

J. W.

What If My Child Has a Learning Disability or Other Special Need?

If you are the parent of a severely handicapped child, you may tend to shy away from trying to give him or her an awareness of God and heaven. With little or no way of gauging your child's response, you may find yourself asking, "Am I really getting through?"

Although your child might not grasp the message of salvation, he or she *can* grasp the love of God. He or she can learn a great deal about God's love without needing to understand every aspect of doctrine. Soak your child in love.

Make the most of any and every opportunity to share spiritual truth with your child. Scripture clearly tells us that we are of incredible worth in God's sight. Physical infirmities don't change that. God's love for your child is no different than it was for David, who wrote:

> *You created my inmost being; you knit me together in my mother's womb. I praise you because I am fearfully and wonderfully made; your works are wonderful, I know that full well. My frame was not hidden from you when I was made in the secret place. When I was woven together in the depths of the earth, your eyes saw my unformed body. All the days ordained for me were written in your book before one of them came to be.* (Psalm 139:13–16)

Someone Special

When my daughter Emily was little, I had no idea how much she would ever know or grasp. She was born with Down's syndrome and was a masterpiece of God's hand. Daily I would talk to her about everything. "Emily, this is a can," I would say to her as I took a can of green beans from the grocery store shelf. "This is a pencil. It's made from wood. Wood comes from a tree that God made."

And I would look directly into her eyes and tell her, "Emily, you have Down's syndrome. That means God gave you something extra—an extra chromosome. And He made you exactly as He wanted you to be. You are special, made in His image."

When her brother was born three and a half years later, we named him Abraham and spent many hours praying for him. Emily heard all these prayers for her and for her brother.

One day when Abraham was two, he crawled into bed with me. "Where's Emily?" I asked.

"In my bed," Abraham replied.

I sent Daddy to look, and sure enough, Emily was there. "What are you doing in Abraham's bed?"

"I sing and prayed."

"What?"

"Prayer, Jesus," she said.

And then we realized she was singing and praying for her brother.

B. F.

Take the best

parts of both

of your

backgrounds

and move

forward with

those elements.

Regardless of whether or not your child is able to understand, pray over him or her, read from the Bible, and sing hymns or other Christian songs to him or her. King David's young baby became ill and David spent seven days fasting and praying for him. The baby died, but David gave him to the grace of God and said only, "I will go to him, but he will not return to me" (2 Samuel 12:23b). Even though his child was clearly unable to have a mental awareness of God before he died, David was comforted because he knew he would one day be with his baby in God's presence. You can have this same confidence as you try to give your child an awareness of God's love.

What If My Spouse and I Are from Different Church Backgrounds?

The key might be to change your focus from where you've come from to where you're going. What do you want for your children? Every tradition has positive things to offer. Take the best parts of both of your backgrounds and move forward with those elements.

This question often comes up with regard to choosing a church to attend. In that context one of the most important issues to consider is community and how the church can benefit your children. The goal is to give them a positive experience where they can grow and participate. The main thing is to discover what works for your family. If there is a Christian church close by that has a good children's program and you or your children already know people who go there, it may not line up with either of your backgrounds, but it may be the best place for your family.

It is the same with spiritual training at home. Carefully consider each of your backgrounds and what they offer. For example, if one person's background includes a traditional, liturgical church with its rich use of ceremony to convey the teaching, then bring that forward and teach your children the wonderful depth and richness of that tradition. If the other spouse comes from a more casual, relaxed faith background, have him or her bring that more relational "everydayness" into the mix.

The key is to find what works for your children and to give them the solid foundation they will need to live for God and have a wonderful, fulfilling life.

What If I Don't See the Need for All the Facts and Doctrine? (I just want my children to love God.)

Knowledge deepens and informs love. The more your children know about God and the more they know how amazing and wonderful He is, the more reason they will have to love Him. "Make every effort to add to your faith goodness; and to goodness, knowledge" (2 Peter 1:5). "Faith comes from hearing the message, and the message is heard through the word of Christ" (Romans 10:17).

If doctrine and biblical facts were all there was to it, Christianity would be boring indeed. But if emotion based on experience were all there was, your children would have trouble when "experience" said God wasn't worth loving. Your children need a solid foundation upon which to build their relationship with God, their understanding of His Word and principles, and their lives on. Everything that God has shown us about Himself, His plan, or the way He created things to work has practical applications to our lives and relationship with Him.

This book and plan will help you cover the three major areas or types of spiritual training your children need in order to grow a solid Christian life:

♦ **Knowing:** Children need to know what they believe and why, and to understand their faith so that they're solidly

Knowing What We Believe

Knowing what and why we believe is critical in order for our children to have a solid spiritual foundation. Putting these beliefs into contexts our children can understand is not always easy. It takes creativity.

My nine-year-old son Kyle is encountering different religions and faiths. In fact, we're right around the corner from a huge Mormon church.

One day Kyle told me that a friend had pointed to the church and said, "My mommy says that's the church where the bad people are."

I realized the need to explain other religions and beliefs in a way that did not portray the believers as "bad people." I took my son to breakfast to explain different views of God in a way he could understand. For example, I said that many people believe in the "Up There God"—the God who loves us and cares for us, but never came down to die for us on the cross. These are not "bad people" but people who do not know or believe in Jesus. I explained the "Man God"—the belief that God was once a man and is now a god, and that everyone can also become a god. This view, held by the people who attend the Mormon church near our house, doesn't make the members "bad people" but "confused" or "misguided" people. I contrasted these and other views with "Our God"—the belief in the one and true God who created us and came down to earth to die for our sins.

K. B.

The foundation of your children's upbringing should be learning and applying God's truth in every area of life.

grounded and can answer the objections they'll face. (They *will* face them.) They need to know who God is and what He's done, primarily as shown in the Bible, but also in your family history and the lives of others.

♦ **Loving:** Children need to love God, grow in relationship with Him, and know how to develop that relationship, increasing their personal knowledge of our loving heavenly Father.

♦ **Living:** Children need to learn how to live out their faith and apply what they know and experience of God and His principles. The Bible isn't just a lofty book of knowledge—it's life's instruction manual.

As discussed in chapters 1 and 2, the Bible says that we are to bring our children up in the training and instruction of the Lord. In other words, the foundation of their upbringing should be learning and applying God's truth in every area of life.

What If We've Already Tried Something Like This and It Didn't Work?

It's a good thing Edison didn't quit trying to get his lightbulb to work! Over 70 publishers rejected Dr. Seuss before his first book was accepted. And really, if you haven't failed, you haven't tried. The issue in spiritual training isn't perfection; it's God-honoring persistence. It's starting again after situations or struggles have turned off the switch. Most attempts at training kids fail because parents *don't* have a plan, or they didn't have a plan that worked for their family. If you have no goals and the going gets tough, or when you're trying to push something at your family instead of pulling together, it's easy to turn on the TV or "wait until a better day." Even with the plan that specifically matches your family that you're about to develop and embark on, you'll have days when it just doesn't work.

Don't use a slip or even many slips as an excuse to quit. Reward whoever says, "Hey, we should do our family time!" with a "Great idea!" not a groan brought on by guilt. Thank God for the reminder of the importance of what you're doing, and get back in the battle.

Now that you know the priority and common obstacles to spiritual training, you're almost ready to put together your unique family portrait and your Spiritual Growth Plan. But first, every effective plan is preceded by a conscious commitment.

NOTES
1. Ralph Keye, *Timelock* (New York: Harper Collins, 1991), 20.

CHAPTER 5

Making a Commitment You Can Keep

Suppose one of you wants to build a tower. Will he not first sit down and estimate the cost to see if he has enough money to complete it? For if he lays the foundation and is not able to finish it, everyone who sees it will ridicule him. (Luke 14:28–29)

Take a moment to reflect upon the last few months. Were you busy? Too busy? Did you have unexpected interruptions—perhaps sick kids, unplanned phone calls, nagging headaches, or car trouble? Were there last minute assignments at work, special church meetings, parent-teacher conferences, soccer practices, music lessons, dentist appointments, and a hundred other activities that filled up your calendar?

Now ask yourself this: Do you honestly think it will be much different during the next few months?

How about the next year?

How about the next 10 years?

Let's face it, hurry and overcommitment are part of life. There is nothing on the horizon that will magically take away all the activity or give us a 32-hour day. So, more than ever, we must become intentional about teaching our children the values we consider important. It is not a matter of when we will have the time but whether we will commit ourselves to the process.

No doubt you agree that the spiritual development of your child is critically important. And we know it won't happen without your intentional involvement in the process. This is one area of parenting that you can't delegate. Yet how can you add another thing to your long list of "to dos"?

Let's walk through a simple process.

Step 1: Recognize the Need

When we become Christians, our number-one life priority becomes our relationship with God. When we get married, we make a commitment to love, care for, and spend time with our spouse. When we have children, we make a commitment to care for, love, and raise them. Their spiritual training is to be the number one focus of that commitment.

Step 2: Assess the Level of Commitment Required

The plan for getting started that's outlined later in this chapter is taking your children to church on Sundays, spending one hour every other week doing a family spiritual training activity, and spending five to ten minutes with each child five days a week.

Step 3: Acknowledge God's Grace

In order to make and keep this commitment, you need to tap into God's grace. Making a commitment in the context of God's grace doesn't mean committing to never failing or falling down. It means committing to continually trusting God to keep getting you up and moving you forward. Don't let the "But I . . .s" or the "But what if . . .s" stand in your way. God's grace will get you started and keep you going.

Step 4: Make a Decision

Even after we agree that something is a priority and we know what we should do, we sometimes fail to get on with it because we postpone the decision to start. Pray, then read and sign (or first photocopy) the commitment card on the next page. This is your personal commitment as a parent or as parents to spiritually train your children. Put it where you can see it.

PARENT'S COMMITMENT CARD

On this _____ day of _____, 20_____,

I am making a commitment before my God.

I, _____, the parent

in this home, commit to fulfilling my calling as the spiritual trainer of my

child[ren]. With God's help I will take up this God-given task. I will keep God's

ways on my own heart and "impress them on my child[ren]. I'll talk about

them when I sit at home, when I walk along the road, when I lie down and

when I get up" (per Deuteronomy 6:6–7).

Signed by my hand—held in the heart:

_____

Your commitment to begin is an important first step in what the scriptures describe as a process that can have a profound and lasting impact.

We will not hide them from our children; we will tell the next generation the praiseworthy deeds of the LORD, his power, and the wonders he has done. He decreed statutes for Jacob and established the law in Israel, which he commanded our forefathers to teach their children, so the next generation would know them, even the children yet to be born, and they in turn would tell their children. Then they would put their trust in God and would not forget his deeds but would keep his commands. They would not be like their forefathers—a stubborn and rebellious generation, whose hearts were not loyal to God, whose spirits were not faithful to him. (Psalm 78:4–8)

Future generations are waiting on us to start the cycle, to teach them the faith that will give them an anchor for living. As we look back from eternity, may we hear that our children, grandchildren, and those beyond "put their trust in God" thanks to the effort we put forth today.

On behalf of future generations, thank you for making an effort to teach your children!

How to Get Started

Congratulations! Your decision to develop a plan for passing on your spiritual heritage is a gift that will enrich your family for generations to come.

Start Now!

Research shows that starting your plan within four days after making a decision is vital to its success. Waiting longer to be intentional about passing on a spiritual heritage means there's a 90 percent chance of never doing it at all. Start small, but start today!

Building a spiritual heritage takes time, effort, and creativity. How do you make it meaningful and make it last?

First, look at your current activities and see which align with the spiritual plan. Second, choose some new activities to make your family's spiritual heritage stronger (see example plan on the next page). Here are some ideas to help you get started—and keep going.

Build a Custom Plan for Your Family's Spiritual Heritage!

SPIRITUAL HERITAGE PLAN			
Pray Daily	**Weekly Family Activities**	**Capture the Moment**	**Attend Church Activities**
Currently: • Pray together at mealtime • Pray with child at bedtime	• Watch favorite TV show together	• Read a bedtime story	• Attend weekly as a family
Plan: • Provide daily prayer covering for family • Pray together for family as husband and wife at end of day	• Choose one night a week to hold "Family Night" (see chapter 21)	• Read devotional stories at dinner • Let children listen to *Adventures in Odyssey* tapes from Focus on the Family after bedtime prayers	• Get children involved in Sunday school and/or youth groups
Your Plan:			

Make Prayer a Priority

It starts with you! As a parent, the responsibility for covering your household in prayer belongs to you. Make a list of your family's prayer needs and lift them up before God each day, whether there's a crisis or not. Keep in mind spiritual needs as well as physical or material needs; for example, your children's protection from negative influences, their desire to learn about God and so on. There's never a day when your family doesn't need your prayers.

◆ **Teach your children to pray.** Spend time with your kids one-on-one to talk about why prayer is important. Let them know that prayer is a personal conversation with God and that they can tell Him everything—their hopes, their worries, their needs. Pray with them to start and then let them voice prayers on their own. You may want to use *The Power of Family Prayer* (National Day of Prayer) booklet as a starting point.

◆ **Pray together as husband and wife.** Starting and ending the day in prayer is a wonderful way to strengthen your marriage and family life. In some families, each parent may choose to fast one day a week.

◆ **Pray together as a family each day.** Whether at mealtimes or at bedtime, find a time to come together and unite in prayer as a family. This daily commitment will draw you closer and reinforce the importance of prayer in your household.

Build Fun and Faith with Family Activities

◆ **Watch videos and/or go to movies together.** Afterward, talk about the themes of what you just saw. Which parts were consistent with your Christian beliefs? Which were not—and why?

◆ **Volunteer together as a family.** It's important for your children to see your beliefs in action by volunteering your time and efforts to those less fortunate. The lessons of sacrificial giving will stay in your children's hearts as you venture into God's mission field together.

◆ **Have a weekly family night.** Use object lessons to teach biblical principles in a fun and memorable way. Many children won't remember all your words to them, but most will remember an activity that teaches them lasting truth. Heritage Builders' Web site (www.heritagebuilders.com) and products offer great ideas.

Family Moments

These are the moments in everyday life that give you an opportunity to capture and create spiritual lessons. They show your family that faith is not something to be saved for Sunday but to be lived out each day.

◆ **Bedtime prayers.** Use this time to remember loved ones who may live far away, missionaries, the hungry, and the homeless. Keep pictures of these people nearby if possible to help your child remember them. Then let your child choose who to pray for each night.

♦ **Mealtime prayers and devotional stories.** Share stories from a good Christian devotional to illustrate godly principles and hold your attention at the same time. After reading the story's setup, have them guess the outcome or tell how they would react in a similar situation. Then read the ending and discuss it.

♦ **Drivetime moments.** Use the time in the car running errands or going to activities to listen to Focus on the Family's *Adventures in Odyssey* or *Radio Theatre*—or just spend the time talking about what's on each other's minds and hearts.

Church Activities

♦ **Commit to attending church as a family.** In addition to Christian fellowship and your own spiritual development, your church will reinforce the lessons you've been teaching at home.

♦ **Involve your children.** Get them into groups geared for their ages at church. Let them discover how much fun church can be! The spiritual and social benefits will be great.

♦ **Consider a family missions trip.** It's an unforgettable experience to serve in another culture. Prayerfully consider whether this might be right for your family.

Keep in mind that there's no "right way" to develop your family's spiritual heritage. The main thing to remember is to be *intentional* and *consistent*, using everyday experience as a tool to teach your children. Don't get too elaborate or lengthy—make it enjoyable for the whole family. Once you get into the habit, you'll see that building a spiritual heritage is not as difficult as you thought.

Visit our Heritage Builder's Web site! Log on to (**www. heritagebuilders.com**) to discover new resources and updated worksheets, and to learn what other families are doing to pass on a spiritual heritage. Or contact Focus on the Family, Colorado Springs, CO 80995 (in Canada, write to Focus on the Family, P.O. Box 9800, Station Terminal, Vancouver, B.C. V6B 4G3).

PART II

How to Pass On Your Spiritual Legacy

Section A: Your Family's Portrait
Section B: Your Children's Ages and Stages
Section C: Methods and Ideas You Can Choose From
Section D: Designing Your Family Spiritual Growth Plan

How to Pass On Your Spiritual Legacy

Parents have faced the same struggle for years. In most cases they were familiar with just one or, at most, two methods of reaching young hearts with God's Word. The mere words "family devotions" can still strike something close to terror into the hearts of many adults as the memory snapshots show Mom or Dad reading from the Bible (or from a book of devotional readings) and praying while the kids are bored and fidgety. About the only interaction livening up these family devotions was Dad warning Suzie to sit still or Mom telling Charlie to quit making faces at his brother. It's almost as if there was an unspoken rule: "If everyone's done it this way for generations, then it's good enough for our family!"

Apart from the question of whether this kind of family devotions was ever effective for many families (for some, it undoubtedly was), the times have changed. We can no longer assume that simply telling or reading our kids something about God will have an impact. We live in a society where our kids (and we) are daily bombarded

There is no "typical" way in which to pass on your faith to your children.

with words and images. We *must* make the effort to think about how we can pass on our spiritual legacy to our children in a way they'll actually hear and grasp. If we don't, we may well find that the Word is being drowned out by words.

Spiritual training must take into account the individuality of each person. After all, the foundation of the Christian faith is an individual relationship with God, who has made each person unique and has a special, unique spot in His heart for each one. That means there is a particular, wonderful, one-of-a-kind relationship with God that only you can have. And the same is true for each of your children. God loves each one individually and equally. He doesn't assign kingdom membership numbers or treat all people the same. He knows each person inside and out—He designed and planned for every child from long before their parents ever considered having them.

And since each member of your family is one-of-a-kind, it follows that your family, and every other family, is also unique. Each family goes through life in its own particular way as a unique combination of people, relationships, dynamics, interests, and hobbies.

There is no such thing as a "typical" family—and there is no "typical" way in which to pass on your faith to your children. Since your faith is expressed through the one-of-a-kind life your family leads, your plan for passing on your faith to your children should match who you

are as a family. What will work for someone else's family may not work for yours at all. Don't try to fit your family and your children into a one-size-fits-all training program. Use a program that not only considers their differences but uses them and builds on them. Then you will have the joy of seeing them grow in faith as they make Christianity their own and learn to apply God's principles to their particular situations.

What's Ahead

Part II of the book will help you begin to develop a plan of spiritual training designed specifically for your family. At the end of some of the chapters, and at the end of each of the first three sections, there is a chart you can fill in (or photocopy and fill in), so that you have all the notes identifying your family and family members in one place. In the fourth section you'll put it all together into one plan. (All planning forms are available online at www.heritagebuilders.com.)

♦ You begin with a simple **family inventory** that helps you identify what your family and children are like and in what ways your family is unique ("Your Family's Portrait," pages 65–100). Each of the four chapters in this section deals with one aspect and will give you examples to help you identify which family yours is most like and will provide you with possible strengths and weaknesses of each.

♦ The second section will help you focus on who **your children** are from a developmental perspective ("Your Children's Ages and Stages," pages 101–136). It will give you a brief overview of a child's progress physically, mentally, and especially, spiritually. This will help you understand what concepts your children can grasp at what age. Children are dealt with in four broad age groups or stages of development: 0–4 years, 5–6 years, 7–9 years, and 10–12 years.

♦ Once you've identified the unique traits of your family, you can use them to look at a number of **ideas and methods** from which you can choose (or adapt) those that are most suited to your particular family ("Ideas and Methods You Can Choose From," pages 137–228).

♦ Finally, you can put all the insights from the first three sections into a **plan for passing on your spiritual legacy**—a plan that will enable you to train your children in their relationship with God without "drilling" them or using methods that are unsuited to their personalities. This plan will keep your spiritual training alive and relevant, exciting, and interesting ("Designing Your Family Spiritual Growth Plan" pages 229–266).

Your Family's Portrait

What Is Your Family's "History of Faith"?
What Pace Does Your Family Live At?
What Are Your Family's Interests?
Identifying Your Family's Unique Personal Strengths
Your Family Portrait: Putting It All Together

CHAPTER 6

What Is Your Family's "History of Faith"?

Understanding your own "history of faith" can make a huge difference in how you approach your children. To help you see how to take advantage of your background, ask yourself what "generation" you are as a Christian.

Are You a "First Generation Christian"?

Jim and Deborah are both "1st Generation Christians." Neither grew up in a home with a strong commitment to Christ. Jim darkened the door of a church with about the same frequency as Halley's comet brightens the sky. Deborah had a bit more exposure to church but never heard about a personal relationship with Jesus. However, they both became Christians in high school.

On the negative side, neither of them came into parenting with an idea of "this is how my parents did it"—good or bad. They're plowing new ground. Nor is there much support from relatives. The opposite in fact: At family gatherings their faith is sliced up alongside the turkey as the family criticizes and mocks Christianity. Jim and Deborah also face the residue of their lives B.C. (Before Christ) and have little "built-in" knowledge to draw on.

Although 1st Generation Christians have hurdles to cross with no tangible models of faith to follow, they bring definite advantages to the table. First is their zeal and enthusiasm for Christ. For example, Deborah and Jim were saved out of difficult pasts. They longed for a heavenly

Tell your children you're in the learning process too, and celebrate discovering answers together.

Father and couldn't be quiet about the changes inside when they met Him. As a result, they both have a tremendous burden for their children to know the Lord and for them to avoid the heartache and pain they themselves had growing up. Another great advantage is that when they are developing their Spiritual Growth Plan they have a clean slate to plan from and they can tailor their plan to their family without any but-that's-not-the-way-we-did-it problems.

Perhaps you're the first in your family to take faith in Christ seriously. If that's the case, congratulations. Your burden and passion as a 1st Generation Christian can be contagious, and even without a positive pattern or role model to draw on, the task is within your grasp. You'll find the Spiritual Growth Plan presented in this book especially helpful. It can provide structure and age-specific answers to your questions about your children's spiritual readiness.

Also, you get to learn some of the great lessons of the faith alongside your children. Don't let pride or embarrassment keep you from teaching them. Let's say your seven-year-old asks, "What's the difference between Jesus and an angel?" or "What's heaven really like?" If you don't have a good answer ready, admit it—and promise to find out.[1] If you can't find an answer right away, don't panic. Tell your children you're in the learning process too, and celebrate discovering answers together. Not only are you helping your child find an answer; you are also modeling honesty, humility, and the all-important attitude of always wanting to learn and grow. Later, when picking methods and tools for your Spiritual Growth Plan, make sure you pick ones that will systematically help your family understand the basic truths of the faith. These truths will add strength and knowledge to your zeal.

Are You a "Second Generation Christian"?

Second-generation Christians grew up in a household of faith, often going to church regularly and having family devotions. If that's your spiritual background, there are many positives to it. For example, you have some knowledge of the Bible, you have a personal history with God, and you have seen people trying to live out their faith in the everyday world.

But there are challenges where faith is a given. Danny Warfol, quarterback for the University of Florida and eventual Heisman Trophy winner, said, "I hate to admit it, but I had a serious drug problem growing up. My father was a pastor, and I got *drug* to church on Sunday morning, *drug* to church on Sunday night, *drug* to church on Wednesday night."[2]

That's in many ways a positive "drug" problem! But he also faced very real challenges because of being surrounded by so much positive spiritual input. As Warfol hit the teenage years, he struggled over whether he had made a personal, individual decision for Christ or had simply adopted a lifestyle that his parents expected. Second Generation Christians need to answer the question "Is this real to me?" Just because a parent's life was changed dramatically is no guarantee that the children will respond. Exposure to spiritual truth isn't enough, any more than exposure to lots of flour makes someone a loaf of bread. And exposure to spiritual truth that is not backed up by a living faith may end up having a negative effect because it's so easy to reject as a mere formality.

Often 2nd Generation Christians don't have passion for God because Christian parents take their faith for granted. The Israelites of Joshua's generation certainly knew God's power, but they got comfy and fat in the Promised Land and stopped growing in their faith. They didn't actively teach their faith to their children—in spite of Moses' warnings and commands recorded in Deuteronomy 6:4–9—and the next generation rejected God (Judges 2:10).

Or take the example of Eli in 1 Samuel 2–3. Eli was at least a 2nd Generation Christian, an Old Testament priest whose life reflected a genuine faith in and love for the Lord. Yet he fell down badly on the job of communicating his faith to his children and made only mild attempts to correct their blatant sin. "Eli's sons were wicked men; they had no regard for the LORD" (1 Samuel 2:12) (see also vv. 22–25). In contrast, Hannah, also a devout follower of God, trained Samuel in the few years she had him so that, even under Eli's lax care, he continued to follow God (1 Samuel 1:1–2:11, 18–26; 3:1–21).

When parents lose their passion and neglect their calling to spiritually train their children, the children usually walk away. They don't understand their faith or see it as something that makes a difference in their parents' lives or as connected to their own lives.

Danny Warfol's experience is normal. Everyone must sooner or later examine the reality of his or her faith. If Christian parents teach their children about this and help them understand how to get through it, they can come out more committed than ever. As a 2nd Generation Christian, if you press on and keep growing, you'll get more excited about your faith, and you'll also have a seasoned Christian maturity that will help you teach your children and grow with them. If this is you, as you're moving through this book pick methods and tools for your Spiritual Growth Plan that you think are original and exciting. Ask God to help you get your spark back so you can start a fire in your kids.

Are You a "Third Generation Christian"?

Third-generation Christians have the advantage of having two (or more) generations before them who loved and followed the Lord. In some cases being a 3rd Generation Christian means having grandparents who know and love the Lord but parents who don't. If that's your situation, in many ways you're like a 1st Generation Christian, choosing to love the Lord without the benefit of parents who are living out their faith. But you still have a tremendous advantage: Grandparents who love the Lord provide a stabilizing influence for you to draw on.

If your parents followed the model above and you're an excited 3rd Generation Christian, you're ahead of the game. You have a solid foundation of Christian living and can see, in your parents and grandparents, how the whole cycle of passing on a genuine, vibrant faith works. You have mature mentors to help and guide you—and you can probably mentor other parents. It will be exciting for you, as you go through these chapters, to find new, fresh ways to train your children and help you branch out from the ways your family used in the past, adding new zest and passion.

If you and your spouse have two different backgrounds—for example, you are a 1st Generation Christian and your spouse is a 3rd Generation Christian—use your differing strengths to your advantage when making your plan. For example, let the one who is more excited about the Spiritual Growth Plan lead the charge, while getting input from the one who may have experience from his or her own childhood.

The Spiritual Background Sheet

With these three generations in mind, take time to fill in your spiritual history checklist on the next page. (You may want to photocopy the form first—it's also available online from www.heritagebuilders.com.) If you're doing this as a couple, use different colored pens. Take a few moments to consider the strengths and struggles listed for your generation. Mark the ones that apply. Add any others you can think of in the spaces provided.

Let the one who is more excited about the Spiritual Growth Plan lead the charge.

SPIRITUAL HISTORY SHEET

❏ **I'm a "first generation Christian."**

Strengths this gives:

___ Passion

___ Enthusiasm

___ Willingness to learn

___ No negative spiritual habits or routines to break

___ No preconceived or "taken-for-granted" ideas

___ Chance to learn along with children

___ Personal knowledge of God's saving power

___

Struggles it brings:

___ Little knowledge

___ Little support

___ No positive habits of Bible study/reading

___ No godly heritage of faith

___ Difficult past to recover from

___ Bad habits to conquer

___

❏ **I grew up as a "second generation Christian."**

Strengths:

___ Bible knowledge

___ An example to follow

___ Experience with positive spiritual training

___ Personal experience with God

___ Knowledge of the effectiveness of God's ways

___ Spiritual support

___

Struggles:

___ Is it real for *me?*

___ Take God for granted

___ Parents assumed my knowledge

___ Parents lost their vibrant, growing faith

___ Faith unconnected to daily life

___

❏ **I'm a "third generation Christian."**

Strengths:

___ Generations of spiritual wisdom and maturity

___ Solid foundation of knowledge

___ Experience of positive spiritual training

___ Positive support and role models

___ History of God's active goodness

___ Personal experience with God

___

___

Struggles:

___ Passion has grown cold

___ Knowledge disconnected from daily life

___ Stale: "This is how it's always done."

___ Pressure to believe without freedom to question

___ Possible negative spiritual experiences

___

___

NOTES

1. Part III, "The Content of Your Spiritual Legacy," provides basic answers with Bible references, and Part IV contains a number of questions parents face. (See also *801 Questions Kids Ask About God* [Wheaton, Ill.: Tyndale, 2000]).

2. Fellowship of Christian Athletes Outreach Breakfast, Phoenix, Arizona, 1998.

CHAPTER 7

What Pace Does Your Family Live At?

Germany is known for its beautiful countryside, lush forests, and incredible chocolate—and its Autobahn, every wannabe race car driver's dream. It's a world-class highway system between major German cities with no speed limit. That's right—*no* speed limit. Have you ever been driving 100 miles an hour and had someone pass you like you were parked with the hood up? There you are, cruising along with traffic at a brisk 100 miles per hour. The first car passes you going, conservatively, 145 miles an hour. Then another blur roars by on your left. Then a third. You think it was two Porsches and a Ferrari, but they went by so fast they could have been guided missiles!

For some of us, life's like that. You think you're moving at a pace that qualifies your family to be poster children for running flat out—until another family passes you on the activity scale like you were sitting in a stroller. This chapter will help you determine which pace your family lives at: in a carriage in the slow lane; in a steam engine, steadily plodding along the track; or in an F-16 fighter, moving faster than the speed of sound. These three paces are not, like the three bears' porridge, "too cold," "too hot," and "just right." Any of them can be "just right" for your family.

Why look at your family's pace? Every family is different. You need to figure out who your family is in order to make a program that will work for *you*. Many Christians think that spiritual training is sitting down weekly or even daily (probably for up to an hour) to read and study the Bible together. But they struggle with this because it just does

To build an effective Spiritual Growth Plan and to choose the right tools for your family, you need to know what your family pace is.

not fit their family life. They think they have to change their family to meet their ideal of how to spiritually train their children.

Wait! Turn that around: Change your ideal to meet who your family is! Spiritual training needs to be effective, not something you can tick off your list for this week. So, to build an effective Spiritual Growth Plan and to choose the right tools for *your* family, you need to know, among other things, what your family pace is. Using the wrong methods and tools leads to frustration and guilt. The key is to identify your family's pace and then match your Spiritual Growth Plan to it so that your plan works.

(The three families below are fictional but based on the real-life experience of many families.)

The Carriage Family: Life in the Slow Lane

Donna and Jim are nothing if not laid-back. They ambled through college and finished their three-year courses in four years. After all, life is to be enjoyed, and Donna's trip to Europe and Jim's time with Youth With A Mission (YWAM) were well worth it. They graduated, found jobs, and married, content. They stroll through life enjoying things, nature, and people. Life doesn't revolve around cramming appointments into a schedule book marked in half hour lots. They use one simple calendar to put down occasional events or excursions. Their children's arrivals threw them into a tizzy, since they weren't sure how to deal with the changes, but they gradually adapted and returned to their laid-back lifestyle.

The carriage family operates at a lower stress level because the clock does not tyrannize them. "Life is too short," Jim would say. They take time to think, reflect, read, and discuss issues—instead of thinking that's something they'll do after retirement. The carriage family has the time and often the family setting to put in place a wonderful Spiritual Growth Plan. They are also usually quite good at starting slowly and spending more time with things, and that's great.

A couple of the obstacles a carriage family may face are structure (sometimes too much of it, sometimes not enough) and the fact that they are often resistant to change. If you are a carriage family, you may have your life and schedule well protected and organized to keep yourself at your current pace. You also may be a carriage family because you are very laid-back and have little structure, if any. Either way, a carriage family tends to resist changing or adding any new responsibilities. This causes them to ease slowly into any new thing they decide on. These two "obstacles" will balance each other out: If you make decisions and start slowly, you'll have the time to adjust your well-organized schedule or slowly add a little structure to your more relaxed life.

The Steam Engine Family: Life in the Fast Lane

Remember the "little engine that could"? It kept chugging along until it saved the day. That's Ron and Julie Smith. Their steam engine family is characterized by steadiness, consistency . . . and increasing commitments. Like adding more and more cars to the train, they keep adding responsibilities. Everyone knows they can count on Ron and Julie. They're reliable, always there when there's a job to do.

The Smiths like to plan things in advance so that they know what's expected when, and so they can be prepared. Their schedule is kept on a large calendar with lots of room to write: One color is for family events, one for work, and one for church.

Problems come when a steam engine family takes on more than they can properly handle, continually adding cars to their train. Ron is liked by everyone, is good at nearly everything he tries, and has difficulty saying no. Julie can't say no to herself. Often she doesn't even wait to be asked. Her attitude is "Why go to AWANA or the Wednesday night kids program when you can *lead* it?" No one else stepped up to be the "den mother" or "room mom or dad"? No problem, Ron and Julie will add that car to their train. After all, "Somebody has to do it!"

The steam engine family, once convinced that the spiritual training of their children is important, will be quick to add the spiritual training boxcar to the train. That's good, but if you are a steam engine family, you'll probably want to start with a bang, putting a full-blown plan in place immediately. The second problem is that your train is probably already pulling too many cars, and adding this new one may lead your family into burnout, if you're not already heading there.

Here are a few tips: First, no matter how large the temptation, begin with the basic Spiritual Growth Plan (discussed on pages 55–58 and in section D). You can add to the plan later when you get more comfortable with this new boxcar and it's fitting into your schedule.

The second tip is clear out some other boxcars. If you don't make the spiritual growth of your family a priority, or if you push yourself to burnout, all your good-hearted helping could backfire on your own family. Don't just quit a bunch of stuff; pray about and discuss with your family which things you should probably not be involved in, at least for a while. Then give ample notice and finish your current term or commitment. If you start slowly with your Spiritual Growth Plan and start to clear out a few cars, you'll do this with relative ease.

The F-16 Family: Life at the Sound Barrier

Then there are those whose lives are constantly on fast-forward. Jim and Tanya met, fell in love, and were married in less than four months. Activity is their hallmark. Their lives are fast-paced and full of quite a bit of everything. They can deal with multiple issues at once and handle a variety of information and circumstances.

Between work, church, and kids' programs, Jim and Tanya can't miss two stoplights in the morning without running behind. Their days start with the "preflight" briefing the night before as they check their mental lists, calendars, and Palm Pilot to make sure they aren't forgetting anything, and to figure out how to handle the double-booked stuff. With the "preflight" done, they move out to accomplish their "mission." On a good day, they hit multiple targets (grocery store, dry cleaners, school adviser, oil change, dog groomer, business meetings, music lessons, and more), and that, of course, is over and above the long hours at work. Finally, there's the "debriefing" at 10 or 11 P.M., a check-in that becomes the "preflight" for the next day.

F-16 families struggle to find time in their frantic pace to teach systematically. Boredom can come easily, consistency is a challenge, and getting the family together is a rarity—unless it's in the car while on the move between activities. The children are addicted to activity and used to being entertained, so the parents need to raise the ante whenever they teach. An F-16 family usually runs at this pace because they want it that way. They need to know that committing to spiritual training doesn't mean they have to sit down in one spot for a long time and drudge away in boredom.

If this is you, this book will show you how to redeem the time you're already spending, such as drive times, those occasional meals together, and bedtimes. And it will help you do more in-depth training without adding much to your F-16 pace. Make the commitment to spiritual training and develop a plan that works with your family without trying to change it into something it's not.

Consider your family's pace without trying to change it.

The Right Tool for the Job

No matter which family pace best describes your situation, make sure that as you move forward in this book and develop your family's plan, you consider your family's pace without trying to change it. (If you're currently running at a pace that is not right for your family, or if you just want to change, treat that as a separate issue. Using your Spiritual Growth Plan to accomplish a pace change could cause your family to resent the plan.) Considering your pace is especially important when choosing the method, times, tools, and resources that you will use with your family. An F-16 family using a tool that best suits the carriage family is just asking for failure. They could get bored with the length and feel that they don't do it often enough. Similarly, using a steam engine or F-16 tool when you're a carriage family leads to frustration. You enjoy sitting down and discussing things, playing board games, and so on. The wrong tools leave you feeling rushed and dissatisfied.

Whatever pace your family moves at, it doesn't have to keep you from spiritual training. That's why we've provided a variety of resources and described over a dozen types of methods, times, and aids you can use. Among them will be those that match your family. The key is to use the right tool for the job. A professional photographer uses top-quality cameras and film. Using a disposable camera will get her frustrated at her lack of progress, inability to get clear images, and failure.

Family "Pace" Assessment

Ready to get a picture of the pace your family is keeping? On the form on the next page (or a photocopy of the form—also available at www.heritagebuilders.com), check off your pace. Look through the strengths and challenges listed and mark any that apply to you. Add others that come to mind as you think and pray about it.

FAMILY PACE SHEET

❏ **We're a Carriage family.**

Strengths:

___ Relaxed

___ Enjoy life and experiences

___ Time for reflection and thought

___ Low stress

___ Time to study and plan

___ Depth of understanding

___

Struggles:

___ Too little structure

___ Too much structure

___ Don't plan things out

___ Haphazard approach to training

___ Dislike change and the unexpected

___

___

❏ **We're a Steam-Engine family.**

Strengths:

___ Steady

___ Consistent

___ Committed

___ Reliable and willing

___ Plan things, organized

___ Competent, can handle a lot

___

Struggles:

___ Overcommitted

___ Tend to overdo things

___ Dislike change and new things

___ Difficulty saying no

___

___

___

❏ **We're an F-16 family.**

Strengths:

___ Can handle lots at once

___ Love variety and trying new things

___ Great at juggling lots of tasks

___ Accomplish a lot

___ Very organized

___ Learn quickly

___

Struggles:

___ Not systematic

___ Boredom comes easily

___ Need to be entertained

___ Inconsistent

___ Little family interaction

___ High stress

___

CHAPTER 8

What Are Your Family's Interests?

When you channel-surf the networks, where do you end up? Nature shows? Baseball games? Classic movies? Believe it or not, the answer can significantly affect your Spiritual Growth Plan! Television programming has become so focused on special interests that it's a good illustration of how you can assess your family's hot buttons to spiritual advantage! But first, a word from our sponsor . . .

Passion Is a Better Predictor of Success

Ever taken an aptitude test? Job placement experts used to give people aptitude tests to determine their abilities or aptitudes. Now experts have discovered that a person's passions are a better predictor of vocational success. In other words, the more passionate you are about something, the more time, energy, and effort you'll put into doing that thing and doing it well. Similarly, what excites your family is an open door to their hearts, and connecting your spiritual training to that gives you a huge head-start!

There are two ways to look at your family's interests and passions:

- What your family as a unit loves: Playing board games? Reading or watching movies? (What kind?) Sports events or plays? Making or fixing things? More intellectual pursuits?
- What your individual family members love: History? Mysteries? Science? Woodworking?

Find and use anything related to your family's interests! God, Christianity, and the Bible are interesting when they're related to your family's and your children's passions.

This chapter will help you discover your family's interests so that you can link them to spiritual truth and tailor your spiritual training accordingly. For example, if you like playing board or video games, surfing the Net, watching videos, or reading books, find and use ones with spiritual content. Or if you're a more active family that loves hiking, camping, being outside, and doing sports, use related materials and activities in your spiritual training. In fact, find and use anything related to your family's interests! God, Christianity, and the Bible are interesting when they're related to your family's and your children's passions. When you use methods, tools, and explanations that make this connection, you will help them see God as enjoyable, Someone they want to be around and learn about—and that's much more than half the battle!

"Network Listings" for Your Family

Consider the "networks" below. They all represent activities and communication media that can be used for teaching and training. The list isn't exhaustive, so feel free to add your own.

The Discovery Network

Does your family love science, animals, and creation? Do you camp and go for hikes to get close to nature? Use that love to teach about the Lord. For example, Gary Richmond's book *The View from the Zoo* (Word, 1987, out of print) links stories from his time at the Los Angeles Zoo with biblical principles. There was the time Gary helped the head herpetologist capture the angry king cobra that was shedding its skin—and got it caught over its head! Afterward Gary mentioned how fortunate they were in not getting bitten when they picked up the snake. The snake expert replied, "Most people don't get bitten picking up a snake—they're bitten when they try to put it down."

Gary illustrates the spiritual principle by tying in a lesson on sin. People often "pick up" bad things, ignoring the verses that say, "Don't steal, lie, covet, etc." While they may get away with "picking up" something negative, when they try to put that sin down, it can bite them. This is a good example of how an interest in animals can be an avenue for lessons of faith.

If you're a Discovery Network family, you probably like things explained "straight up" and logically or scientifically. Use a book like *Genesis for Kids: Science Experiments That Show God's Power in Creation*

(Nashville: Tommy Nelson, 1997) to have fun while learning. Focus on Bible stories about creation, nature, and God's wonderful power and creativity. Go to zoos, game parks, or science fairs. Go for hikes and explain how nature points to God. Use nature metaphors (such as sin being like a snake's bite—it can poison your whole system) as you teach. Give your child who also loves biographies books on scientists who are Christians.

The Sports Network

If your family is interested in sports, use that to make learning spiritual things relevant and fun. Focus on the stories of athletes or heroes in the Bible. Find books on Christian sports stars. Send your kids to sports camps run by Athletes in Action (an organization of Christian athletes) or to Kanakuk Kanakomo Kamps (run by Joe White in Branson, Missouri). Take them to hear Christian athletes. Play sports together and talk about fairness, sportsmanship, and so on, relating the topics to God and the Christian life. Use sports metaphors; for example, tell them how a team practices "plays" until they're almost second nature and work smoothly to score for them. Similarly, Christians need to practice "plays" such as telling the truth, being loving, giving to the church, obeying, and so forth, until they become second nature.

Your family will probably want their spiritual training more activity- than book-oriented. They might be more interested in doing physical things than things that require long periods of physical inactivity. Be aware of this as you choose tools and design your program.

The Arts Network

Are you an artistic family? Do you have budding Da Vincis or soon-to-be-famous actors, ballet dancers, writers, interior designers, or fashion designers under your roof? Will the next Pavarotti or Elvis spring from your den? Are museums, theaters, and art galleries favorite outings? If your family is interested in the arts, by all means use that interest! There was a time when the greatest art came out of the church, when churches were the "galleries" where "cutting edge" art was displayed.

Link the budding artists in your family with artists who match the talent God gave them with a deep and real love for Jesus. Introduce them to the artists of the past who excelled and credited God. Focus on biblical stories about such things as the making of the temple or the artist Bezalel (Exodus 31, 35–37). Go to museums, plays, and art galleries and then discuss how they display biblical principles (or not). Get your family involved in what your church is doing in these areas—choir, band, drama (acting, backdrops and settings, costumes). Paint a family mural of Bible events on your den wall.

Creative people don't connect well with logical, step-by-step, left-brain presentations. Instead, find ways to explain things using the right side of the brain: intuition, images, stories, pictures, patterns, and designs. Regular Bible studies, and the left-brain logic behind them, won't work.

The Biography Network

Is your family people-oriented? Are you "social butterflies" or "party animals"? If so, then people are where it's at for you! Being with people, talking about people, reading about people, enjoying people—there are numerous opportunities to link faith lessons with people from the past or present. For example, Corrie ten Boom's book *The Hiding Place* (Baker, 1996 [25th Anniversary edition]), which has inspired millions, shows the reality of one woman's faith among the terrors of the Holocaust.

If you're a biography family, focus on Bible characters and what they did, how they followed God, why they made the right (or wrong) choices. Use biographies of Christian heroes, martyrs, and scientists. Invite missionaries, pastors, and visiting speakers over. Get involved in helping the needy or in your church's other outreach programs. Make some of your family's times with God social events by including friends and adding a party. Cloak your teaching in people-oriented stories, illustrations, and metaphors. Relate what you're studying to your children's interactions with friends and help them apply it to school and clubs. They'll be more comfortable thinking about "what this means to me and my friends" than "what this means about sin or obedience."

And So Forth

We could go on listing "networks" that show your family's interests or passions. For example, your passion may be travel (plan a trip to a place rich with opportunities to learn of God's wonderful work or history, such as a National Forest or the Nation of Israel), photography (do a series of photos with Christian themes), intellectual learning (discuss books or take classes together), or any number of other things. These ideas will get you going, but it's up to you to fill in the blanks. The main point is not to bore your family but to get them excited.

Your Passion Assessment

Ready? It's time to note what interests you. You can use the form on the next two pages in two ways (feel free to make photocopies—the form is also available at www.heritagebuilders.com): Fill one out for (or with) each family member, and one for your family as a group. Discuss and write down what network or networks interest you. Check off things under as many networks as apply. The point is to record your family's areas of interest so that you can capitalize on them when designing and implementing your Spiritual Growth Plan.

The main point is not to bore your family but to get them excited.

PASSIONS (NETWORK) CHART

Name_____

❏ **I/We love the Discovery Network.**

I/We love:

___ animals
___ creation/nature
___ science
___ gadgets
___ environmental issues
___ camping
___ gardening
___
___

I/We can use these to teach or learn:

___ books/stories
___ hikes
___ camping
___ videos
___ a garden
___ clubs (e.g., 4-H)
___
___

___ trivia
___ experiments
___ board games
___ trips/outings
___ science camps/contests
___
___
___

❏ **I/We love the Sports Network.**

I/We love:

___ watching sports
___ playing sports such as:
___
___
___ trivia
___ competitions
___ team sports
___ solo sports
___
___

I/We can use these to teach or learn:

___ books/stories
___ Christian sports camps
___ playing sports together
___ videos
___ activities
___
___
___

___ trivia
___ board games
___ trips/outings
___ Christian athlete speakers
___
___
___

❏ **I/We love the Arts Network.**

I/We love:

___ visual arts (painting, mural)

___ 3-D arts (clay, carving, fabrics)
___ written arts (stories, poetry)

I/We can use these to teach or learn:

___ trips to places such as:
___ museums
___ art galleries
___ the theater

___ art camps
___ board games
___ videos
___ trivia

PASSIONS (NETWORK) CHART

___ movement (dance)   ___ books/stories   ___

___ drama (acting, props)   ___ camping (with paints, etc.)   ___

___ music (playing, singing) ___ art classes together   ___

___ watching artists   ___ church choir, drama, etc.   ___

___   ___   ___

___   ___   ___

❏ **I/We love the Biography Network.**

I/We love: *I/We can use these to teach or learn:*

___ watching people   ___ books/stories   ___ trivia

___ being with people   ___ videos   ___ board games

___ parties: ___ social events   ___ clubs

    ___ going to them   ___ charitable works   ___ outreach

    ___ planning them   ___ visitors   ___ trips/outings

___ helping others   ___   ___

___ games   ___   ___

___ discussions   ___   ___

___   ___   ___

___   ___   ___

❏ **I/We love other Networks.**

I/We love: *I/We can use these to teach or learn:*

___ travel   ___ books/stories   ___ trivia

___ photography   ___ trips/outings   ___ videos

___ reading/studying   ___ board games   ___ camps

___ history   ___ speakers   ___ activities

___   ___   ___

___   ___   ___

___   ___   ___

___   ___   ___

___   ___   ___

CHAPTER 9

Identifying Your Family's Unique Personal Strengths

Each child comes with his or her own unique identity and personality, or their "bent." Even look-alike kids can be markedly different. John and Jeff are identical twins. They switched classes in grade school without the teachers suspecting, and they could still do the Doublemint Gum commercials today. But their personalities seem to come from different planets! Jeff's a morning person; John's a night person. Jeff skips dessert; John starts with dessert. Jeff has a sock drawer; John has a sock room. Jeff starts his papers the day they are assigned; John starts looking for the assignment sheets the night before they are due. Jeff starts a savings account and balances it to the penny; John starts a checking account and switches banks to discover his balance!

Because of these differences, effective spiritual training for the twins couldn't have been more varied. Jeff likes to sit down, read, and reflect. John wants to learn "along the way," listen to a tape, or do an activity.

The Personal Strengths Survey is a way of "measuring" what traits your children (and you) came equipped with. The survey was carefully designed to help you pinpoint your strengths.

Taking the Personal Strengths Survey

Each of the four boxes in the survey on page 89 contains 14 descriptions and one phrase. For example, in the "L" box you'll find "Takes charge" and "Determined" with the phrase "Let's do it now!" Circle each one that describes who you tend to be as a person. Count up and *double* the

Each child

comes with his

or her own

unique identity

and personality,

or their "bent."

number you circled, then record that score in the box. If you circled five words and the phrase "Let's do it now" in the "L" box, that's six circles. So your score is 12. Do the remaining boxes in the same way. When you're done, transfer your scores to the graph below the survey, putting each score on the matching line. Once you've transferred all your scores, connect the dots to produce your graph. (Feel free to photocopy the survey for your family's use. The forms are available online at www.heritagebuilders.com.)

You and your older children can take the survey yourselves. Have any younger children take the child's version of the survey on page 90, or simply fill it out for them. (**Do the tests before reading on.**) Ready? Get out an egg timer or look at your watch and give yourself three minutes to complete the survey. You're looking for a "first guess" response, so that's plenty of time.

PERSONAL STRENGTHS SURVEY

Name _____

L

Takes charge	Bold
Determined	Purposeful
Assertive	Decision maker
Firm	Leader
Enterprising	Goal-driven
Competitive	Self-reliant
Enjoys challenges	Adventurous

"Let's do it now!"

Double the number circled = _____

B

Deliberate	Discerning
Controlled	Detailed
Reserved	Analytical
Predictable	Inquisitive
Practical	Precise
Orderly	Persistent
Factual	Scheduled

"How was it done in the past?"

Double the number circled = _____

O

Takes risks	Fun-loving
Visionary	Likes variety
Motivator	Enjoys change
Energetic	Creative
Very verbal	Group-oriented
Promoter	Mixes easily
Avoids details	Optimistic

"Trust me! It'll work out!"

Double the number circled = _____

G

Loyal	Adaptable
Nondemanding	Sympathetic
Even keel	Thoughtful
Avoids conflict	Nurturing
Enjoys routine	Patient
Dislikes change	Tolerant
Deep relationships	Good listener

"Let's keep things the way they are."

Double the number circled = _____

Sample: L=8, B=24, O=12, G=4

CHILD'S PERSONALITY SURVEY

Name _____

For your younger children, read the following descriptions aloud.
Circle or put the child's initial by each description that is a consistent character trait.

L	B
Is daring and unafraid in new situations	Is neat and tidy and notices little details
Likes to be a leader; often tells others how to do things	Sticks with something until it's done; doesn't like to quit in the middle of a game
Ready to take on any kind of challenge	Asks lots of questions
Is firm and serious about what is expected	Likes things done the same way
Makes decisions quickly	Tells things just the way they are
Total relevant statements = _____	**Total relevant statements = _____**
O	**G**
Talks a lot and tells wild stories	Always loyal and faithful to friends
Likes to do all kinds of fun things	Listens carefully to others
Enjoys being in groups; likes to perform	Likes to help others; feels sad when others are hurt
Full of energy and always eager to play	Is a peacemaker; doesn't like it when others argue
Always happy and sees the good part of everything	Patient and willing to wait for something
Total relevant statements = _____	**Total relevant statements = _____**

Sample: L=4, B=1, O=3, G=2

Adapted from *The Two Trails*, © 1998 by John Trent and Judy Love (Nashville: Tommy Nelson, 1998).

What Does It Mean?

Now that your surveys are completed, what do the letters stand for? They stand for four personality types represented by four animals: Lion, Beaver, Otter, and Golden Retriever.

Lions (High "L" People)

Lions are take-charge, assertive, go-for-it people. If you have children who are Lions, they're the ones letting you live at home! They like leading and being in charge—even of you. Just watch Lion children when a friend comes over: They'll greet the friend at the door with "Glad you're here. Now let's get moving, we've got a lot to do!" That's because they're the boss—or at least they think so. And they often do grow up to be bosses.

You rarely have to motivate Lions—just point them in a direction. As adults, they're decisive. Tell them, "That's impossible," and then stand back and watch them do it. Perhaps that decisiveness is one reason why many Lions think stoplights are a tool of the devil. Instead of stopping, they'll drive through the parking lot of a mini-mart just to keep the car moving!

When a Lion's strengths are pushed out of balance, they become too strong or assertive and insensitive in their words or actions. They can become so intent on a project that they communicate that the project is more important than the people involved. But when a Lion's strengths are balanced with loving sensitivity, they make wonderful leaders, great friends, and some of the best parents.

Approach Pointers for Lions

Approach Key: Emphasize God's purpose for the world and their life. They want to know why and how it all works.

Spiritual Training: Let them "lead," have a say in how things are done, and help develop the program, and they'll be committed to it.

The Bible: Use Bible stories about leaders such as Moses or David. These are a Lion's heroes!

Salvation: Explain God's One Big Story, including His purpose and plan. Lay it all out for them from Adam and Eve to Jesus' death, resurrection, and eventual return.

Tip: Give their faith a purpose—they need to understand the goal and have something to strive for. Get them involved in helping, leading, and teaching others—even siblings. They love this.

Otters (High "O" People)

If this is you, you're "a party waiting to happen"! Otters love having fun. If you've ever seen a real otter, you know how playful they are. They eat floating on their backs, are extremely social, and sleep a lot—mostly so they can eat and play. That description fits Otter people too. Otters love life and especially people. They're tremendous networkers. They know people who know people who know people—they just don't know anybody's name! And in spite of not remembering names, *everyone* is their best friend! They have a "best work friend," "best neighborhood friend," "best church friend," and "best elevator friend." They just love people!

Otters usually aren't into details. In school, they often start their term papers the night before (why hurry?). On the job, "quarterly" reports become "semiannual" reports (I'm busy building relationships, not filling out forms!).

Like the Lions, their strengths can be pushed to an extreme. Their tendency to be late or to put off doing routine things needs to be balanced with responsibility and an understanding of the pressure their lateness puts on others. With some added structure, their sensitivity can be a tremendous asset, especially when they serve as a spiritual leader in a home or ministry.

Approach Pointers for Otters

Approach Key: Emphasize relationship with God and others; that's what interests them. To them, life is all about people.

Spiritual Training: Vary Otters' spiritual training and put the emphasis on fun. If something becomes routine, they'll lose interest. They need to learn discipline, but that's easier when they're having fun.

The Bible: Use Bible stories about people—Esther, Peter, and King Joash, for example.

Salvation: Explain God's desire for relationship, His love for people and desire to save everyone.

Tip: Make sure you plug Otters into a good social structure and make their faith fun.

Golden Retrievers (High "G" People)

These are the people who buy 20 boxes of Girl Scout cookies every year! Sensitive and caring, Golden Retrievers have difficulty saying no. They're compassionate, wonderful team players, and are very loyal and loving. They care about *individuals* and want everyone to feel included. They're adaptable and willing to go with the flow. While the Lion often challenges the status quo and suffers the consequences, Golden Retrievers watch others make mistakes and avoid them (thus avoiding the pain).

Laura is a pure-bred Golden Retriever. One night while her family was watching TV, six-year-old Laura stood up, said, "Oh no!" and walked down the hall.

"Laura," her father called, "where are you going?"

"I just remembered I did something wrong at school today . . . and I'm sending myself to time out." (You can be sure Lions rarely send themselves to time out! They're more likely to send you to time out.)

When they're older, Golden Retrievers can be called on to "put out fires" and make those around them feel loved and accepted. But these children can have their feelings easily hurt (they're not weak, just sensitive). And parents, please note: If you have Golden Retrievers, their sensitivity can mean that they soak up friction in the home like a sponge. If there's major disharmony between parents, even at age five or six these children can try to "solve" their parents' problems or take on emotional burdens far beyond their years.

> ## *Approach Pointers for Golden Retrievers*
>
> ***Approach Key:*** Emphasize God's personal love and care for them and the world. Love, acceptance, and individual care are the keys to their hearts.
>
> ***Spiritual Training:*** Put the emphasis on your relationship with them. When you're doing this together, they'll feel safe and take part eagerly. They need the context of personal relationships.
>
> ***The Bible:*** Use stories about God or people taking care of people; e.g., the Good Samaritan, Jesus healing people, and Paul's missions to help people know Jesus.
>
> ***Salvation:*** Explain John 3:16, emphasizing that God so *loved* the world that He *gave* . . . That's where it's at—love and commitment.
>
> ***Tip:*** Help Golden Retrievers establish right friendships. Lead them in praying and caring for others (let them help in the church nursery). Make their faith a caring faith.

Beavers (High "B" People)

Any *Jeopardy* fans out there? "The animal on the class ring of MIT." That's right! "What is a beaver?" Why would the most prestigious technical university in the United States pick that furry friend? Because beavers are God's little architects. When a beaver does something, it does it right and by the book. If a beaver builds its house across your stream, you can choose between abandoning the stream and blowing up the dam!

Beavers are detailed and organized. They do things "right." They tend to start, *and complete*, a few projects each year. (Otters start a thousand new projects or hobbies each year and let Beavers finish them.)

Beavers are wonderful to have at Christmas parties because they remember to bring the food (it was on their list—something very important to Beavers). And if you talk long enough, they'll begin to clean up.

Beavers have a way of mentally filing things so they can always find them. This inner filing system includes details and experiences. For example, they remember what you said precisely a year ago—and what you were wearing at the time.

They're very good at analyzing and taking things apart. But when their strengths are pushed to an extreme they can be so good at it that they take people apart as well. There is no critic like a Beaver—and that includes how they view themselves. They set high standards and can be very hard on themselves if they don't reach those goals. Overall, however, Beavers are wonderful to have on a family or work team. They follow through, are predictable, and make lasting contributions.

Approach Pointers for Beavers

Approach Key: Emphasize truth and right (as opposed to wrong) and you'll grab them.

Spiritual Training: Be consistent and predictable (almost the opposite of Otters). They like to know what's coming and when. This provides safety and security for them.

The Bible: Use stories where principles are foremost and the right and wrong ways of doing things are contrasted, such as Adam and Eve or the Pharisee and the tax collector. Beavers know there *is* a right way and a wrong way. Use it.

Salvation: Explain the whys and hows of salvation. Beavers want the details and they want to know that the truth is based on solid fact.

Tip: Make their faith make sense—find the specific answers to their questions. Explore apologetics, the reasons and "proofs" for beliefs and doctrines.

Using This Information

Use the knowledge of your children's strengths as a means of praising them. Particularly if their personalities are different from yours, recognize that their unique makeup can be a wonderful way of blessing and building into their lives.

As you develop the plan for your family, look for methods and tools that match your children's unique strengths. The key, as with their interests and passions, is to use things in your spiritual training that they connect with and enjoy. For example, there is nothing a Golden Retriever likes better than to have Mom or Dad read them a story. Doing this at night is a great way to send them happily to sleep. Lions want to help design and develop what you do with them, so give them options to choose from. Otters do better with a fun family training time that happens during a commute time or over a Christian board game where others are involved. With a Beaver, consistently and systematically go from A to B.

If your family is a strong mix, you'll face challenges. For example, try getting a Beaver to play a competitive board game with a Golden Retriever who wants to help *everyone* win and thus be happy ("people's feelings are more important than rules"). For a Beaver, the rules are there for a purpose, and if someone's losing, well, that's part of the game. The Lion agrees—the point is to *win* after all; competition is healthy. As for the Otter, she just wants to have fun—if the game goes on too long, she might quit and do something else.

Remember that your own personality strengths influence how *you* approach things— including teaching your children. Consider how to match your strengths with your children's learning style needs. (This chapter may have given you some insight into why you've been having difficulty getting through to one or more of your children.) If two of you with different personality types are doing the training, take advantage of that. If you're alone, adapt your teaching style to using a variety of approaches. (After all, the most mature and balanced personality is a mix of all four types.) Take your own strengths, needs, likes, and dislikes into account. And remember the watchword: *Grace*. Be patient with yourself and remember that God is with you, helping you, and cheering you on!

Pulling It Together

The following form is for you to record your family members' personality strengths. (Again, you may want to photocopy it or get it from www.heritagebuilders.com.) Be aware that most people are a combination of personality types. Go through the form, checking off which statements are true for the person you're considering. They can help you (Lions and Golden Retrievers will want to help, with Beavers coming a close second to make sure you *do it right*).

PERSONAL STRENGTHS CHART

NAME: _____

❏ Lion

Strengths:	*Struggles:*	*Things to use to teach them:*
___ assertive	___ too assertive	___ explain "why"
___ leader	___ insensitive	___ leader stories
___ takes charge	___ bossy	___ involve them in designing the
___ loves a challenge	___ runs over others	plan
___ responsible	___	___ give them a goal
___ goal-oriented	___	___ let them mentor others
___ bold	___	___
___ motivated	___	___
___	___	___

❏ Otter

Strengths:	*Struggles:*	*Things to use to teach them:*
___ loves people	___ dislikes details	___ relationships
___ playful, fun	___ undisciplined	___ variety
___ social/networker	___ irresponsible	___ fun
___ enthusiastic	___ "shallow" relationships	___ people stories
___ sensitive	___ needs structure	___ other people
___ spontaneous	___	___
___	___	___

❏ Golden Retriever

Strengths:	*Struggles:*	*Things to use to teach them:*
___ compassionate	___ oversensitive	___ one-on-one times
___ team player	___ easily hurt	___ love and care
___ loyal	___ takes on stress	___ people helping people stories
___ easygoing	___ could compromise values	___ outreach
___ adaptable	___ people pleaser	___ good friendships
___ peacemaker	___	___ "together"
___ deep friendships	___	___
___	___	___

❏ Beaver

Strengths:	*Struggles:*	*Things to use to teach them:*
___ high standards	___ critical	___ what is right
___ detailed	___ perfectionist (standards	___ consistency
___ organized	too high!)	___ principle stories
___ finishes things	___ rigid	___ how and why
___ good memory	___ dislikes change	___ details
___ predictable	___	___
___ reliable	___	___
___ discerning	___	___
___	___	___

CHAPTER 10

Your Family Portrait: Putting It All Together

Now that you know about your family's history of faith, preferred pace, best learning environment (interests and passions), and God-given strengths, you can pull together all that you've discovered in the last four chapters by transferring the information from each chapter's form onto the Family Portrait Summary Sheet (photocopy it or get it from www.heritagebuilders.com).

This "family portrait" helps you determine the types of materials and approaches that will work most effectively for your family and will help you choose those tools as you move toward a concrete, practical Spiritual Growth Plan that matches your family's characteristics.

Armed with the information you've gathered, move to Section B, "Your Children's Ages and Stages," for a look at their level of spiritual readiness. You'll consider where they are developmentally so that you'll know what content they can handle. (The content itself you'll find in Part III, after you've developed your plan and are ready to work with it.)

FAMILY PORTRAIT SUMMARY SHEET

Spiritual History:

We're a _____ generation family.

This gives us these strengths: And these struggles:

Family Pace:

We're a _____ family.

This gives us these strengths: And these struggles:

Passions and Networks:

We're primarily a _____ family.

We love: We can use these to teach:

Personality Strengths:

Our family contains _____ animals.

Name: _____ is a _____

Strengths: Struggles: We'll use these to teach:

FAMILY PORTRAIT SUMMARY SHEET

Name: _____ is a _____
Strengths: Struggles: We'll use these to teach:

Name: _____ is a _____
Strengths: Struggles: We'll use these to teach:

Name: _____ is a _____
Strengths: Struggles: We'll use these to teach:

Name: _____ is a _____
Strengths: Struggles: We'll use these to teach:

Name: _____ is a _____
Strengths: Struggles: We'll use these to teach:

Your Children's Ages and Stages

Ages 0–4: Laying the Foundation

Ages 5–6: Establishing and Teaching About Relationships

Ages 7–9: Giving Them the Reasons for Their Faith

Ages 10–12: Helping Them Make the Right Choices

Your Children's Ages and Stages

When you look at all your children need to learn—the Bible, who God is, what He's like and has done, how to have a personal relationship with Him, and what all of that means for their lives—it can seem as if you're standing behind a fully loaded dump truck as the driver raises the back. Out fall doctrine, parables, wisdom, history, truths, prophecy, miracles, guidelines for conduct, God's kingdom, faith, belief, sin and its consequences, laws, discipline, character development, and more—4,000-plus years of revelation about God, God's dealings with humanity, Christian experience, and doctrinal development! And you have to pass all this on to your children in creative ways that take into account your family's uniqueness?

Don't panic! It's not as overwhelming as it seems. For one thing, you have your kids for two to four years at each stage in their development, and for another, the charts in this section (which you'll also find in Part III) are more of a what-they-will-learn-if-you-get-started-and-keep-moving list than a what-you-must-teach-them list. Relax. Your children will learn these things as you follow your plan, starting with a commitment to as little as an hour a week.

And, as we mentioned before, *you're not alone!* God is also at work in your child's life with the full arsenal of His training tools: events, relationships, experiences, answers to prayer, insight, love, and compassion. Furthermore, children (especially young ones) learn as much from watching you live out your own faith as from more formal teaching. A big part of your task is simply to follow God, continue to grow in relationship with Him, and get started sharing that with your children.

A Word of Encouragement

Before getting started with the chapters in this section, look at some of the things you may already be doing: mealtime prayers of thanks, bedtime Bible stories and prayers, Advent calendars at Christmas, Sunday school where Bible stories and songs about Jesus are taught, prayers for illnesses and "owies." All of these are having an impact on your children and teaching them that God is approachable, loves them, gives them food, cares when they feel bad, and tells about Himself in His Bible. (On the following form, record what you're doing and how it's working. Feel free to get the form online at www.heritagebuilders.com or to photocopy it.)

Each of the following four chapters is divided into five sections:

♦ ***Developmental Distinctives*** (Physical and Mental Development, and Spiritual Development)

♦ ***Key Ways to Prepare Their Hearts***

♦ ***Common Reflections of Faith at This Age***

♦ Creating a "Memory Marker" (see pages 111–112 and chapter 23)

♦ ***Things About God They're Ready to Learn at This Stag***e

You may find that your child moves more slowly or quickly through some or all of the material than the age brackets in these chapters would indicate. That's okay. No two children are alike, so move at their pace.

Warning: Don't get so excited about spiritual training that you push your children or teach them beyond what they can grasp. The Christian faith isn't an exam

SPIRITUAL TRAINING ASSESSMENT

We're already using:

What our children are learning:

___ Bedtime Bible stories

_____

___ Bedtime prayers

_____

___ Effective Sunday school program

_____

___ Christian songs

_____

___ Mealtime prayers

_____

___ Prayers for "owies"

_____

___ Family times focused on God/Bible

_____

___ Summer camps, VBS, etc.

_____

___ Christian clubs: _____

_____

_____

_____

___ Casual conversations

_____

___ Christian music tapes

_____

___ Christian videos

_____

___ Memory verses

_____

___ Seasonal celebrations

_____

___

_____

___

_____

___

_____

___

_____

___

_____

you can cram for—it's a relationship with God that works its way into your children's hearts over time. Be patient and move with them. If you have a developmentally challenged child who will never be able to grasp some of the more abstract concepts, give this special child what he or she *can* handle, such as the reality of God's love shown through you.

CHAPTER 11

Ages 0–4: Laying the Foundation

Your key task in the earliest stage of your children's lives is to lay the solid foundation of love. They need to know that they are loved, accepted, and wanted. This is also the best time to build in them the knowledge of God's reality, care, and power.

Developmental Distinctives

Children start out helpless and totally dependent, needing love and nurture. But by the time they are four, they bear little resemblance to that helpless, incommunicative baby.

Physical and Mental Development

Newborns aren't idle layabouts. They are hard at work learning about their bodies and this strange place they're in. And they are working on a number of key tasks: forming an attachment bond (first with Mother), learning they are accepted, developing autonomy or independence and a sense of initiation—the ability to go ahead and discover things. Throughout this stage they gain about four pounds and grow two-and-a-half to three-and-a-half inches a year.

By age two they have a brain that is 75 percent of its adult size. They walk, run, climb, pedal a tricycle, use objects to represent other objects, play alone while interacting little with others, develop a recognizable personality, begin to talk, and are mental sponges.

By three they have a vocabulary of from 500 to 1,000 words, form

Simply thank God out loud for your children.

sentences of five and more words, add about 50 words a month to their vocabulary, and are still mental sponges.

At age four they skip awkwardly; have greater strength, endurance, and coordination; draw shapes and stick figures; paint pictures; build with blocks; play interactively; have laid the basic foundations of life; are in a growth spurt so need lots of exercise; discover friends; feed themselves; almost completely dress themselves; go to the bathroom alone; express emotions that change from minute to minute; can think of God in a personal way, and can trust Him with a simple faith.

Spiritual Development

When it comes to spiritual growth, each child has an empty photo album that needs pictures. Although God created them as unique individuals, from the first moment you hold them you are adding to their album and forming their picture of the world. When you protect them and love them by caring for their basic needs, they learn that they are loved and the world is a safe place. They need to know this is also true spiritually, so you need to demonstrate, with actions and words, that God is like you: He also cares for them, keeps them safe, and makes sure that their needs are met. When they hear and see this repeatedly, they begin to build a world view with a Christian foundation that sets them up for life. (If this foundation isn't established here, they establish others—such as "I have to take care of myself.")

In these early years they are dependent on you to feed and nourish them spiritually. As soon as you know you're pregnant, pray for them, and pray simple, short prayers over them that affirm God's love and care. When you consistently pray for them, they learn what prayer is and that God is interested. You can begin this even before they know what talking is. Simply thank God for them out loud, pray that He gives them a good sleep, and thank Him for putting them in your life. In doing this you are giving them the basics of the Christian faith: God is real, He made them and loves them, He takes care of them, and prayer is talking to God (see Part III, Topic Nos. 9 and 10 for more). You are giving them their first snapshots of life. It's probably a collage of impressions: love, comfort, security, smiles and frowns, happiness, care—all pieced together within a bright border that says, "Mommy, Daddy, and God love me. I'm special." What a way to start off their life's photo album!

Key Ways to Prepare Their Hearts

These children are receptive. You are doing all the work of preparing them for a lifelong relationship with God—loving, nurturing, reassuring, and caring for them. Children are all very different, but they are similar in their needs, what they can understand, how they develop, and what approaches work best.

◆ *Be consistent.* An important element of love and nurture, both physical and spiritual, is consistency. Make a habit of telling your children of your love and God's. Consistency is key because it's impossible to say when any child starts to understand what you're doing. But if you're constantly modeling a positive attitude to God and a loving relationship with Him, you will be doing that when your child starts to notice. And you will also be modeling who God is: faithful and continuously present.

◆ *Model God's love as you show your love.* In this love and nurture stage, it's impossible to overemphasize the importance of modeling. Growth is a continuum.

  ❖ It begins with you modeling who God is and what a relationship with Him is like as you demonstrate your and God's love. You do this as you care for them, talk with them, and show them what love is. They observe and take it in.

  ❖ As they start understanding language, you verbally communicate that you and God love them. Then you gently move them to where they begin to be active before God. Even before they can comprehend what you're saying, you continually explain the basic truths to them (such as what prayer is and when you're doing it). Your intentional modeling raises questions for them that you can answer in a nurturing, loving environment.

  ❖ Finally, they try to imitate you. It's a natural cycle of growth especially obvious in this stage.

◆ *Connect with where they are and what they're interested in.* This growth continuum happens in all areas. They learn most when your teaching connects with where they are and what they're interested in. For example, you pray over your children, explain what you're doing, and encourage questions. Then you let them join you. This might be as simple as asking them what they want to pray about and then praying their prayers for them, such as, "Dear God, thank You for loving me. Help me go potty in the potty and sleep well." This prayer connects with them because it deals with *their* concerns and it's short and simple enough for them to grasp. (Their prayers can be longer and cover more ground than this one.) The key is to never go beyond their attention span—always stay at their "heart level." Gradually, as you explain and answer questions, they will want to pray their own prayers.

◆ *Teach obedience.* At this stage, it's also important to establish the principle of obedience to parents, in the context of love and nurture. One of the ways God loves and cares for His children is by teaching them and giving them guidelines. You teach your children to be obedient to God because you know He loves them and is trustworthy. They should also obey you because, like God, you love them and want the best for them. Children live so much out of their emotions and are so intent on exploring their world, learning the limits, and becoming independent that obedience is hard for them at first. They will need help. Gently walk them through the right response again and again—and again (see Topic No. 15, *God Wants You to Obey Your Parents* in chapter 29).

◆ *Keep learning exciting.* Make God attractive by using different media such as simple Bible videos or music tapes. Spice things up by adding actions, playing games, or giving them a snack during their video. Use variety to increase their enjoyment and keep their interest high. Use Bible stories that are suited to their level. Talk with them about the pictures and what they mean. Relate what you're talking about to their lives.

◆ *Make church attractive.* Work with your church to ensure that the care area is bright and exciting and that children aren't being babysat but are learning simple songs and Bible stories. Volunteer to help in the nursery. Work to make church an enjoyable experience for your kids.

Common Reflections of Faith at This Age

As your children grow, they move toward the next stage, where they'll become more actively involved in their own faith and learning. On the way there, they'll enjoy the various things you're doing together with them and God, such as praying, reading Bible storybooks, and singing songs, and they'll begin to want to "do it myself" rather than having you do it all for them. They'll start to grasp some of the basics about God and the Christian faith: They'll understand certain things about how God wants them to be and behave, know that God loves them and made them (and everything else) on purpose, and know that they can talk to Him.

Memory Markers

In the Old Testament, Joshua's first day on the job included a faith-stretching task. Taking over from Moses, he was to lead the people across the Jordan River at flood stage. Years earlier, God had enabled Moses to part the Red Sea so Israel could escape slavery. Now God told Joshua and the priests that He would part the waters again. Not only did almighty God provide a way of *escape* from Egypt, He parted the waters for their *entrance* into the land that He'd promised to Abraham so long ago.

Once Joshua and the priests had everyone safely across, God commanded His new leader to set up a "Memory Marker." Twelve stones from the middle of the riverbed were to be made into a special marker to commemorate what God had done. But the stones weren't just to celebrate that day—and they weren't just for Joshua and the people who crossed the river.

And Joshua . . . said to the Israelites, "In the future when your descendants ask their fathers, 'What do these stones mean?' tell them, 'Israel crossed the Jordan on dry ground.' For the Lord your God dried up the Jordan before you until you had crossed over. The Lord your God did to the Jordan just what he had done to the Red Sea when he dried it up before us until we had crossed over. He did this so that all the peoples of the earth might know that the hand of the Lord is powerful and so that you might always fear the Lord your God." (Joshua 4:20–24)

The "Memory Marker" Joshua was commanded to put up was a picture for the children. That pile of rocks became a testimony to what God

They'll begin to want to "do it myself" rather than having you do it all for them.

111

had done, and an opportunity for parents and children to focus on God's greatness and love. It was a snapshot of God's faithfulness that they could look at and talk about.

A major help in spiritual training is the creation of Memory Markers for your family and the members of your family.

Creating a Memory Marker: The Dedication

Just as Hannah, the mother of Samuel, dedicated her son to the Lord (1 Samuel 1) and Mary presented Jesus to God (Luke 2:21–38), so you can commit your children to God and commit yourself to raising them with His help. Children will, of course, decide for themselves eventually, but in dedicating them to God, you also commit yourself to doing everything you can throughout their lives to teach and train them to follow God, lead a Christ-centered life, and develop a personal relationship with Him. By dedicating them to God, you are dedicating yourself to taking up the calling God has given you and making your own commitment to love and nurture them. By giving your children to God, you are acknowledging His partnership in the parenting process and asking for His help and wisdom.

Although your children won't remember it, create a memory for them for later. (Make it a Memory Marker for you and your own commitment as well.) Many churches have dedication services for infants that you can take advantage of. Make this into a memory by buying your child a special outfit, taking pictures, having a family gathering afterward, and so on. Put the pictures in their baby books with comments and notes about the occasion.

Consider choosing a "life verse" to read at your children's dedications. This Bible verse can embody your hopes and prayers for them. Write it in their books beside the pictures. When the children are old enough to understand, recreate the moment, showing them the pictures and explaining how you dedicated them to God and promised you would train them in His ways.

Things About God They're Ready to Learn

This chart shows the truths your children are ready to learn.

◆ The "Knowing" columns contain truths about their faith, God, and what He has done;

◆ The "Loving" column is about developing their relationship with God; and

◆ The "Living" columns are about living out in their person and actions who God wants them to be.

In each of these three areas, topics and concepts are listed that they can grasp (see Part III for the details). As you intentionally implement the plan you'll develop at the end of Part II (chapter 28), your children will learn all the things listed here. Surprised? Don't be. Remember, they're sponges!

Ages 0–4

KNOWING		LOVING	LIVING	
A. Who God Is	**B.** What God Has Done	**C.** You Can Have a Relationship with God	**D.** You Can Be All God Wants You to Be	**E.** You Can Do All God Wants You to Do
1. God exists. 2. God loves you. 3. Jesus loves you. 4. God wants to take care of you.	5. God created everything. 6. God created you. 7. God gave us the Bible. 8. God's Son, Jesus, died for your sins so you can be with God.	9. Prayer is talking to God in Jesus' name. 10. You need to talk to God regularly. 11. You need to regularly listen to stories about God and Jesus from the Bible.	12. God wants you to be good, kind, and loving, just like Him and Jesus. 13. God wants you to see and think good things.	14. God wants you to go to church. 15. God wants you to obey your parents. 16. God wants you to learn to share your things with others.

CHAPTER 12

Ages 5–6: Establishing and Teaching About Relationships

Your key task during this stage is to help your children have a growing relationship with God and others. Thus far you have been doing everything for your children, but now they're ready for the next step where you take them to God and actively train and teach them to do their part in the task of learning, doing, and growing. It's time to help them become committed to God and develop their own relationship with Him. (For help with how to do this, see chapters 15–28 and Part III.)

When you make God a natural, consistent part of your lives, developing a relationship with Him will come easily for your children as they, too, fall into the practice of including Him. The key is to ensure that God has a significant place in their lives and to make sure that they understand how important healthy relationships (with God and others) are, and that they know what those healthy relationships look like and how to build them.

Developmental Distinctives

Children at this age are becoming social creatures, and although their physical growth is slowing down, they are still developing a vast number of skills and abilities.

Physical and Mental Development

At age five, children have doubled their birth length, weigh from 35 to 40 pounds, feed themselves using cutlery, and dress and undress themselves. They're active and agile, print their names in large letters, and have a vocabulary of about 2,000 words, although they understand more. They are friendly and enjoy playing with others. Adult approval and praise is very important, and they will cooperate to get it. They are curious, eager to learn, and have stable emotions.

Six-year-olds start to lose their baby teeth and grow permanent ones, have proportions similar to those of an adult, need lots of opportunity to move, can sometimes ride bicycles, and have a preference for using their right or left hand. Their emotions are very near the surface; in fact, they can be puzzled and alarmed by their own yo-yo feelings. They often become bossy and like to make rules and have them obeyed—by others.

These children can reflect on the past and future, want to know about their parents' past (although the sequence of events means little), can take on and complete small chores, and can think about how one activity will affect another. They sing well and read, often with a finger following the words on the page. They learn that others have rights too, and they begin to express their emotions in socially accepted ways.

Spiritual Development

Age five to six is an important time of learning about relationships and how they work, with both God and people. Here is where they need to establish a strong foundational understanding of why relationships are so important and how they affect them, others, and their daily lives and interactions.

Children this age are no longer so passive. They are ready to be pulled into active involvement in their own development. It's important for them to learn that it is not just your relationship with God—it's *theirs* (just as they have their own relationships with other children). So they can, for example, begin to say their own prayers, and they need to read regularly from their Bible storybooks with you.

At this age, expect that children will want to do other things rather than pray, read the Bible, and so on. This is normal. When given the choice between work and learning or fun and relaxation, they'll often pick the latter (as will many adults!). How do you handle this? Be careful not to make learning about God seem like work—something you have to do but would like to get done with. Your own positive attitude will help enormously here. When you read Bible stories to them or pray with them, give them your full and undivided attention. If they have questions or comments, listen to them. If something bothers them, take the time to talk about it and pray about it. Don't let what you planned to do become so rigid that you can't shift gears when it's needed. This is how God listens to us, and this is how we can model to our kids that God listens.

Key Ways to Prepare Their Response

At this stage growing autonomy is the name of the game. If their life snapshots until now have always included you front and center, now they're starting to include their friends and growing social contacts—often with you in the background. The key is to make those snapshots positive pictures.

♦ *Talk about how they like to be treated.* Keep in mind that children have to be taught *how* to have relationships with God and others. They need to learn what acceptable treatment of others is, how to talk nicely, how to share, when to apologize and why. They need to learn to respect others and their wills, rights, and property. They need to learn it all from someone—you. Similarly, they have to learn how to develop a relationship with God through prayer, worship, reading His Word, and learning to trust and follow Him. As you teach them, remember that they are unique. Be sensitive to their individual characters and development.

♦ *Use your relationship and rapport with them.* You are developing your own unique relationship and rapport with your children as their personalities become evident and more defined. You're beginning to know who they are. Use this rapport and love to show them what a relationship with God is like. For example, help them see that if they never talked to you, or vice versa, you wouldn't know each other very well, nor would you be able to meet their needs properly. It's the same with God.

Remember to keep the focus on relationship. The relationship with God they establish here will be with them for the rest of their lives. It's important to establish the right basis for it: love, concern,

Give your children your full and undivided attention.

active care, and interest. For example, when they are worried about monsters under the bed, remind them that God cares for them—they can trust Him.

◆ *Have them start saying their own prayers.* Until now you have been praying over them or saying their prayers for them. They need to move increasingly into making their prayers their own. You can still help them decide what to pray for, but now they can pray for the things on their list in their own words. As they grow in this, you could alternate—one night you pray, the next they do, gradually increasing the nights they do it.

◆ *Talk about reasons for obeying.* Children have already been working on obeying you; now they can understand that they obey because of their relationship with God—He wants them to. Let them know that you have to obey too: You have to obey God, your boss, etc. Explain how cooperation and obedience make things work better. And always give them the reason for obedience: because God loves them and knows what's best. He tells them to do things that will benefit them and others around them. This keeps God from becoming the "heavy" or the disciplinarian in the sky. Focus rather on the good things about God: His love for them, His ability and willingness to care for them, His desire for their best.

Common Reflections of Faith at This Age

When your children are ready to move on to the next stage, they will have a solid foundation of the bigger picture of the Bible and a relationship with God and will begin to see how the pieces fit together. They will understand that life is all about relationship: between God and them and between them and others. They'll have basic social and spiritual skills and will be ready to learn more.

Creating a Memory Marker: Introducing the Gospel

For this Memory Marker, you will have to do some preparatory work. (For an explanation of the "Memory Marker," see pages 111–112.) Read simple Bible stories about Jesus to your children and help them work their way through their Bible storybooks. As they do, they will begin to see the context of how their relationship with God fits into life. As their knowledge of Jesus grows, introduce them to the gospel. They will be able to grasp the simple message of their relationship with God being broken because of sin; of Jesus, God's Son, dying in their place; of their need to accept what Jesus did; and of living with Him forever.

Respond to their curiosity about accepting Jesus. Since they won't become curious about information they don't have, use a variety of stories, situations, and media to talk about salvation. Use times like Christmas and Easter or church baptisms to reinforce the story and expand their knowledge. When they know Jesus died on the cross, they'll want to know why. What a great opportunity to help them understand salvation! (For help leading your children to Christ, see chapter 30, Topic No. 22, *God Sent His Son, Jesus Christ, to Die for You.*)

They won't understand all of it, at least not in the same way they will as adults, but many children ask Jesus into their hearts at this age or younger. The Spirit of God draws them to Himself, and He knows when they're ready—and He will keep drawing them throughout their lives. Jesus said, "Let the little children come to me, and do not hinder them" (Matthew 19:14). He also quoted Psalm 8:2: "From the lips of children and infants you [God] have ordained praise" (Matthew 21:16). And finally, there can be great wisdom in the simplicity of a child's understanding of the "deep things of God"!

Many children ask Jesus into their hearts at this age or younger.

The Things About God They're Ready to Learn

This chart shows the information your children are ready to learn during this stage. In each area, topics that they can grasp are listed (see Part III for more details). Make an effort to always bring the topic back to the practical: How does this affect their lives? What does this mean to them where they are now and in their relationships? As you intentionally implement the plan you'll develop in Section D (pages 229–268), your children will learn all the things listed here.

Ages 5-6

KNOWING		LOVING	LIVING	
A. Who God Is	**B.** What God Has Done	**C.** You Can Have a Relationship with God	**D.** You Can Be All God Wants You to Be	**E.** You Can Do All God Wants You to Do

A. Who God Is

17. God is your loving Father. He wants to guide, teach, love, protect, and provide for you.

18. In some ways, you are just like God. He has feelings and thoughts. He can understand you. Jesus showed us who God is and what He's like.

19. In other ways, you are very different from God. He is everywhere, He can do anything, and He knows everything.

20. Jesus has always been with God and is God.

B. What God Has Done

21. God tells you about Himself, His Son, Jesus, and His plan for you in the Bible: The One Big Story.

22. God sent His Son, Jesus Christ, to die for you.

23. God has prepared a place for you in heaven. Jesus is coming back for you.

C. You Can Have a Relationship with God

24. You can have a relationship with God by accepting what Jesus did for you: Salvation.

25. God wants to have a relationship with you.

26. You can talk to God through prayer.

27. You can thank God and Jesus for all They've done and still do for you.

28. You can ask God for wisdom and guidance.

29. You can read about God and His Son, Jesus, in the Bible or in a Bible storybook. You begin to have personal Bible reading and time with God.

D. You Can Be All God Wants You to Be

30. God has a plan for you.

31. The Bible tells you the kind of person God wants you to be.

32. God's way works best. You can be all God wants you to be by following Jesus.

33. God wants you to put only good things into your heart.

34. When you sin, you should ask God to forgive you—and He will.

E. You Can Do All God Wants You to Do

35. God wants you to spend time with other Christians, both at church and in the community.

36. God wants you to help others and be nice to them.

37. God wants you to obey Him and follow Jesus in everything.

38. God wants you to share and take good care of everything He gives you: Stewardship.

39. God wants you to understand and memorize Bible verses.

CHAPTER 13

Ages 7–9: Giving Them the Reasons for Their Faith

Your children need to know they can trust God and that their relationship with Him rests on His consistent character. They need the assurance that, when they grow up in God's presence with a solid personal relationship with Him, He will be their foundation. Children need to have God's trustworthiness, love, care, and provision reinforced to them. They are now also ready to begin understanding the basis of their faith and to learn the reasons for what they believe.

Developmental Distinctives

In this stage, children are beginning to think for themselves. They are ready to understand more and believe more.

Physical and Mental Development

Children's forebrains undergo a growth spurt during this stage, so that by age eight their brains are 90 percent of their adult size. They begin to internalize values and integrate moral principles, buying into what you've taught them and developing good habits. Family is still the most important influence, but peer groups are gaining.

Seven is the "eraser age": Children want to do perfect work to gain approval, so they often try to erase their errors. They become more coordinated and graceful (a good time for sports), and they need to overcome being sore losers and telling tales. To children eight and nine, rules are decided by adults and should therefore be kept. Hero worship is big, based on their acceptance of adult authority. They express themselves through writing, enjoy reading, remember several things at once, have a good concept of time (they understand months and years), and remember facts longer. Self-esteem is high: They believe they can do anything they set their minds to.

These children can think systematically and logically; deal with concrete, real ideas; are independent, industrious, and willing to perfect new skills. Friendships form and gender differences begin to matter. They want to belong to clubs, play games, and enjoy childhood rituals (like avoiding stepping on cracks in the sidewalk). They want to please and be good, will endure the consequences of their actions, and take responsibility. Their attention span is longer—they can work on a project for weeks. They have the beginnings of empathy, can see another's point of view, and discriminate somewhat between good and bad.

Spiritual Development

This is the "age of reason." Children are beginning to think for themselves. They want to know "why" and "how" and explore options. It's important to explain things to them in preparation for the next stage, when they will start making their own decisions. If you don't know the answer, search for it with them. Teach them how to find answers and show them that you can always learn and grow. (See Part III *The Content of Your Spiritual Legacy* and Appendix I *Topical Questions and Answers* for help with answers.) Don't simply say, "I don't know" or "Because I said so." At this stage children need the foundations of their faith solidly grounded.

These children need to be taken seriously as intellectual beings. This is a great time to teach them the underlying reasons for how they can know the Bible is God's book, how it's the manual for life from life's Manufacturer (see chapter 31, Topic Nos. 47–50), how they can be sure Jesus is God (Topic No. 44), how you know God cares (Topic No. 46), and so on. They need to know that their faith is both *reasonable* (there are good reasons behind it) and *real* (it works in *their* lives). Teach them these things now to ensure that, when they hit their preteens and teens, they'll make choices based on what they know, rationally and experientially, to be true.

Children also need *relational* reasons. That is, they need to experience the results of actively trusting their loving God. They don't always connect an answer to prayer with a specific prayer they prayed earlier. You can play an important role by keeping track of these, showing them that their faith is real and practical. When they pray to find friends or for help on a test, show them the answers when they come. When they choose to tell the truth or not to steal, show them how it worked out because God's way works best. When they see concrete evidence of God's care, their beliefs about life become firmly established. They'll get into the habit of doing things God's way and going to God for help—because they'll know from experience that it works! They will have a growing collection of snapshots of God's faithfulness and the reliability of His principles.

When you show your children that what they believe is reasonable, their faith is given a solid anchor. When they experience God's love, their faith is real and practical.

Key Ways to Prepare Their Minds

In the last stage, most of your children's snapshots had to do with people, relationships, and their expanding social world, with you always there in the background. As their lives expand, so do the experiences and memorable moments that form the basis of their lives and fill their albums. So now their pictures tend to focus on objects, experiences, and all manner of things they're curious about. And there, somewhere at the edge of the pictures, you can still be seen—your hand, eye, shoulder, or smile visible and supportive.

◆ *Continue to let your children in on the parenting process.* Tell them that your job is to prepare them to do things themselves: have their own quiet times with God, read and study the Bible, choose God's way when no one is watching or there's pressure to do the opposite. Your job is to continue encouraging and loving them, but also to insist that they do their part. Their job is still to learn and take the next step. You'll be there to show them how and make sure they understand where they're going. And God is always nearby.

◆ *Encourage and try to answer your children.* Their questions will cover a lot of areas:

Children need to experience the results of actively trusting their loving God

Children will start to understand that Bible stories are more than just stories—these stories help them know how to live.

❖ Why certain behaviors are important, right or wrong
❖ Why God answers some prayers and not others
❖ Who God is and what He's like
❖ Why people do bad things
❖ Why some of their friends aren't Christians
❖ Why some who are Christians don't always act like it
❖ Why church is important
❖ Why God doesn't just do stuff without them praying
❖ Why Jesus had to die

These foundational truths are best taught in the context of making their faith real and reasonable, with an emphasis on God's love and care.[1]

● ***Show them examples from the Bible that address their concerns.*** Children at this age need to know that they can trust the Bible and God. When they understand these things, in the next stage they'll be ready to hang on and trust because they know God is in control and is working things out for their good. They'll start to understand that Bible stories are more than just stories—these stories help them know how to live. By the end of this stage, when they are grounded and growing, they will be able to tell their friends about who Jesus is, why Christianity works, what happened to them, and why they know it's real.

● ***Prepare your children for what's coming.*** Each child develops differently and is ready to do more on his or her own—at his or her own pace. Match your approach to your children's needs and readiness. Be prepared for them to have very different concerns, speeds of learning, degrees of willingness to step out alone, and desire for your support. Whenever they move toward more autonomy, they're in transition to the next stage. Prepare them for what's coming in the various areas and give them a date, such as a specific birthday. Make the change something to look forward to. For example, if you're planning to change your evening prayer times, tell them, "On your seventh (or eighth) birthday, you're going to start praying on your own—with us still helping and listening." On that day, if they're not ready, try alternate ways. You might say the prayers and have them repeat them after you. The next day, come up with their prayer list together and then have them say their prayers. You could alternate until they're ready to do it almost on their own. Be patient, go at their pace, but be insistent that they keep moving toward the next stage. Growth takes place one step at a time, not overnight.

Near the end of this stage your children will begin to yield to God and put themselves in His hands. They'll begin developing their own relationship with God. You will still do most of it with them, but toward the end of this stage they may want to start doing some of it on their own. Let them choose what time of day to do it—they might prefer after school or in the morning. The structure needs to work for them. This helps them move toward taking ownership in their relationships with God.

Common Reflections of Faith at This Age

As your children approach age 10, they need to be equipped with reasonable answers (geared to their level of understanding), a reasonable faith that they know is true, and the rationale behind the way they view the world. They'll be able to say, "I believe this. I'm going to build my life on God's way." They'll be ready to face the questions their expanding world will confront them with. They'll be moving toward reading their Bibles and going to church because they want to, and toward enjoying their times with God. They will get all the input you can possibly give them and know where to go for more (Sunday school, the pastor, other Christian leaders and adults, the Bible).

Creating a Memory Marker: Exploration and Expressions

A lot of exploration of their faith is going on, and your children are beginning to find ways to express their own personal relationships with God. It's important to formalize this by creating Memory Markers for them. (For an explanation of the Memory Marker, see pages 111–112.)

Near the end of this stage, you could set aside a specific time with each of your children. Make it significant in some way—a special meal out or a dedicated evening just for them. During your time together, affirm their faith. Remind them of any previous Memory Markers, such as their dedication or their prayer for salvation. Give them any additional explanations about salvation they may need. Now that they can understand it more fully, they may have questions. Reaffirm their commitments to follow and obey God. Remind them of answered prayers they've experienced and emphasize that their faith is true and God is real. Ask them about their experiences with God and some of the events that have helped them truly know God is with them. Tell them your own faith story.

You may mark this occasion by preparing gifts for them. Give them a certificate (or framed Bible verse or special quote) with the date and a couple of sentences of explanation or a significant answered prayer. Let them choose the frame so it can become part of their decor and life. Then give them a "Faith Stories Journal" to track their relationship with God. (This is a notebook or blank book set aside specifically to write down their experiences with God and prayer.) You can start it by entering the dates of their Memory Markers (see pages 111–112), including this one, and recording some of the answers to prayer you've seen in their lives, and perhaps a dedication. Encourage them to take over and record in it

- the things God does for them;
- what they learn as they continue to grow in their relationship with Him;
- prayers and their answers;
- how God blesses them;
- things they want God's help to understand; and so on.

When they make these records of their spiritual lives, they will be able to look back through them and see God's faithfulness alongside their own growth.

Things About God They're Ready to Learn

This chart shows the information your children are ready to learn. In each area, topics they can grasp are listed. Along with giving them an understanding of the "whys" and "hows," make an effort to always bring the topic back to the practical: How does this affect their lives? What does this mean to them where they are now? As you intentionally implement the plan you'll develop in Section D, your children will learn all the things listed here.

Ages 7-9

KNOWING

A.
Who God Is

40. You can be sure that God is real.

41. There is only one God.

42. God exists in three Persons: Father, Son, and Holy Spirit. This is called the "Trinity."

43. God (Father, Son, and Holy Spirit) is eternal.

44. Jesus is both God and Man.

45. Nothing exists apart from God.

46. God's character is true, honest, loving, compassionate, generous, selfless, forgiving, merciful, trustworthy, faithful, just, impartial, and holy.

B.
What God Has Done

47. The Bible is true. It is God's Word, and you can trust it.

48. God made sure all stories in the Bible together tell the One Big Story.

49. The Bible you have is exactly what God wanted to give you.

50. God wants you to learn and study the Bible.

51. The world is full of sin. There is an enemy in the world (Satan). Not everyone obeys God.

52. Jesus died to save you from the penalty for sin.

53. Jesus defeated sin and Satan.

54. Jesus is the only way to God.

LOVING

C.
You Can Have a Relationship with God

55. You read the Bible to learn about who God is (Father, Son, and Holy Spirit) and what He has done and is doing.

56. You can pray your own prayers with your parents.

57. Prayer benefits you in many ways.

58. Keep praying: persistence, tests, and trials.

59. You can trust God and turn your life over to Him.

60. You should learn to seek God.

61. Jesus gives you peace.

LIVING

D.
You Can Be All God Wants You to Be

62. God wants you to learn and grow and become like Jesus.

63. Growth is a learning process.

64. Your character should match God's character.

65. God wants you to develop your talents.

66. God wants you to develop the Fruit of the Spirit.

67. God wants you to mature and develop your personality.

E.
You Can Do All God Wants You to Do

68. Church is God's idea. Jesus is the head of the church. At church you learn about God and encourage each other to follow Jesus.

69. God wants you to understand what a blessing people and good relationships are.

70. God has taught you right from wrong. He did this to keep you safe and to give you a good life.

71. The Ten Commandments are a good guide for life.

72. God wants you to share your faith.

NOTES
1. See Section IV for help answering these questions. In addition, Josh McDowell Ministry has a number of materials on "right from wrong." See also the Resource List under *Apologetics and Archaeology*.

CHAPTER 14

Ages 10–12: Helping Them Make the Right Choices

Children this age need to learn to submit to God. This is a crucial time as they learn what the Bible says about how they should live, what choices they need to make, and what God expects of them. They are moving into greater autonomy in their spiritual lives.

Developmental Distinctives

This is a time of great personal growth and increasing independence.

Physical and Mental Development

At this age, children are working hard at growing up. A number of tasks begun earlier continue, such as internalizing values and forming friendships. Peer groups become increasingly important. These children have a keen sense of loyalty, enjoy making things, want things to do, are on the move, like to compete, enjoy team games and hobbies, have good memories, and are collectors. They can think logically and reason about their experiences. They are capable of dealing with abstractions. They experience rapid changes in growth and development, continuing to gain two inches in height and six to seven pounds a year. They are still at the stage where they generally don't like the opposite sex. They show a marked increase in physical coordination and an increased attention span. They need extended physical activity as heart and lung capacity grow. They learn how to resolve conflict fairly and notice when their needs are different from those of others. This is a time to explore their abilities and talents and see where they fit.

Emotions are relatively stable until the end of this stage, when they can swing wildly as hormones build and sexual development begins. Girls generally mature physically a year ahead of boys, often reaching puberty in elementary school. Both sexes are becoming conscious of their bodies. Lack of self-confidence grows along with self-consciousness and the deep longing for acceptance and approval. For this reason they may be tempted to associate with popular people—regardless of the morals of these people. They need your ongoing acceptance and affirmation. If they don't get it, they'll look for acceptance and affirmation elsewhere. They are shifting from being good because you say so to being good on their own.

During this time, it can be helpful to prepare them in advance for what puberty will bring: the changes in their bodies, emotional ups and downs, the importance of friends, greater independence, and the dangers of peer groups. It will seem like everything is changing, but assure them that your love and God's love are constant.

Spiritual Development

The main goal in raising children is to ensure that, by the time they leave home, they have incorporated God's values into their lives and have a fully developed and mature relationship with God. Age 10 to 12 is an important transition period in their growth toward that goal. These children are moving from dependence to independence. Naturally, your involvement doesn't stop when they hit 13, but it changes. Your children realize, *I'm a person in my own right. These are my thoughts. This is my life. **This is my faith.*** They see the need to take ownership of developing their own spiritual life and being responsible for their walk with God.

These children are really beginning to think for themselves. They have a lot of information and are ready to make choices based on it. Your job is to help them learn to make the right choices. You need to begin letting go and allow them to test their wings and make decisions in the controlled, safe environment of home—especially about things that don't matter in the grand scheme of things, such as what hairstyle to have, how late to stay up on weekends, when to spend time with God, and so on. Knowing your standards and how you arrived at them will give them the rationale for making good choices. It can also help you, as these smaller things remind you that changes are necessary and are happening.

In addition, children need to know that the disciplines they are establishing will benefit them their whole lives—just as going to school will. They know that they need to learn and are aware of the benefits of good grades: they can go to college, become good at a profession, find fulfilling work, or start their own business. They may not always enjoy school or the process of learning, but they know why they need to be disciplined and study. Similarly, they can now understand that while there are occasions when spending time with God seems to have less immediate appeal than playing a video game, the long-term importance is far greater. Understanding this helps them develop their spiritual lives as they would a talent or skill they're excited about.

Key Ways to Prepare Their Choices

The snapshots that fill this section of your children's photo albums are chock-full of all kinds of things, from school to clubs to friends to church. Their lives are expanding and so are the "pictures" they take—they're beginning to include things from the wide world and show your children's growing experiences and confidence. You still appear in the background of some of the shots, but your presence is becoming less central. In fact, it's time to move purposefully out of the way.

♦ ***Encourage them to take more responsibility by easing them into it.*** Even so, don't just let go and tell your children, for example, to have their own times with God. If you remove your involvement in their spiritual lives too soon or too suddenly, devotional times could stagnate or disappear. Instead, gradually give your children more and more rope. Encourage them to take increasing responsibility for your devotional times together. If you have been using the time just before bed as your time with God, then it has also become an important relational time between you and your child. Don't abandon it—change its function. Morph it gradually into a time to visit, to talk about what's happening in their lives, and to discuss what they want to pray about. You might pray for a few things together and then let them pray quietly about others. When they can get through the prayer time without input from you, or when they say, "I want to do

Children need to know that the disciplines they are establishing will benefit them their whole lives.

Children need to begin to discern between cultural "truths" and God's truth, and they need to understand why scripture is the standard.

it on my own," they are ready for you to pull back. That's a good sign. They're getting personal with God.

- ◆ ***Remind them of their times with God and help them plan them.*** You will need to help them make their times with God consistent, just as you remind them to brush their teeth: You don't stand over them while they brush but you help them to remember to do it and to be consistent.
- ◆ ***Show your children how to find answers in the Bible.*** The same process of withdrawal and transition happens in all areas of their spiritual growth, such as Bible reading. They're too old for Bible storybooks, so replace them with age-appropriate full-text Bibles of their own. When they have questions, direct them to a part of the Bible that will help them. Let them choose what Bible books to read. You can offer suggestions, such as Genesis or one of the Gospels, or perhaps Esther or Ruth for girls. Read the same book independently then discuss what you've read. Ask them what they learned and share what you got out of it. It's important for them to discover how to get direction for and insight from their reading. After all, the goal of Bible reading is learning and application. But don't force it. Trust God to work in their lives and speak to them.
- ◆ ***Encourage their participation in church activities by making it easy for them to get there.*** Church is becoming increasingly important to children this age. They are getting more involved in church, attending extra meetings, helping out, joining clubs, going on trips or missions excursions, and making their key friends there. Church provides a wonderful, safe place for them to explore autonomy in their faith.
- ◆ ***Let your children see what's outside the Christian bubble.*** They need to be exposed to other ideas and ways of thinking and believing so they'll know how to handle them. They need to begin to discern between cultural "truths" and God's truth, discover what to do with new ideas, and learn to compare them with scripture. And they need to understand why scripture is the standard.
- ◆ ***Share with your children what you're learning.*** As your children grow older, your relationship with them changes into that of travelers on the same road sharpening one another. Ask them to pray about your concerns, such as work, and ask them what concerns of theirs they want you to pray for. Explain that you are growing with God together. Let them know that you value them as growing, maturing people. Then, when they finally leave home, they will be people who can speak into your life as you speak into theirs.

Common Reflections of Faith at This Age

By the time your children leave this stage and head for their teens, they will know who they are, how they fit into God's story, and what choices they're responsible for. They will have a history of good decision making and be comfortable with the idea that they have made and can make right choices and discipline themselves to have times with God. With this foundation they will grow into people who want to know and learn more about the Christian life, grow in their relationship with God, and take responsibility for it.

As your children move toward their teens, they face greater temptations. They must be ready to resist them and hang on to the truth. The key is for them to know that their relationship with God is the foundation and cornerstone of the rest of their lives. When they understand this, their view of life through their teen years will be molded by it. They will, with your ongoing help, be able to weather many storms and use the right tools to make good decisions.

Creating a Memory Marker: Commitment

A great time for a Memory Marker is when children leave their childhood and enter their teen years. (For an explanation of the Memory Marker, see pages 111–112.) Not only are they becoming teens, they are ready to make an informed, personally chosen commitment to God and His ways. Talk to them ahead of time about whether they are ready to make a serious commitment to follow God for the rest of their lives. This will deepen their commitment to obedience and a biblical lifestyle. When they are ready, create an event they'll remember. (This will be especially important for those who were so young when they made their original commitment that they don't remember.)

Create a Memory Marker for them through a special ceremony and celebration. Many churches have occasions you can use for this, such as confirmation, baptism, Sunday school graduation, or another rite-of-passage ceremony. If your church doesn't have one, make a special occasion with friends and family for your children as they commit to follow God. Take pictures, buy a new outfit, have a special meal, give them something to represent their new commitment.

Things About God They're Ready to Learn

This chart shows the information your children are ready to learn now. As you ensure they have what they need to make informed choices, always bring the topic back to the practical: How does this affect their lives? What does this mean to them where they are now?

Ages 10–12

KNOWING		LOVING	LIVING	
A. Who God Is	**B.** What God Has Done	**C.** You Can Have a Relationship with God	**D.** You Can Be All God Wants You to Be	**E.** You Can Do All God Wants You to Do
73. Not everyone believes the truth about God, but there are ways you can respond to their objections. (Handling contrary opinions about God: basic apologetics; other religions)	74. God wants you to explore the One Big Story. 75. God put the Bible together in a fascinating way. 76. You need to learn how to study the Bible. 77. God lets His people serve Him and express their worship of Him in different ways. 78. God gave us an accurate record of His Son, Jesus. 79. God wants you to tell others about what Jesus has done. 80. Jesus will return as Judge and there will be a new heaven and a new earth.	81. You can pray on your own. 82. You can read the Bible on your own. 83. You can learn to worship God and Jesus on your own or in a group.	84. God wants you to choose to grow, learn, and seek His wisdom. 85. God's grace: You don't have to do it on our own. God is working in you by His Holy Spirit. 86. God wants you to find and follow His will for your life.	87. God wants you to choose to commit your entire life and everything you have to Him. 88. God wants you to choose His way because you love Him and want to be like Jesus. 89. God wants you to learn to seek and follow His Spirit's leading. 90. You need to learn how to resist Satan and temptation. 91. You need to get involved in church and find your place in the body of Christ.

The Teen Years

At the end of this 10–12 stage, you need to be letting your children progressively take more responsibility for their own spiritual growth. The teen years they are heading into are an entirely different phase of life, and your role as a parent needs to change to match it. Your role moves toward becoming more like a coach, as opposed to an instructor and trainer. You now need to walk alongside them and assist in their growth and discovery.

Young teenagers are beginning to have their own ideas of what they want and how to do things. They are in the process of formulating their identity: who they are in relation to you, their friends, and the world around them. They want to walk on their own two feet and be independent. Teens have strong opinions and are often confident that they can do quite well on their own, thank you very much. They are eagerly seeking signs that you approve of their growing independence as you give them more responsibility for making decisions and following through on them. For all these reasons, when your children hit their teen years, it is important to walk with them, coaching and guiding them, rather than always telling them what to do and how to do it.

The strong foundation that you have laid in their lives through spiritually training them in the early years will protect them and help them make the right decisions. The understanding of God, His ways and love, will keep them following and seeking God. They are not entering a time when they know it all (in spite of what teens often think) and no longer need to grow and advance spiritually. They still need to have a personal relationship with God, read and study the Bible, be a part of a church, and live God's way. The difference is that they are now taking on responsibility for these things themselves with you encouraging them.

Be careful not to just let your teenagers go completely. Every coach checks up on the progress of his or her athletes or players. As your kids' coach, you need to watch their progress too. Here are three ways to do this.

1. Keep in touch with their progress by having regular conversations with them as a fellow learner. Tell them what you are learning, going through, and talking to God about, and then encourage them to include you in their spiritual lives.
2. Recruit them to assist you in teaching and helping with the spiritual growth of their younger siblings.
3. Encourage them to get involved in assisting with Sunday school classes at your church.

Ideas and Methods You Can Choose From

• Church • Mealtime • Drive Time • Bedtime • Fun Time
• Teachable Moments • Family Nights • Family Devotions
• Meaningful Memories • Blessing Ceremonies
• Holidays • Quiet Time • Exploration Time

Ideas and Methods You Can Choose From

Spiritual training can fit your family and your schedule to a "T." All you need to do is find out what will probably work best for you and design a plan around that. (If after a few months you find that what you thought would work doesn't, you can always change the details of your plan.) This section describes a number of ideas and methods for you to choose from. Then, in the next section, you'll take everything you've discovered about your family (in Sections A and B) and match it with some of these methods and models to form a unique plan for your family.

The Dreaded "D" Word

When you hear the phrase "family devotions," a memory snapshot probably comes to mind at once, especially if you're a second- or third-generation Christian. There you were, sitting at the table with piles of delicious-smelling food just waiting to be eaten, innocently assuming that dinner was the main item on the agenda. But before you could begin, your father got out his Bible or devotional book and

began reading. He waxed eloquent for a time about what the passage meant, while the aromas of pot roast and potatoes made you dizzy with hunger. The rumbles in your belly and the tantalizing odors made concentration difficult. Finally Dad said, "Let us pray." You bowed your head, hoping for something about the length of "Rub-a-dub-dub, thanks for the grub." Instead, he prayed for each member of the family, extended family, church family, missionary community, political party, and justice and educational systems. By the time he said, "Amen," the food was cold and the gravy had congealed into globs.

This is not to knock your parents' deep desire to pass their faith on to you. They used what was available and what they knew. Unfortunately, the "traditional" method doesn't work for every family. Now you're a parent and wondering what you can do differently so your kids will have positive instead of negative snapshots. Perhaps you're a first-generation Christian and had no model at all for spiritual training.

Vary Your Recipe

Take heart. There are many methods available for passing on your faith to your children. Consider the lowly potato. If the only way you served potatoes was boiled or mashed without any salt, pepper, butter, or gravy, your family would quickly tire of eating them. But if you go through your recipe books, chances are you could come up with a different way to serve potatoes every night of the week, probably for several weeks in a row, and your family would never get sick of them. You could make french fries; potato salad; baked potatoes with sour cream, chives, and bacon bits; even potato pancakes. You'd be using the same basic ingredient every night—potatoes—but the different spices you add and the variety of presentations would keep your family's taste buds begging for more.

In a similar way, spiritual training has a number of basic ingredients (Bible reading, teaching, discussion, prayer) and a single purpose (to develop mature Christians). But just as there are countless ways to serve potatoes, so there are countless ways in which the ingredients of faith training can be combined with other elements and presented in such a way that each session is challenging, exciting, and rewarding for everyone. Perhaps it's time to change your spiritual training "recipe" and look at new, enjoyable, and exciting ways to train your children in their Christian faith.

Teach Sitting, Walking, Lying Down, Getting Up

If you reduce the Bible to its essentials, all of the doctrine, examples, stories, principles, laws, warnings, cautions, dos, don'ts, and truths amount to one thing: *life*. That's the subject of all Christian teaching and training. Life is the context in which that training is carried out and the goal toward which it aims. Jesus said, "I have come that they may have life, and *have it to the full*" (John 10:10, italics added). Since this is true, it makes sense to teach Christianity right in the midst of everyday life.

In the next 13 chapters we explore tried-and-true ideas and methods for the formal instruction of your children, as well as methods that will help you get the practical training done in the routine of everyday living. Over the years, many tools have been developed to help you accomplish this task, and some new ones have been developed to be used with the methods and ideas presented in the following chapters. We recommend using a wide range of tools whenever they are appropriate to the method and model we are describing. Simply put, this section will give you lots of great ideas that will help you get the job done and will suggest many tools and resources to assist you.

As you are reading this section, *remember to be flexible*. Use different methods with different children. Choose models and tools that are fun and interesting and fit your family and lifestyle so well that your kids look forward to them. Achieving the purpose is more important than the methods you use. And that is exactly what this section is designed to help you with.

Read through the various models and start thinking about which methods and tools suit your family. These will become part of your plan (in Section D, pages 229–268). You'll begin replacing that snapshot of "family devotions" we gave you at the beginning of this introduction with ones that will work for your kids.

You're probably already using some of the ideas and methods mentioned in the following chapters, while others will be new to you. Remember, the purpose is

I
D
E
A
S

A
N
D

M
E
T
H
O
D
S

to help your children on their way to a mature, lived-out, growing faith in God. Whatever forms, ideas, or methods can accomplish that purpose for your unique family—those are the ones to use.

Here is a list of the models we will discuss:

- **Church-Related Spiritual Training**
  Church (page 143)

- **"On-the-Spot" Spiritual Training**
  - Mealtime (page 149)   • Drive Time (page 155)
  - Bedtime (page 161)   • Fun Time (page 167)
  - Teachable Moments (page 173)

- **Ideas, Methods, and Tools for the Family**
  - Family Nights (page 177)   • Family Devotions (page 185)
  - Meaningful Memories (page 189)

- **Special Times and Events**
  - Blessing Ceremonies (page 197) • Holidays (page 203)

- **Ideas, Methods, and Tools for Individual Growth**
  - Quiet Time (page 213)   • Exploration Time (page 221)

Read through these chapters prayerfully and with an open mind. Don't skip a particular chapter simply because the title doesn't appeal to you. Look at all the possibilities before you make your choices.

Each of the chapters begins with a one-page summary that shows you that method at a glance. This will help you more easily find those methods that seem to suit your family particularly well. The chapter then presents an overview of the method and a related sample for you to try with your family. Each one also points you to tools that can help you implement that chapter's approach. The chapters are not intended to be complete manuals for the methods presented but an introduction to them.

Please note that some of the tools listed may no longer be available. You can find up to date resource lists from the Focus on the Family (www.family.org) or Heritage Builders (www.heritagebuilders.com) Web sites—or check your local Christian book store. You're sure to find a resource that will work in your family's unique situation. See the Resource List in Appendix II for even more tools.

CHAPTER 15

Church

Summary: The frontline support for spiritual training is your local church. Get involved in and support the various programs offered, such as worship services, Sunday school, vacation Bible school, Bible clubs, etc.

Impact: God has given believers the local church as a place for corporate worship, teaching, service, encouragement, and accountability. When we consistently demonstrate the priority of attending church, our children learn to place a high priority there as well. An additional benefit is that children are more likely to meet and make the right friends through church.

How long does it take? Usually an hour or two each week.

Where does it happen? At your local church.

When should we do it? Weekly.

Who is involved? The entire family, along with your local congregation.

Parental effort required: Modest (the stress of getting everyone ready without losing your cool).

Spiritual growth impact rating: High.

I D E A S   A N D   M E T H O D S

The Church: A Parent's Greatest Ally

As a parent, the church should be your greatest ally and a key partner in helping you pass on your Christian faith to your children. While we've talked a lot about choosing different methods and models to suit *your* family, church attendance and participation should be part of *every* family's Spiritual Growth Plan. With the support of Sunday school, vacation Bible school, youth groups, and other church-sponsored ministries, you will be able to more effectively instruct and train your children.

To the Heart

I don't remember what the Sunday school teacher said during class that Sunday. I was only four years old. Whatever the teacher said simmered in my young heart all the way home in the car. And I vividly remember what happened next.

Dad barely got the front door unlocked when I ran into the house. I ran to the family room and slammed the door. The coat hangers jangled on the back of the door as I turned my chin upward. "Jesus," I said out loud, "You'd better come into my heart *right now!"* Then I smiled. I knew Jesus would do what He promised. And I knew He now lived in my heart. And now, many, many years later I know, and have never doubted, that He has lived in me ever since that moment.

L. H. J.

Keys to Success

There are many practical things you can do to take full advantage of what your children are learning in Sunday school, vacation Bible school, or youth group. The following are a few suggestions.

♦ *Pray together.* Help your children build an expectation that God will teach them during Sunday school by praying with them in the car on the way to church. You might pray something like "Dear God, help us today to learn more about You, grow closer to You, and encourage and help others to do the same."

♦ *Follow up.* After church or vacation Bible school, reinforce what your children learned by asking them about it. Look at their take-home sheets. Interview the teachers at the beginning of each term and find out what general topics will be covered and what the memory verses will be. Take time during the week to pull out the Sunday school papers, memory verses, and Bible stories and review them. This doesn't have to take long. Perhaps you can do it as a special bedtime activity on Sunday nights.

◆ *Be patient with young children in church.* If a young child has to sit with you during church service, there will probably be times when he is not engaged, especially during the sermon. Some churches have special bulletins for children with simple activities to keep them engaged during the sermon. If your church doesn't have that, bring a coloring book or activity book for the child to use when he gets restless. Or bring a colorful Bible storybook for him to look at when your Bible is open.

◆ *Get involved.* For parents with young children who are looking for a church, one of the best things you can do is sit in on the Sunday school classes and see what is being learned, what the atmosphere is like, and whether your children are being taught or just babysat. Better yet, get involved and teach a Sunday school class yourself. If you're already in a church and you're unhappy with the direction your Sunday school is headed, get involved and help out. But you don't have to teach to get involved. You can sit on the Sunday school board, lead games or singing, or help out with crafts. Don't complain about what's going on in your church—jump in and help.

◆ *Say thanks.* Most church volunteers are overworked and underappreciated. Make a point of thanking and encouraging your children's teachers, and teach your children to do the same. Thank-you cards and gifts at the end of each term and on special occasions, such as Christmas and birthdays, are a good way to do this.

Tools

FaithTraining: Raising Kids Who Love the Lord by Joe White (Focus on the Family, 1994).

This book is designed to help parents train children of all ages to love the Lord. One section features 365 ways to tell your child "I love you" without saying the words.

I Want to Know About the Church by Rick Osborne and K. Christie Bowler (Zondervan, 1998).

This book will help your child discover what the church is and learn its story, learn about how God cares and provides for the church, and find out ways he or she can serve God in the church. For ages 8–12.

See the Resource List in Appendix II for more tools to help you.

Sunday School Helps

Here are two forms that can help you reinforce Sunday school lessons at home. Both forms can be photocopied or found at www.heritagebuilders.com. (They can also be used for other church activities that involve teaching.)

Sunday School Teacher Interview Form

This form is a guide to asking questions; it is not a tool of the Inquisition. Listen with an open, supportive spirit to the teacher's responses to the questions. Be sensitive—your children's teachers may not be used to having parents get involved. So be sure to clarify your intentions up front and assure them that you're not there to criticize them or ask them to do extra work. You simply want to enhance what they're doing by reinforcing it at home.

Sunday School Learning Log

This form will help you and your children keep track of what they learn in Sunday school each term, including memory verses, Bible stories, and the main lesson learned each week. At the end of the term, review with them what was learned and pray with them, thanking God for what He has taught them about Himself.

SUNDAY SCHOOL TEACHER INTERVIEW FORM

Teacher's name: _____ Birthday: _____

Class name: _____

Number of students (on average): _____

Do you have a theme for this term that I can reinforce at home? _____

_____

Are there any subthemes that you plan to cover? _____

_____

Are you planning to study any particular Bible book(s) or stories?_____

_____

Will you give the children memory verses? If so, do you have a list you can give me, or is there a way

I can get involved in helping the children learn? _____

Do you have any special classes or events planned—such as field trips, plays, or parties—that will

require extra help from parents? _____

   If so, when are they? _____

What can I do to help? _____

Can I help by supplying snacks or other supplies during the term? _____

Is there anything else I can do to help? _____

_____

_____

IDEAS AND METHODS

IDEAS AND METHODS

SUNDAY SCHOOL LEARNING LOG

Name: _____

Term: _____ Fall _____ Winter _____ Spring _____ Summer

	Lesson	Key Verse/ Memory Verse	Bible Story
Week 1:	_____	_____	_____
Week 2:	_____	_____	_____
Week 3:	_____	_____	_____
Week 4:	_____	_____	_____
Week 5:	_____	_____	_____
Week 6:	_____	_____	_____
Week 7:	_____	_____	_____
Week 8:	_____	_____	_____
Week 9:	_____	_____	_____
Week 10:	_____	_____	_____
Week 11:	_____	_____	_____
Week 12:	_____	_____	_____
Week 13:	_____	_____	_____

CHAPTER 16

Mealtime

Summary: Take advantage of the time spent eating meals together to discuss spiritual topics in an enjoyable, unforced manner.

Impact: Incorporating spiritual conversations into the natural flow of life, such as during a meal, allows your children to overcome the notion that spirituality is just a "church thing." It also allows you to take advantage of time already spent together and make it even more meaningful.

How long does it take? Usually no more than 10 minutes.

Where does it happen? At the table.

When should we do it? At any and every meal, once a day, or at least once a week.

Who is involved? The entire family.

Parental effort required: Very little (three–five minutes preparation time).

Spiritual growth impact rating: Moderate.

IDEAS AND METHODS

A Perfect Opportunity

It's dinnertime, and as usual, the father leads the family in prayer. Everyone bows their heads, expecting the normal wording, something like "Lord, bless this food to our bodies' use, and us to your love and service." But tonight Dad surprises them by saying, "Father, thank You for the glorious sunrise this morning. What a wonderful evidence of Your glory! Everything we have comes from You, including this meal for which we give You thanks tonight."

As Mom serves up the casserole and Dad begins passing the rolls, the kids are already diving into their food. After a couple of bites, Dad says, "Did anyone see the sunrise this morning?"

One of the kids says, "Dad, only you get up that early." An older one jokes, "If God wanted us to see the sunrise, He'd have scheduled it later."

Dad laughs along with the family, then begins to describe the sight. "Fingers of gold and orange clouds came up from the horizon. And all above me, it was as though a great painter had stroked the most colorful clouds. It was so beautiful, I had trouble concentrating on driving. It was one of the most beautiful sights I've ever seen, and it reminded me again that all of the natural beauty around us is a reminder of God, and that He is the Creator."

Such conversations are common in this household. Mealtime is a chance for this family to connect about their day and activities. But it's also a chance for Dad or Mom to comment on God's work in their lives. This evening Mom tells about a family who had been in a car accident

Ten Commandments

"Kelsie," I said one evening at dinner, "can you list the Ten Commandments?"

"Don't lie," she said, putting her fork down next to her plate. "Don't murder."

"Thou shalt not commit adultery," my wife Diane chimed in.

I wrote the answers down between bites. I couldn't remember them all either, and had hesitated even bringing up the subject if I didn't know the answer.

"Thou shalt not steal," Kelsie added.

Diane said, "Don't take the Lord's name in vain."

"Keep the Sabbath day holy," I said as I wrote it down. Once we thought we had all 10, we tried to list them in order. We got as far as we could on our own, then got a Bible to check our answers. Together we said them aloud a few times. From there, we closed the Bible and had a contest to see who could list them the quickest.

By the time we finished, we had the scripture memorized—and we had fun doing it!

J. M.

recently. In fact, the kids had prayed for them. "I saw Beth this afternoon at the grocery store," Mom reports. "She is looking great. Considering that the car was totally destroyed and they should have been killed, it's a miracle that all of them are on the road to full recovery. She is praising God for His goodness to them."

In our culture, meals are often eaten on the run in many homes. Or they are consumed in front of a television set. But for the family that regularly gathers for a meal and uses the time for casual spiritual conversation, the results are memorable with children.

Keys to Success

If your mealtimes are already full of fun, laughter, and togetherness, don't suddenly try to make them "spiritual" or turn them into sermon times. Your children will resent it. Allow time for that interaction to take place, but also direct the content of some interactions toward the Christian life and a mature faith. Here are some keys to making a successful mealtime discussion.

◆ *Personalize it.* Tell your children how you learned the truth under discussion or how you experienced what you are talking about. For example, if the discussion is about how God can be trusted to provide for one's needs, relate a time that He did that for you. Perhaps you lost your keys, prayed, and suddenly remembered where you'd put them. What about the time you needed a new outfit for a job interview and someone lent it to you or gave you a gift that enabled you to buy one? Tell a story about when you were a kid and learned about the topic.

◆ *Time it right.* Start after people have begun eating the meal, when the first hunger pangs are stilled and people are ready to talk. If you try to do it too early, you'll encounter only the sound of tummy rumbles. However, if you wait too long, they'll just be thinking of getting to their next task.

◆ *Keep it short.* If you can see your family is interested and there's a lively discussion happening, keep it going. But if the discussion falters and there's little interest in pursuing it further, end it. When this happens, don't assume your children aren't interested; just leave the seed planted and move on to other things of more immediate interest to them. God's truth can take care of itself—it will keep working in them and nudging their thoughts.

If one child is interested but the others aren't, let everyone go and keep talking with the interested child, or promise to talk some more later, perhaps when tucking him or her into bed.

◆ *Keep it relevant.* Make your topics fit what's happened that day. If something comes up that your children are concerned about and you had planned to focus on a different topic, change your plan. It will be easier for them to get involved and take it in when they can see why it's important.

Tools

Here is a tool designed specifically around mealtimes.

Mealtime Moments by Tricia Goyer and Crystal Bowman (Tyndale, 2000).

This resource contains a variety of mealtime discussions. Each day's entry includes similar basic features, but there is enough variety throughout the book to keep it from becoming ho-hum. Each mealtime starter begins with an attention-grabbing newspaper-type headline. Features include the following:

- Mealtime Prayer
- Appetizer (starting things off with an activity, joke, or crazy discussion)
- Main Course (the entree that serves as a transition from the appetizer into the biblical topic)
- Table Talk (a series of questions that directs and rounds out the discussion, leading to the lesson and application—through a fun discussion)
- Vitamins and Minerals (a key verse that encapsulates that day's lesson and is good for memorizing, if you want to use it that way)

This book also includes suggestions for special holiday meals and a section on theme meals, like "Take Out," "Fondue," "TV Dinners," and "Desserts," each with related activities or discussions. This tool gives you roughly six months' worth of activities (based on using five or six per week). Here is a sample for you to try.

Plain Ol' Vanilla

Mealtime Prayer

Let each person at the table offer his or her own kind of prayer—short or long, silent or aloud. Have the last person who prays thank God for your different tastes in prayer—and food!

Appetizer

Which of these ice cream flavors is the top seller: strawberry, cookies 'n' cream, chocolate, or vanilla? (*Answer: vanilla.*) What's your favorite flavor?

Main Course

Why isn't there just one flavor of ice cream? If you were a flavor of ice cream, which would you be: Mysterious Mocha, Cheery Cherry, Quiet Kiwi, Grumpy Grape, or Outrageous Orange? Why?

Why didn't God make just one kind of person? Just like ice cream, all of us have different "tastes." Your flavor is what makes you unique. Each person has a different way of talking, walking, thinking—even praying and worshiping God.

Table Talk

Take a vote on the following questions:
- Would you rather sing a praise song with motions or without?
- Would you rather pray while standing, sitting, kneeling, or bowing with your face to the floor? Why?
- Now that you've voted, should you all have to sing and pray in the way that got the most votes? Why or why not?

Vitamins and Minerals

"There are different kinds of service, but the same Lord" (1 Corinthians 12:5).

See the Resource List in Appendix II for more tools to help you.

CHAPTER 17

Drive Time

Summary:	Between school, doctor visits, grocery shopping, music lessons, and athletic contests, you probably spend hours each week in the car or minivan with your children. Redeem some of the time by using it to intentionally teach spiritual truth, fulfilling the modern-day equivalent of teaching "when you walk along the road" (Deuteronomy 6:7).
Impact:	Instead of remembering boring hours in the car, children may actually anticipate this time. This is a chance to let a child talk about what is on his mind, bring up a topic you want to discuss, or have them listen to Christian music or drama.
How long does it take?	Five minutes to an hour—it depends on the length of your trip.
Where does it happen?	In your car.
When should we do it?	Anytime you go on a trip and want to pass the time in a productive way. If your family has several car trips per day, you might pick one time, such as the morning commute, to concentrate on spiritual training.
Who is involved?	Your entire family.
Parental effort required:	Very little. (Have tapes ready or prepare a couple of questions).
Spiritual growth impact rating:	Moderate.

IDEAS AND METHODS

155

One for the Road

Anna hustled her three children, ages 6, 9, and 11, into the van for a drive across town. She would drop one child off for soccer practice, then take another to a baseball game, where her husband would join her. She had a plastic pail and shovel for the youngest, who would dig in the sandbox in the play area near the ball field.

But first there was 25 minutes of city driving. The kids were noisy and fidgety. Anna had a headache. This could be the worst time of the day. Or the best!

"Hey Mom," yelled the nine-year-old, "can we listen to *Adventures in Odyssey*?"

Mom smiled despite the pain in her head. "Nathan, you can't hear anything when you're this noisy."

"We'll be quiet," promised Nathan.

The other kids chimed in: "Yeah, Mom, we'll be quiet."

"Okay, I'll start the tape as soon as you're all quiet." Instantly, there was silence in the car. Mom pulled a cassette tape out of an album and popped it into the tape player. Later, as they pulled up to the soccer field, the show's moderator was wrapping up the story. On the way to the baseball game, Mom discussed the show's lesson with her oldest child. From there, the youngest daughter would ride home with Dad, who would play a couple of songs from *The Singing Bible*. The little girl had many of the songs memorized but never tired of hearing them again.

The result? What could have been a horrendous time in the car had become a peaceful respite for Anna and her family. Her children actually looked forward to this time, and she knew they were learning important biblical truths.

Keys to Success

◆ *Get them while they're hot.* Use drive time as an on-the-fly family meeting time to deal with any problems that have just come up. For example, if right before you left the house there was a conflict between two of your children over who should use the bathroom first, deal with the issue while you're on the way to the next event. This is an excellent opportunity to catch something while it's happening and apply biblical principles on the spot. Remember, this isn't lecture time, so try to keep things relatively light.

◆ *Keep it simple.* If your children are arguing over who gets to sit in the front seat, it's not the time to launch into a theological treatise about the difference between right and wrong. Instead, talk to your children about what the Bible says in regard to looking out for the needs of others before we look out for our own. After you share this with your children, you might tell about a time when applying this principle worked for you, or you might remind them of a story they heard that teaches this truth.

◆ *Make it fun.* One of the best ways to diffuse anger or conflict is with humor. If your children get into the car and they are in the midst of an argument or they are just cooling off from a conflict in the house, this is probably not the best time to talk to them about how to apply God's principles to resolve the issue. Instead, why not get everyone to roll down their windows and have a contest to see who can yell the loudest? You go first. This may alarm the neighbors, but it will provide your children with a positive way to channel their negative energy—and hearing you yell can show them how ridiculous they sound. Once everyone is worn out and the bad feelings have subsided a little, take a moment to talk with your children about the conflict and how they can resolve it.

Overcoming Obstacles

Drive time is a great time to talk to your children about God, and there are some excellent tools to help you in this task. But don't become so tool-oriented that the tools themselves become an obstacle to learning. Sometimes your children just want to relax, goof off, and have fun. Be sensitive to their wants and needs instead of always trying to squeeze in one more kernel of wisdom. This is also a good time to talk

IDEAS AND METHODS

I
D
E
A
S

A
N
D

M
E
T
H
O
D
S

to your children from your heart—or to just listen.

Your children may not be responding to your efforts to teach them during drive time because you may be using the wrong tool. For example, you may want to have a conversation, but your children just want to listen to the songs from *The Singing Bible* (see page 160). Give your kids a choice from among the different tools that are available. This will ensure their interest. If they can't agree on which tool to use, let them take turns choosing.

Tools

Joy Ride! by Jacqueline Lederman (Tyndale, 2000).

Within the pages of this book you will find a variety of new and interesting ways to help you teach your children while you enjoy quality time together on the road. The goal of this book is to provide families with a good Christian growth resource to use in the car. It includes fun discussion starters, travel games, and other activities that will help your children learn spiritual and biblical content while having a good time. The following are a sample game, trivia question, and discussion starter from *Joy Ride!*

The License Plate Game

In this game, players are to come up with Bible words using letters from the license plates of other cars on the road. Most license plates contain letters and numbers. If players can take the letters from five cars and come up with the name of a person or place in the Bible, they get five points. (If they can spell Zerubbabel, they get an extra 1,000 points for having performed a miracle.) If they can make the name of a Bible book, they get three points. If they can make a word that is found in the Bible or is related to the Christian life (in other words, not just words like *first*, *go*, or *work* that might appear in the Bible but aren't particular to Christianity), they get two points. And if they can only make a "normal" word, they get one point.

You can make the game go for as many rounds as you want. A good idea is to set the winning score at 20 and give a prize to whomever gets there first. Note: Younger children may need a bit of help from their parents or older siblings for this game.

Trivia

What Place Am I?

Clue #1: I cannot be found on a map.

Clue #2: Gates must be entered to come here.

Clue #3: Only people who have trusted in God see me.

Clue #4: There is a Book of Life here that contains the names of every person who will ever live here.

Clue #5: God's people will live with Him forever here.

(*Answer: Heaven*)

Discussion Starter

Moving at the Speed of Light

Jump Start:

Imagine yourself having a secret identity with strength and powers beyond human abilities—such as soaring through the air with lightning speed, seeing with X-ray vision, or having the power to pick up buildings! What other abilities would you want? What would you do if you had them?

Speeding Up:

- Know of anyone who has those kinds of abilities? (Yes, you do!)
- Imagine a supervillain and a superhero. What would they do with their power?
- Power alone doesn't make you a superhero. What makes the difference between a supervillain and a superhero?

Look at the Map:

Psalm 147:5: "Great is our Lord and mighty in power; his understanding has no limit."

Travel Plan:

Okay, so God is the greatest superhero of all time! He's all-powerful and can do anything! So what does He do with His power? He has X-ray vision, you know—how does He do that? Can you trust Him?

Adventures in Odyssey (Focus on the Family).

These dramatized audiotapes take kids ages eight and up through all sorts of exciting adventures and teach important lessons about God, the Bible, and the Christian faith. Whether it's traveling through time in the Imagination Station or just hanging out and having a soda at Whit's End, you never know what's going to happen next in the fictional town of Odyssey. After you've finished listening to an adventure, discuss the main teaching points and reinforce the lesson taught by personalizing it to suit your children's lives. At approximately 25 minutes each, these tapes are ideal for long or medium commutes. For vacation trips, an album will last the average family about 400 miles! For a current list of Adventures in Odyssey video and audio tapes, see the Resource List in Appendix II.

The Singing Bible by Richard and Elaine Osborne (Tyndale House Publishers).

Children ages 2 to 7 will love *The Singing Bible*, which sets Bible stories and facts to music with over 50 sing-along songs! New from Heritage Builders, a ministry of Focus on the Family, it introduces your kids to people like Jonah and the whale and Daniel in the lion's den, making *The Singing Bible* a fun, fast-paced journey kids will remember.

See the Resource List in Appendix II for more tools to help you.

I D E A S   A N D   M E T H O D S

CHAPTER 18

Bedtime

Summary: Many families already have some sort of bedtime routine, and these are ideal opportunities for spiritual training, affirmations of love, and prayer. Bedtime activities have very high value for the time spent.

Impact: The end of the day is a natural time for families to talk about their triumphs, defeats, anxieties, and dreams. By spending a few minutes in the evening, parents can help children start each day with a clean slate of hope, anticipation, and joy. Your relationship with each child will be affirmed and your faith in God reinforced.

How long does it take? Usually no more than 10 to 15 minutes.

Where does it happen? At home, in the bedroom.

When should we do it? As often as possible, hopefully every night.

Who is involved? Ideally you meet one-on-one with each child, but it can be done as a group.

Parental effort required: Minimal.

Spiritual growth impact rating: Very high.

A Perfect Time to Share God's Love

In our culture, bedtime has become a time when most parents spend a few moments reading to their children, talking to them, and even praying with them before tucking them in for the night. Because of this, bedtime is also the perfect opportunity to start mentoring and teaching your children about developing the habit of a daily time with God in order to get to know and love Him. This simple practice will help your children begin to understand and develop the two main aspects of daily times with God: Bible reading and prayer.

This nightly routine is also important because of what it demonstrates about God's love. One of the most powerful ways to share God's love or character with your children is by loving them and modeling God's character to them yourself. Spending time with your children each day at bedtime is an effective way to demonstrate God's desire to spend time with them. It shows them that you care enough about them to take time out of your schedule and to make them a priority—and that God wants to be with them just as you want to. Bedtime is a good time to teach your children simple things about God, but the emphasis should be on getting to know Him and helping your children develop a relationship with Him. (This is an excellent time to focus on the loving aspect of training.)

An easy way to start is to choose a good Bible or Bible storybook and begin working through it with your children. End the time with a short prayer asking God to help your children get to know Him. But before prayer time, take the time to tell your children that God is listening to them and that He cares about them and can look after all of their needs. As they approach God, He'll draw closer to them. Help your children understand that their relationship with God takes time and consistency, just like any other relationship. A good way to explain this is by asking them if their closest friends would be very good friends if they just passed by each other all the time with a quick hello. Obviously, any friendship grows by purposely planning and enjoying time together. The same is true of their relationship with God.

Try to spend time with each child individually. Even if you read the Bible and pray together as a family, time alone with each of your children is still important. It is this *sense of wanting to be with them as individuals* that you want them to carry over into their relationship with God. It's not enough to know that God loves the world and gave His only Son—each of your children needs to know that He loves him or her *as an individual* and that He wants to be with him or her *individually*.

Keys to Success

Bedtime is a real no-brainer when it comes to looking for opportunities to build a quiet time with God into your children's daily routine. But it doesn't come without its challenges. There are teeth to be brushed, toys to be put away, and tomorrow's lunches to be made. Here are some tips to help you make bedtime a rewarding experience for all of you.

◆ *Be open to change.* As your children grow older, their time with God will change. They may want to start doing their own quiet time, and they may want to do it in the morning or after school. When your children are mature enough to take this step (usually starting around age 10), encourage it. But it's still good to spend a bit of time with them at bedtime to continue demonstrating God's love and your love for them. During this time, you can talk to them about their time with God and continue coaching them forward.

◆ *Keep it interesting.* Developing a relationship with God should not be a boring event where the same routine is followed time and again. Variety, laughter, and fun make learning enjoyable and memorable. They also reflect a wider view of God: He isn't just about serious learning; He likes to have fun, too. He created humor and enjoys variety and creativity—so make sure there's plenty of it in your children's bedtime routine.

◆ *Keep it focused on the child and his or her needs.* Use this time to affirm your children and their worth as a creation of God and

163

member of your family. This is not the time to press a parental agenda. Find out what your child's concerns are so you can focus on them in your prayers. Allow your child to change the agenda every once in a while. Don't be afraid of spontaneity. Keep your prayer times and Bible readings relevant to your children's needs and experiences.

The *Adventures in Odyssey* and other audiotape series (see the Resource List in Appendix II) are also a way to add variety to your bedtime routine. Your children can listen to these tapes beforehand, or you can listen to them together and then link your prayer to the story you heard on the tape.

Overcoming Obstacles

If you have a large family, it may be difficult to spend time individually with each child every night. This is especially true if you are a single parent. If you find this to be a problem, perhaps you can try doing the Bible reading with your children as a group and then pray separately with each one. If two parents are involved, share the responsibility, but make sure you "rotate" the children so that both of you regularly spend time with each child. If one-on-one time is just too difficult, a group prayer is still a good option.

Tools

The basic tools for bedtime include a good Bible storybook with engaging art and age-appropriate stories, along with some sort of devotional book and/or prayer book for children. The following tools were specifically developed to help you with your children's bedtime.

Bedtime Blessings by John Trent (Tyndale, 2000).

This is an especially helpful book for children ages 7 and under. It contains six months' worth of relational activities you will engage in with your children. Each session ends with a blessing prayer meant to affirm your love (and God's) for your child and the high value you place in him or her. It is a practical tool, designed to help you bless your child on a daily basis.

Try out this sample blessing from the book.

Let's Look at Nature

(You will need a flower.)

What can you learn from this flower?

One day when Jesus was teaching, He taught by using flowers. He said, "Why do you worry about clothes? See how the lilies of the field grow. They do not labor or spin. Yet I tell you that not even Solomon [who was a very rich king] in all his splendor was dressed like one of these. If that is how God clothes the grass of the field, which is here today and tomorrow is thrown into the fire, will he not much more clothe you?" (Matthew 6:28–30).

Do you ever worry? Whenever you do, look at the flowers. What is God saying to you through them?

Prayer:

Dear God, Thank You for flowers and the lesson they teach: the comforting lesson that You are going to take good care of us. Amen.

Other Resources

The Resource List in Appendix II contains many excellent tools to help you create an effective bedtime routine for your children. Here are some highlights:

The God Loves Me Bible by Susan Elisabeth Beck (Zondervan, 2000).

This colorful Bible for children ages 2–4 emphasizes the overriding theme of the Bible: God loves His world, His people, and me!

My First Bible in Pictures by Kenneth N. Taylor et al. (Tyndale, 1990).

This best-selling Bible for children ages 6–10 features bright, full-color illustrations and 125 meaningful stories that capture children's attention.

The Amazing Treasure Bible Storybook (Zondervan, 1997).

This unique Bible storybook for ages 6–12 takes readers on an archaeological adventure throughout the entire story of the Bible—a story unearthed room by mysterious room in dramatic lessons that make Bible truths come alive.

IDEAS AND METHODS

Tips on Choosing a Bible for Your Child

Your children will probably go through four to six different Bibles between the day they're born and the day they leave home. This is not only practical, since their reading skills, comprehension levels, and interests change, but it also encourages kids to see that they are progressing in their knowledge of God.

In the past, choosing a Bible or Bible storybook for children was a relatively simple task because the choice was limited. Times have changed. Now there is a dizzying variety of Bible storybooks and regular Bibles to choose from. They all come with illustrations, study notes, and other special features. But which one is the best one for your child? Here are some general tips to help you make your choice:

- Each of your children should have his or her own Bible. Owning a Bible shows them how important God's Word is and how it should always be on hand as the practical guidebook for life.
- Let your children have a say in choosing what type of Bible to buy. Ownership in this decision will increase their interest in reading it.
- When your children are old enough to want a whole-text Bible, choose a translation that uses modern language. Some versions are deliberately made for children's use. If you're not familiar with the various modern translations, pick out a few verses from different parts of the Bible and compare how they read in different versions.
- Finally, look for children's and teens' Bibles that contain the whole text of the Bible as well as additional materials to help your children understand and apply what they read. Choose a Bible with all or some of the following features: a simple concordance, explanatory notes in the text, introductions to each book of the Bible, maps of Bible lands, cross-references, and Bible facts or trivia.

Here are a few hints for choosing a Bible storybook or a Bible by age group:

- **Preschool:** Buy a Bible storybook, with simple illustrations, that covers key Bible stories and has a small number of simple words per picture.
- **Beginning Readers:** Choose a storybook that contains simple illustrations and more stories than a preschool storybook. It is best if beginning readers have a storybook that takes two pages or more to tell each story.
- **Grade Schoolers:** Fewer pictures, more words is the key at this level. Make sure the illustrations are interesting and up-to-date. Simple Bible reference lists and an index are also good features to look for at this age level.

CHAPTER 19

Fun Time

Summary: Making use of Christian media and events is an easy and fun way to teach spiritual lessons. You'll use them throughout your life, but they are especially helpful for people who are just beginning spiritual training. These activities can be deliberate or spontaneous, as complex as searching for just the right book or video to achieve a specific goal, or as simple as mixing Christian storybooks into your reading routine with your child.

Impact: It may be fun, but children capture many spiritual lessons in the midst of reading, listening to, and watching Christ-centered media or events.

How long does it take? As long as you want it to, from a few minutes to a few hours.

Where does it happen? Anywhere your family likes to have fun.

When should we do it? Anytime your family gets together for recreation.

Who is involved? Your entire family.

Parental effort required: Easy. Who doesn't like having fun?

Spiritual growth impact rating: Medium to high.

IDEAS AND METHODS

Too Busy for Fun?

"Mommy, come play with me."

"Oh, sweetie, I can't. I'm making dinner."

"Daddy, will you come push me on the swing?"

"I'm in the middle of changing the oil on the car. Can you wait?"

How many times have you had to say no to your child? It seems we have to say no more times than we say yes. Yet the relationship you nurture with your child *is* the legacy you're passing on to him or her. One of the best ways to develop that relationship is by having fun together. While you are having fun, we encourage you to seek opportunities to do two things:

❖ teach spiritual lessons in the midst of your fun time and

❖ seek opportunities for fun time that involves spiritual content.

Here are some specific ideas:

◆ ***Read, listen to music, and watch videos together.*** In some cases, the media should have Christian content; in other cases, the media offers the opportunity for a discussion on being Christlike. As a rule of thumb, younger children need more overt messages while older children are ready for less concrete messages.

◆ ***Attend Christian events*** like concerts, church plays, and youth rallies together.

◆ ***Spend active time*** riding bikes, hiking, fishing, swinging, rolling down hills, and jumping into piles of leaves with your children. Watch for teachable moments. (See chapter 20.)

Keys to Success

There are a number of practical things you can do to make sure your fun times are both entertaining and meaningful for your children.

◆ ***Be sensitive to your children's needs.*** Children learn in many different ways. Some learn best by listening, some by talking, and others by doing. You need to keep this fact in mind when planning your family's fun times. Vary your approach. Watch a video, play a board game, or surf Christian Web sites

together. Go with the flow of your children's energy and interests. Make sure your methods stimulate as many senses as possible. The more senses you stimulate, the more your children will remember the fun and/or the lesson.

◆ ***Don't get complicated.*** Fun time can be a great time to let someone else do the teaching. Resist the temptation to add to what is already being said. Your children need to see that you are not the only one who believes this Christian stuff. They also need to learn to discern, digest, and decide on their own. So relax, and let fun time be fun for you, too. If you are the teacher, keep it light.

◆ ***Let fun times happen.*** Your children will often take the lead by asking you to play a game, watch a video, or listen to music with them. You never know what might come out of it.

◆ ***Make up your own fun time.*** Some families have done some crazy, outrageous fun things, such as having shaving cream fights (everyone gets his or her own can of shaving cream), or playing hide-and-seek in the dark. (See the end of the chapter for more ideas.)

Or you can put a unique, crazy twist on everyday activities. One family put their clothes on backward to take a "backward walk." Another family had a "sharing dinner" where everyone fed the person on his or her left. No one was allowed to feed him or herself. How about an impromptu raw egg toss in the kitchen before Saturday breakfast? Or how about teaching your children how to make faces out of bologna?

Overcoming Obstacles

Creating fun times for your family is a practical way to begin intentional spiritual training. If you're a beginner at all of this, fun times can be based upon simple goals like watching a video with Christian content without being too concerned about the specific topic—you just know it's good and glorifies God. As you become more adept at spiritual training, you might begin seeking fun opportunities to convey a specific message or teach a certain principle. This technique is incredibly flexible but can still be an excellent way to pass on scriptural truth.

Don't fall into the trap of thinking that your children should only play games or watch videos that explicitly teach them about God. Monopoly and other "family-approved" board games or videos should not be banished to the closet or the secondhand store just because they don't contain a blatantly Christian message. Instead, add some good Christian games and videos to the mix. Also, you never know what opportunities might arise in the midst of even the simplest games; the key is often just being around your children when the opportunity presents itself.

Tools

There are many tools available for fun time activities, here are some ideas to get you started. See the Resource List in Appendix II for more or go to www.heritagebuilders.com for a larger list of ideas.

Video and Audio Products

Adventures in Odyssey (Focus on the Family audio, video and other resources; see pages 406–408).

These dramatic presentations are an excellent addition to fun times with the children.

Board Games

Children love board games. They are a great way to teach your children about their faith while letting them cut loose and have some fun.

House Rules (Tyndale, 1999).

This is a highly interactive family game that will help your children learn how to apply biblical principles to their relationships and to the running of the household. It is designed to provide lots of opportunities for discussion on how your family works.

Magazines

Clubhouse (Focus on the Family).

Intriguing and entertaining, this magazine for kids ages 8–12 reinforces traditional values and promotes family closeness with hands-on activities, challenging puzzles, and exciting stories.

Clubhouse Jr. (Focus on the Family).

Children ages 4–8 love to learn with the fun stories, games,

CHAPTER 19: FUN TIME

and puzzles in *Clubhouse Jr.*, the activity-filled magazine that emphasizes family values while teaching character.

Other Ideas for Fun Activities

- Make tunnels and tents throughout the house with blankets, card tables, chairs, boxes, and whatever you can find. These are especially great during thunderstorms when you're armed with a flashlight and a big bowl of popcorn to eat. Read Psalm 91 and talk about how God covers us with His love.

- Have a shaving cream fight. Buy the cheap stuff at a discount store, one can for every member of the family. Generally, it leaves no marks and smells yummy. Don't use whipped cream; it stains. It also stinks days later (forever!) if you miss cleaning a spot.

- Eat a backward dinner—dessert first, then the main course. Wear clothes backwards and try to eat with the utensils upside down.

- Have a cooperation dinner—everyone must feed the person to his or her left. As Christians, we are to encourage and help one another.

- Walk on the ceiling with mirrors. For this, you take a hand mirror and hold it about waist height. Look down into it and you will see the ceiling. Begin to walk through the house. Step over any obstacle you see in the mirror. This works best in homes with lots of doorways and ceiling beams. Walking down stairs is a real challenge! Your family can learn that basing your life on man's ideas is much like walking "on the ceiling," while walking in the truth is like seeing life as it really is.

- Snuggle into a sleeping bag and slide feet first down the stairs. Have someone time everyone to see who has the best time.

- Dress formally for dinner. Have an elegant dinner using a tablecloth and candles. Everyone must address each other as "Sir" or "Madam," or Mom and Dad can be "Princess" or "Prince" and the children (if only two) can be addressed as "King" and "Queen." Everyone must talk in overdone formal voices.

- Dress silly for dinner. Or wear dress-up clothes that have been saved for the kids to play in. Even Mom and Dad must wear something from the dress-up box—including wigs, silly glasses, outrageous clothes, etc.

- Make hats out of paper plates and wild and silly objects: toys, dry food, crafts—the more outrageous the better. Everyone must wear his or her hat to dinner and tell a story about the hat. Go to McDonald's or out for ice cream wearing the hats. Pretend to be very serious while people stare at you. Remind your family that everyone is to be prepared to share about the hope that is within them. Their relationship with Jesus makes them "different," and sometimes people might wonder about it.

- Throw a birthday party for a pet and invite all the neighbor kids. For a dog party, serve "dog kibble"(Chocolate Kix); for a cat, serve Goldfish crackers; for a bird, serve sunflower seeds. Show how all God's creation is special and worth celebrating.

- Paint faces with glow-in-the-dark paint. Stand with your eyes closed in front of a light for about 60 seconds, then go into the bathroom and turn off all the lights. Look into the mirror at the funny things on your faces.

- Make your own play dough, and squish around in it a while. (There's nothing better than warm play dough.)

- Make up skits, or find a book of simple skits and perform them for each other.

- Throw a half birthday party for a friend who needs cheering up.

- Paint thumbs to look like faces. Sometimes you can dress them. Have them sing songs from a favorite musical such as *The Sound of Music*, *Mary Poppins*, or other favorites.

- Tuck the thumb under the first finger making a sort of fist. When the thumb is wiggled, the slit between the two digits looks like a mouth. Paint it to look like a mouth. Paint eyes on the hand so that you have a face. Make your hands sing and talk to each other.

- Have someone lie on his back on a table or bed with his head dangling just over the edge. Cover his face above the nose with a light cloth (so he can breathe easily). Then paint the chin so the eyes are at the very bottom of the chin and nose, between the edge of the chin and the mouth. Have the person talk or sing in a silly voice.

- Play "Arms." This takes two people. One person stands in front of a table with items on it, like a phone, a bowl of applesauce or cereal, and a pen and piece of paper. This person clasps her hands behind her back. A second person hides behind her and puts his arms through the sleeves of the person in front of him. Now have the standing person speak and tell a story, or say things that involve the items on the table. The "arms" must pick up the phone and hold it to the person's ear, feed her, make hand motions as if he is the person speaking, and so on. If you have a video camera, this is a great one to videotape.

- Play hide-and-seek in the house with all the lights out. Tell everyone they have to scream loudly when they are found.

See the Resource List in Appendix II for more tools to help you.

CHAPTER 20

Teachable Moments

Summary: One of the easiest methods to begin using in spiritual training is capturing teachable moments. These are moments when you are with your child and something occurs that offers an opportunity to teach something about God. It's as simple as paying attention to the world around you and presenting it from a godly viewpoint.

Impact: The best learning is that which takes place in the context of real life. The impact of using teachable moments can vary from minimal to exceptional, depending on the lesson learned.

How long does it take? From mere moments to entire discussions.

Where does it happen? Anywhere a teachable moment occurs.

When should we do it? Anytime an opportunity presents itself.

Who is involved? Your entire family.

Parental effort involved: Moderate. (The big thing for parents is awareness.)

Spiritual growth impact rating: Medium to high.

In the Middle of Life

In the middle of your responsibilities and commitments, planning times to impart knowledge to your children and to train them to apply this knowledge seems like just one more pressure. We have good news for you: Not everything has to be planned. Life is happening all around you, whether you plan it or not. And many events in life are ready-made opportunities to teach and train your children. The key is *recognizing the moment.* God referred to this approach when He told the Israelites in Deuteronomy 6:6–9 to use every part of life to teach their children (see pages 9–12). This model focuses on the *living* side of the Christian life: application in the midst of life.

Some of the best times to train come when your children ask questions or are dealing with life and its problems and their interest level is high. That's when children are primed and ready to learn. Two minutes of solid teaching at that moment will stay with them better than a dozen lectures. Use their interest and curiosity to your advantage. Be on the lookout for that God-given opportunity where truth and life collide to create a real-life teachable, trainable moment.

Modeling or teaching by example is another way to teach and train children in the midst of everyday life. They watch what you do in both

The Cookie Sheet

As a single mom with three very active, very verbal children, I often got distracted on shopping trips. Trying to keep the children close and behaving well captured all my attention.

One day I unloaded the contents of my cart onto the conveyor belt. I answered the kids' endless questions while the checker scanned the items and dropped them into bags.

I handed a bag to each child and we all trooped out to the car. Then I drove home, where everyone carried his or her bag inside. As we unloaded the bags, I checked the purchases against the receipt. "Oh, no," I groaned.

"What's wrong, Mommy?" Stacie asked.

"She only charged me for one cookie sheet. I guess they stuck together and she didn't notice there were two."

Stacie shrugged. "So? You got a free cookie sheet."

I could have simply returned to pay for the cookie sheet without anything more said, but at that moment I realized this was one of those moments when I could teach my children what the Bible says. I silently sent up a quick prayer for wisdom. "But it's not right to keep it," I told her. "God wants us to be honest in all that we do."

"The store will never know," Trevor added.

"Maybe not. But we know and God knows," I told them. "God wants us to always do what is right, even if no one else is watching."

We all piled back into the car and returned to the store, where the lesson in honesty was emphasized by the manager's gratitude and surprise at our honesty.

L. H. J.

IDEAS AND METHODS

good and bad times. Don't think you can teach something only if you've mastered it. Letting them watch you learn is a great teaching tool. Children notice your responses to temptation, frustration, windfalls, and shortages. They know more about your honesty, diligence, and handling of money than you realize. Do they watch you keep that extra change or gossip about a colleague? Or do they see you return the change, pray for that colleague, or work extra hours without grumbling? Whatever you're doing, they're learning. Guaranteed.

Keys to Success

Here are some effective teaching and training principles to keep in mind as you help your children learn in the midst of everyday life.

- *Keep it short and simple.* Don't turn every teachable moment into a lecture, and stay off your soapboxes (we all have them). In fact, it is sometimes best to let the moment speak for itself or revisit a moment at a more appropriate time.

- *Be proactive.* If errors are the only teachable moments you are capturing, you are preaching when you should be coaching. Try to find positive lessons to teach that affirm your child and your relationship with him or her. This doesn't mean you should not correct; it does mean you should correct constructively and in love.

- *Don't go it alone.* God has given you the privilege and responsibility of helping to form your children into wonderful human beings. But He's their heavenly Father and wants to help in the parenting process. When you choose to raise your children in partnership with Him and ask for help and wisdom, He is right there with His grace. Ask Him to help you recognize teachable moments, know what to do when they arise, and show you whether you should be thorough, brief, or silent.

Overcoming Obstacles

Perhaps the greatest obstacle in this area is lack of balance. If you were hit over the head with Bible verses when you were growing up, as a parent you'll most likely have a tendency to focus more on your role as a nurturer than on your role as a teacher, trainer, and discipline manager—especially in the area of spiritual training.

On the other hand, if you feel acutely the lack of any consistent training in the Christian faith as you were growing up, you may tend to the other extreme: more instruction than nurturing—especially if you are a Lion/Beaver combination.

In attempting to train your children on the go, it's especially important that you find the balance between your dual roles as parent. Neglecting to train your children in and for life is setting them up for failure. But taking a balanced approach that is full of love and grace is essential for the training to be effective.

Tools

The following will help raise your awareness so that you recognize teachable moments when they arise in the course of your daily life.

The Learning for Life Series by Rick Osborne et al. (Moody, 1999).

The titles in this series are *Your Child and Jesus, Your Child and the Bible*, and *Your Child and the Christian Life.* These books will help equip you with what you need so that you can effectively take advantage of teachable moments. They offer encouragement, wisdom, and practical advice for teaching your children in the midst of everyday life. They include Bible stories, Bible trivia, memory verses, games, riddles, quotes, and jokes to make teaching your children natural and enjoyable.

See the Resource List in Appendix II for more tools to help you.

CHAPTER 21

Family Nights

Summary: Create meaningful opportunities for spiritual training by setting aside an evening for fun activities and object lessons to drive home a spiritual truth.

Impact: When children enjoy time with their parents, they are far more motivated to embrace the values and beliefs we hope to teach them. Object lessons and activities have proven to be one of the most effective ways to create meaningful memories while engaging your children in the learning process.

How long does it take? Usually no more than one hour per family night.

Where does it happen? At home.

When should we do it? Once a week, if possible. Once a month at least.

Who is involved? The entire family.

Parental effort required: Minimal (20–30 minutes preparation time).

Spiritual growth impact rating: Very High.

I D E A S   A N D   M E T H O D S

177

Intentional or "Oops"?

There is toothpaste all over the plastic-covered table. Four young children are having the time of their lives squeezing the paste out of four tubes—trying to get every last bit out of them, as Dad had told them to.

"Okay," says Dad, slapping a twenty-dollar bill onto the table. "The first person to get the toothpaste back into their tube gets this money!" Little hands begin working to shove the peppermint-flavored pile back into the rolled-up tubes, but almost no toothpaste makes it back through the narrow opening.

"We can't do it, Dad!" protests the youngest child.

"Ah, that's just like your tongue. Once the words come out, it's impossible to get them back in. You need to be careful what you say because you may wish you could take it back, but you can't. That's why the Bible says we must watch our tongue."

Jim Weidmann and his wife Janet did this with their children and it made a lasting impression. A few days after the lesson, one of their children said something negative. Janet responded, "That sounds like some toothpaste leaking out."

"Oops!" said the child, who quickly covered her mouth.

A few years ago, Jim and Janet Weidmann began setting aside time to intentionally impress upon their children their values and beliefs through a weekly ritual called Family Night. They play games, talk, study, and do things that reinforce the importance of family and faith.

The power of Family Nights is twofold:

◆ They create a structured setting within which you can intentionally instill beliefs, values, and character qualities in your children.

◆ Twenty to 60 minutes of structured fun and instruction can set up countless opportunities for informal reinforcement—at the dinner table, in the car, or while watching TV. Once you have addressed a given Family Night topic, you and your children will naturally refer back to those principles during the routine of everyday life.

Keys to Success

There are several keys to having effective Family Nights.

◆ *Make it fun.* Enjoy yourself, and let the children have a ball. They may not remember everything you say, but they will always cherish the time of laughter—and so will you.

◆ *Keep it simple.* The minute you become abstract or complicated, you've missed the whole point. Don't try to create deeply profound lessons; just try to reinforce your values and beliefs in a simple, easy-to-understand manner.

◆ *Don't dominate.* Pull your children into the discovery process as much as possible. If you do all the talking, you've missed the mark. Ask questions, give assignments, invite participation in every way possible.

◆ *Go with the flow.* It's fine to start with a well-defined outline, but don't kill spontaneity by becoming overly structured. If an incident or question takes you in a different direction, great! Some of the best teaching opportunities are completely unplanned and unexpected.

◆ *Mix it up.* Don't allow yourself to get into a rut. Keep the sense of excitement and anticipation through variety. Experiment to discover what works best for your family. Use books, games, videos, props, made-up stories, charades, songs, music or music videos, or a family outing.

◆ *Do it often.* We tend to find time for the things we feel are really important. It is best to set aside one evening per week (the same evening if possible) for Family Nights. Remember, repetition is the best teacher. The more impressions you can create, the more of an impact you will make.

Overcoming Obstacles

If you're an F-16 family, your busy lifestyle may make regular Family Nights difficult. This problem will be compounded as your children get older and become more involved in activities outside the home. This doesn't mean that you won't be able to have Family Nights; it just means you will have to be more creative about how you schedule your Family Nights.

For example, Saturday mornings may be the best time for your family to get together. If that's the case, go for it. "Family Mornings" can be as effective as Family Nights. You also might find that once a week is too much for your family; if so, try biweekly or monthly. The key to successful Family Nights is to establish a pattern that works for your family and then stick to it.

Tools

Family Nights Activity Books.

Heritage Builders has a series of tools that will get you started on your own Family Night activities. Each book contains a dozen or more complete Family Night sessions, including a list of items that will be needed, the main teaching point(s) to get across during each session, and detailed explanations and tips to help parents lead each session. Here is a complete list of Family Nights activity books:

- *An Introduction to Family Nights* by Jim Weidmann et al. (Chariot Victor, 1998).
- *Family Nights Tool Chest: Basic Christian Beliefs* by Jim Weidmann et al. (Chariot Victor, 1998).
- *Family Nights Tool Chest: Christian Character Qualities* by Jim Weidmann, et al. (Chariot Victor, 1998).
- *Family Nights Tool Chest: Holidays* by Jim Weidmann et al. (Chariot Victor, 1998).
- *Family Nights Tool Chest: Larry Burkett's Money Matters* by Jim Weidmann et al. (Chariot Victor, 1998).
- *Family Nights Tool Chest: Proverbs* by Jim Weidmann et al. (Chariot Victor, 2000).
- *Family Nights Tool Chest: Ready for Adolescence* by Jim Weidmann. (Chariot Victor, 2001).
- *Family Nights Tool Chest: Simple Science* by Jim Weidmann et al. (Chariot Victor, 1999).
- *Family Nights Tool Chest: The Ten Commandments* by Jim Weidmann et al. (Chariot Victor, 1998).
- *Family Nights Tool Chest: Wisdom Life Skills* by Jim Weidmann et al. (Chariot Victor, 1998).
- *New Testament Bible Stories for Preschoolers* by Jim Weidmann and Kirk Weaver (Chariot Victor, 1999).
- *Old Testament Bible Stories for Preschoolers* by Jim Weidmann and Kirk Weaver (Chariot Victor, 1999).

Try This!

The following are two sample Family Night activities. Read them over and think about how this model could work for your family. Then try them out! (They are adapted from the Heritage Builders Family Nights Tool Chest series by Jim Weidmann and Kurt Bruner (Chariot Victor, 1997).)

God Cares for Me

Target Age: 3–7 years old.

Goal: To teach that God loves and cares for those who love Him.

Scripture: Genesis 6:5–8:19; 9:12–16

Materials:

1. Children's Bible or children's book or video of the story of Noah.
2. Large box that the children can fit into.
3. Stuffed animals or cutout paper animals.

Family Lesson and Discussion

I. Open in prayer

II. Do activities and discussion

Setup: Place a box big enough for the children and their stuffed animals to fit into (suggestion: a wardrobe box used in moving) in the middle of the room before Family Night. Place a doll in it to be Noah and have the box completely taped up when placed in the center of the room. (The presence of the box will raise children's excitement.) Hide all the family's stuffed animals around the house.

Read: Read the story of Noah from the children's Bible, or tell it in your own words.

Activity 1: Tell the children that you will now make an ark together. Bring out the crayons and a knife (for Mom or Dad) to cut the windows and door. Draw the boards with brown crayon on the sides and cut windows and an opening for the animals to climb through and the children to fit through. Once you're finished and have discovered Noah in the ark, tell your kids that now you need the animals. Tell them that you have hidden them in the house and they are to find them and bring them back two by two. With multiple children, send them out one at a time. At some point slip Noah out and hide him. With all the animals in the ark, have the children climb in with the animals. Then ask, "Where is Noah?" (They will have to go and find him before you shut the door.)

Question: While they are in the box, ask the children why Noah had to build the ark.

Answer: Only Noah chose to love God; the others chose to turn away from God and not to love Him. They were wicked people. God wanted to clean all the world of wickedness. So He sent the Flood, and Noah needed the ark to keep safe from the Flood. He told Noah just how big to make the ark to be safe.

Point: God cares for those who love Him.

Activity 2: Now ask each child to name his or her favorite animal. Then for five seconds while they are still sitting in the box, all together make the sound of that animal. Ask how it must have sounded in the ark for Noah and his family. Next, tell your children the rains are starting, and tap lightly on the box. Then tell them the waves are coming and roll the box from side to side.

Discussion: God promised Noah and us that He would never send another Flood. And He showed us this promise through the rainbow.

Read: Genesis 9:12–16 from a children's Bible, or restate it in own words.

Memorize: Noah was safe from rain and sea. God cared for him; God cares for me.

III. Close in prayer. Then have ice cream or some other treat.

Why Obey?

Target Age: 3–10 years old.

Goal: To show that obedience is for our own protection and good.

Scripture: Exodus 20:12; 1 Samuel 15:23.

Materials:
1. Paper and crayons for drawing a picture.
2. Soft objects to throw at one another (such as balls or rolled-up socks).
3. A long rope, string, or stick.
4. An umbrella.
5. A bowl of candy.

Family Lesson and Discussion

I. Open in prayer; review last Family Night lesson.

II. Do activities and discussion.

Question: Is it better to obey or disobey?

Read: Read 1 Samuel 15:23; then ask why God rejected Saul as king.

Answer: Because he didn't obey God.

Read: Read Exodus 20:12; then ask, "Why do you think God gives us rules to obey?"

Answer: For our protection.

Activity 1: Have the kids draw a picture of your family under an umbrella. Write the word "obey" on the umbrella to represent obedience to parents and to God's rules. Draw a strong rain-storm falling around the umbrella—representing the "hard knocks" of life when we take ourselves out from under God's protective instructions. List together some of the bad things that can happen when we disobey (such as getting hit by a car when running in the street).

Activity 2: Have the kids stand under an umbrella with Mom while Dad gets above them on a ladder or chair. Throw soft objects at the umbrella. No harm is done. Then entice the kids to leave the protection of the umbrella with a bowl of candy while Mom instructs them to stay put. As soon as the kids step out from under the umbrella, nail them with the soft objects over and over until they return to the umbrella. (Repeat this activity until laughter!)

Activity 3: Place a "line" across the floor using a rope, string, or stick. Tell the kids they will be fine so long as they don't cross that line. Place the bowl of candy just beyond reach to tempt the kids. Turn around. As they cross the line to get the candy, peg them with a soft object. Take turns crossing the line and throwing the objects.

Point: It is better to obey because it protects us.

Memorize: If you don't cross the line, you'll be just fine!

III. Close in prayer. (Eat the candy or have ice cream or some other treat.)

See the Resource List in Appendix II for more tools to help you.

I
D
E
A
S

A
N
D

M
E
T
H
O
D
S

CHAPTER 22

Family Devotions

Summary:	Devotions are a time for a family to stop and reflect together on a passage of scripture.
Impact:	This can be very positive if done effectively—relating scripture to the children in their daily lives. This is also a great way to help them store the Word in their hearts.
How long does it take?	Approximately 10 minutes.
Where does it happen?	At home.
When should we do it?	Once or twice a week. You can do it right after supper, before breakfast, or whenever works best for your family.
Who is involved?	Your entire family.
Parental effort required:	Minimal—the time to read from a devotional. More time will be needed if you decide to create your own material.
Spiritual growth impact rating:	Moderate.

Whose Turn Is It?

The Johnson family is finishing dinner. There are two teenagers and two elementary aged children at home, and all have had their chance to tell what is happening in school. Since no one has a tremendous amount of homework, there is no quick exit from the table tonight. So Dad suggests, "Let's read from *LifeTraining*."

"It's my turn to read," says Nancy, the fourth grader.

"No, you read last time," says one of her teenage brothers.

"I think it's Matt's turn," Mom agrees.

Dad smiles—he's not aware of too many families where the kids are eager to take turns reading from a devotional book. "Nancy, you can

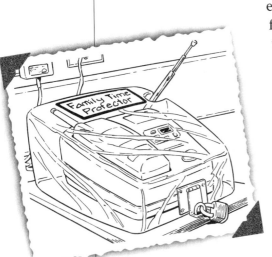

read the prayer card," Dad says. The Johnsons end each devotional time with a time of prayer for a persecuted Christian. There are 52 cards they rotate through, each telling about a specific country, the condition of the church there, and a prayer request for a specific person who is suffering for their faith.

The whole process takes about 10 minutes. Dad and Mom participate in the discussion, but the kids feel it's their time because they read the selection and lead the discussion. All the parents did was choose the tools.

Devotions can be a very helpful vehicle for spiritual growth in a family. But because there are often negative connotations to it, we suggest that if you are going to use this tool, you bring your whole family into that process in a family meeting. Briefly go over with your family the different approaches we've suggested in this book. Let them choose the approaches they think will work best in your situation. If it turns out that your family wants to try something new, be willing to replace the family devotions you've been doing. (Remember, it's the information and training that's sacred, not the method you use to communicate it.)

An effective family devotional time should include at least three of the following four basic activities:

1. Read a scripture passage first.

2. Read a devotional story or reading from a family devotional book (see examples of such books under Tools).
3. Ask questions based on the two readings. Discuss your answers. Strive to be uplifting and encouraging during this time. Don't squelch answers.
4. Pray together. Go around the circle and have everyone contribute a suggestion or two for what you should pray for. Review past prayer requests and update the family on how things are going. Once you have all the prayer requests in, you can either get one person to pray or have everyone take turns until everything you mentioned has been prayed for. However, don't force your children to pray beyond where they are comfortable. Use willing participants and give them short, age-appropriate things to pray for.

Keys to Success

◆ *Start small and build slowly.* If you're just beginning to introduce family devotions to your home, ease your family into the routine. Perhaps you can start by doing devotions once a week and then gradually increasing their frequency. The key is not to rush your family. It will be a big change for them, and change is accepted best when it happens slowly.

◆ *Share responsibility.* You can help your children feel more ownership of the devotional time by making each of them responsible for a different aspect of your routine. For example, have one child read the Bible passage, another child read the devotional reading, and a third child write down the prayer requests that everyone brings forward.

◆ *Set a time limit.* Decide ahead of time how much you'll read and how long the devotional will take. Tell your kids ahead of time and stick to it.

◆ *Encourage discussion.* Remember, the more you get your kids to question and think, the more they will internalize what you're reading and talking about. Don't always jump in with the answers.

IDEAS AND METHODS

Encourage all kinds of thoughts and questions. Whenever you can, answer a question with a question to help them come to the right conclusions themselves.

Overcoming Obstacles

How a teacher approaches a lesson can make all the difference. Think back to your days in school. Which teachers did you like the most? Why were they so effective? Chances are they made learning more than a rote exercise that everyone was obliged to endure. They kept it lively and interesting by adding humor and by constantly relating what was being learned to real life to show that it was both interesting and practical.

Taking your cue from this, make it a priority to keep your family devotion times fun and exciting for your children. You can do this by adding humor, making the teaching relevant to your children's lives, using a variety of approaches and materials, focusing on their questions and interests, and employing the KISS method: "Keep It Simple and Sincere."

Tools

Family Walk: Love, Anger, Courage, and 49 Other Weekly Readings for Your Family (Zondervan, 1991).

Family Walk Again: Family, Friends, Self-Esteem, and 49 Other Weekly Readings for Your Family (Zondervan, 1993).

These family devotionals are a compilation of daily Bible studies from Walk Thru the Bible Ministries' *Family Walk* monthly devotional guide. They are carefully designed to help parents train children to apply biblical truths to everyday situations. Each book tackles 52 weekly topics. They are ideal for families with children from ages 6–12.

The Family Walk Devotional Bible by Bruce H. Wilkinson (editor), et al. (Zondervan, 1996).

This Bible combines the full NIV Bible text and the best of the *Family Walk* devotional series. If you've struggled to have devotions as a family, this Bible will bring that special time to life.

LifeTraining by Joe White (Zondervan, 1998).

This devotional is designed primarily for parents and teens. However, younger children that have teen siblings will also benefit. Volume one covers Matthew, Luke, John, Acts, James, and Revelation. Volume two covers the rest of the New Testament. Each volume also contains 100 scripture memory verses.

See the Resource List in Appendix II for more tools to help you.

CHAPTER 23

Meaningful Memories

Summary:	Passing down stories about God's grace and intervention in your life is an excellent way to teach your children that God loves them and cares about what happens to them.
Impact:	Faith stories do two things: (1) they glorify God; and (2) they increase your family's trust in God and His provision.
How long does it take?	Usually just a few minutes.
Where does it happen?	Anywhere.
When should we do it?	On special occasions for your children or your family, or whenever the opportunity presents itself.
Who is involved?	Your entire family or possibly just you and your child one-on-one.
Parental effort required:	Minimal—the effort to tell a story.
Spiritual growth impact rating:	Medium.

Faith Stories

Every family has a story. Whether it's the one about the time Uncle Norman dared his little brother to eat an earthworm (and he actually did it!) or the story of your wedding, your children will be transfixed as they sit and listen to you talk about the way things used to be or how things came to be. These family stories are a great way to connect your children's faith to reality by showing them "snapshots" of God's involvement in your life and the lives of other family members.

One of the best types of stories you can tell is a "faith story." Faith stories are just that: stories of God's faithfulness that helped to increase your faith in Him. Deuteronomy 6:20–24 says:

> In the future, when your son asks you, "What is the meaning of the stipulations, decrees and laws the LORD our God has commanded you?" tell him: "We were slaves of Pharaoh in Egypt, but the LORD brought us out of Egypt with a mighty hand. Before our eyes the LORD sent miraculous signs and wonders—great and terrible—upon Egypt and Pharaoh and his whole household. But he brought us out from there to bring us in and give us the land that he promised on oath to our forefathers. The LORD commanded us to obey all these decrees and to fear the LORD our God, so that we might always prosper and be kept alive, as is the case today. And if we are careful to obey all this law before the LORD our God, as he has commanded us, that will be our righteousness."

The great acts of God that Moses refers to in this passage are the actual personal and immediate stories of how God worked in the lives of His people at that time. While it is good to tell your children the stories of God's incredible deeds recorded in the Bible, you also need to tell them how God has worked in your own life. Doing this will help to strengthen your children's faith and show them that obedience to God and trusting in Him bring us the blessing of God's loving provision. Facts and details about God become very real to your children when they can see and hear how God has worked in the lives of your family members.

Keys to Success

- *Document your life of faith.* If you find yourself wracking your brain right now trying to come up with faith stories to share with your children, don't sweat it. Take a moment to sit down and relax. Let your mind wander back over your life and call up times when you saw God at work. Pray and ask God to help you remember. These stories don't have to be spectacular tales of divine intervention, just the everyday miracles that God does in each of our lives. Once you've thought of a few stories, write down the main points and keep them on hand for when a suitable opportunity arises to tell them to your children.

Let your faith stories become part of your family's story—a story that is continuously growing as God works in the lives of each generation. After a while, your children will want to tell their own faith stories. That's great. Encourage them to write them down so they can share them with their children.

◆ *Seize the day.* Don't let an opportunity to pass on a snapshot of God to your children pass you by. Get out your calendar and mark down significant days and events that you can use to build up their faith in God. Whether it's birthdays, holidays, or anniversaries, telling the stories that go behind the events can be very meaningful for your children. For example, if you and your spouse were Christians when you got married, use the occasion of your anniversary to tell the story of how you relied on God to help you choose the person you would marry. If you were not Christians then, talk about how God has worked in your marriage since you both started following Him.

Overcoming Obstacles

When you're telling your children faith stories, you need to be careful not to glorify your wild past or bumpy youth. Children often don't have the discernment to separate the lesson from the story. They may want to do what you did rather than take it as a warning to do as you say. Think through your faith stories. Are there some things you should edit out for a younger audience? You can get into more detail when your children are older. As a general rule, stick to the stories of how you trusted God and what happened when you did.

Memory Markers

In the Old Testament, Joshua's first day on the job included a task that stretched his faith. After taking over from Moses, his first job was to lead the people across the Jordan River—while it was in flood stage, filling its banks to overflowing (as explained in chapter 11). Many years before, Moses had obeyed God and parted the Red Sea so Israel could escape the Egyptian army. Now God told Joshua and the priests that He would part the waters again. Almighty God not only provided a way of *escape* from Egypt, He opened the way for the Israelites to *enter* the land that He'd promised Abraham so long ago.

Once Joshua and the priests had everyone safely across, God commanded His new leader to set up a "Memory Marker." So they gathered twelve stones from the middle of the riverbed and piled them in a special way to commemorate what God had done. But the stones weren't only to celebrate that day, and they weren't just for Joshua and the people who crossed the river.

> *And Joshua . . . said to the Israelites, "In the future when your descendants ask their fathers, 'What do these stones mean?' tell them, 'Israel crossed the Jordan on dry ground.' For the LORD your God dried up the Jordan before you until you had crossed over. The LORD your God did to the Jordan just what he had done to the Red Sea when he dried it up before us until we had crossed over. He did this so that all the peoples of the earth might know that the hand of the LORD is powerful and so that you might always fear the LORD your God." (Joshua 4:20–24)*

The "Memory Marker" God told Joshua to put up was a picture for the children and the generations who would follow. That pile of rocks became a testimony to what God had done, and provided an opportunity for parents and children to remember and focus on God's greatness and love. It was a snapshot of God's faithfulness that they could look at and talk about.

Creating your own Memory Markers for your family and for each child can be a great help in spiritual training. You could make a pile of stones in your front yard every time you want to help your children

IDEAS AND METHODS

remember what God has done, but this may not be too effective. Besides, the neighbors might complain. So, what can you do to capture and celebrate your family's spiritual highlights? There are lots of opportunities for you as parents to make spiritual events into significant life-changing memorials—if you are willing to make them a priority.

First, as we discussed earlier in the book, you can use Memory Markers to mark each stage of your child's spiritual development.

- 0–4: Dedication
- 5–6: Introducing your child to the Gospel
- 7–9: Exploration and expressions
- 10–12: Commitment ceremony

These ceremonies and events can be powerful rites of passage that communicate to children that they are moving from one stage of life to the next and taking on more responsibility for their spiritual walk. Special church services such as confirmation, communion, baptism, and graduation are natural opportunities to remind your children about their faith and call them to dedicate their lives more completely to God. Take advantage of these circumstances to make a lasting impression on your children.

There are many other great opportunities to create Memory Markers in your family. One example of such a monument occurred in a family where the father bought a real sword and engraved his and his son's names on it. Then, at a special ceremony, he passed it on to his son. The sword represented God's Word and the ceremony represented the 13-year-old son taking responsibility for his spiritual growth. Any time a child of yours takes a small or significant step forward spiritually, you can mark it with a special meal or gift that helps establish the moment. Come up with your own ideas that match your family. If you get stuck, don't worry; the resources listed on pages 194–195 are full of ideas that will help you mark these special occasions for your children.

IDEAS AND METHODS

Keys to Success

Life is full of occasions that you can inject with spiritual meaning for your children. For example, particularly important milestones to mark are your children's spiritual birthdays—the day they became Christians. If you can't remember the exact date, choose one that's close and use the day to celebrate the goodness God has shown to you and your family. You can do this same thing with other significant dates in your children's spiritual lives, such as the day they were baptized. Help your children out by writing down the day they become Christians, including any relevant circumstances, so they have that story to pass on to their children. You may want to celebrate your or your family's spiritual birthdays on one day, such as a day when a significant spiritual event took place for your family, or a day leading up to Christmas or Easter. The Bible says the angels of heaven celebrate when a person comes into God's kingdom through Christ. You could continue the celebration with an annual party.

Overcoming Obstacles

If you don't sit down and consciously plan traditions and milestone celebrations, they simply won't happen. You need to be very intentional about this. It may take a bit of work up front to sit down and plan how you can create new traditions or use existing ones. But remember, you shouldn't look at this as an onerous duty. Rather, see it as a tremendous opportunity to share your faith with your family, and to fill their big pictures with many crystal clear, wonderful little snapshots that will remind them of God's goodness and their growth in His grace. Your example will inspire your children to carry on the legacy when they become parents.

Tools

Faith stories notebook.

An essential tool to help you record your family's faith stories is a notebook that you can use to jot down facts, details, and lessons learned from events in your past. Buy one for yourself and another one for your family. Keep it in a convenient place so it is always available when a faith story comes to mind.

Family Traditions by Otis J. Ledbetter and Tim Smith (Chariot Victor, 1998).

Healthy traditions are a key component of a godly heritage

because they strengthen the family's identity. This book will help you renew your sense of appreciation for the role of tradition in family life by introducing fresh, meaningful impressions to under-gird traditions you may already celebrate. From typical holiday traditions, this book branches out to important milestones or monuments in the Christian life and adaptations of wonderful biblical traditions. They include practical, intentional guidelines for developing a traditions "blueprint" for your children that ensures you are instilling all the qualities you value by the time your children reach maturity.

Let's Make a Memory by Gloria Gaither and Shirley Dobson (Word, 1983, 1994).

In this book Shirley Dobson and Gloria Gaither have gathered a collection of their families' favorite traditions and ideas for building togetherness at home. You can simply use the traditions as they are presented, or use them as an inspiration to create your own.

Scrapbook Storytelling: Journaling, and Your Own Creativity, Save Family Stories and Memories with Photos by Joanna Campbell Slan (Writer's Digest Books, 1999).

This inspiring, visual book offers crafters, family historians, and proud parents dozens of great ideas for documenting family stories and events with "scrapbooking." Following easy-to-understand steps, readers will learn new ways to discover and recover favorite stories and combine these stories with cherished photos, collages, fabric art, mosiacs, and illustrations.

See the Resource List in Appendix II for more tools to help you.

IDEAS AND METHODS

CHAPTER 24

Blessing Ceremonies

Summary: The biblical model for blessing ceremonies (parent to child) includes five specific elements: (1) appropriate, meaningful touch; (2) spoken words of love and acceptance; (3) the attaching of high value to the child; (4) the envisioning of a special future for him or her; (5) a genuine commitment from the parent.

Impact: In the eyes of young children, their parents are direct reflections of God. If they see you as loving, concerned, and committed, they will also view God that way.

How long does it take? A few minutes is all that is usually needed. "Rites of Passage" blessings may take longer.

Where does it happen? Most likely at home.

When should we do it? On special occasions or transition moments for your children.

Who is involved? Your entire family or just you and your child one-on-one.

Parental effort required: Moderate to high. (Some blessings are conveyed during daily routines; others are planned events to celebrate a special event or milestone.)

Spiritual growth impact rating: High.

IDEAS AND METHODS

The Gift of the Blessing

The greatest gift you as a parent can give your children is a combination of words and actions that leaves them with a deep sense of being loved, accepted, and valued by you. And even more important, it can also open them up to God's love! This gift is a biblical tool called "the blessing." In Bible times it was a longed-for, life-enriching gift from a parent, grandparent, or loving friend to a child. When a parent blessed a child, it was a specific opportunity for a loved one to communicate high value and worth to him or her. Today, you can use this tool to encourage your children's faith. Let's look more closely at the five things parents did, and at how you can use those same elements in a special blessing ceremony for your children.

♦ *Appropriate and meaningful touch.* In the Bible we see fathers and grandparents "laying their hands" on their children and grandchildren. The Bible also contains many other examples of appropriate touch, including when Jesus "took the children in his arms . . . and blessed them" (Mark 10:16).

♦ *Words of love and acceptance.* In many homes today, children grow up with an undefined feeling that they are loved—yet they never hear the words. If that's the case, then they've never gotten their parent's blessing. They may have been put through school, or had a parent stay up and type a paper for them—but without words of love and acceptance, it's not a blessing.

♦ *Attachment of high value to the child.* The words used in the Bible were ones that attached high value to the child. They were words of praise and honor which painted a beautiful picture of parental love that was imprinted upon the child's memory.

♦ *A special future.* A key part of blessing a child in biblical times was the way parents would consider each loved one and pick out a character trait that they felt God could use or affirm in the future. Children have always looked to parents for affirmation about their future. The blessing was a powerful way of encouraging a positive look at who they could be, backed by a parent's belief in them.

◆ *A genuine commitment.* Finally, the blessing assumed that these actions and words were serious and backed with the genuine commitment of a parent to stand behind the words and actions.

Here is a sample blessing ceremony that you can try out on one of your children.

An Evening of Blessing for Your Child

Goal: That your children will know and experience your love for them in a special setting and in a unique way.

Possible Elements

1. *Give Notice:* Give your child several days' notice before his or her blessing ceremony. Some parents tie it in with a birthday, graduation, or other special event. For children, half the fun of an event is anticipating the evening designed just for them!

2. *Ask for Input:* Ask your child ahead of time what his or her favorite meal would be and use that as your guide for a festive dinner to begin the event. Be prepared for peanut butter and hot dogs as a main course, topped off with chocolate cake for dessert. Feel free to sneak in a vegetable or something nutritious, but involve your child in planning a meal that reflects some things he or she has specially picked out.

3. *Employ Meaningful Touch:* Before the meal is served, have everyone in attendance gather around and hold hands while you thank the Lord for the food. (Remember the meaningful touch!)

4. *Communicate High Value and a Special Future:* After dinner, your goal is to communicate verbally the high value and special future you picture for your son or daughter. Some ways to do that could be the following:

   • Put together a slide show or picture album showing each year of the child's life. Kids love seeing pictures of themselves and of you with them!

   • After the slide or picture show, have each parent, sibling, or special friend in attendance list three or more specific things that they appreciate about the child being honored. (If you have more than one child, do a separate blessing ceremony for each one—even if they're twins!)

   • Have each person share a story that illustrates a character trait they like in the child. If several people pick the same trait, that's fine.

- Pick out an everyday object that can become a "picture" for the child of how you view him or her. For example, one father picked a sponge to describe how he viewed his son. "Henry," he said, "this past year you've reminded me of a sponge. You've soaked up so many neat things from God's Word and then squeezed them out all over your mom, me, your brothers, and your sister."

- Finally, have each person gather around the child being blessed and pray for him or her. If that sounds threatening, then here's a suggestion that is a wonderful way to close a blessing ceremony: Pick a Bible verse or psalm that is meaningful to you, or says something you'd like to say to your child and pray it over him or her.

Keys to Success

♦ *Make blessing your children a common practice.* As you spend time with your children, practice the blessing principles described above. Also, don't limit your blessings to your children only. Bless others you come in contact with, especially your extended family members.

♦ *Use transition events.* In biblical times, blessing ceremonies often signaled a major transition in a child or young adult's life. For example, when Jacob left home to seek a wife, he was given a special blessing before he left. Today, a blessing ceremony could mark your son becoming a teenager, or your daughter going from grade school to junior high. You could do a blessing ceremony before your children go to kindergarten, go to church to be baptized, or head off to high school or college.

Overcoming Obstacles

One of the challenges of any relationship is to express your love in ways that make sense and connect with the other person—and to learn to receive the other's love in the ways he or she express-es it. So take the time to discover what things your children understand as being signs of love. And then build your blessing around them.

If one child sees love only in terms of time, then even words, if unaccompanied by the evidence of your desire to spend time with him or her, will sound hollow. For that reason, making a special evening with that child where you do something with only him or her and *then* provide the special blessing, will really do the trick. Tailor the blessing ceremonies to your children's individual needs.

Tools

Bedtime Blessings by John Trent (Tyndale, 2000).

This is an especially helpful book for children ages 7 and under. It contains six months' worth of relational activities for you to engage in with your children. Each session ends with a bless-ing prayer meant to affirm your love (and God's) for your child and the high value you place in him or her. It is a practical tool, designed to help you bless your children on a daily basis.

The Gift of the Blessing by Gary Smalley and John Trent (Thomas Nelson, 1993).

In this book Gary Smalley and John Trent detail the five ele-ments of the parental blessing, the greatest gift a mother or father can give a beloved child: meaningful touch, the spoken word, the expression of high value, the description of a special future, the application of genuine commitment.

Pictures the Heart Remembers by John Trent (Waterbrook Press, 2000).

We are called to be a blessing. But being a blessing is not merely our calling; it's a choice we need to make daily with regard to our past and with regard to each person who comes across our path. But how do we choose to bless when the events of our past evoke emotions of failure, shame, or deep disap-pointment? How can we bless the people around us today when their actions make us want to respond not with a blessing but with a curse? In this book John Trent shows us how we can face the painful pictures of our past and choose to live—and give—God's blessing. With poignant vignettes from scripture, from the lives of everyday people, and from his own struggles to face a painful, disappointing past, Trent paints a vivid picture of the powerful impact of choosing to bless those around us.

See the Resource List in Appendix II for more tools to help you.

CHAPTER 25

Holidays

Summary: Holidays are an ideal opportunity for spiritual training, especially since so many of them have their roots in Christianity. Take the time to teach children the true meaning of each religious holiday (Thanksgiving, Christmas, Easter) and the virtue in secular holidays (Labor Day, Veterans Day, days honoring great people).

Impact: Holiday traditions are the type of things that are handed down from generation to generation. In some cases, your family traditions and the way you celebrate holidays will become icons of your family legacy.

How long does it take? It varies greatly depending on your involvement. It may be as simple as telling a story or as complex as volunteer service.

Where does it happen? Anywhere your family celebrates the holiday.

When should we do it? On holidays and special occasions.

Who is involved? Your entire family.

Parental effort required: Modest to significant effort, depending on the occasion.

Spiritual growth impact rating: High.

IDEAS AND METHODS

Primed to Learn

Nearly every child in America lies awake in bed on Christmas Eve, eagerly anticipating the gifts he or she will get to open the following morning. And every child looks forward to Easter break and the long Thanksgiving weekend. Holidays, especially the three just mentioned, provide excellent opportunities to strengthen your children in the basics of the faith. Not only do these holidays have profound religious significance for Christians, but the excitement and anticipation involved put children in a frame of mind where they are primed and ready to learn. Here are some ideas to help you make the most of these golden opportunities.

As Christians who know what Jesus has done for us, we have many reasons to celebrate during the holidays. But in our culture, Santa Claus and the Easter Bunny have all but taken the place of Jesus when it comes to celebrating Christmas and Easter. Because of this, you might be tempted to say, "Humbug," and have nothing to do with the holidays rather than go along with the commercial traditions associated with them. But even though the holidays have become highly secularized and commercialized, there is no reason for Christians not to celebrate them. In fact, it makes celebrating them even more important so you can help your children see the truth behind the tinsel.

The Origin of Santa Claus

Santa Claus is based on St. Nicholas, who was bishop of Myra (in modern day Turkey) in the fourth century A.D. Legend has it that Nicholas was a shy but very generous man who went around secretly doing good for the poor and unfortunate. After his death, the stories about him became famous around the world. Over time, they grew into their modern day versions, and Nicholas's name was changed to Santa Claus, which comes from the word Sinterklaas, a Dutch variant of the name "Saint Nicholas."[1]

Instead of taking all of the fun out of the holidays for your children, use the occasions to emphasize the true reason for the season: the birth, death, and resurrection of Jesus Christ. The more fun you make your celebrations, the more positively the real message behind them will be reinforced in your family. Christians have more to celebrate during these holidays than anyone else does. Jesus came to earth to set us free from our sins and restore our relationship with God. As a Christian, you've accepted this wonderful truth and been given eternal life.

Christmas and Easter are the official days to celebrate the events that made this possible.

Children enjoy Santa Claus, presents, Easter eggs, and so on. Just because these symbols are widely used by the secular community does not mean they cannot be incorporated into your Christian celebrations. Many of these symbols have Christian roots that have been glossed over through the years.

You don't have to dig far below holiday symbols to discover their Christian origins. For your children's sake, take a balanced approach to your holiday celebrations. Find enjoyable ways to emphasize the true meaning of the season. Build exciting family traditions around them. But let your children also have fun with some of the secular traditions. They will thank you for it and be more open to receive the true reason for the seasons.

Keys to Success

You can do several things to turn holidays into meaningful opportunities to share your faith with your children.

- *Get involved.* Make time to get involved in your church's Christmas and Easter programs. Don't leave programs to the Sunday school and youth group to perform. Set a positive example by taking an active role in these important church celebrations. If you're gifted musically, help lead or accompany the children's choir. Help direct the Christmas play, or bake desserts for the coffee time afterward. Find a role that suits you and get plugged in.

- *Don't be heavy-handed.* Santa and the Easter Bunny get too much credit when it comes to holiday fun. Do your best to make the Christian symbols of Christmas and Easter as enjoyable as the secular symbols. An excellent way to do this is to focus your celebrations around historic Christian traditions such as Advent, the twelve days of Christmas, or setting up the Nativity scene. For resources on how to do this, see the Tools section.

IDEAS AND METHODS

- *Do unto others.* Christmas and Thanksgiving are excellent times to teach your children about helping people who are less fortunate. Why not take time to get your family involved in a food hamper or shoebox campaign through your church, or help your local food bank collect or distribute food? When you're doing this, keep in mind that while it is good to teach your children to share with others, this should add to their joy and experience, not be at the expense of it. Instead of saying, "Sorry, kids, you don't get any presents this year because we gave all the money we would have spent on gifts to charity," the time or money you donate to charity should be above and beyond what you do for your children.

- *Start new traditions.* Make a family tradition of reading the Christmas and Easter stories together. This tradition can be combined with games and food to make it a fun time for everyone. However, doing this on Christmas morning right before gift opening, or on Easter morning right before the Easter egg hunt, can backfire because the kids may view it as the boring part. Find a time that works for your family and adds to your children's celebration instead of colliding with other parts of it.

- *Watch it on video.* As the holiday seasons approach, make a tradition of watching your family's favorite film about Jesus. You can make this a fun event by including food, friends, games, and discussions. See the Resource List in Appendix II for a list of family holiday videos.

Overcoming Obstacles

With so much emphasis put on fancy decorations, expensive gifts, and food, you may be tempted to gripe about the commercialism of the holidays. But instead, why not take advantage of the opportunities Christmas and Easter provide to have fun with presents, food, parties, and decorations? Don't knock secular ways of celebrating the seasons; rather, be positive, showing your excitement about the holidays and what they signify about Jesus.

It's natural for children to be excited about presents. Don't put gifts at odds with the true meaning of Christmas. Instead, when your children are getting excited about the approach of Christmas and the presents they will receive, showing them how the giving of gifts fits into the Christmas narrative. For example, you can talk about how salvation is the ultimate gift offered to us by God through Jesus, or about how the wise men brought Jesus gifts when they came to worship Him.

Tools

Family Nights Tool Chest: Holidays by Jim Weidmann et al. (Chariot Victor, 1998).

This excellent family night book put out by Heritage Builders is full of activities to help you inject Christian truth into eight traditional holidays, from Christmas to Valentine's Day to Halloween. It's full of creative ideas and activities that have been tried and tested on families just like yours. They are designed to make lasting impressions on children of all ages. You'll find a sample (for Easter) below.

Let's Make a Memory by Gloria Gaither and Shirley Dobson (Word, 1983, 1994).

The authors share a wealth of ideas on how to make family traditions reinforce lasting values in your home. The suggestions include holiday activities, vacation ideas, and relationship builders.

Easter—God's Plans

I. Warm-up

Open with Prayer: Begin by having a family member pray, asking God to help everyone in the family understand more about Him through this time.

Share: "Today we're going to talk about how Jesus' death was God's plan to save us and that if we confess our sins, Jesus will forgive us and cleanse us."

II. Activity 1: God's Plan

Point: **Easter was God's plan for Jesus.**

Supplies: You'll need paper and pencils or pens, materials to make a large cross (wood, hammer, nails), and a Bible.

Activity: Ask your children to describe what a plan is and how one is made. Here are some responses kids might give:

- A plan is something for the future.

IDEAS AND METHODS

- A plan is something you make when you're getting ready to do something.
- A plan is a list of things you need to do.
- A plan is like a recipe.

After helping to clarify what a plan is, ask family members to think of some event you should plan for. This could be anything from a spring or summer trip to a birthday party to a visit to the grocery store. With your family's help, make a plan for that event, listing your ideas on paper.

Then read aloud John 3:16. Consider these questions:

- What does this Bible passage tell us about God's plan for Jesus? (God planned to send Jesus to die on the cross.)
- What does this Bible passage tell us about God's plan for us? (God wanted to save us; God loves us; God wants us to live forever.)

Discuss how God made a plan to save us and to make us His sons and daughters. Explain how God planned for Jesus to come, die on the cross, and be raised from the dead.

Read or summarize Romans 3:23 and 6:23. Explain that those who sin against God will be separated from God forever. Then read or summarize Colossians 2:13–14. Explain how God takes our sins and nails them to the cross.

Have your family members help you create a wooden cross. You can do this by cutting an eight-foot two-by-four into five-foot and three-foot lengths, then nailing them together to form a cross.

Have family members each write their names on a sheet of paper along with the word "sins." Then nail the papers to the cross. You may need to help younger children with this activity.

Share: When Jesus died on the cross, He took all of our sins with Him. Because of this we get to be a part of God's family.

III. Activity 2: Confession

Point: If we confess our sins, Jesus will forgive us and cleanse our hearts.

Supplies: You'll need a magic slate, candies (such as M&M®s), paper, pencils, bathrobe ties or soft rope, items that can be used to weight someone down, and a Bible.

Activity: Announce to your family that you're going to have a fun time playing games. Then take out the magic slate (you may want more than one, if you have more than one child). Take turns playing tic-tac-toe using the slate. Award two candies to each winner and one to each loser. Point out how you can clear the slate by just lifting the front plastic sheet.

NOTE: If you can't find a magic slate, use a small blackboard and chalk or a reusable note board that can be wiped clean with a cloth.

After you've played a few games of tic-tac-toe, give a family member the magic slate and whisper to him or her the name of an animal. Have that person draw the animal while other family members attempt to guess it. Repeat this activity until each family member has had at least one turn. Don't forget to clear the magic slate after each turn!

When you're finished with the animal drawing game, take the magic slate and write on it something you've done wrong, then hold it in front of you. For example, you might write, "I yelled when I was angry." Then have family members entangle you with a bathrobe tie or soft rope and give you something heavy to hold (such as a big book). Attempt to walk around the room. Then add another item to the slate or simply tell family members about another time you did or said something wrong. Once again, have family members wrap you with more bathrobe ties or soft rope and give you another heavy item. Repeat one or more times, with family members adding more ropes or heavy items each time. Explain how Hebrews 12:1 says that sin (or things we do that are wrong) entangles us and weighs us down, just like the ropes and heavy objects. Then have someone read aloud 1 John 1:9 and explain that when we confess (or tell Jesus about) our sins, Jesus will forgive us and clean up our hearts. Go ahead and ask Jesus for forgiveness for the things on the magic slate, then have someone lift the plastic sheet to make them disappear. Also, have family members help you remove the ties and weights.

If appropriate, repeat this activity with each family member taking a turn being entangled by sin.

After everyone has had a turn, form a circle and discuss these questions:

- What did it feel like to be tied up and weighed down? (I couldn't move; I didn't like it; I thought it was fun at first, but then it wasn't.)
- How is that like what it feels like after you've sinned or done something wrong? (It's the same—I don't like it; when we do something wrong, sometimes it seems fun at first, but then it isn't.)

Share: When we sin against God, we get all tangled up. But because God sent His Son to die on the cross, we can ask Him to untangle us and forgive us for the wrong things we say and do. If we confess our sins, Jesus will erase the mess and make us clean again!

IV. Wrap-up

Gather everyone in a circle and have family members take turns answering this question: What's one thing you've learned about God today?

Next, tell kids you've got a new "Life Slogan" you'd like to share with them.

Life Slogan: "Jesus' death is the key to unlock God's plan for me." Have family members repeat the slogan two or three times to help them learn it. Then encourage them to practice saying it during the week so they can talk about it at your next Family Night session.

Close in Prayer: Allow time for each family member to share prayer concerns and answers to prayer. Then close your time together with prayer for each concern. Thank God for listening to and caring about us.

Remember to record your prayer requests so you can refer to them in the future as you see God answering them.

Easter Resurrection Eggs

One of the best ways to merge a traditional fun activity with the goal of teaching your children about Jesus is to incorporate "Resurrection Eggs" into your egg-hunting plans. Number a dozen plastic eggs (the kind that open for placing candy or other items inside) up to 12, and place the items listed below inside. Hide the eggs along with the candy or real eggs and begin the search. Once all the eggs have been found, have the children open each "resurrection egg" in order and recount the story of Christ's death, burial, and resurrection. You can make this part of your egg hunt extra exciting and special by giving a prize to the child who either finds the most resurrection eggs, or finds the tomb egg (egg 12).

Egg 1: A small cup and cracker (symbols of the Last Supper described in Matthew 26:26–28)

Egg 2: Three coins wrapped in foil (symbols of the betrayal by Judas described in Matthew 26:14–15)

Egg 3: A small whip made of a toothpick with string or rubber band strips (symbol of the flogging described in Mark 15:15)

Egg 4: A tiny robe pattern cut from purple cloth (symbol of the robe described in Mark 15:17)

Egg 5: A thorn (symbol of the crown of thorns described in Mark 15:17)

Egg 6: A cross (symbol of the cross described in John 19:17)

Egg 7: A scroll with "King of the Jews" written on it (symbol of the scroll described in Matthew 27:37)

Egg 8: A nail (symbol of the nailing of Jesus' hands to the cross as described in John 20:25)

Egg 9: A piece of sponge (symbol of the vinegar given to Jesus as described in John 19:29–30)

Egg 10: A spear made of toothpicks (symbol of the spear used to pierce Jesus' side as described in John 19:34)

Egg 11: A small rock (symbol of the stone used to cover the tomb as described in Luke 24:2)

Egg 12: Nothing! (symbol of the empty tomb after the resurrection described in Luke 24:6)

Other Holiday Books

The following books will help you show your children the Christian significance of some of your favorite holiday traditions.

The Legend of the Candy Cane by Lori Walburg (Zonderkidz, 1998).

One dark November night, a stranger rides into a small prairie town. But who is he? And what is he doing? The townspeople wish he were a doctor, a dressmaker, or a trader. But the children have the greatest wish of all! Will their wish come true? In the tradition of the best-selling *One Wintry Night* and *Tale of Three Trees*, this sensitive and imaginative story introduces children to the Christian symbolism of their favorite Christmas candy—the candy cane.

The Legend of the Easter Egg by Lori Walburg (Zonderkidz, 1999).

Featuring the beloved setting and characters from *The Legend of the Candy Cane*, this moving new story takes us deeper into the mystery of Christianity. From the darkness of Good Friday to the light and life of Easter, this story reminds Christians that because of Christ's sacrifice and resurrection, we too will conquer death and receive the glorious gift of eternal life.

See the Resource List in Appendix II for more tools to help you.

NOTES

1. "Nicholas, Saint", Britannica CD, version 97 (Encyclopedia Britannica, Inc., 1997.)

IDEAS AND METHODS

IDEAS AND METHODS

CHAPTER 26

Quiet Time

Summary:	This is time for each individual member of the family, ages 10 and older, to spend time with God. For younger children, their time with God is the time they spend with you at bedtime (see chapter 18).
Impact:	Time with God needs to become a habit, and the best time to develop that habit is as a child.
How long does it take?	From 15 to 30 minutes, depending on the ages of your children.
Where does it happen?	In the bedroom or some other quiet place.
When should we do it?	At a regular time each weekday. Ideally, first thing in the morning or right before bed.
Who is involved?	Everyone in your family over the age of 10 or 11 should do this on his or her own (or partly on his or her own).
Parental effort required:	Initially, significant. It will taper off as your child becomes more independent.
Spiritual growth impact rating:	Potentially high.

IDEAS AND METHODS

I
D
E
A
S

A
N
D

M
E
T
H
O
D
S

The Key to Every Good Relationship

You don't have to be married or in any other relationship for long to realize the importance of spending time alone with your spouse, friend, or child, just enjoying each other's company and growing closer together. Children need to learn that the same thing is true in their relationship with God. They need to spend time alone with Him if they want their relationship with Him to grow.

Until your children are approximately nine years old, the time you spend with them reading Bible stories and praying is their time with God. But as they get older, they will start to outgrow Bible storybooks and your regular bedtime routine with them. It's important to recognize this and help them move toward having their own daily quiet time alone with God, which should consist of Bible reading, prayer, and perhaps some sort of devotional reading. (This is the primary time for teaching the *loving* aspect of the Christian life—where they get to know God personally.)

One of the first things you need to teach them is that developing a regular quiet-time habit is not a law or a duty—it's a wonderful opportunity to have a relationship with the God who loves and cares for them. God is their heavenly Father who wants to guide, protect, and instruct His children, provide for them, and gradually reveal His love, character, and presence to them.

Your children can grow and learn every day through the normal circumstances of daily life. But it's important for them to step away from the clutter and busyness of life and sit quietly with God on a regular basis. When they do this, they will grow closer to Him and get to know Him better. They will experience His presence, sense His direction, and receive His wisdom.

Quiet time can be explained to your children as special time spent with God, just as they would spend time with you or a close friend. No one looks at spending time with a friend as a duty or burden. Rather, it is something wonderful, enjoyable, and necessary for strengthening the relationship. By establishing a regular quiet time habit, you are essentially saying to God, "I love You. You're important to me. I enjoy spending time with You and I want to get to know You better."

Finding, planning, and maintaining a regular time slot for quiet time is vital to establishing this habit. One way to help your children with this is to talk about your own time with God. Tell your children how and when you do it, and share some things you've learned about God from your quiet-time experiences.

If your children have all grown beyond enjoying Bible stories at bedtime, you may want to establish a daily quiet time for the entire family. This could be a set time each day when all other activities cease. The TV is shut off, homework and toys are put away, and everyone goes to his or her room or another private place and spends from 15 to 40 minutes (depending on your children's ages) praying and reading the Bible.

If you still have a younger child, you could do your quiet time at another time and spend this family time with him or her while everyone else is doing their own. You could do this in the morning, after supper, or just before bed, whichever time best suits your family. Before bed is ideal because it will help your younger children make a smooth transition from their bedtime routine to quiet time. By building this time into the family schedule, you will help your children establish this discipline in their own lives and demonstrate to them that spending time alone with God is a top priority for you—the key to your relationship with Him.

Keys to Success

Helping your children establish a regular quiet time will take consistent effort, especially if you're not the type of person who likes routines or schedules yourself. The following practical tips will help you be more effective in helping your children establish this life habit.

♦ **Start with baby steps.** Let's face it, until your children begin experiencing the benefits firsthand, convincing them to give quiet times a chance can be a real challenge. Start by providing opportunities for them to enjoy their quiet times and see immediate results.

You'll probably want to start with only a few minutes and extend the time as they are ready.

♦ *Give them ownership.* Help your children understand from an early age that they are responsible for developing their own quiet time with God. As they get older, let them begin to take more and more control of their regular Bible reading and prayer while you are still doing it with them. You can do this by letting them choose the Bible stories or books they read and what they should pray about. Work gradually and purposefully from reading to them and praying for them when they are young to listening to them read and pray, with your guidance, when they are older. Always affirm that this is *their* time with God, which they will have for the rest of their lives. Let them know they'll do it completely on their own one day.

♦ *Show and tell.* As your children get older, begin sharing more of your own spiritual life with them. Seeing how you do things will help them when it comes to establishing their own routines. Begin by talking about your own quiet time and asking them about theirs. You may even want to read the same book of the Bible in your individual quiet times and discuss it together. Come alongside and talk with your children as people who are all growing in your relationships with God. By mentoring your children in this

Bibles and Pizza?

Every morning the alarm rings. Kyle, age nine, and Shaun, age seven, get out of bed on their own, make their beds, get dressed, and read their Bibles. Kyle is reading a couple of stories every day from his *Comic Bible*. And Shaun reads one story from the *Beginner's Bible*. While the boys get ready and have their quiet time, Mom has her own.

How did this happen?

Mom decided she needed to do two things. First, she needed her own quiet time every day. Second, she needed to teach her children responsibility and get them started with their own quiet time. So one day she and the boys made a wheel that looked like a colorful pizza. Each "slice" had a prize on it that the boys had chosen. One piece offered a dollar. One was an extra 30 minutes of television. One stated that Mom would make their beds for three days. Other pieces of pizza offered different prizes. If the boys did all four things on their list every morning, on Friday night they got to pitch a penny onto the pizza. Wherever the penny landed, that was the prize they received.

The boys love it and Mom never has to nag. Because Shaun is so young, she spent the first three days showing him exactly what she expected. They read the Bible story together and answered the questions. Some days she still goes into his room to encourage him. Kyle, being older and a self-starter, needed only the prize at the end of the week to motivate him.

K. B.

way, you will encourage them to follow your example. It's very important that you have open communication with your children and allow them the dignity of growing up and launching out on their own.

♦ *Help them live what they learn.* When teaching your children about quiet time, emphasize that, first of all, this is a special time for them to grow in their relationship with God, to experience His love, and to love Him in return. But they also need to learn how to apply what they learn to their everyday life. It's vital that you emphasize this connection between seeking God, knowing Him, and letting their relationship with Him transform their lives. For example, if they are learning about forgiveness in their daily Bible reading, help them to apply what they learn by pointing out situations that call for forgiveness and guiding them through the forgiveness process. Doing this will help your children understand the practical value of spending time alone with God.

Overcoming Obstacles

Probably the biggest obstacle to helping children establish a consistent quiet time is that many parents tend to cut their kids loose too soon. Your children need supervision and support, not just when they're starting out but all the way until they leave home (and even thereafter). When you're busy, it's tempting to leave them to do it on their own. But you need to stay with them until they're mature enough to do it alone. If you cut them loose from your regular, supervised bedtime or other quiet-time routine too early, they'll get discouraged and will likely begin to dread quiet time rather than look forward to it.

A second major obstacle is trying to get children to sit down and concentrate long enough on their own to have a quiet time. There are too many things to distract them, such as little brothers or sisters, toys, video games, or TV shows. Even though you've taught them for years how to do it and why they should do it, they will still need practical help

IDEAS AND METHODS

actually doing it and being consistent. It's just like brushing teeth. Your children have good intentions, and they want their teeth to be clean, but when you're a child it's very easy to get distracted.

Help your children by coming alongside them and making the family schedule as conducive to quiet time as possible. Be flexible and keep things fun. You want your children to think of quiet time as a joyful activity that really benefits them. Don't nag them! Instead, be positive about quiet time.

One idea is to discuss with each of your children an order of things to do before they go to bed that includes, for example, personal play or reading time, brushing their teeth, washing their face, 10 minutes of Bible reading, and 10 minutes of prayer. Help them decide what time they will start their routine and when they need to move from one event to the next. Once they've decided on the routine, help them do it each evening.

Be sure to be flexible if they want to adjust their plan. Also remember to allow variety. Perhaps once a week their Bible reading can be done in the form of a Bible audio or video cassette. You may also decide that Sunday's Bible reading is covered at church. Listen to your children's unique objections, concerns, and ideas, and help them overcome obstacles and plan a time they look forward to. By structuring their bedtime in this way you will do a great deal toward helping them develop a regular, effective quiet time habit.

A further obstacle to effective quiet times is the lack of tools for children ages 10–12. By this age most children are too old for Bible storybooks, but they're not old enough to attack the Bible on their own. Your children need guidance and support in their quiet time, especially when they're starting out on their own. Some devotional books simply give a reading or provide a prayer for the children to read, doing everything for them, including giving them a list of lessons they can learn from each day's reading. However, you are trying to get your children to the place where they are going to the Bible itself and are praying from their hearts. For that purpose, the best devotional books act as an addition to or an inspiration for a personal quiet time with God apart from the book. Look for quiet time resources that allow your children to take ownership of their own quiet time and heighten their interest level. This will also help them continue to grow in their relationship with God.

Tools

The following books will be effective tools to help your children ages 8–12 take a proactive approach to their quiet time.

The NIrV Kids' Quest Study Bible (Lightwave, Livingstone, Zondervan, 1999).

This full-text Bible for children aged 6–10 brings together the easy-to-read New International Reader's Version and the best-selling *101 Questions Children Ask* series to create a study Bible that answers children's questions about God's Word while they're reading the verses that make them wonder. It responds to their big questions about God, life, and the world around them with answers straight from scripture.

My Time With God by Jeanette Dall et al. (Tyndale, 2000).

This book of devotionals are quiet-time primers or "coaches" for your children aged 8–12. Like a traditional devotional, it walks children through the main elements of a fulfilling quiet time with God—prayer, Bible reading, and personal reflection. Included are tips and tools to help them make their quiet times effective and enjoyable. But unlike traditional devotionals, this book does not do all the work for your children. It merely serves as a guide and a stepping-off point for quiet times. For example, this book includes prayer starters and prayer suggestions, but children have to come up with their own words and speak from their hearts when it comes time to pray. It also includes Bible reading suggestions that children have to look up and find in their own Bibles.

My Time With God contains six months' worth of daily quiet-time starters. Each reading includes similar features, as seen in the sample below.

The sample quiet time starter from *My Time With God* on the next page will give you an idea of how the book works. Feel free to photocopy this example and let your children try it out on their own.

IDEAS AND METHODS

Windblown Waters and Wiped Out Warriors!

Could you swim across a large lake? What if someone were chasing you? This was the exact situation the Israelites were in. To find out how things turned out, read Exodus 14:9–31.

Think About It

• Try to imagine the confusion and noise, and all the people, both adults and children, crying as the Israelites are trapped by the sea. How would *you* be feeling?

• Then how would you feel when Moses raised his staff and the way was clear for you to cross?

• Think of a "hopeless" situation you're facing. Which do you think is harder for God: holding back the Red Sea or solving your "hopeless" problem? Why?

Go Deeper

Exodus 14:1–15:20; Psalm 91:14; John 14:14; 1 Corinthians 10:1–2.

Prayer Starter

Along with your other prayers, thank God for helping you through a tough experience. Tell Him honestly how you feel about the difficult problem you were thinking about and trust Him to do what's best for you.

Facts and Fun

A teacher told his students that the parting of the Red Sea wasn't a miracle because the water was only three feet deep. "That would have been even more of a miracle!" a student said. "How so?" his teacher asked. The student answered, "It would take some doing to drown the entire Egyptian army in only three feet of water!"

Coming Up Next

How would you like to eat exactly the same food every day, and have to scrape it off the ground every morning? Learn how the Israelites felt about their meals . . . next time!

See the Resource List in Appendix II for more tools to help you.

CHAPTER 27

Exploration Time

Summary:	As children mature intellectually and spiritually, they will become more amenable to exploring and growing in the knowledge of their Christian faith. Introducing them to this practice in their preteen years is a good start toward making this a lifetime habit.
Impact:	Ideally, family learning will continue for as long as your child lives in your home. However, personal study and dedication will become important as your children gain their independence.
How long does it take?	From 15 to 30 minutes, depending on the ages of your children.
Where does it happen?	In the bedroom or some other quiet place.
When should we do it?	Perhaps once a week.
Who is involved?	Initially, parents will do this with their children, often by using some of the other methods outlined in this book. As they become ready, children will begin personal study, usually directed by the parent.
Parental effort required:	Significant.
Spiritual growth impact rating:	High.

Equipped for Life

Learning about the Christian faith should be something that happens all the time right in the midst of everyday life. But we need to teach our children the importance of taking a special time each day or each week to grow in the knowledge of their faith. You can explain that it is just like mathematics. You use your math skills every day, and you can become better at math by applying what you know to everyday situations. (How much change should you get? How long will it take you to save for that special item? How long until your birthday?) But if you don't spend time at school expanding your knowledge and skills, you'll be limited in the kinds of mathematical problems you can solve, and could end up giving someone the wrong change, miscalculating schedules, or being cheated.

Many people who have grown up in the church have not been taught their "spiritual numbers"—the basics of the Christian faith. Their Bible knowledge is limited to a few simple Bible stories and a handful of platitudes. As a result, their faith has little impact on their lifestyle. Worse, they may leave the faith, or even be led astray by a cult because they are unable to recognize erroneous teachings.

In 2 Timothy 2:15 Paul writes, "Do your best to present yourself to God as one approved, a workman who does not need to be ashamed and who correctly handles the word of truth." Many Christian young people experience profound spiritual struggles in university or college because they don't have a proper grounding in their faith to enable them to successfully battle the daily onslaught of conflicting and anti-Christian ideas they encounter. By teaching your children to regularly read, explore, and study God's Word, you are equipping them to use the truth to deal with their own doubts and questions and with people and information that challenge their faith. This is why the knowing part of your training is so important. This chapter focuses on exactly that.

1. The first step in this process is to **teach your children what the Bible is**. It can be explained in the following four ways:

   ❖ *As God's autobiography.* The Bible tells us about God's character and values so we can begin to understand Him.

   ❖ *As God's plan.* The Bible tells us the story of God's plan for the world.

   ❖ *As a love letter.* The Bible tells us how, because of His love,

God dealt with sin and made a way for us to be together with Him forever.

❖ *As life's instruction manual.* God made the world to work according to particular principles. The way to have the best life is to follow those principles. God wrote them down for us in the Bible so we'd know how to live life to the fullest.

These things, taken together, are the foundation of our Christian faith, and the Bible is the handbook of that faith.

Knowing what the Bible is intended to be will affect how your children read and study it. For example, when you pick up an autobiography, you are looking for different things than when you pick up an instruction manual. Often, when we read through the Bible, especially during our time alone with God, we get to know God better. But when we are looking for instructions for life, on subjects such as love, prayer, or doctrine, we need to use and study God's Word as His instruction manual for life. Some excellent resources to help your children in their Bible exploration are included in the Tools section as well as in the Resource List in Appendix II.

2. The second step is to **help your children develop a regular pattern of Bible study and exploration.** This time is different from their quiet time in that exploration time focuses on learning about the Christian faith (*knowing*), whereas the focus of quiet time is knowing God and growing in your relationship with Him (*loving*). That's not to say that one can't learn about God during quiet time or grow in one's relationship with God during exploration time— just that the focus of each is different. Teach your children that regular Bible study and learning about their faith is important because it will help them grow as they come to understand more about God, His character, and the kind of life He wants them to live.

When your children are still quite young, work with them to develop regular times when they learn about their faith and grow in their knowledge and understanding of doctrine. This will probably start out with you and them working through a Bible storybook together. As your children get a little older, they need to develop their own regular exploration times. By the time they hit their teens, they should have a well-developed habit of learning and growing in the knowledge of the Bible and the Christian faith. Even so, encourage your children to never stop learning.

3. The third step is showing your children the importance of **applying what they learn to their lives.** Good teaching is one thing, but it is only half of the equation. Your children will have nothing but theories if they don't apply what they learn to their lives. The other half is training. Help your children in the learning process by showing them how what they learn from their Bible exploration time can equip them for a fulfilling life.

Keys to Success

Encouraging your children to develop a regular habit of Bible exploration may sound like a daunting challenge, especially if you're not much of a scholar yourself. (Very few adult Christians apply themselves to learning the Bible and the elements of their faith beyond casual Bible reading or church attendance. If you're one of these people, then doing exploration time with your children is a great opportunity for you to learn as well!) The following practical tips will help even nontheologians to motivate their children toward this goal.

◆ *Make it rewarding.* Don't be afraid to reward your kids for growing and learning, because life also rewards us for doing this. You may want to set up a system where they earn extra allowance or a special treat when they do their Bible study for the week. By rewarding your children for learning, you are demonstrating how life works. When you reward them, you can even say something like "We are rewarding you to show you that learning and living by God's principles will help you in life."

- **Be teachable.** If you've been a Christian for a long time, you have probably been to hundreds of church services and seen or read dozens of Christian books. If you're not careful, you can get into the habit of hearing a sermon or seeing a book and saying, "I've heard that a hundred times already." As a parent, you need to ask God to help you resist this temptation, because if you adopt an unteachable attitude, your children (who are always watching you) will do the same. Instead, when you hear a message, don't have the attitude that you know it all already. Remember, if you're growing as a Christian, you should get something new from God's Word each time you hear it. Be open to the Spirit and believe that God can always teach you something, even from the simplest messages. This attitude will have a positive impact on your children when the time comes for them to learn.

- **Keep it interesting.** Don't limit your idea of study time to 30 minutes spent in seclusion with the Bible and some dry, academic tome. Learning about the Bible can and should be fun. Instead of having your children read a book, why not rent a video on the Bible or a biblical topic and then discuss it with them afterward over a snack? Or play a Bible-based game, such as *The Book Game* that will teach your children basic facts about the Bible. (Check out the Tools section and the Resource List in Appendix II for more ideas.)

- **Make it relevant.** Your children aren't going to care how many ephahs of grain God required the ancient Israelites to give for a fellowship offering, but they will be fascinated with the story of how Delilah tricked Samson into revealing the secret to his incredible strength. When helping your children develop a Bible exploration program, make sure it caters to their interests and teaches them principles they can immediately apply to their lives. Bible exploration should never be just a dry academic exercise. Show them how applying what they learn can lead to benefits that they can see, touch, and taste.

- **Seize every opportunity.** While personal study tools are key, don't hesitate to let your children take advantage of other opportunities to learn about the Bible in Sunday school, vacation Bible school, or summer camp.

IDEAS AND METHODS

225

Overcoming Obstacles

One of the biggest obstacles you'll face when it comes to exploration time is convincing your children to sit down and do it. After all, they sit in school all day, and probably the last thing they want to do when they get home (after they've completed their homework) is more studying. This calls for sensitivity on your part.

For example, don't pull them away from something they enjoy, such as playing outside or working on a hobby, to do Bible study. They will only resent it. Instead, build exploration time into their regular program so that it does not intrude on their fun. You might even want to let them out of doing a chore, such as supper dishes, one night a week so they can do their Bible study. This can be a powerful incentive. Another idea is to take a break once in a while and do the Bible exploration as a family. This is a great time to pull out a game or a video. Creativity and sensitivity will be your keys to success in this area.

Another common obstacle is for your children to adopt the attitude of "been there, done that." In other words, once they've done one study on love, they might think that they've learned everything they need to know about it. Your challenge as a parent is to show your children that their learning can't stop at one lesson. They have to go on learning. This means going beyond the course or book they're working on and learning about the topic directly from the Bible. And they shouldn't stop there. Get them excited about other resources, such as books, games, and Web sites that are available.

And help them see that learning does not stop when study time ends. Constantly refer back to what they are learning. For example, if they ask you a question about war, say, "Let's find out what the Bible says." Teach your children that learning is a lifelong process. They should approach learning about the Bible as they would anything else they want to be good at: with dedication, practice, and perseverance.

Tools

Exploration time is vital for every family, no matter what your personality, passion, or pace is. But no two children are alike when it comes to choosing a Bible study program that's right for them. Some children learn best on their own; others like to learn in a group. Whatever your children's wants or needs are, the following list of tools will help you find a program that works best for them.

The Adventure Bible Handbook by Ed Van der Maas (Zondervan, 1997).

This unique Bible handbook combines a rollicking fictional adventure through time with fascinating Bible facts about key Bible people, places, and events. It is the perfect resource to help your children understand the Bible better.

The I Want to Know . . . series by Rick Osborne and K. Christie Bowler (Zondervan, 1998–1999).

This comprehensive introduction to the basics of the Christian faith is an excellent tool to use with your children ages 8–12. This fun, informative series is packed full of fascinating facts, full-color photos, cartoons, illustrations, and activities. The set covers basic Christian doctrines concerning God, Jesus, the Holy Spirit, the Bible, the church, prayer, the Fruit of the Spirit, and the Ten Commandments. By the time your children have finished these books, they will have an excellent understanding of the foundation of the Christian faith.

Kidcordance by Rick Osborne et al. (Zonderkidz, 1999).

This fun, challenging Bible reference book for children aged 7–12 defines and explains 300 key words and concepts from the Bible.

The following is an example of how your children can do a topical Bible study (taken from *I Want to Know About the Bible*).

How to Study the Bible

Reading the whole Bible gives us the overall story of God's plan for the world and why Jesus came. It also shows us who God is and what He is like. But in order for us to understand the whole Bible, we first need to study its individual parts, whether they are books, passages, characters, key words, or topics. By looking at some of these little pictures in the Bible, we will be better able to take in the big picture of God's revelation to us.

One approach to understanding the Bible is to do a topical study of a key word or idea. The following steps will show you how to do this for the word "love." Once you've gone through these steps, try doing your own study on a different word or topic, such as prayer, friendship, money, or honesty.

Step One: Get a notebook and call it your "Treasure Chest." You'll fill it with the "gold" of wisdom and the "jewels" of knowledge that you find in the Bible.

Step Two: Choose one of the Bible's "treasures" to study, say love.

Step Three: Pray. God understands the Bible better than anyone, so it's important to ask for His help when you study it.

Step Four: Find a part of the Bible that teaches about your topic. A great section on love is 1 Corinthians 13. Read through the passage, then take a few minutes to think about it. Ask yourself questions about the passage. For example, what does "is not self-seeking" mean? Make note of any questions you have about what you've just read.

Step Five: One good way to find answers to your questions is to find out what other parts of the Bible say about love. Many Bibles have cross-references, little notes beside verses that point to other verses on the same topic. In your Bible, look up the cross-references for 1 Corinthians 13:5. If there aren't any, look up the following verses: Job 14:16, 17; Proverbs 10:12; 17:9; Matthew 5:22; 1 Corinthians 10:24; 1 Peter 4:8. Based on what you've read in these verses, what do you think "is not self-seeking" means?

Step Six: Most Bibles have a small concordance in the back. A concordance lists key Bible words and the verses they can be found in. If your Bible has a concordance, look up some of the verses it lists under the word "love." Choose three Old Testament verses and three New Testament verses. If you don't have a concordance, look up the following verses: Genesis 20:13; Exodus 34:6; Numbers 14:19; Matthew 5:43; Romans 5:8; 1 Corinthians 8:1. Read the verses around each verse to see how they fit into what the writer is saying. Who is loving? How is love shown? Write your answers in your "Treasure Chest."

Step Seven: Bible dictionaries are another type of Bible study tool. Like concordances, they're alphabetical and easy to use. If you have a Bible dictionary, look up "love" and see what you find. If you're into computers, you'll find many Bible study tools online or on CD-ROM. Do a search or find on "love" and see what the computer brings up. Dig deep. Treasures are there to be found!

Step Eight: Now it's time to live out what you've learned. In your notebook write down the names of five people you would like to show love to. Then write down five ways that you can show love to each person on your list. Pray and ask God to help you be more loving. Then go out and do it!

See the Resource List in Appendix II for more tools to help you.

IDEAS AND METHODS

Designing Your Family Spiritual Growth Plan

Putting It All Together in a Plan

CHAPTER 28

Putting It
All Together
in a Plan

You have reached the most important section in this guide.

In chapter 1 we gave you a plan for getting started. In this chapter we will take you to the next level, using simple, easy-to-fill-out questionnaires and a planning system that can be completed one step at a time. When you finish, you will have a customized, flexible spiritual growth plan that fits your unique family.

Don't Put the Bar Too High!

Before we move forward to help you create a spiritual growth plan for your family, rewind your memory bank to 1992.

In anticipation of the summer Olympic Games, Reebok™ invested over $15 million in pre-Olympic coverage ads, asking whether the world's greatest decathlete would be Dan O'Brien or Dave Johnson. As a result "Dan or Dave?" became a common watercooler topic across the country. Each was considered a slam dunk to make the Olympic team, compete in Barcelona, and stand on the medal platform.

At the U.S. Olympic trials, the two were indeed neck and neck in points—until the pole vault. The competition started at 14'5¼". O'Brien had jumped this height, and higher, literally hundreds of times in practice and competition. He considered the pole vault one of his best events.

So he decided to pass at 14 feet. He didn't even take off his warm-ups until the bar had inched to over 15 feet. His first jump came at 15'9".

Starting and staying with a few things and building on them is far better than planning many things and following through on none.

On his first attempt, he went *under* the bar. No problem. On his second attempt, he knocked the bar off coming *down*. Now everyone in the stands, especially the Reebok executives, began to think, *Maybe there is a problem.* On his third and final attempt, he ran down the runway, planted his pole . . . and went *under* the bar again.

If O'Brien had just cleared the *opening height and no more*, he would have earned enough points to finish second and he would have made the Olympic team. Instead he spent the 1992 Olympics in the broadcasting booth rather than on the field.

The lesson is simple but critical: failing at spiritual training doesn't come when parents start slowly, act intentionally, and enlist supportive friends to keep them on course. Rather, parents often fail because they choose a world record height to begin training their children. None of this "now-I-lay-me-down-to-sleep" stuff. They're going to start out spending an *hour minimum* studying and praying with each child *twice* a day. Forget using books that could help them—that's canned material! They're going to develop their *own* spiritual growth materials (worthy of winning literary awards) for each child!

But when reality sets in and they find they've fallen far short of their grand expectations, they (or their children) often get so frustrated that they throw up their hands and give up altogether.

The key thing to remember is this: **Most families will do far more by doing less.**

That's especially true in the beginning. It doesn't mean that we don't expect great things from our kids, or that we shouldn't challenge them to do and be their best. What it does mean is that starting and staying with a few things and building on them is far better than planning many things and following through on none.

This is a wonderful encouragement. God has always made a point of honoring those who start out and are faithful in using the "few things" that He has given them. In Matthew 25:14–30 we read Jesus' Parable of the Talents. In that familiar story, the master (God) praises the two faithful stewards for working with what He had given him (five talents to the one, two talents to the other): "Well done, good and faithful servant! You have been faithful with a few things; I will put you in charge of many things. Come and share your master's happiness!" (v. 23). The amount each had received did not matter—what counted was their faithfulness in using and applying what they had been given. (The master did not expect a return of five talents from the servant to whom he had given only two talents; his expectations were based on what he had entrusted to each.)

But the third servant, who had received only one talent, looked at the limitations of what he had to work with and gave up without even trying. The master expected him to use what little he had been given.

Therefore, in this chapter, we're going to encourage you to come closer to the Lord as a family by starting out with "low-bar" stuff: things like praying with Suzie before she goes to school in the morning, or reading Steven a Bible story at night. Things like following through on a Family Night activity every other week, and going to church as a family on Sunday. Low-bar stuff to start with. Later you'll be able to raise the bar—when the family is ready for it.

Here's the plan for this chapter:

1. First, we take you briefly through seven reminders—things to keep in mind as you create your plan.
2. Next, we give you three examples of how families in different situations might put their plan together, and we show you how one of these families completed their forms.
3. Then, in seven steps, we take you through the process of putting it all together. When you get done with this, you will have a Basic Plan (a low-bar starting level plan) and a Support Plan (which focuses on how to sprinkle your family entertainment times with spiritual content and use creativity, holidays, special times, and the teachable moments that crop up).
4. Finally, we challenge you to become a gold medalist spiritual trainer.

So, let's jump into a great, God-honoring adventure—setting up a Spiritual Growth Plan for your family!

Seven Reminders for Creating Your Family Spiritual Growth Plan

Be Committed

In an earlier chapter (chapter 5), you signed a commitment card. That is a personal "Memory Marker" of your decision to be intentional about passing down your faith.

There will be times when it's inconvenient, you're tired or busy, or you feel inadequate or unprepared to do what you said you would. It's your commitment to the process that will help get you through negative feelings, keep you on track, and help you see positive results in the end.

So if you haven't already done so, we urge you to pray over and sign your commitment card today, before you go through the process of actually creating your Family Spiritual Growth Plan.

Be Realistic

As important as it is to be committed, it's equally important to be realistic about how much you should put on your (and your family's) plate. Start with the bar low with what we call the Basic Plan. A minimum workable commitment would be the following:

- Go to church;
- Set aside a total of one hour each week—or every two weeks—with your family. Remember, that's an hour *total*. The time can be divided up in many ways among, for example, drive time and mealtime discussions and family time activities; and
- Spend five minutes with each child, five times a week. (The time will be longer the older the child is.)

It may be wise to get the family together and get everybody on board. The decision to have a Family Spiritual Growth Plan (and Individual Spiritual Growth Plans for each family member) is, of course, not negotiable, but it will help enormously in the long run if you can get the whole family to agree on what is realistic. It will especially help if you also make it clear that you'll involve them in evaluating the plan after a specific period of time, perhaps three months.

Be Specific

For some of us who don't like details, it's easy to skip the part where you write down the specifics of your family profile, the profiles of your children, and the details of your plan. We encourage you not to skip this part.

If you write down the details from the start, the process of putting the plan together now, and of revising it later, will continue to be easy to complete. If you skip some of the details, the process will start becoming more difficult because you haven't considered everything you need to develop a plan that will truly work for your family and each individual in it.

Having a specific plan (even if you think it's too specific) will help you know where you started from and what you've committed to.

Be Creative

This is where the Support Plan begins. You may not think of yourself as creative, and you may find it especially difficult to be creative when it comes to teaching spiritual truth. But as you complete your plan, you can be creative in your choices and decisions.

◆ The problem may in part be your spiritual "comfort zone"—the feeling that spiritual things should be presented in a serious and solemn manner, much like they were in Sunday school when you grew up. When you get to choosing what methods and models you will use with your family, make sure you decide on the basis of what matches and will work for your family, not on what matches what you've done before or what falls within your comfort zone.

◆ Get resources that help you get the job done. There are many books that give ideas for teaching your kids. But there are also videos, software, Web sites, and music and audio tapes of every description. Vary your tools and approach.

◆ Use your kids' creativity. Let your children know about all the different models and methods outlined in this book. Let them get excited about the ones they like. Even after you've decided on a method and a plan, stay open to creative suggestions and alternative ideas. Give them options and ask them how they would like to approach learning a certain topic or doing family time learning. They may suggest some off-the-wall things like learning about spiritual warfare by playing laser tag; but if you go with it,

Teachable moments happen; you can't manufacture them.

they'll never forget the experience or the lesson.

- ◆ Never forget that God has given us the gifts of humor and laughter. No matter how dry the activity or lesson, slow down and relax enough to let in some joking around, a little wrestling or tickling with your younger kids, and maybe some humorous storytelling with your older ones. Sometimes you may end up on an entirely different topic, but the time together and the wisdom shared won't be forgotten.
- ◆ If your children have musical gifts, why not let them use music in their spiritual growth? Have them write a song about God's love or about a particular aspect of their relationship with God and perform it on a family night. If they are artistic, why not encourage them to try to give expression to God's forgiveness by drawing on paper or sculpting with clay? This will establish a connection between your kids' talents and the things of the Spirit.
- ◆ Get together, talk, and share ideas with others who are intentional about spiritual training.

Be Alert

As you implement your Family Spiritual Growth Plan, you'll find that more and more you'll begin to see ways to teach spiritual truth in every-day teachable moments. The things you do as a regular part of your plan will raise all kinds of questions for your kids, and there will be opportunities during the everyday moments of life to extend, explain, illustrate, and reinforce what was taught. Watching for and recognizing these opportunities is one part of being alert.

A word of caution: Teachable moments happen; you can't manufacture them. They are moments in which God's Spirit makes our hearts especially receptive. As a parent, be alert to the working of the Spirit and work *with* the Spirit and His timing. If you try to turn everything into an opportunity to teach a spiritual lesson, your family will soon quit listening.

Be Connected

Don't go it alone. We can't stress enough how important it is to have supportive friends come alongside you in this high calling. Whether it's a Sunday school class that decides to go through this book together, a small group of friends, or even one friend you can share your plan with, there is tremendous strength, encouragement, insight, and creativity that comes from linking with others. Perhaps you can get together, with children or without, twice a month at your church or at someone's home.

The important thing is that you share with someone else your Spiritual Growth Plan, and ask them to ask you the hard questions: "How did you do this week in following through on your commitments?" Like iron sharpening iron, committed friends can make all the difference in helping positive goals become everyday realities.

Be a Light

Finally, there is no better way to learn than by teaching. Once you have gone through the process of prayerfully putting together your Family Spiritual Growth Plan, share it with someone else. Offer to help a family in your church go through the same process.

One way to do this is to find a family who's interested and buy them a copy of this book to get them started. (Suggest that they do the same for someone else once they have built and begun implementing their plan.)

You could photocopy an extra blank set of all the forms in this book that you used to put together your plan and take the other family through the plan step-by-step. (Normally photocopying copyrighted material is illegal, but *we give you permission* to photocopy the charts and forms in this book or download them from www.heritagebuilders.com.)

Or you can give them a copy of the book and then offer to help them and talk it through with them.

The Seven Steps in Creating a Family Spiritual Growth Program

Three Sample Family Plans

Once upon a time there were three very different families. Each had different needs and children of various ages, but all had the same commitment—to see their family and their children grow in Christ. Let's look at how each of these three families with their unique situations decided on and implemented their first Family Spiritual Growth Plan and Individual Spiritual Growth Plans. One thing you'll see is that each wisely began with a "low bar" approach, based on the Basic Plan below. These families are fictional, but they are based on the real-life experience of many families who have begun to be intentional about passing on their faith.

Basic Plan (Starting Point)
- Go to church;
- Set aside a total of one hour each week—or every two weeks—for family spiritual growth. Remember that that's an hour total. The time can be divided up in many ways among, for example, drive time and mealtime discussions, and/or Family Nights; and
- Spend an average of five to 10 minutes with each child, five times a week. (The time spent with each child will vary depending on his or her age and what you've planned to do with each one.)

Support Plan
- Begin to sprinkle your family fun and entertainment times with spiritual content.
- Look for everyday opportunities in the middle of life to reinforce what you're learning.

Family One: The Bilby's

The Bilbys are a blended family with a 16-year-old from Raye Ann's first marriage, two six-year-old twin boys, and a mile-a-minute two-year-old.

While most families don't pick a specific day to commit to a plan together or to sign their commitment card, the Bilbys did. Raye Ann's first husband had walked out on her when their daughter, April, was only six. That's a tough age to lose a father. Yet when the news came little more than a year later that he had been killed while driving drunk, it was like replaying every shattered emotion a hundred times over.

Another year would pass before Raye Ann met Mike at work. A steady, caring Golden Retriever, he slowly demonstrated a patient and caring heart that won Raye Ann's love. They were married at the end of a year, and the following year, when April was 10, the twins came along. And although Jacob—or Jake, as they call him—wasn't entirely planned or expected, he was welcomed into the family four years later.

Mike had worked hard at being a good husband and father since he married Raye Ann. He was the one who picked Father's Day to make their commitment, wanting to make a point. Namely, as long as the Lord gave him breath, he would "be there" for Raye Ann, April, Jason, Jeffrey, and Jake.

The Bilbys decided they were definitely an "F-16" family. With a teenager, twins, and a toddler, and with Raye Ann back working part-time as a nurse, it seemed that life was always stuck in "full throttle." They'd been praying and talking about some kind of consistent method for teaching their children about the Lord at home. Mike and Raye Ann had quite different backgrounds, and they had some difficulty agreeing on what they should do. When they looked at the Basic Spiritual Growth Plan, they were thrilled to have a basic plan laid out for them. They also loved the options presented in Section C (pages 145–236) and found it easy to find ones they could agree on.

The Bilby family was basically a zoo when it came to personality types. Mike was the Golden Retriever and Raye Ann was an off-the-chart Otter. April was a Beaver's Beaver, keeping her room and closet immaculate. That wasn't true for Jason, the older twin (by an entire seven and a half minutes). Jason was a pure-bred Lion who raced through a room like a whirlwind, while his identical twin, Jeffrey, was as much a Golden Retriever as his father. It was a little hard to tell with Jake, since he was so young, but after reading the qualities and traits of the different personality types, they were convinced this little ball of energy was following in his mother's Otter footsteps.

Mike and Raye Ann knew that April was an avid reader who loved fiction of all genres. Jason and Jeffrey were primarily tuning in to the sports channel even at their young ages, and Jake couldn't get enough of both books and playing ball. Having completed the family and individual profiles, they were ready to move to the next step. They looked at the Basic Plan and began developing their family and individual plans.

Getting Started:

- *Church attendance*—no problem. They were already regular attenders.
- *Set aside a total of one hour each week—or every two weeks—for family spiritual growth.* This is where Mike and Raye Ann both were excited and wholeheartedly agreed to begin Family Nights. It just seemed natural for them, and they even found a free night that was perfect for everyone.
- *Spend an average of 5 to 10 minutes with each child, five times a week.* What they would do for the twins and Jake seemed pretty straightforward, but they wanted to talk to them about it before getting

any resources. They would use bedtime to do some Bible storybook reading and praying with them.

They knew it was going to be a little more tricky to get their 16-year-old on an individual plan, especially since she had been too old for a few years now for bedtime prayers and Bible stories. So even though they had bought her a Bible, they really had not done anything to help her continue her personal time with God. They decided to talk to her to find out what she'd like to do.

Additional Support:
- *Begin to sprinkle your family fun and entertainment times with spiritual content.* This one was easy, because the twins and Jake loved videos. They all loved to play board games, and Christian fiction would be great for April.
- *Look for everyday opportunities to reinforce what you're learning.* Mike and Raye Ann decided that the most important on-the-go training was to take time to answer their children's questions when they asked them, so they made a commitment to do so even if they had to look up the answers.

Next they had a family meeting and discussed the importance of having a Spiritual Growth Plan. They committed to doing a spiritual Family Night activity every other week on Thursday evenings. Then they chose one of the *Family Nights Tool Chest* books to use for lessons, structure, and ideas. Seeking to get everyone involved, they put Jason in charge of rounding up the family when it was time. Like any good Lion, he took charge and made sure everyone was at the kitchen table when they should be.

April, the avid reader (and Beaver), would read with her mom about the activity they'd do and help prepare any special materials that the lesson called for (paper plates, balloons, shaving cream, paper, etc.).

Raye Ann would lead the activity, using her Otter personality, and Mike would wrap it up, explaining and making sure that everyone understood the main point of the lesson. Then Jeffrey chipped in as Mom's activity assistant and would get the snacks and refreshments from the kitchen when the activity was finished. Everyone helped keep Jake entertained and focused. (That division of labor didn't always work perfectly, and there were times when they traded roles. However, they had so much fun learning that Family Nights soon became a favorite for parents and children alike.)

Mike also liked the idea of using all of the commute time driving the kids around as an addition to their family plan. He got the *Joy Ride!* book by Jacqueline Lederman (Tyndale, 2000) and began having enjoyable learning while playing games in the car.

Next, they needed to go over their individual plans. Raye Ann and Mike started this part of the family meeting by discussing how they had come to the conclusion of how important it is to spend time with God every day and by telling the kids what they scheduled for themselves. Then, even though they already had them pegged, they had the children take the personality tests and helped them fill out their individual charts. The kids loved this part. Mike and Raye Ann explained some of the options and suggestions. Both boys wanted to expand their bedtime prayer to include going through a Bible storybook with their dad. Raye Ann liked the idea of bedtime blessings for Jake, but the twins wanted them as well, so she agreed to do bedtime blessings with them when Dad had to work late or was busy.

April didn't want to do devotions on her own at first but definitely wanted to pray on her own. They decided that Raye Ann was going to read through the book of Matthew with her, a chapter or two a night, and suggest some prayer topics for her to pray about on her own before going to bed. April usually liked to read before bed, so the Bible reading and prayer took place after pleasure reading, just before lights-out.

Looking to connect with April in her last two years before heading to college, Mike took April through a special father/daughter quiet time on nights when Raye Ann was unavailable. He found a book designed for dads and daughters, *She Calls Me Daddy: Seven Things Every Man Needs to Know About Building a Complete Daughter* by Robert Wolgemuth (Focus on the Family), as a topical study guide each week.

Basic Plan

The Bilbys decided to start with a very simple Family Spiritual Growth Plan and Individual Spiritual Growth Plans:

- Once a week: Attend church as a family.
- Once every other week: Do a family activity. They chose Tuesday evenings. Resource: *Family Nights Tool Chest* books by Jim Weidmann et al. (Chariot Victor).
- Once a day, Monday through Friday: Spend 10 minutes with the twins at night reading a Bible story or bedtime blessing together and praying with them individually. Resource: *Bedtime Blessings* by John Trent (Focus on the Family, 2000).
- Once a day, Monday through Friday: Spend 15 minutes reading the Bible or a devotional book with April and talking to her about prayer (just before

lights-out). Resource: *She Calls Me Daddy* by Robert Wolgemuth (Focus on the Family). (She already had a Bible).

Support Plan

Both Mike and Raye Ann looked for ways to sprinkle their family entertainment with spiritual content and reinforce in everyday life the biblical principles they were teaching. They were challenged immediately with their commitment to answer questions, and the next day they took a trip to a Christian bookstore to add spiritual content to their family entertainment. That summer they also enrolled the twins in a Christian sports camp, which they loved.

Mike and Raye Ann were assistant leaders in their adult Sunday school class, making it easy to get connected with like-minded parents. In fact, it just so happened that their class needed a curriculum for the next quarter! That term, after hearing what Mike and Raye Ann were doing, they went through the material in this book, filled in the family and individual charts, and developed their Family Spiritual Growth Plans as a class project. But what became most helpful was allowing time for couples to talk about their experiences at the end of class. The last 15 minutes of class became "sharing time," with couples assigned to small groups. These group times became the highlight of the class for Mike and Raye Ann. In fact, the four couples they met with weekly continued meeting at their home even after the class had moved on to other topics.

Mike and Raye Ann could tell that as their family grew closer to the Lord, their extended family and some of their friends could see a major difference, which resulted not only in comments but also questions. Several in-depth spiritual conversations took place between Raye Ann and a once "very closed" sister, who wanted to know more about their Family Nights—this was a minor miracle!

A TO F. OUR FAMILY PROFILE

A. History of Faith (circle):

You: (1st) 2nd 3rd Generation   Your Spouse: (1st) 2nd 3rd Generation

B. We are a   ❑ Carriage family   ❑ Steam engine family   ☒ F-16 family

C. Family Interests:

Sports	*Games*
Reading	
Videos	

D. Ages of Children

	0-4	5-6	7-9	10-12		0-4	5-6	7-9	10-12	13-16
Jake	☒	❑	❑	❑	*April*	❑	❑	❑	❑	☒
Jason	❑	☒	❑	❑		❑	❑	❑	❑	❑
Jeffrey	❑	☒	❑	❑		❑	❑	❑	❑	❑

E. Family Members' Personalities
(Lion, Otter, Beaver, Golden Retriever, or combination)

Mike	*G.R.* /		*Jason*	*Lion* /
Raye Ann	*Otter* /		*Jeffrey*	*G.R.* /
April	*Beaver* /		*Jake*	*Otter* /

F. As a family, we are already doing the following:

Activity: *Going to church*	est. time per week: *60* minutes.
Activity: _____	est. time per week: _____ minutes.
Activity: _____	est. time per week: _____ minutes.
Activity: _____	est. time per week: _____ minutes.
Activity: _____	est. time per week: _____ minutes.

Total estimated time per week: *60* minutes.

G. FAMILY ACTIVITIES

BASIC PLAN

☒ *Church*
❏ *Traditional Devotions*
   ❏ Resource book
   ❏ Family Bible
   ❏ Other _____
❏ *Bedtime*
   ❏ Discussions
   ❏ Resource book
   ❏ Bible or Bible storybook
   ❏ Other _____
❏ *Mealtime*
   ❏ Discussions
   ❏ Discussions resource book
   ❏ Other _____
☒ *Drive Time*
   ☒ Discussions and games
   ☒ Discussions and games resource book
   ❏ Audio tapes
   ❏ Music
☒ *Family Nights*
   ☒ Family Nights resource books
   ❏ Other _____

SUPPORT PLAN

☒ *Fun Time*
   ☒ Board games
   ☒ Videos
   ❏ Audio tapes
   ❏ Software
❏ *Special Times and Events*
   ❏ *Holidays*
      ❏ Gospel storybook
      ❏ Gospel story video
      ❏ Children's holiday storybooks
      ❏ Other _____
   ❏ *Celebrations, Events, Ceremonies*
      ❏ Activity ideas resource books
      ❏ Other _____
☒ *Teachable Moments*
   ☒ Idea resource books
   ☒ Question and answer resource books
   ❏ Other _____

H. OUR FAMILY SPIRITUAL GROWTH PLAN

BASIC PLAN

Regular activities we plan to do (or continue to do):

Activity: _Church_

How often? _1_ times per _week_   Specific day(s) or night(s)? _Sunday_

Estimated time per activity: _60_ *minutes; estimated time per week:* _60_ *minutes*

Activity: _Family Spiritual Growth Night_

How often? _1_ times per _2wks._   Specific day(s) or night(s)? _Tuesday night_

Estimated time per activity: _60_ *minutes; estimated time per week:* _30_ *minutes*

Activity: _Commuting Time Discussion_

How often? _3_ times per _week_   Specific day(s) or night(s)? _weekdays_

Estimated time per activity: _10_ *minutes; estimated time per week:* _30_ *minutes*

Activity: _____

How often? _____ times per _____   Specific day(s) or night(s)? _____

Estimated time per activity: _____ *minutes; estimated time per week:* _____ *minutes*

Total estimated time per week: _120_ *minutes*

SUPPORT PLAN

Fun Times (ideas) _Videos, Board games_

Resources? _WWJD?, House Rules, Adventures in Odyssey_

Special Times and Events (ideas) _Start celebrating spiritual birthdays with natural ones_

Resources? _____

Teachable Moments (ideas) _Answer children's questions on the spot_

Resources? _801 Questions Kids Ask About God_

A TO G. INDIVIDUAL SPIRITUAL GROWTH PLAN

Name: _Jason_

A. Age: _6_

B. Stage: _5-6_

C. Interests:
  Reading
  Playing ball
  Dinosaurs/insects

D. Personality: _Lion_ / _____
  Strengths: _Leadership qualities,_
  self-starter, has good
  ideas, motivated.

  Potential weaknesses: _Cooperation_

E. Special Characteristics: _Smart._
  Strong sense of right
  and wrong.

F. Where he or she is at in terms of spiritual growth: _Open to learning._
  Needs more and higher
  level things to challenge him.

G. Things I (we) need to do or give special attention to: _____
  Teaching him to pray.

H TO I. INDIVIDUAL SPIRITUAL GROWTH PLAN

Name: _Jason_

H. INDIVIDUAL ACTIVITIES

☒ *Church Related*
- ☒ Sunday school
- ☐ Vacation Bible school
- ☐ Church clubs/groups
- ☐ Other _____

☐ *Quiet Time (ages 10-12)*
- ☐ Prayer
- ☐ Devotional
- ☐ Bible reading
- ☐ Other _____

☒ *Bedtime (ages 0-9)*
- ☒ Blessings
- ☒ Bible stories
- ☒ Prayer
- ☐ Audio
- ☐ Devotions
- ☐ Other _____

☐ *Exploration Time*
- ☐ Study tools
- ☐ Kid's study Bible
- ☐ Other _____

I.

Regular Activities We Plan to Do (or continue to do):
(Remember, 5-10 minutes per child per weekday)

Activity: _Bedtime Blessings_

How often? _5_ times per _week_   Specific day(s) or night(s)? _weeknights_
Estimated time per activity: _5_ minutes; estimated time per week: _25_ minutes

Activity: _Bible stories_

How often? _5_ times per _week_   Specific day(s) or night(s)? _weeknights_
Estimated time per activity: _10_ minutes; estimated time per week: _50_ minutes

Church-related (involvement and ideas): _Sunday School_ _____

Exploration Time (ideas): _(Consider next time)_ _____

Resources for exploration time: _(See if we can find a Christian book on dinosaurs or insects)_

Memory Markers and Special Events: Dedication ____ Salvation _X_ Confirmation _X_ Baptism ____
Birthday _X_ Spiritual birthday _X_ Starting faith journal ____ Other _____

Activity: _Spiritual & Natural birthdays (same date)_   Date: _June 1_

Activity: _____   Date: _____

Activity: _____   Date: _____

ACTION STEPS

BASIC PLAN

- When will you start (specific date and time)? _Monday, Nov. 20, 2000, 6:30pm._

- What do you need to get started, such as books, videos, or other materials for your family plan and individual plans? To help you make this simple, on pages 256–257 is a Specific Resource Checklist with books, tools, and materials we've recommended earlier in the book.
  Family Nights Tool Chest: Basic Christian Beliefs.
  Adventures in Odyssey Tapes.
  Family Reference Guide.

- What is needed by way of preparation for the first event?
  On Sunday, go over first Family Night activities. Make sure we have the props we'll need. Put tapes in car and tape deck in house.

SUPPORT PLAN

- What fun time things do you need?
  House Rules game.

- What are you going to do to prepare for or remind yourself of teachable moments?
  Look through 801 Questions Kids Ask About God.
  Put notes on the fridge and bathroom mirror.

- What do you need to do to get your support person or group in place? By when?
  Invite the Johnsons over for dinner and talk about it.
  Next Friday night.

- After you have been using your plan for a period of time, which family would you like to share your experience with? _James and Marie Sherbrooke_

Family Two: The Wootenbergs

Marsha Wootenberg was approached by her favorite neighbor and invited to join a small group of parents going through this material. Marsha was a single parent with an 11-year-old daughter, Beth, and an eight-year-old daughter, Chelsey.

Even though she had been considering taking her kids to church, she had declined the invitation at first, thinking that it would be just one more thing that took her away from the kids. But when she heard that in this group the children met at the same time in a different part of the house (supervised by one member's college-age daughter who always had a Bible lesson and activity for the kids), she decided to try it out.

After their first meeting, she signed her commitment card, but wrote in large letters "For three months only" at the bottom. That way, she could leave herself an escape if it became too burdensome.

Right away, Marsha had to vary the Basic Plan, which bothered her. In her job, she had to work one weekend a month, which meant that going to church that weekend wasn't possible. (Later, the church she joined started a Saturday night service which the family could attend on the weekends she was working.)

She identified her threesome as a "steam engine" family. As a single, working parent she was careful not to overcommit. So even though they had a lot going on, it was manageable, and she always tried to make spending time with her kids a priority.

Beth, her 11-year-old, was an extra-sensitive Golden Retriever. She couldn't quite decide on Chelsey, but with her radiant smile and the way she talked to everyone, Marsha thought she was an Otter.

Marsha had always made an effort whenever possible to sit down together as a family and talk at mealtime, so she decided with her children that mealtimes would be when they did their family time. She kept it short and read through the mealtime devotion and went through the activity. If the topic struck a chord and everyone got into it, she would let it go on. If not, she would end it before it got boring and move into their regular conversation. Marsha and her girls filled out the individual charts and decided together what they wanted to do. First of all, since they were all relatively new to the Christian faith, the girls told their mom that they wanted to go to the new believers' class at church with her. After discussing the need for personal time with God, Beth decided on getting and working through one of the books that some of the other kids her age were using, *My Time With God* (Tyndale, 2000). Chelsey wanted to work through Bible stories and begin to pray with her mom before bed.

Basic Plan

Marsha's first plan was simple:
- Once a week: Attend church (three times a month due to her work schedule).
- Once every other week: Do a Family Night activity (on Thursday nights).
- Once a day: Pray for the children (in the morning).

Support Plan

Attending the parenting meeting in her neighborhood soon became a highlight for Marsha and her children. Not only was she learning from several of the veteran parents in the group, but she could tell that her children liked their teacher as well as the neighborhood children who were their ages.

After she had done this for a while, Marsha began to think of ways to share her experience. As she shared with a colleague what she was doing with her children, she discovered that her office friend was a backslidden Christian. She told her friend what a phenomenal change there was in her two girls and the fun they were having. Soon her friend was asking where she could get books and other resources to help her family!

As far as sprinkling fun through her spiritual training went, her family was into music and it didn't take long for them to find out from their group which CDs they would enjoy and where on the dial they could find a Christian radio station. Chelsey really liked *Adventures in Odyssey*. And Marsha found that doing their Family Spiritual Growth plan during the meal each night also served as a way of connecting the topics to the real-life stuff they were each going through, because that's where the conversations led quite naturally.

Family Three: The Bannisters

Kevin and Cindy Bannister were the typical SITCOM family (Single Income, Three Children, Oppressive Mortgage). They were also strong Christians with a deep desire to communicate their faith to their children.

The Bannisters had moved to a part of the country that was at a polar extreme to their Bible Belt upbringing. They hadn't been able to find a strong local church, nor a neighbor who seemed interested in spiritual things. Except for Cindy's parents, who were committed Christians and lived only 45 minutes away, they felt in many ways cut off and alone when it came to their faith.

Kevin and Cindy decided that even if they had to do it alone (which eventually they didn't), they would be intentional about strengthening their family's faith. In a way the move was great because they realized how much they had more or less assumed that their children's spiritual growth was taken care of at church.

While they hadn't lived like a "carriage" family before, they did now. A benefit of moving to the relative isolation of their new home was that they found themselves off the "F-16" pace they'd been on and had all been suffering under. They had always been a carriage family but overcommitted and traveling at an F-16 pace. With Cindy at home now, they decided they could realistically modify the Basic Plan slightly to begin.

The Bannisters had a son, Nathan, who was seven; a second son, David, who was five; and a daughter, Brianna, who was three. Nathan was quiet and introspective, and had struggled in school. As a result, Cindy was home-schooling him, and he was having his best year of learning yet. David was also being home-schooled for his first year. Kevin and Cindy's best guess was that he was a Beaver. Brianna was a bundle of energy, and at three, seemed to be a Lion/Otter combination of fun and determination!

While deciding where to go was a tough decision, the Bannisters did agree to commit to attending a local church. What made the decision so difficult was that their previous church had been very good, and nothing they could find seemed to measure up to their experience there. However, they realized that they needed the support and fellowship, so they picked a small church that had a great kids' program and decided to plug in there. After attending for a few weeks, Cindy found out that the church had a home-school support group, which they joined immediately. Kevin and Cindy set an evening aside, after the kids were all in bed, to put together their initial plan.

The first thing they discussed was how they could support each other in getting their own daily time with God back on track. They decided that Kevin would get up a little earlier in the morning and Cindy would take on more of the morning routine so that he could be alone. Cindy wanted time alone right after dinner, so Kevin agreed to take on more of the after dinner cleanup and play with the kids so she could have that time. For the Family Spiritual Growth Plan, Cindy wanted to try Family Nights, but Kevin really liked the idea of giving the kids a basic foundation of the whole Bible story by singing through it. So they planned on doing a Family Night once every two weeks and Kevin got some good audio tapes and started playing them for the kids whenever they were in the car together. (The kids liked both so much that Family Nights moved quickly to a weekly affair and eventually the tapes were in every available stereo, whether in the car, the house, or Grandma's house.)

For the individual plans they decided, since all their children were in the Bible story age, that they would sit down together as a family before bed and read Bible stories. (They chose a good Bible story-book—see "Tips for Choosing a Bible for Your Child" on page 166—and got everyone ready for bed before reading. The anticipation of this time actually helped speed up the getting-ready-for-bed routine. Since there were three kids, and since Dad had only two knees, David usually ended up on his dad's head.)

Then, to reinforce the idea that each of their children needed a daily time with God, they separated the kids for their own prayer time. They staggered their kids' bedtimes so they could start with the youngest and move to the oldest and still have everyone down on time. Nathan usually read another Bible story out of his own early reader Bible while he waited for Mom or Dad to get to him. Mom used *Bedtime Blessings* to help her with Brianna's alone time, and Dad told another story to David or answered his questions about the one they had just read. Kevin and Cindy got the *My Prayer Calendar* by Shirley Dobson (Gospel Light) so that they would be sure to move their children forward consistently with their prayers.

Basic Plan

They also started out slowly:
• Once a week: Attend church.

- Once a week (usually on Wednesday nights): Do a spiritual training time with each child.
- Once every other week (on Friday): Have a family activity night.
- And once a day: Pray for each child (at bedtime).

Support Plan

To make sure that they were taking every opportunity to incorporate spiritual training naturally into their everyday routine, Cindy spent some extra time going through the book *Your Child and the Christian Life* by Rick Osborne with K. Christie Bowler (Moody), which gave her lots of ideas and practical helps in that area.

The one problem they faced was that they had not found anyone with whom they could share their efforts to help their family grow spiritually and who could be a support to them. Here's where the Bannisters had to be creative.

They had Cindy's parents over for dinner and explained what their Family Spiritual Growth Plan was and asked if they could help in some way. Her parents were excited and offered to help by supporting them in prayer and contributing to the family fun part of the Spiritual Growth Plan. Whenever presents were being purchased for the kids, they made sure that fun things with spiritual content were included: videos, games, audio tapes, magazines, software, and picture books, all from the Christian bookstore. They also came over from time to time and got involved in the Family Night activity, spending time telling their grandkids about the things God had done for them in their lives.

Now It's Your Turn to Create Your Family Spiritual Growth Program

Step 1: Review and Make Sure You Have All Your Information

Before going to Step 2, make sure you have completed all the forms and charts in the earlier chapters in Part II. You will need all the information to complete your family and individual Spiritual Growth Plans. You'll save time by collecting it all now rather than trying to locate it as you go. The best way, if you have access to a photocopier, is to copy all the completed forms and put them together in a folder or binder. This helps you as you complete your plan now, and it will be readily available for future reference when you find that you want to revise your plan at a later date.

Step 2: Put Together the Family Spiritual Growth Plan

Once you have all the information filled in and gathered together from the previous charts, start filling in Our Family Profile and Our Family Spiritual Growth Plan in the charts that follow. Be as detailed as you can. As you fill out these charts, you may want to do them in pencil first. Some of what you write down you may want to adjust once you've met with the whole family to discuss it (see Steps 4 and 5).

Completing Your Family Spiritual Growth Plan

The first thing to do is to bring forward the information you have put together in the preceding chapters. In the chart on the opposite page, fill in your family's profile:

A. Your family's history of faith (from page 72);

B. Your family's pace (from page 78);

C. Your family's passions (from pages 84–85)

D. Your children's ages and stages;

E. Your family members' personalities (from page 96).

Now move from your family's characteristics to your family's activities.

F. Write down what you are already doing as a family that falls under the umbrella of spiritual growth training, such as going to church and Sunday school, praying with your children at bedtime, and so forth. Include approximately how much time you spend per week on each and how much time altogether. These activities should be added later in your plan with the things you will commit to doing.

On page 256 you will begin to plan what you are actually going to do: which methods, models, and tools you will use. Choose ones that match or complement the profile of your family from page 255. For example, if you have identified yourself as an F-16 family, don't pick methods and tools that require sitting still together for long periods of time. If you find yourself having trouble matching methods and tools to your family, re-read the three examples of families who did this on pages 237–253. Then come back and complete your plan.

A TO F. OUR FAMILY PROFILE

A. History of Faith (circle):

You: *1st   2nd   3rd*   Generation   Your Spouse: *1st   2nd   3rd*   Generation

B. We are a   ❏ Carriage family   ❏ Steam engine family   ❏ F-16 family

C. Family Interests:

_____   _____

_____   _____

_____   _____

D. Ages of Children   0-4   5-6   7-9   10-12   0-4   5-6   7-9   10-12

_____   ❏   ❏   ❏   ❏   _____   ❏   ❏   ❏   ❏

_____   ❏   ❏   ❏   ❏   _____   ❏   ❏   ❏   ❏

_____   ❏   ❏   ❏   ❏   _____   ❏   ❏   ❏   ❏

E. Family Members' Personalities
(Lion, Otter, Beaver, Golden Retriever, or combination)

_____   _____/_____   _____   _____/_____

_____   _____/_____   _____   _____/_____

_____   _____/_____   _____   _____/_____

F. As a family, we are already doing the following:

Activity: _____   *est. time per week:* _____ minutes.

Activity: _____   *est. time per week:* _____ minutes.

Activity: _____   *est. time per week:* _____ minutes.

Activity: _____   *est. time per week:* _____ minutes.

Activity: _____   *est. time per week:* _____ minutes.

Total estimated time per week: _____ minutes.

255

G. FAMILY ACTIVITIES

BASIC PLAN
- ❑ *Church*
- ❑ *Traditional Devotions*
  - ❑ Resource book
  - ❑ Family Bible
  - ❑ Other _____
- ❑ *Bedtime*
  - ❑ Discussions
  - ❑ Resource book
  - ❑ Bible or Bible storybook
  - ❑ Other _____
- ❑ *Mealtime*
  - ❑ Discussions
  - ❑ Discussions resource book
  - ❑ Other _____
- ❑ *Drive Time*
  - ❑ Discussions and games
  - ❑ Discussions and games resource book
  - ❑ Audio tapes
  - ❑ Music
- ❑ *Family Nights*
  - ❑ Family Nights resource books
  - ❑ Other _____

SUPPORT PLAN
- ❑ *Fun Time*
  - ❑ Board games
  - ❑ Videos
  - ❑ Audio tapes
  - ❑ Software
- ❑ *Special Times and Events*
  - ❑ *Holidays*
    - ❑ Gospel storybook
    - ❑ Gospel story video
    - ❑ Children's holiday storybooks
    - ❑ Other _____
  - ❑ *Celebrations, Events, Ceremonies*
    - ❑ Activity ideas resource books
    - ❑ Other _____
- ❑ *Teachable Moments*
  - ❑ Idea resource books
  - ❑ Question and answer resource books
  - ❑ Other _____

Completing Your Family Spiritual Growth Plan (continued)

G. On the checklist to the left, check off the activities you have chosen as most suited to your family's personality and needs.

Then, under each activity you've chosen, check off the type of tools you would like.

Later, under Step 6, Action Steps, you'll find a specific checklist of books and other tools that you can use as resources.

H. You are now ready to fill in your Family Spiritual Growth Plan on the opposite page. As you fill in this page, remember:

Basic Plan

- It is okay to have only one or two activities in addition to going to church if you think that works best for you. Don't set the bar too high at first. You will probably achieve more by doing less initially.
- Be specific about days and times. The less specific you are, the greater the chance that some of these activities will simply fall by the wayside, perhaps without anyone noticing.

Support Plan

- *Fun Times.* Make sure you choose some things from Fun Time (such as games, videos, etc.) so that as an informal addition to your plan you can sprinkle your family fun and entertainment times with spiritual content.
- *Special Times and Events.* Even if holidays (Christmas, Easter) are still far in the future, select an activity now and put it into your plan at the next family meeting.
- *Teachable Moments.* You will not need to commit to a certain amount of time. Rather, it is good to be ready for spiritual training opportunities by preparing yourself for your children's questions and problems.

H. OUR FAMILY SPIRITUAL GROWTH PLAN

BASIC PLAN

Regular activities we plan to do (or continue to do):

Activity: _____

How often? _____ times per _____   Specific day(s) or night(s)? _____

Estimated time per activity: _____ *minutes; estimated time per week:* _____ *minutes*

Activity: _____

How often? _____ times per _____   Specific day(s) or night(s)? _____

Estimated time per activity: _____ *minutes; estimated time per week:* _____ *minutes*

Activity: _____

How often? _____ times per _____   Specific day(s) or night(s)? _____

Estimated time per activity: _____ *minutes; estimated time per week:* _____ *minutes*

Activity: _____

How often? _____ times per _____   Specific day(s) or night(s)? _____

Estimated time per activity: _____ *minutes; estimated time per week:* _____ *minutes*

Total estimated time per week: _____ *minutes*

SUPPORT PLAN

Fun Times (ideas) _____

_____

Resources? _____

Special Times and Events (ideas) _____

_____

Resources? _____

Teachable Moments (ideas) _____

_____

Resources? _____

Step 3: Put Together the Individual Growth Plan for Each Family Member

Your Kids

In Step 2 you dealt with the things your family can do together as a family. Here your focus is on each individual's characteristics and differences. The steps are similar to those in Step 2. Remember the low-bar approach—that is, keep the bar low by your *child's* standards, not yours! Also, make sure that you base your choice of ideas and tools for use in the individual plan on your child's personality and needs as you've determined them in the earlier chapters.

You

Complete a plan with or for each child—and complete a chart for yourself (have your spouse complete one as well if yours is a two-parent family). Just as you give your children time and help in growing spiritually, so God wants to give you time to grow. Your needs are different from those of your children, but if you want to give them what they need spiritually, you must also receive spiritual renewal and refreshment. You may need, in addition to your daily Bible reading and prayer, an hour during the week by yourself to pray, study the Bible in more depth, or just sit quietly in God's presence. Or you may need the support you gain from attending a small fellowship group or Bible study group once every two weeks. Meeting your own spiritual needs is part of your responsibility in training your children.

You and Your Spouse

If yours is a two-parent family, set up your own and your spouse's plan together so you can give each other support and encouragement in sticking with your plans. Discussing your individual plans with each other may also give you both an opportunity to get a deeper insight into each other's spiritual and personal needs.

Completing the Individual Spiritual Growth Plans

Completing the Individual Spiritual Growth Plan is similar to completing the Family Plan.

A–D. Simply bring forward the information you've gathered in the first sections of Part II.

E. Since each individual is unique, he or she may have special characteristics that could have an impact on the individual's Spiritual Growth Plan. These could include things such as special needs or special strengths.

F–G. As we have said a number of times, a person's chronological age does not necessarily reflect his or her spiritual age. This applies especially to the area of *knowing*. A child of 10 may be ready to understand more complex concepts than a child of 3, but if the 10-year-old has never been exposed to Christian truth before, it is necessary for him or her to go back and learn the basics of the Christian faith first.

A TO G. INDIVIDUAL SPIRITUAL GROWTH PLAN

Name: _____

A. Age: _____

B. Stage: _____

C. Interests:

❏ _____

❏ _____

❏ _____

❏ _____

D. Personality: _____ / _____

   Strengths: _____

   _____

   _____

   _____

   Potential weaknesses: _____

   _____

   _____

E. Special Characteristics: _____

   _____

   _____

   _____

F. Where he or she is at in terms of spiritual growth: _____

   _____

   _____

   _____

G. Things I (we) need to do or give special attention to: _____

   _____

   _____

   _____

   _____

Completing the Individual Spiritual Growth Plans (continued)

H. Now go through the list and check off those things you want to do with this child. The Bedtime category is for kids ages 0–9, the Quiet Time is for kids 10–12. In these two categories, checking off prayer and one of the Bible-related selections would be a minimum.

You'll have an opportunity to select specific books and other resources later (in Step 6, Action Steps), as well as a Bible that is appropriate for your child's age.

I. Finally, you're ready to get specific and fill out the actual Individual Spiritual Growth Plan.

Step 4: Have a Family Meeting

At this point, it is good to discuss Our Family Spiritual Growth Plan, its details as well as its importance, with the whole family. Rather than it being something you impose on them (a recipe for failure), getting the family's input will make them part of the decision as to what the plan will look like. Make this discussion an enjoyable time. (The *only* thing that should not be open for discussion is whether or not you'll have a plan.) Then ask for everyone's input and listen to what each person says. Be willing to modify the plan, especially in its details.

Also, emphasize to the kids that the details of the plan are not a forever thing. Set a time—perhaps one, two, or three months in the future—when you as a family will review the plan to see if it is working and, if necessary, come up with new ideas and changes. Remember to discuss the family fun times ideas as well. Your kids will find it easier if there is a fun part to look forward to.

Use your best judgment as to whether you want to deal with the kids' individual plans strictly on a one-to-one basis or share them with the rest of the family. In some situations (and for some kids) confidentiality is extremely important and sharing an individual plan with the rest of the family could violate trust. You can also decide whether to share your own individual plan with the rest of the family.

Have a photocopy of the Family Commitment Card (on page 262) ready. Once you've decided on the details have everyone sign the card before serving or going out for a favorite family treat to celebrate. This celebration becomes a great Memory Marker.

H TO I. INDIVIDUAL SPIRITUAL GROWTH PLAN

Name: _____

H. INDIVIDUAL ACTIVITIES

❏ *Church Related*
  ❏ Sunday school
  ❏ Vacation Bible school
  ❏ Church clubs/groups
  ❏ Other _____

❏ *Bedtime (ages 0–9)*
  ❏ Blessings
  ❏ Bible stories
  ❏ Prayer
  ❏ Audio
  ❏ Devotions
  ❏ Other _____

❏ *Quiet Time (ages 10–12)*
  ❏ Prayer
  ❏ Devotional
  ❏ Bible reading
  ❏ Other _____

❏ *Exploration Time*
  ❏ Study tools
  ❏ Kid's study Bible
  ❏ Other _____

I. SPECIFICALLY. . .

Regular Activities We Plan to Do (or continue to do):
(Remember, 5–10 minutes per child per weekday)

Activity: _____

How often? _____ times per _____ Specific day(s) or night(s)? _____
  Estimated time per activity: _____ *minutes; estimated time per week:* _____ *minutes*

Activity: _____

How often? _____ times per _____ Specific day(s) or night(s)? _____
  Estimated time per activity: _____ *minutes; estimated time per week:* _____ *minutes*

Church-related (involvement and ideas): _____

_____

Exploration Time (ideas): _____

_____

Resources for exploration time: _____

_____

Memory Markers and Special Events: Dedication ____ Salvation ____ Confirmation ____ Baptism ____
Birthday ____ Spiritual birthday ____ Starting faith journal ____ Other _____

Activity: _____ Date: _____

Activity: _____ Date: _____

Activity: _____ Date: _____

FAMILY COMMITMENT CARD

On this _____ day of _____, 20_____,

we are making a commitment before our God.

We, the family in this home, commit to fulfilling the task of spiritual training.

With God's help we will take up this God-given task. We, the parent(s) will

keep God's ways on our heart(s) and "impress them on our child[ren]. We'll

talk about them when we sit at home, when we walk along the road, when

we lie down and when we get up" (per Deuteronomy 6:6–7).

Signed by our hands—held in the heart:

_____   _____

_____   _____

_____   _____

Step 5: Finalize the Family Plan and the Individual Plans

On a blank photocopy of the form (or on the form you've been using, after erasing what you have written in pencil), write down the activities you have all agreed on, with times and dates where applicable. You could put it on the refrigerator or frame it and put it next to the signed commitment card in a place where you'll see it regularly. In the same way, finalize the individual plans.

Step 6: Decide on Action Steps

The specific action steps depend, of course, on the activities you have chosen as part of your plan.

ACTION STEPS

BASIC PLAN

- When will you start (specific date and time)? _____

- What do you need to get started, such as books, videos, or other materials for your family plan and individual plans? To help you make this simple, on pages 264–265 is a Specific Resource Checklist with books, tools, and materials we've recommended earlier in the book.

  _____

  _____

  _____

- What is needed by way of preparation for the first event?

  _____

  _____

  _____

SUPPORT PLAN

- What fun time things do you need?

  _____

  _____

- What are you going to do to prepare for or remind yourself of teachable moments?

  _____

  _____

- What do you need to do to get your support person or group in place? By when?

  _____

  _____

- After you have been using your plan for a period of time, which family would you like to share your experience with? _____

SPECIFIC RESOURCE CHECKLIST

C – Children's Resource   **P – Parenting Resource**   **F – Family Resource**

CHURCH-RELATED SPIRITUAL TRAINING

❏ *I Want to Know About the Church* (p. 402) C

TOOLS FOR THE FAMILY

Family Nights

❏ *An Introduction to Family Nights* (p. 409) F
❏ *Family Nights Tool Chest: Basic Christian Beliefs* (p. 409) F
❏ *Family Nights Tool Chest: Christian Character Qualities* (p. 409) F
❏ *Family Nights Tool Chest: Holidays* (p. 409) F
❏ *Family Nights Tool Chest: Larry Burkett's Money Matters* (p. 409) F
❏ *Family Nights Tool Chest: Proverbs* (p. 409) F
❏ *Family Nights Tool Chest: Ready for Adolescence (available 2001)* (p. 409) F
❏ *Family Nights Tool Chest: Simple Science* (p. 409) F
❏ *Family Nights Tool Chest: The Ten Commandments* (p. 409) F
❏ *Family Nights Tool Chest: Wisdom Life Skills* (p. 409) F
❏ New Testament Bible Stories for Preschoolers (p. 409) F
❏ Old Testament Bible Stories for Preschoolers (p. 409) F

Mealtime

❏ *Mealtime Moments* (p. 423) F

Drive Time

❏ *Adventures in Odyssey*** (p. 407–408) C
❏ *Joy Ride!* (p. 423) F

Bedtime

❏ *Amazing Treasure Bible Storybook, The* (p. 402) C
❏ *Bedtime Blessings* (p. 422) C
❏ *Teaching Your Child How to Pray* (p. 419) P

Traditional Devotions

❏ *FaithTraining* (p. 417) P
❏ *Family Walk Devotional Bible, The* (p. 423) F
❏ *Family Walk Devotional Series, The* (p. 422–423) F

Fun Time
Audiocassettes and CDs

❏ *Adventures in Odyssey*** (p. 407–408) C
❏ *Bible Eyewitness—New Testament*** (p. 408) C
❏ *Bible Eyewitness—Old Testament*** (p. 408) C
❏ *Legend of Squanto, The*** (p. 406) F, C
❏ *Lion, the Witch, and the Wardrobe, The*** (p. 406) F, C
❏ *Magician's Nephew, The*** (p. 406) F, C

Videos

❏ *Adventures in Odyssey* (p. 407) C
❏ *Jay Jay the Jet Plane* (p. 404) C
❏ *Last Chance Detectives, The* (p. 404) C
❏ *McGee and Me* (p. 405) C
❏ *StoryKeepers, The* (p. 405) C
❏ *Veggie Tales* (p. 405) C

SPECIFIC RESOURCE CHECKLIST

C – Children's Resource   P – Parenting Resource   F – Family Resource

Board Games

- ❏ *Book Game, The* (p. 406) F, C
- ❏ *House Rules Game* (p. 406) F, C
- ❏ *Sticky Situations* (p. 406) F, C
- ❏ *The Money Matters for Kids Game* (p. 408) F, C
- ❏ *WWJD? Game, The* (p. 406) F, C

TOOLS FOR INDIVIDUAL GROWTH

(See page 166 for tips on choosing a Bible)

- ❏ Bible for _____: _____
- ❏ Bible for _____: _____
- ❏ Bible for _____: _____
- ❏ Bible for _____: _____
- ❏ Bible for _____: _____
- ❏ Bible for _____: _____

Quiet Time

- ❏ *NIrV Kids' Quest Study Bible, The* (p. 403) C
- ❏ *My Time With God* (p. 423) C

Exploration Time

- ❏ *801 Questions Kids Ask About God* (p. 417) P
- ❏ *Adventure Bible Handbook* (p. 402) C
- ❏ *I Want to Know . . . series, The* (p. 402) C
- ❏ *Kidcordance* (p. 403) C
- ❏ *NIrV Kids' Quest Study Bible, The* (p. 403) C

SPECIAL TIMES AND EVENTS

Holidays

- ❏ *A Christmas Carol* * * (p. 406) F, C
- ❏ *Family Nights Tool Chest: Holidays* (p. 410) F
- ❏ *Your Child and Jesus* (p. 418) F

Meaningful Memories

- ❏ *Family Traditions* (p. 409) P
- ❏ *Let's Make a Memory* (p. 415) F

Blessing Ceremonies

- ❏ *Bedtime Blessings* (p. 422) C
- ❏ *Gift of the Blessing, The* (p. 423) P
- ❏ *Pictures the Heart Remembers* (p. 423–424) P

Teachable Moments

- ❏ *801 Questions Kids Ask About God* (p. 417) P
- ❏ *Your Child and Jesus* (p. 418) F
- ❏ *Your Child and the Bible* (p. 418) F
- ❏ *Your Child and the Christian Life* (p. 418) F

* *Audio products

Step 7: Celebrate Your Success!

God will bless you and your family as you seek to help them grow spiritually, one little picture at a time. Remember to undergird your family and their spiritual growth each day in prayer.

Going for Bronze, Silver, and Gold!

Once you begin your Family Spiritual Growth Plan, it helps to have a special celebration after completing the first three months, the first six months, and the first year (or whatever intervals you decide on). Award yourselves a medal or a certificate, created by one or more members of the family. This certificate can be placed alongside your commitment card and your signed plan on the refrigerator (or wherever you put yours).

At a family meeting at the end of the designated period, take a short time to evaluate your family plan and your individual plans. Let everyone say what they like and suggest any changes they would like to see. Be prepared by reviewing Section C (Ideas and Methods, pages 137–228) beforehand, so that you can suggest other things you might try.

If one of your children has a significant problem with his or her individual plan, let the child know that the two of you will talk it over and come up with some alternate suggestions.

Remember that you want your whole family to take ownership of and responsibility for their spiritual growth. The more input you allow them, the more they will feel that this whole program is theirs.

You may also need to talk about consistency if you haven't been as regular about following your plan as you would have liked. Don't get heavy-handed with this; often it's small or practical things—such as having chosen a difficult night—that cause this to happen. Just ask for ideas and suggestions from everyone on how you can overcome the obstacles, and then adjust your plan.

Now quickly get on to celebrating your victories—have a great dessert and break out the craft supplies or the computer to create a Memory Marker together.

The point of the certificate is not that it be a work of art. Nor does it have to look like a solemn Sunday school award. Rather, it can be a way to involve the younger members of the family. They can use clip art, crayons, pictures cut from magazines, or whatever it takes them to create a cheerful certificate. You can decide on the text together and write it longhand or create the certificate on the computer together with your kids (and let the younger kids add their crayon touches to it). Don't worry if you end up with a certificate that looks like a Picasso reject. What matters is marking the achievement and involving the family in this unique Memory Marker.

May God bless, keep, encourage, and strengthen you and yours as you seek to better know and love and live for Jesus!

PART III

The Content of Your Spiritual Legacy

From Hugs to Hosannahs: What Your 0–4-Year-Old Can Learn

From Friendships to Faith: What Your 5–6-Year-Old Can Learn

From Bikes to Bibles: What Your 7–9-Year-Old Can Learn

From Wrestling to Worship: What Your 10–12-Year-Old Can Learn

Truths Worth Teaching: What Your Children Need to Know

"When I saw it," says John, a father of two, "I couldn't believe it."

There he was with his son, playing air hockey at one of those pizza-and-game emporiums. As the plastic puck clicked back and forth, he spied something strange over by the Skee-Ball—a boy who'd climbed atop one of the lanes. Instead of rolling the balls, the boy was striding to the end of the alley and dropping them directly into the "100" hole. With each bogus bull's-eye he fooled the machinery into reeling out yards of unearned prize tickets.

Where did this kid get the idea that cheating and stealing are okay? John wondered. His question was answered minutes later when he and his son ventured to the Skee-Ball themselves. By now the young cheater had stopped playing, but his little sister and brother were toddling down alleys of their own, dropping balls into holes, churning out more tickets. Nearby sat the person who'd taught all three children this scheme. She was giving specific instructions and launching the kids toward their targets, apparently unconcerned about whether anyone might be watching.

Who was she? Their mother!

"I just stared," John recalls. "I thought parents were supposed to *discourage* this sort of behavior, not *direct* it."

As John saw that day, knowing *how* to teach isn't the only thing a parent needs to know. That mom was an effective tutor—but the values she was passing on to her children were warped indeed.

What you teach your children can make all the difference—especially when it comes to spiritual training. That's why you'll find in this section the "what" of your spiritual legacy; key truths of the Christian faith you'll want to pass on to your children.

Here you'll see answers to questions like these:

◆ What are my children ready to learn and understand at their ages?
◆ How can I be sure I've covered the essentials?
◆ What are some practical ways to teach each of these truths?

As you scan this section, you may wonder how you could ever teach this many truths in a lifetime, let alone during your children's preteen years. You may fear that you're supposed to make your kids memorize and recite the content, like a catechism. You may feel your children's abilities or interests don't fit those described for their age levels. You may believe some topics have been overemphasized—and others left out.

No problem! Rest assured that

◆ You can cover the topics as you like, in the order that suits you, at your own pace. It's a good idea to read through the chapters covering your children's ages in order to get an overview, but feel free to start by choosing just one or two topics that especially interest you and your children now.
◆ The truths are meant to be communicated in your own words, reflecting your style and feelings. Your children need to understand and apply them, not memorize them and recite them back to you.
◆ Every child is unique, developing at his or her own speed. Don't worry if your kids don't seem able to grasp a topic that's listed at their age level. Simply wait until they can. The important thing is for them to grow in their relationship with God, not just to learn facts.
◆ Your outlook, experience, denominational background—all these will influence how you choose to emphasize, de-emphasize, or add to the topics in this section. Great care has gone into their selection, but the list is not exhaustive.

You'll find truths arranged under five headings:

These headings are the same for all stages—ages 0–4, 5–6, 7–9, and 10–12. The first two headings, "Who God Is" and "What God Has Done," deal with *knowing about God*. The third, "You Can Have a Relationship with God," addresses *loving God*. The last two, "You Can Be All God Wants You to Be" and "You Can Do All God Wants You to Do," deal with *living with and for God*. Listed under each of these five headings are the topics that children in that age group can grasp.

To find a particular topic, check the charts on the following pages. Then flip through the chapter that corresponds to the age group listed to locate the topic you want.

If you're new to spiritual training and your child is older than four, you'll want to read the chapter(s) covering previous age levels, in case there are truths you need to catch up on. If your child is about to move from one stage to another, try reading ahead to prepare yourself.

As you read, you may discover truths you didn't know. That's great! See this as an opportunity to learn along with your children. Spiritual training isn't just for children; it's for all of us who want to better know and serve the God who loves us.

Ages 0–4

KNOWING		LOVING	LIVING	
A. Who God Is	**B.** What God Has Done	**C.** You Can Have a Relationship with God	**D.** You Can Be All God Wants You to Be	**E.** You Can Do All God Wants You to Do
1. God exists.	5. God created everything.	9. Prayer is talking to God in Jesus' name.	12. God wants you to be good, kind, and loving, just like Him and Jesus.	14. God wants you to go to church.
2. God loves you.	6. God created you.	10. You need to talk to God regularly.	13. God wants you to see and think good things.	15. God wants you to obey your parents.
3. Jesus loves you.	7. God gave us the Bible.	11. You need to regularly listen to stories about God and Jesus from the Bible.		16. God wants you to learn to share your things with others.
4. God wants to take care of you.	8. God's Son, Jesus, died for your sins so you can be with God.			

Ages 5-6

KNOWING		LOVING	LIVING	
A. Who God Is	**B.** What God Has Done	**C.** You Can Have a Relationship with God	**D.** You Can Be All God Wants You to Be	**E.** You Can Do All God Wants You to Do

A. Who God Is

17. God is your loving Father. He wants to guide, teach, love, protect, and provide for you.

18. In some ways, you are just like God. He has feelings and thoughts. He can understand you. Jesus showed us who God is and what He's like.

19. In other ways, you are very different from God. He is everywhere, He can do anything, and He knows everything.

20. Jesus has always been with God and is God.

B. What God Has Done

21. God tells you about Himself, His Son, Jesus, and His plan for you in the Bible: The One Big Story.

22. God sent His Son, Jesus Christ, to die for you.

23. God has prepared a place for you in heaven. Jesus is coming back for you.

C. You Can Have a Relationship with God

24. You can have a relationship with God by accepting what Jesus did for you: Salvation.

25. God wants to have a relationship with you.

26. You can talk to God through prayer.

27. You can thank God and Jesus for all They've done and still do for you.

28. You can ask God for wisdom and guidance.

29. You can read about God and His Son, Jesus, in the Bible or in a Bible storybook. You begin to have personal Bible reading and time with God.

D. You Can Be All God Wants You to Be

30. God has a plan for you.

31. The Bible tells you the kind of person God wants you to be.

32. God's way works best. You can be all God wants you to be by following Jesus.

33. God wants you to put only good things into your heart.

34. When you sin, you should ask God to forgive you—and He will.

E. You Can Do All God Wants You to Do

35. God wants you to spend time with other Christians, both at church and in the community.

36. God wants you to help others and be nice to them.

37. God wants you to obey Him and follow Jesus in everything.

38. God wants you to share and take good care of everything He gives you: Stewardship.

39. God wants you to understand and memorize Bible verses.

Ages 7-9

KNOWING

A. Who God Is

40. You can be sure that God is real.

41. There is only one God.

42. God exists in three Persons: Father, Son, and Holy Spirit. This is called the "Trinity."

43. God (Father, Son, and Holy Spirit) is eternal.

44. Jesus is both God and Man.

45. Nothing exists apart from God.

46. God's character is true, honest, loving, compassionate, generous, selfless, forgiving, merciful, trustworthy, faithful, just, impartial, and holy.

B. What God Has Done

47. The Bible is true. It is God's Word, and you can trust it.

48. God made sure all stories in the Bible together tell the One Big Story.

49. The Bible you have is exactly what God wanted to give you.

50. God wants you to learn and study the Bible.

51. The world is full of sin. There is an enemy in the world (Satan). Not everyone obeys God.

52. Jesus died to save you from the penalty for sin.

53. Jesus defeated sin and Satan.

54. Jesus is the only way to God.

LOVING

C. You Can Have a Relationship with God

55. You read the Bible to learn about who God is (Father, Son, and Holy Spirit) and what He has done and is doing.

56. You can pray your own prayers with your parents.

57. Prayer benefits you in many ways.

58. Keep praying: persistence, tests, and trials.

59. You can trust God and turn your life over to Him.

60. You should learn to seek God.

61. Jesus gives you peace.

LIVING

D. You Can Be All God Wants You to Be

62. God wants you to learn and grow and become like Jesus.

63. Growth is a learning process.

64. Your character should match God's character.

65. God wants you to develop your talents.

66. God wants you to develop the Fruit of the Spirit.

67. God wants you to mature and develop your personality.

E. You Can Do All God Wants You to Do

68. Church is God's idea. Jesus is the head of the church. At church you learn about God and encourage each other to follow Jesus.

69. God wants you to understand what a blessing people and good relationships are.

70. God has taught you right from wrong. He did this to keep you safe and to give you a good life.

71. The Ten Commandments are a good guide for life.

72. God wants you to share your faith.

Ages 10–12

KNOWING

A.
Who God Is

B.
What God Has Done

LOVING

C.
You Can Have a Relationship with God

LIVING

D.
You Can Be All God Wants You to Be

E.
You Can Do All God Wants You to Do

73. Not everyone believes the truth about God, but there are ways you can respond to their objections. (Handling contrary opinions about God: basic apologetics; other religions)

74. God wants you to explore the One Big Story.

75. God put the Bible together in a fascinating way.

76. You need to learn how to study the Bible.

77. God lets His people serve Him and express their worship of Him in different ways.

78. God gave us an accurate record of His Son, Jesus.

79. God wants you to tell others about what Jesus has done.

80. Jesus will return as Judge and there will be a new heaven and a new earth.

81. You can pray on your own.

82. You can read the Bible on your own.

83. You can learn to worship God and Jesus on your own or in a group.

84. God wants you to choose to grow, learn, and seek His wisdom.

85. God's grace: You don't have to do it on our own. God is working in you by His Holy Spirit.

86. God wants you to find and follow His will for your life.

87. God wants you to choose to commit your entire life and everything you have to Him.

88. God wants you to choose His way because you love Him and want to be like Jesus.

89. God wants you to learn to seek and follow His Spirit's leading.

90. You need to learn how to resist Satan and temptation.

91. You need to get involved in church and find your place in the body of Christ.

CHAPTER 29

From Hugs to Hosannas: What Your 0–4-Year-Old Can Learn

Who God Is

Topic Nos. 1, 2, 3, 4

God Exists; God and Jesus Love You; God Wants to Take Care of You.

What do infants and toddlers need most? To be loved, accepted, and safe. Affirming that God loves and cares for them can begin the day your children are born. As you hold them, love them, feed them, and keep them warm, you establish that their world is good and safe. In time, as you tell them that God loves them and looks after them, they make the connection.

God Exists. (See Topic No. 40, *"You Can Be Sure That God Is Real."*)

❖ *"In the beginning God"* (Genesis 1:1).

❖ *"For since the creation of the world God's invisible qualities—his eternal power and divine nature—have been clearly seen, being understood from what has been made, so that men are without excuse"* (Romans 1:20).

God and Jesus Love You.

❖ *"We love because he first loved us"* (1 John 4:19).

❖ *"For God so loved the world that he gave his one and only Son "* (John 3:16).

KNOWING
A. Who God Is

1. God exists.
2. God loves you.
3. Jesus loves you.
4. God wants to take care of you.

277

God Wants to Take Care of You.

❖ *"Look at the birds of the air; they do not sow or reap or store away in barns, and yet your heavenly Father feeds them. Are you not much more valuable than they? . . . See how the lilies of the field grow. They do not labor or spin. . . . If that is how God clothes the grass of the field, which is here today and tomorrow is thrown into the fire, will he not much more clothe you, O you of little faith?"* (Matthew 6:26, 28, 30).

Hints and Helps

◆ One time to affirm God's existence and love is at bedtime. Try talking aloud to God as you rock your baby or give your toddler a back rub. At first your children won't know who God is because they can't see Him. But as you affirm His existence and love with verbal, visible, and emotional demonstrations, they'll take His reality for granted.

◆ How can you teach your children that God loves them? With hugs, smiles, and telling them *you* love them! Thus they learn what "love" means. As you add that God loves them, they'll know what that means too.

◆ When your children feel sick, affirm God's care and provision by comforting them, saying *you* care and that you want them to feel better. They'll see what "caring about them" means. When you add that God cares and wants them to feel better, they'll understand.

◆ If you're feeling uncertain about God's love and care yourself—perhaps due to money problems, illness, or other tough times—allow yourself to deal with your doubts. Try reading in the Gospels (Matthew, Mark, Luke, and John) to discover through the example of Jesus that God is loving, compassionate, kind, welcoming, forgiving, generous, healing, and providing. He desires to be all these things in your family's life. You may also want to work through your uncertainties with your pastor or a Christian counselor. Ask God to help you trust Him so that you can aid your children in doing the same.

What God Has Done

Topic Nos. 5, 6

God Created Everything; God Created You.

We all need to know that we're wanted and unique. So even before your children understand, tell them that God made them special. This shows His care for them and strengthens their sense of value. Let them know that God not only made them but that He made them purposefully and lovingly.

Tell them that God made everything else, too. This fact is your children's first glimpse of God's power and bigness.

❖ *"In the beginning God created the heavens and the earth"* (Genesis 1:1; see also 1:2–31).

❖ *"For you created my inmost being; you knit me together in my mother's womb"* (Psalm 139:13; see also 139:14–16).

Hints and Helps

◆ When you pray for and over your children, thank God for making them so special and for giving them to you and your family. Be as specific as you can. For example, at the end of a day in which your toddler built an especially tall tower of blocks, thank God for giving him or her a steady hand and a creative mind.

◆ Do your children like to see how tall they are, perhaps standing next to you or a height chart, or just looking in the mirror? Use these times to point out specific things about your children that God designed, such as eyes and mouth, ability to laugh and have fun, nose shape, and hair color.

◆ "God made everything" can be a tough concept for children at the younger end of this age group to grasp, since "everything" is so vast. So be concrete, pointing out individual items He made—a tree, flowers, mountains, other people, a pet. Choose things your child likes or is curious about.

KNOWING

**B.
What God Has
Done**

5. God created everything.

6. God created you.

7. God gave us the Bible.

8. God's Son, Jesus, died for your sins so you can be with God.

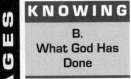

AGES 0–4

KNOWING

**B.
What God Has
Done**

5. God created everything.

6. God created you.

7. God gave us the Bible.

8. God's Son, Jesus, died for your sins so you can be with God.

Topic No. 7

God Gave Us the Bible.

Why do your children need to know early on that the Bible is God's book? Because it will be so basic to their relationship with God. It's a one-of-a-kind book that only God could have written (see Topic Nos. 47, 75). And He wrote it for you and your family!

Children also need to know that God's book is true—not just a storybook like others they look at or have read to them. Except for certain stories, such as parables, the events in the Bible really happened—and the people in it were real.

❖   *"All scripture is God-breathed"* (2 Timothy 3:16).

❖   See also Psalm 33:4; 119:160; John 5:39; 1 Thessalonians 2:13.

Hints and Helps

◆   As your children start with the simplest board books, give them simple Bible storybooks, too. Let them see your "grown-up" Bible and those of older siblings, explaining what these are and how you enjoy them. Help your toddler look forward to getting older and owning a Bible that has more of God's story in it.

◆   When possible, choose Bible storybooks that take your children from the beginning (creation and Adam and Eve) to the end (Jesus' resurrection, the growth of the church, and Jesus' return)—and that introduce the Bible's main characters. This helps youngsters to see that God's Word is more than a collection of unrelated events and people.

◆   Help your children understand the idea of "true" stories by saying something like, "I'm your Mommy (or Daddy). You're my child, and you live in Mommy (and/or Daddy's) house. That's a true story." Recount a recent incident involving the child and explain that this, too, is a true story. This prepares children to understand what you mean when you say that the Bible and the stories in it are true.

Topic No. 8

God's Son, Jesus, Died for Your Sins So You Can Be with God.

At the upper end of this age group, most children can grasp a very basic story. It might be expressed this way: "Everyone, even you, does some wrong things. These wrong things are sin and make God sad. But God loves us so much that He sent His Son, Jesus. Jesus died for us so that we could be forgiven and could be God's children. Just as you need to tell me you're sorry when you've done something wrong, you need to tell God you're sorry for doing wrong things and ask Him to forgive you because of what Jesus did. He will. From then on, you are God's child. And if you do anything wrong after that, you can ask God to forgive you and help you do better—and He will."

❖ *"For God so loved the world that he gave his one and only Son, that whoever believes in him shall not perish but have eternal life"* (John 3:16).

❖ *"For all have sinned and fall short of the glory of God, . . . The wages of sin is death, but the gift of God is eternal life in Christ Jesus our Lord"* (Romans 3:23; 6:23).

Hints and Helps

◆ Younger children may be baffled by the idea that Jesus "died on the cross," especially if they don't understand what death is. If you sense that a discussion of death would scare your preschooler, rather than inform, concentrate on talking about the love and actions of Jesus, especially the fact that He came to rescue us. When your child is ready to understand what it meant for Jesus to give His life, explain that part of the salvation story.

◆ Do you use time-outs, spankings, or lost privileges to discipline your child? Try mentioning these as you explain the concept of sin and how Jesus paid the price for ours. Children will understand how wrong acts displease God because they know how you respond when they disobey. Explain that wrong actions put a wide space between your children and God—one that they can't cross alone. That's why Jesus came—to make a way for them to cross back to God and be forgiven. If your children have already accepted Jesus, emphasize that they can go to God anytime, about anything, and ask Him to forgive them when they've done something wrong.

KNOWING

**B.
What God Has
Done**

5. God created everything.

6. God created you.

7. God gave us the Bible.

8. God's Son, Jesus, died for your sins so you can be with God.

AGES 0–4

LOVING

C.
You Can Have
a Relationship
with God

9. Prayer is talking to God in Jesus' name.

10. You need to talk to God regularly.

11. You need to regularly listen to stories about God and Jesus from the Bible.

You Can Have a Relationship with God

Topic Nos. 9, 10

Prayer Is Talking to God in Jesus' Name; You Need to Talk to God Regularly.

How do young children learn about relationships? By watching and interacting with you! Explain that just as the closeness between you and your children grows as you spend time talking, so closeness to God grows through prayer—which is simply talking to Him. You'll want to mention that prayer has its differences; for instance it often helps to close your eyes when you do it, to help you concentrate. And prayers often include the words "in Jesus' name" because Jesus is the One whose sacrifice made it possible for us to be close to God.

Let children know that God hears them and wants to help them, just as you hear and want to help. But God is much bigger than you are, and He knows best how to take care of them. They can talk to Him about anything; God loves to hear from them, just as you do. And since being close to God is so important, talking with Him needs to go on the list of things we do every day.

❖ *"In everything, by prayer and petition, with thanksgiving, present your requests to God. And the peace of God, which transcends all understanding, will guard your hearts and your minds in Christ Jesus"* (Philippians 4:6–7).

❖ *"Pray continually"* (1 Thessalonians 5:17).

Hints and Helps

◆ Before your children have learned to speak, let them hear you pray as often as you can. In addition to mealtimes and bedtimes, try praying at "odd" times—perhaps carrying them from the car to their room as they're falling asleep, or when you encounter a beautiful cloud formation during a walk. As you establish the habit, they'll be more likely to pick it up.

◆ As much as possible, let praying be easy and enjoyable—even fun!

While uncontrollable giggles can spoil a prayer time, feel free to pray about funny things that happened during the day, for example, thanking God that you got to share a "Knock, Knock" joke or see the dog chasing its tail. To fit attention spans at this age, try keeping your prayers short and to the point.

- Be yourself! Prayer doesn't have to be formal or use certain words. When you pray with your children, favor words and language that are part of their normal, everyday speech—and yours. Requiring formal, unfamiliar language implies that God is "foreign" and unknowable, and that children must put on an act in His presence. Allow your prayers to reflect your feelings, too; if you're excited, for instance, let it show!

- At the younger end of this stage, it's likely that you'll say the prayers and your children will listen. Let them know that these are *their* prayers, and that you are praying in order to show them how it's done. Ask children what they'd like you to pray about. As children progress through this stage, move them toward praying with you. Near the end of this stage, help them begin to pray their own prayers.

- Pray about anything and everything, especially things that already interest your children. For example, if a child is learning to clean up his toys, pray, "Dear God, help Jimmy to be a big boy and put his toys away." This leads children to realize that God cares about the things that are important to them.

- From time to time, take a break from prayer itself to remind children why you're praying—and to whom. Remind them that God is really there, listening, and that they don't have to work hard to get their prayers through to Him. He's ready and willing to answer.

Topic No. 11

You Need to Regularly Listen to Stories About God and Jesus from the Bible.

Even at this age, children can spend time each day focused on God. As consistently as you can, read to them from a Bible storybook—or tell a Bible story yourself! When you do, remind them why you are

LOVING

C.
You Can Have a Relationship with God

9. Prayer is talking to God in Jesus' name.

10. You need to talk to God regularly.

11. You need to regularly listen to stories about God and Jesus from the Bible.

LIVING

D.
You Can Be All
God Wants You
to Be

12. God wants you to be good, kind, and loving, just like Him and Jesus.

13. God wants you to see and think good things.

doing it: to learn more about God and to get to know Him. Explain that God's Book tells them what He's like, how He acts, and how He wants them to act.

❖ *"The unfolding of your words gives light; it gives understanding to the simple. I open my mouth and pant, longing for your commands"* (Psalm 119:130–131).

❖ *"And how from infancy you have known the holy scriptures, which are able to make you wise for salvation through faith in Christ Jesus"* (2 Timothy 3:15).

Hints and Helps

♦ If you can tell Bible stories on your own, make the experience fun! Let your children add sound effects (stomping feet for thunder, slapping knees for rain, etc.). Include as much drama and expression in your voice as you can. Older children in this stage may also be able to tell the stories back to you!

♦ To remind your children that a Bible or Bible storybook is different from other books, approach it differently. Before you open it, try asking God to help you and your children understand what you read. This will also serve as a good model later as they begin to read the Bible on their own.

♦ If the Bible storybook you're using provides a lesson, deal with it briefly and try to relate it to the day's events. It's not necessary to pull a "lesson" out of each story, however. Be open to children's questions, allowing time for and encouraging discussion.

You Can Be All God Wants You to Be

Topic No. 12

God Wants You to Be Good, Kind, and Loving, Just Like Him and Jesus.

Your children may learn quickly that there's a right way of *behaving*. But do they know there's a right way of *being*? Correct behavior comes out of correct being. The perfect model for being *and* behavior is God Himself—as Jesus, His Son, has shown us.

❖ *"My command is this: Love each other as I have loved you"* (John 15:12).

Hints and Helps

♦ When your children do something wrong, focus on saying and demonstrating what they *should* have done, not just on what they did wrong. Say something like "Next time we can do it God's way." Be brief with this process, quickly moving on to hugs and fun things that reinforce your expectation that they will want to follow the example of Jesus.

♦ For younger children, you'll need to show what it means to be kind, good, and loving. For example, if two-year-old Marie hits brother Ken on the head, kneel down at Marie's level and give her a brief lesson on the topic of touch. Say something like "When you touch people, you need to be kind and gentle, like Jesus. If you want to touch Ken, this is how you should do it." Take her hand and help her pat Ken's arm. Explain that this kind of touch makes a person feel happy and loved.

♦ When talking with your children about being kind and loving, do it in a kind, loving way. It's easy to be harsh when a child has just done wrong, but that doesn't affirm goodness. If necessary, give yourself a few minutes to calm down before speaking. When you do, try to phrase your guidance as positively as you can. For example, affirm that kindness and goodness are part of your family identity: "Because we love Jesus, this is how we act in our family."

Topic No. 13

God Wants You to See and Think Good Things.

Children this age often can't separate what's going on inside (thoughts and feelings) from what comes out (actions). As they progress through the stage, though, you can begin to help them realize that seeing and thinking good, kind, loving things will help them to *be* good, kind, and loving.

❖ *"The good man brings good things out of the good stored up in his heart, and the evil man brings evil things out of the evil stored up in his heart. For out of the overflow of his heart his mouth speaks"* (Luke 6:45).

Hints and Helps

♦ When listening to music or watching TV with your children, pause occasionally to ask how they're feeling. Use their answers as a springboard to talk about the way we're shaped by what we see and hear. If they're listening to a sad song and feel sad, point out the connection. Do the same if they're upbeat while watching a happy show. Explain that God wants them to see and hear good things

LIVING

D.
You Can Be All
God Wants You
to Be

12. God wants you to be good, kind, and loving, just like Him and Jesus.

13. God wants you to see and think good things.

AGES 0–4

LIVING

E.
You Can Do All
God Wants You
to Do

14. God wants you to go to church.

15. God wants you to obey your parents.

16. God wants you to learn to share your things with others.

♦ What can you do when your children copy the actions of others who fight or speak rudely? In addition to dealing with the disobedience itself, use the incident as a chance to explain how what we see and hear can convince us to do the wrong things. Conversely, cheer your children on when they imitate positive behavior; point out that God wants us to watch and listen to such good examples.

You Can Do All God Wants You to Do

Topic No. 14

God Wants You to Go to Church.

Church is God's idea, and for good reason! It's meant to be part of every Christian's learning and support system. To show your children that church is vital, involve them in it at the earliest possible age. Take them to the nursery or Sunday school; make sure they're comfortable and secure. If your children have trouble staying when you leave, remain and help if you can for the first time or two. Help them enjoy being there so that they'll gain a positive view of church.

As soon as your children can understand, tell them why you go to church: to learn about God, to celebrate His greatness, and to be with others who love Him.

❖ *"Let us not give up meeting together, as some are in the habit of doing, but let us encourage one another—and all the more as you see the Day approaching"* (Hebrews 10:25).

Hints and Helps

♦ Don't have a church? Find one! Your whole family can benefit from the support and the challenge to grow in your faith. Try to find one close enough that your children can participate in activities as they grow. Check out the Sunday school and other children's programs. Look for an enjoyable, exciting environment with an emphasis on helping children learn about God and the Bible.

◆ Get involved in what your children are doing at church. Sit in on some of their classes, helping out if you can. Watch to see that by the time your children are one to two years old, they're learning basic lessons about Jesus through songs, stories, and fun at church. Encourage them to participate in crafts, games, and action songs, and to answer questions when they're able. Try to bring them together with church friends for playtimes, sending the message that it's important and fun to spend time with Christian friends.

◆ Whether your church meets on Sunday morning or at another time, try to make that part of the week special. Create fond memories for children to associate with church time—a favorite breakfast, a simple quiz in the car, a picnic. Plan ahead to avoid rushing. Talk with enthusiasm about what you'll be doing at church, and afterward discuss positively what you learned.

Topic No. 15

God Wants You to Obey Your Parents.

One of the Ten Commandments is to honor mothers and fathers—and honor includes obedience. Those who honor parents are promised long lives (Exodus 20:12; see also Ephesians 6:1–3). Children need to know that obedience is not optional. In fact, learning to obey you is a key to learning to obey God.

> ❖ *"Children, obey your parents in the Lord, for this is right. 'Honor your father and mother'— which is the first commandment with a promise—'that it may go well with you and that you may enjoy long life on the earth'"* (Ephesians 6:1–3).

> ❖ *"Children, obey your parents in everything, for this pleases the Lord"* (Colossians 3:20).

Hints and Helps

◆ Show your children how obedience looks. When you're driving, point out the speed limit sign and how you're obeying the law. When you bring your child to the workplace, explain that you're doing what God wants when you provide for your family. Explain that you need to obey

---

LIVING

E.
You Can Do All God Wants You to Do

14. God wants you to go to church.

15. God wants you to obey your parents.

16. God wants you to learn to share your things with others.

LIVING

E.
You Can Do All
God Wants You
to Do

14. God wants you to go to church.

15. God wants you to obey your parents.

16. God wants you to learn to share your things with others.

too. You obey God, your boss, and the government because obeying is part of God's plan.

◆ As children grow older, they need to trust that when you tell them to do something, you have a good reason for it. When they're able to understand, tell them *why* they have to do something—not "because I said so," but because it will keep them healthy, give them a skill they'll need, and so on.

◆ Say yes to your children whenever you can. Only say no when you have to—when the issue has to do with safety or growing their character, for example. This reflects God's heart. Ask them to do things that are reasonable and for their good, and be prepared to give them the reasons when they're old enough to understand. This, too, reflects God: Everything He tells us to do is reasonable and for our good. This approach to obedience helps children realize as they grow older that God isn't arbitrary or a killjoy. From your example they will begin to see that God's way is the best way.

Topic No. 16

God Wants You to Learn to Share Your Things with Others.

Brianna, like other toddlers, is just learning that her doll doesn't cease to exist when she can't see it. Before she can feel comfortable sharing her doll, she needs to know it's still there, even when it's being used by someone else. She also needs to understand that the doll still belongs to her, and that she'll get it back later. A sense of ownership must precede sharing. So for younger children, emphasize two truths: God lets us have nice things, and He wants us to share them with others.

During much of this stage, children tend to play alone or side by side—not together. For them to share means simply letting another person use their things for a time. Help them know that this makes the other person happy, and that they will get the things back. Begin to instill in them the fact that God will take care of their needs; they can trust Him with their belongings and share them.

❖ *The man with two tunics should share with him who has none, and the one who has food should do the same"* (Luke 3:11).

❖ *Command them to do good, to be rich in good deeds, and to be generous and willing to share"* (1 Timothy 6:18).

Hints and Helps

◆ Rather than forcing your children to share a new toy, give them time to enjoy it first. Once they've played with it, sharing will be easier.

◆ Try trading and taking turns. It's a good way to introduce sharing. If Christopher and Jonathan are playing with their own spaceships, have them trade for a minute or so. As they learn that the ships don't disappear when out of their hands, and that their belongings will be returned, you can increase the trading time. Or sit with your children and play together, taking brief turns with several toys.

◆ Help children to see the difference between *ownership* and *selfishness*. When four-year-old Tanisha refuses to let younger brother Bobby use one of her many crayons, explain why Bobby's request is reasonable. Point out that we need to be in charge of our things without being selfish—just as God has been unselfish with us. In time your children will be able to understand that ultimately God owns everything; just as He shares His possessions with us, He wants us to share with others. This also helps your children start to learn that *relationship* is more important than *things*.

CHAPTER 30

From Friendships to Faith: What Your 5–6-Year-Old Can Learn

Who God Is

Topic No. 17

God Is Your Loving Father.

Children need to understand what "God is your loving Father" means in practical terms. You're probably already demonstrating that every loving parent wants to take care of his or her children, guide them, protect them, teach them, help them grow strong and wise, clothe and feed them, give them advice, help with homework, and more.

Explain to your children that God, their heavenly Father, wants all this for them, too. He made them because He wants a loving relationship with them. As you make it clear that God is loving, children will see Him as approachable and want to move closer to Him.

- ❖ *"Every good and perfect gift is from above, coming down from the Father of the heavenly lights, who does not change like shifting shadows"* (James 1:17).
- ❖ *"How great is the love the Father has lavished on us, that we should be called children of God! And that is what we are!"* (1 John 3:1).

Hints and Helps

- ♦ When your child needs something, involve God in the equation if possible. For example, if your child asks for a glass of milk, you might mention how wonderful it is that God made cows, and helped people make

KNOWING

**A.
Who God Is**

17. God is your loving Father. He wants to guide, teach, love, protect, and provide for you.

18. In some ways, you are just like God. He has feelings and thoughts. He can understand you. Jesus showed us who God is and what He's like.

19. In other ways, you are very different from God. He is everywhere, He can do anything, and He knows everything.

20. Jesus has always been with God and is God.

291

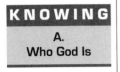
AGES 5–6

17. God is your loving Father. He wants to guide, teach, love, protect, and provide for you.

18. In some ways, you are just like God. He has feelings and thoughts. He can understand you. Jesus showed us who God is and what He's like.

19. In other ways, you are very different from God. He is everywhere, He can do anything, and He knows everything.

20. Jesus has always been with God and is God.

dairy farms and grocery stores. If your child is worried about a sick pet or having trouble breaking a bad habit, pray together about that.

◆ At gift-giving times—Christmas and birthdays, for instance—remind your children that every good thing ultimately comes from God and that He enjoys giving it to them. This doesn't mean that human gift-givers shouldn't get credit; it may mean sending thank-you prayers as well as thank-you notes.

◆ When your children are ill or injured, assure them that God cares—even if He doesn't answer requests for healing right away. You may want to tell the story of how Jesus didn't heal Lazarus immediately, how Jesus cried when He saw how hard the death of Lazarus was on his friends, and how Jesus finally raised Lazarus to life (John 11:1–12:19).

Topic No. 18

In Some Ways You Are Just Like God.

God made people in His image, so your children are like Him in some ways. You can tell your children that, like them, He feels emotions like sadness, anger, and joy; He also laughs, talks, thinks, makes things, and forms friendships. Knowing their "likeness to God" is important to children because it lets them know that God understands them and can help them. It also makes God more real to them—easier to believe in, relate to, and talk with.

❖ *"Then God said, 'Let us make man in our image, in our likeness,' . . . So God created man in his own image, in the image of God he created him; male and female he created them"* (Genesis 1:26–27).

❖ *"Since the children have flesh and blood, he too [Jesus] shared in their humanity . . . Because he himself suffered when he was tempted, he is able to help those who are being tempted"* (Hebrews 2:14, 18).

Hints and Helps

◆ Have a family talent show. Let each child demonstrate an ability—anything from playing the piano to making funny faces. Afterward, talk about God's "talents." Which ones has He "passed on" to humans? Which ones has He reserved for Himself?

- During an upcoming meal, make God your guest. You may even want to set a place for Him as a reminder to your children that He's always there. As you laugh together, thank God for fun. When you mention how proud you are of your children, tell them God is too. When they tell jokes, remind them that God has a sense of humor as well.

- Take your children out one at a time for lunch, dinner, miniature golf, or another activity. As you talk and listen, affirm your interest in your children's lives. Then let them know that God enjoys them too. Remind them that God is thinking about them and likes being with them.

Topic No. 19

In Other Ways You Are Very Different from God.

Though we're made in God's image, we certainly aren't His equals. Let your children know that, unlike us, God can do anything, knows everything, and is everywhere. Nothing is too hard for Him to do or too small for Him to bother with; there is nothing He doesn't understand; no place is out of His reach. Understanding these truths will help your children trust God when the world seems scary, confusing, or out of control.

- ❖ *"You have made the heavens and the earth by your great power and outstretched arm. Nothing is too hard for you"* (Jeremiah 32:17).
- ❖ *"With man this is impossible, but with God all things are possible"* (Matthew 19:26).
- ❖ *"Great is our Lord . . . his understanding has no limit"* (Psalm 147:5).
- ❖ *"Even the very hairs of your head are all numbered"* (Matthew 10:30).
- ❖ *"Can anyone hide in secret places so that I cannot find him? . . . Do I not fill heaven and earth?"* (Jeremiah 23:24).

Hints and Helps

- At this stage children are beginning to discover the vastness of God's creation. They often develop an interest in the solar system, volcanoes, dinosaurs, the undersea world, and other big things God has made. Check out library books and videos that describe the awesome size of Jupiter, the mind-boggling distances between stars, the depth of the seas. Look together at maps and globes that show how large countries and continents are. As you do, talk about how powerful God must be to make such gigantic things.

- Assure your children that they can ask God for big things. He can

---

KNOWING

A.
Who God Is

17. God is your loving Father. He wants to guide, teach, love, protect, and provide for you.

18. In some ways, you are just like God. He has feelings and thoughts. He can understand you. Jesus showed us who God is and what He's like.

19. In other ways, you are very different from God. He is everywhere, He can do anything, and He knows everything.

20. Jesus has always been with God and is God.

AGES 5–6

KNOWING
A.
Who God Is

17. God is your loving Father. He wants to guide, teach, love, protect, and provide for you.

18. In some ways, you are just like God. He has feelings and thoughts. He can understand you. Jesus showed us who God is and what He's like.

19. In other ways, you are very different from God. He is everywhere, He can do anything, and He knows everything.

20. Jesus has always been with God and is God.

handle anything. Hinting that there are some requests they shouldn't make sows doubt and undermines trust. *But what if my kids want it to snow in the middle of summer?* you might wonder. Let them ask! They need to learn to go to God for everything—and trust Him to do what's best. Explain that sometimes this means His answer will be no—just as sometimes you, too, say no because a thing's not good for them, because the time isn't right, or because you have a better plan. (See also Topic No. 58, "Keep Praying: Persistence, Tests, and Trials.")

◆ If you've been disappointed by seemingly unanswered prayer, it may be difficult for you to assure your children that God can do anything. You may worry that you'd be setting them up for disappointment, too. Let your children know that you are learning to trust God. Go to the Bible with them and look up verses about God's attitude toward our requests (John 14:17; Romans 8:31). Spend time meditating on how God is different from you, on how big and powerful He is. Discuss your feelings with a pastor or mature Christian friend if you like. As you gain confidence in God's power, you'll be better able to teach your children trust—in His willingness to answer as well as the wisdom of His responses.

Topic No. 20

Jesus Has Always Been with God and Is God.

The Jesus most children relate to is the Man, their Friend. But they also need to know that He is God, with all the same qualities and abilities as God the Father. He was always alive and with God from before time began. He made everything. When children know that Jesus made everything and therefore knows how it all works, they understand that He knows the very best way to live. (See also Topic No. 32, "God's Way Works Best.")

God Is . . . Checklist (Psalm 103)

Forgiving	Slow to anger	Gracious
Healing	Full of love	Kind
Savior	Merciful	King over all
Faithful	Boundless Lover	Everlasting
Tender	Compassionate Father	Fair
Understanding	Giver of good things	

❖ *"In the beginning was the Word, and the Word was with God, and the Word was God. He was with God in the beginning. Through him all things were made; without him nothing was made that has been made" (John 1:1–3).* (Note: The Word is Jesus.)

❖ *"The Word became flesh and made his dwelling among us"* (John 1:14).

Hints and Helps

◆ When possible, as you read your children Bible stories about Jesus or talk about Him during the course of a day, try to convey the awesomeness of who He is: God the Son, who has always been, who created everything. For instance, while telling the story of how Jesus fed thousands of people, you might say, "Making a big meal out of a few loaves and fish was no trouble for Jesus—He made all the fish in the ocean!" Or, when talking about how Jesus blessed the children, you could ask, "If you were standing in line to see Jesus, would you be nervous? Do you think those children knew that He is God?" Such side notes of awe, wonder, and respect help your children begin to understand the divine nature of Jesus. It's easy to stop being wowed by who He is and what He did. Remind yourself and convey the "wow" to your children!

◆ At Christmas, our celebrations often emphasize the human side of Jesus—the vulnerable baby in the manger. If you want to remind your children that Jesus is also God, an Advent calendar may help. As your children open a little door on the calendar each day during December, wonder together what might have been going on in heaven as God's Son prepared to come to earth in human form.

What God Has Done

Topic No. 21

God Tells You About Himself, His Son, Jesus, and His Plan for You in the Bible.

Once your children know the Bible is God's book, they need to learn why He gave it to them. Let them know that through the Bible they can find out about the God who loves them so much, and about His plan for them. It's their instruction manual for life, prepared by the inventor of life Himself.

KNOWING

B. What God Has Done

21. God tells you about Himself, His Son, Jesus, and His plan for you in the Bible: The One Big Story.

22. God sent His Son, Jesus Christ, to die for you.

23. God has prepared a place for you in heaven. Jesus is coming back for you.

AGES 5-6

❖ *"Your word is a lamp to my feet and a light for my path"* (Psalm 119:105).

❖ *"All scripture is God-breathed and is useful for teaching, rebuking, correcting and training in righteousness, so that the man of God may be thoroughly equipped for every good work"* (2 Timothy 3:16–17).

Hints and Helps

◆ It's a love letter! It's an autobiography! It's a history book! It's a true adventure! Refer to the Bible in a variety of ways so that your children can see that it has a number of purposes.

◆ Bring out the instruction book to your VCR, camera, or other device. Explain that the book helps you know how the device works best and how to get the most from it. Point out that the Bible is our instruction book for life, written by the One who created us. You can do the same thing with other kinds of books—an encyclopedia, where we look up answers to our questions; an atlas, which shows us which way to go on a trip; and so on.

◆ No matter how many Bibles or Bible storybooks you may have in your home, be sure that each child sees a particular one as belonging to him or her. Your children need "personal" Bibles or Bible storybooks. This reinforces the idea that God's special book is for *them*.

◆ If your Bible storybook doesn't link the stories together, try doing this yourself as you read them. Help children understand the order of the stories—for example, that Adam and Eve came before Noah, who came before Abraham, who came before David, who came before Jesus. This adds to their understanding of the overall story. So does learning the names and order of the books of the Bible, which children can begin to do at this age.

◆ Children need to know that even though the Bible is made up of many stories, they add up to the one big story of God's plan for the world from creation to eternity. That plan: to make it possible for us to be His children. Besides giving your children a context for each story, this helps them find their way around the Bible, thereby making it less likely that they'll be intimidated by "big" Bibles later on.

To help your children discover God's One Big Story, try reading the following version to them.

God's One Big Story

In the beginning there were no rocks, trees, animals, stars, or people, only God—the Father, Son, and Holy Spirit. Then God made everything. After He'd made the world and everything in it, God made people, Adam and Eve. God wanted to be a Father to them and have a wonderful, loving relationship with them. He made a beautiful garden for them to live in called Eden. God gave them one rule: Don't eat from the Tree of the Knowledge of Good and Evil.

But Satan, an important angel who became God's enemy, disguised himself as a snake and lied to them. Adam and Eve disobeyed God and ate the fruit from the forbidden tree. That was sin. It changed everything. God sent them out of the garden. He still loved them, but sin separates people from Him. Adam and Eve had a choice to love and obey God, or not. They chose to disobey. They didn't know how awful separation from God would be. Because of Adam and Eve's sin, everyone born after them was born sinful and separated from God, too. This meant people could no longer be God's children as He wanted. But God had a plan to bring people back to Him so they *could* be His children. He just needed one perfect person.

Adam and Eve had children, who had children, and so on until the world was full of sinful people. God was very sad. He decided to destroy everyone. But God found one man, Noah, who loved Him. He told Noah to build a huge boat called an ark. God sent two of most kinds of animals and seven of other kinds into the ark, along with Noah and his family. Then it began to rain. Forty days and nights later, only the people and animals in the ark were alive. And God was still working on His plan.

Noah's children had children, and so on until one day God chose a man named Abraham and his wife Sarah to be part of His plan. He told them He would be their God and sent them to a land called Canaan which He promised to give their children forever. Abraham and Sarah were old and couldn't have children, but God gave them a miracle, a son named Isaac. God promised that one of Isaac's descendants—the Messiah, or Savior—would bless the whole world.

AGES 5–6

297

Isaac's son Jacob, also called Israel, had 12 sons and one daughter. Jacob gave his favorite son, Joseph, a special coat. Joseph's brothers were jealous and sold Joseph as a slave into Egypt. But even as a slave Joseph loved and obeyed God. Years later God helped him explain a dream to Pharaoh, the king of Egypt. The dream said a huge famine was coming. Pharaoh told Joseph to get Egypt ready for the famine by storing lots of food. When Joseph's family came to get food, Joseph invited them to live in Egypt.

The Israelites, Jacob's descendants, came to Egypt and had children who had children and so on. Years later, there were so many of them that the new Pharaoh got worried. He made them slaves and told them that they couldn't keep any of their baby boys. One Israelite mother set her baby boy, Moses, in a basket and put him in the river to escape Pharaoh. Pharaoh's daughter found him, took him to the palace, and raised him.

When Moses was a man, he killed an Egyptian who was mistreating a slave. Moses ran away to the desert. Years later he saw a bush on fire but not burning up. God spoke to him from the bush. He said, "Go to Egypt. Tell Pharaoh to let My people go!" God sent 10 plagues to show He was stronger than Egypt's false gods. In the last plague the oldest child in every family was to die. But God told the Israelites to kill lambs and put the blood on the doorways of their homes so He would pass over their houses and their children would be safe. The lambs died in place of the oldest children. This was called the Passover. That night Pharaoh let God's people go.

The Israelites left in a huge exodus or exit. God led them into the desert and gave Moses the Ten Commandments and the Law, which told the Israelites how to please God and have a good life. Then God led them to the land He'd promised Abraham long ago. God was working out His plan.

Many years later, the Israelites asked God for a king. Their first king, Saul, fought their enemies, the Philistines. One day Goliath, a giant Philistine, made fun of God. A young Israelite boy named David trusted God and fought Goliath with only a sling and some stones. He won! Later God made him the king of Israel. David loved God with his whole heart.

For all those years, God was teaching people what He was like, but no one was ever perfect or sinless. Then, years and years later, God gave Mary, David's descendant, His own Son, Jesus, as a baby. God chose Joseph, Mary's fiancé, to help her look after Him. Because the baby was God's Son, He was born without sin. God sent angels to tell people about Jesus' birth. They came to see this amazing event: God's Son born as a baby!

Jesus grew up in Nazareth. When He was about 30, He began the job God had given Him. He was baptized in the Jordan River, then God led Him into the desert. Satan tempted Jesus to do things his way instead of God's, just as Satan had done to Adam and Eve. But Jesus refused.

Jesus taught people about God and His kingdom. He showed that God loved people by healing the sick, feeding the hungry, and loving those whom others didn't. He taught people how to have a good relationship with God.

The religious leaders were afraid that the people would follow Jesus instead of them, so they decided to get rid of Jesus. Judas, one of Jesus' followers, offered to help them arrest Him. Judas led guards to arrest Jesus. Then Jesus was put on trial for saying He was God's Son. The punishment was death. Jesus was beaten and led out to be crucified. But He asked God to forgive the people because they didn't realize what they were doing. Then, even though He really was the Son of God and He'd done nothing wrong, He died. He was the new Passover Lamb. (Remember the first one?)

After Jesus died, His friends put His body in a tomb. On the third day the tomb was empty! Jesus appeared to many people, proving He was alive again. God had accepted His death as payment for everyone's sins! Just as the Israelites were saved from death when they painted the lambs' blood on their doors, those who trust that Jesus died for their sins are saved. That meant the separation begun with Adam and Eve could be ended. All people could be God's children once again! Jesus was the perfect Messiah, or Savior, that God had promised long ago.

Jesus went up to heaven, but He sent the Holy Spirit to help His followers tell the world about Him and live the way God wanted. The religious leaders tried to stop them, but nothing worked. One leader, Saul, searched out Jesus' followers to have them arrested and killed. One day Jesus appeared to Saul, and he

AGES 5–6

KNOWING

**B.
What God Has
Done**

21. God tells you about Himself, His Son, Jesus, and His plan for you in the Bible: The One Big Story.

22. God sent His Son, Jesus Christ, to die for you.

23. God has prepared a place for you in heaven. Jesus is coming back for you.

became a Christian that day. He changed his name to Paul and traveled the world telling people about Jesus. He started churches and wrote letters to help Christians live as God wanted them to. He also explained the teachings of Jesus and the Bible.

John, another one of Jesus' followers, was sent to an island prison for following Jesus. Jesus gave him a message for the church. In this message Jesus promises to come back and take God's children to be with Him in a new heaven and earth. There will be love and happiness there. No more sadness or pain. You'll be with God as His children, just as He planned before the world began. What a party that will be!

Topic No. 22

God Sent His Son, Jesus Christ, to Die for You.

Knowing the facts of Jesus' life, death, and resurrection is vital for your children. But understanding why these things matter to them personally is even more important. You might want to explain by reading the following to your children.

Jesus Pays the Price

Jesus was the perfect Person God's plan needed. Since He is God's Son, He is the only Person since Adam and Eve's first sin ever to be born without sin. He grew up like you, obeying His parents, doing chores, going to school, playing, and learning things. When Jesus was 30, He began the job God had given Him. He traveled around His country telling people what God was like, showing them that God loved them. He was friends with people others avoided, and He welcomed children. Jesus also showed people that God is powerful. He taught them about God's kingdom, how life works, how to pray, and what things are really important. For example, He said that how you are on the inside is even more important than how you act.

The religious leaders didn't like what Jesus was teaching and doing. They were jealous, so they planned to get rid of Him. They asked Judas, one of Jesus' followers, to help them. One night, when Jesus was talking to His friends, the religious leaders sent Judas with a crowd to arrest Him. They took Him to the ruler of the area and put Him on trial because He said He was God's Son. The ruler tried to free Jesus, but he was afraid of the people and finally gave Jesus to the soldiers to be nailed to a cross and killed.

Jesus had done nothing wrong. He is perfect. He could have stopped the soldiers from killing Him, but He didn't. He didn't need to die at all because He has never sinned. But He died to pay for your sins, and for the sins of everyone who ever lived, so that you could be forgiven and be God's child as God always wanted.

But that's not the end of the story. Jesus didn't stay dead. When He rose from the dead, He showed that God was stronger than death and had accepted His death in place of everyone else's. Jesus told His friends to tell others the truth and then went back into heaven to be with God. One day Jesus will come back for all God's children— those who believe Jesus died for them and who thus have been forgiven. They will all be with God forever. Nothing will ever separate them from God's love again!

Hints and Helps

♦ To help children understand the meaning of Jesus' sacrifice, you can read the preceding story, read them a good storybook about Jesus' death and resurrection, or show them a video on the subject (be sure to screen the video yourself first to make sure it's appropriate for your children). Answer any questions they have; if you don't know an answer, promise to investigate and get back to them. If you can't find the answer in your Bible or this book, consult your child's Sunday school teacher or your pastor.

♦ When your children appear to understand the basics of what Jesus has done for them, simply ask something like "Do you want to pray and ask God to forgive you and make you His child right now?" Using the phrase "right now" makes it easier for you to ask them again later if they aren't ready yet.

♦ If they are ready, have them pray in their own words or repeat a simple prayer after you, such as this one:

AGES 5-6

The Gospel in a Nutshell

All have sinned; the penalty for sin is death; Jesus is without sin and so did not deserve death; Jesus willingly paid the death penalty for everyone else; because of that, all who accept Jesus' death as payment for their sins can be forgiven and have a wonderful relationship with God as His children.

- "For all have sinned and fall short of the glory of God" (Romans 3:23).
- "The wages of sin is death" (Romans 6:23).
- "Without the shedding of blood there is no forgiveness" (Hebrews 9:22).
- "For God so loved the world that he gave his one and only Son, that whoever believes in him shall not perish but have eternal life" (John 3:16).
- "The gift of God is eternal life in Christ Jesus our Lord" (Romans 6:23).
- "If you confess with your mouth, 'Jesus is Lord,' and believe in your heart that God raised him from the dead, you will be saved. For it is with your heart that you believe and are justified, and it is with your mouth that you confess and are saved" (Romans 10:9–10).
- See also Romans 3:21–26; Colossians 2:13–15; Hebrews 9:23–28.

Dear God, I know that I've done wrong things and sinned. I'm sorry. I know that Jesus, Your Son, died for my sins and rose from the dead. Please forgive me and make me Your child. Help me to trust and obey You and make the right choices. Thank You for loving me and making me Your child. In Jesus' name, amen.

◆ How old should children be when they pray to accept Jesus as Savior? Some children as young as three can do this, though most won't understand fully what they're doing yet. If you're concerned that your child has "prayed the prayer" without grasping all the theology, remember that children need only understand the main points. Being forgiven and becoming a Christian is not like a contract signing in which you must be careful to read all the fine print. It is the start of a loving relationship—a foundation on which your children can build throughout their lives.

◆ If your children don't accept Jesus in exactly the same way or setting as you might have envisioned, try not to worry or be disappointed. There is no single "correct" way to come to Jesus. It can happen with you, in church or Sunday school, with a friend, as children are thinking by themselves—anywhere. It might be emotional or matter-of-fact. God wants a unique relationship with each person, and each relationship starts in its own way.

◆ Celebrate with your children when they take Jesus into their hearts. Throw a party! Make it a special occasion to be remembered and treasured. (See the Memory Marker for this age group in chapter 11, page 119.) This can be a "snapshot" your child will have in his or her "photo album" forever.

❖ *"In the same way, I tell you, there is rejoicing in the presence of the angels of God over one sinner who repents"* (Luke 15:10).

❖ *"For God so loved the world that he gave his one and only Son, that whoever believes in him shall not perish but have eternal life"* (John 3:16).

Topic No. 23

God Has Prepared a Place for You in Heaven—Jesus Is Coming Back for You.

Jesus is coming back! The how and when is not as important as the fact of His return. For children, the key is the *reason* He's returning: to take them to be with Him in heaven forever. Tell your children that Jesus is getting a wonderful place ready for them, looking forward to the time they will be with Him there. When you teach your children about what's ahead for them in heaven, you give them hope—and the beginnings of an eternal view that puts things here in perspective.

❖ *"No eye has seen, no ear has heard, no mind has conceived what God has prepared for those who love him"* (1 Corinthians 2:9).

❖ See also Isaiah 35:10; John 14:2–3; Revelation 21:3–4.

Hints and Helps

◆ People often have the idea that heaven is a boring, static place where nothing ever happens and everyone sits around playing harps. If your children have gotten this impression from TV or other sources, they may wonder, *Why would anyone want to go there?* But heaven will be fantastic! The Bible says there will be no crying, no sadness, no pain or hurt. And heaven isn't just the absence of bad things; the apostle Paul wrote that it's far greater than anyone can even imagine. Next time you and your children enjoy an especially delicious meal, thrilling game, or breathtaking view, point out that heaven is even better.

◆ If your discussion of heaven brings up questions about angels, explain to your children that angels live in heaven and are God's helpers. They carry out God's plans and sometimes deliver His messages (as Gabriel did to Mary and Joseph), and God has them look after Christians. For more about angels, see Psalm 104:4 and Hebrews 1:14.

KNOWING
B.
What God Has Done

21. God tells you about Himself, His Son, Jesus, and His plan for you in the Bible: The One Big Story.

22. God sent His Son, Jesus Christ, to die for you.

23. God has prepared a place for you in heaven. Jesus is coming back for you.

AGES 5–6

LOVING

C.
You Can Have
a Relationship
with God

24. You can have a relationship with God by accepting what Jesus did for you: Salvation.

25. God wants to have a relationship with you.

26. You can talk to God through prayer.

27. You can thank God and Jesus for all They've done and still do for you.

28. You can ask God for wisdom and guidance.

AGES 5-6

You Can Have a Relationship with God

Topic No. 24

You Can Have a Relationship with God by Accepting What Jesus Did for You.

Yes, Jesus died for your children so that their sins could be forgiven. But why? So that they could have a close relationship with God, their heavenly Father! Make sure your children know that God is eager to have a relationship with them. He wants a special friendship with them, one He can have with no one else because each child is one of a kind. In this private relationship they get to know God in their own unique way.

Children need to know that deciding to accept Jesus as Savior is the beginning, not the end. Getting to know God is something exciting they'll be doing for the rest of their lives.

❖ *"Jesus answered, 'I am the way and the truth and the life. No one comes to the Father except through me. If you really knew me, you would know my Father as well. From now on, you do know him and have seen him'"* (John 14:6–7).

❖ *"Jesus replied, 'If anyone loves me, he will obey my teaching. My Father will love him, and we will come to him and make our home with him'"* (John 14:23).

Hints and Helps

◆ Let your children see how *your* relationship with God works. Allow them to hear you pray honestly and conversationally; encourage them to pray the same way, even about things that may seem trivial. Tell them about something God has taught you from the Bible. Talk about times when you've felt especially close to God. If you sometimes feel far from Him, admit it; if it's sometimes hard to relate to a Person who's invisible and doesn't speak to you audibly, admit that, too. Tell them what you would miss most if you couldn't have a relationship with God. As children learn that a relationship with God can be very real even if it has ups and downs, they'll have more realistic expectations as they begin their own.

◆ Create visual reminders of the relationship between your children and God. Have children draw pictures of themselves hiking with Jesus, for example. Or cut a picture of Jesus from a Sunday school paper and add it to a family portrait. Post these reminders where your children will see them frequently.

Topic Nos. 25, 26

God Wants to Have a Relationship with You; You Can Talk to God Through Prayer.

It's hard to have closeness without communication. Let your children know that the number-one way to develop their relationship with God is through prayer. At this age they may pray mostly in your presence, at your suggestion. As they move through this stage, however, your goal will be to teach them how to say their own prayers all by themselves.

❖ *"Cast all your anxiety on him because he cares for you"* (1 Peter 5:7).

❖ *"But when you pray, go into your room, close the door and pray to your Father, who is unseen. Then your Father, who sees what is done in secret, will reward you"* (Matthew 6:6).

Hints and Helps

◆ At the start of this stage, depending on your child, you may simply have him or her repeat prayers after you. Or try "Ping-Pong Prayers"—you pray something, then the child does, then you do, and so on. Or use "Starter Prayers"—after you and your child compile a list of things to pray for, you give a one- or two-word clue of something on the list and your child prays about it. This progression will comfortably move children toward saying their own prayers.

◆ How can we talk to someone we can't see? If your children have difficulty with this, help them understand by standing near them and having them close their eyes. Be quiet for a moment. Then ask, "Am I still here when your eyes are closed? How do you know?" Then explain, "It's like that with God. Even though you can't see Him, you'll know with your heart that He is there. You can know He never left because the Bible says He'll always be with you."

◆ As this stage begins, you may be telling your children what to pray about—especially if they have trouble coming up with ideas. Try to make a gradual transition, however, to letting them decide what to talk to God about. Help them make a list by asking questions or making suggestions. Eventually they'll be able to make their own list

LOVING

**C.
You Can Have
a Relationship
with God**

24. You can have a relationship with God by accepting what Jesus did for you: Salvation.

25. God wants to have a relationship with you.

26. You can talk to God through prayer.

27. You can thank God and Jesus for all They've done and still do for you.

28. You can ask God for wisdom and guidance.

29. You can read about God and His Son, Jesus, in the Bible or in a Bible storybook. You begin to have personal Bible reading and time with God.

AGES 5–6

LOVING

**C.
You Can Have
a Relationship
with God**

24. You can have a relationship with God by accepting what Jesus did for you: Salvation.

25. God wants to have a relationship with you.

26. You can talk to God through prayer.

27. You can thank God and Jesus for all They've done and still do for you.

28. You can ask God for wisdom and guidance.

AGES 5–6

with a little help. This transfer of responsibility helps them see that this is *their* relationship with God, not yours.

◆ Variety is the spice of a prayer life, too! Even if your main prayer time is always at bedtime, avoid praying for the same things or in the same way every night. Make each night's prayer as relevant to the day's events as possible. Ask your child to pray for *your* concerns sometimes. Rearrange the bedtime routine occasionally so that prayer isn't just another step toward "lights out." This reinforces the truth that prayer is meant to be meaningful.

◆ Encourage your children to be themselves with God. There's a difference between respect and the *form* of respect. Respect is a matter of the heart, not of the words. Speaking in reverent tones and terms might sound respectful, but God sees the heart. He is much more interested in an honest relationship than in a pious-sounding one.

Topic No. 27

You Can Thank God and Jesus for All They've Done and Still Do for You.

Helping your children to be thankful is one of the greatest gifts you can give them. Thankfulness readies them to receive God's grace, coaches them to expect God's provision and care, and strengthens their faith. An attitude of gratitude leads them to contentment and peace. Being able to recognize blessings in all their forms, large and small, will shape your children's lives and increase their happiness.

❖ *"But in everything, by prayer and petition, with thanksgiving, present your requests to God"* (Philippians 4:6, emphasis added).

❖ *"I know what it is to be in need, and I know what it is to have plenty. I have learned the secret of being content in any and every situation, whether well fed or hungry, whether living in plenty or in want"* (Philippians 4:12).

Hints and Helps

◆ Since they think in concrete terms, children don't always make the connection between their prayers and God's answers. Nor do they always link God with the wonderful things they have. Encourage your children to make a list of their Top-10 favorite things; point out that these are gifts from God. If you keep a prayer list, help children to keep track of God's answers, too.

♦ From time to time, at the end of an uneventful day, talk with your child about the not-so-good things that *could* have happened that day but didn't—getting sick, falling down on the ice, losing milk money on the way to school, an earthquake, etc. Thank God together that these things *didn't* happen.

♦ Let children see your own thankfulness and that you credit your own blessings to God. At mealtime, for example, thank God for more than the food. Modeling gratitude and contentment with what you have gives your children a positive example to follow.

Topic No. 28

You Can Ask God for Wisdom and Guidance.

God wants your children to ask for wisdom—the ability to know the right thing to do in a situation. He has all the wisdom they could ever need! Encourage your children to ask for wisdom on a regular basis during prayer time—and anytime they need to know what to do.

❖ *"If any of you lacks wisdom, he should ask God, who gives generously to all without finding fault, and it will be given to him"* (James 1:5; see also 3:15–17).

❖ *"If you call out for insight and cry aloud for understanding, and if you look for it as for silver and search for it as for hidden treasure, then you will understand the fear of the LORD and find the knowledge of God"* (Proverbs 2:3–5).

Hints and Helps

♦ Use your children's questions and frustrations as an opportunity to teach them how to ask for God's wisdom. If they're upset about not being able to take a toy apart or put it back together, remind them that God is ready to help. Show them how to stop and be still for a moment while they ask God for wisdom. Help them think through their situation and watch the ideas come. If God seems to lead them to ask someone else for help, that's fine. God provides us with wisdom in many different ways and in His time.

♦ Avoid giving your children the answer yourself every time they need guidance. Sometimes it's good to show your children how to do

---

LOVING

C.
You Can Have a Relationship with God

24. You can have a relationship with God by accepting what Jesus did for you: Salvation.

25. God wants to have a relationship with you.

26. You can talk to God through prayer.

27. You can thank God and Jesus for all They've done and still do for you.

28. You can ask God for wisdom and guidance.

29. You can read about God and His Son, Jesus, in the Bible or in a Bible storybook. You begin to have personal Bible reading and time with God.

AGES 5–6

LOVING

**C.
You Can Have
a Relationship
with God**

24. You can have a relationship with God by accepting what Jesus did for you: Salvation.

25. God wants to have a relationship with you.

26. You can talk to God through prayer.

27. You can thank God and Jesus for all They've done and still do for you.

28. You can ask God for wisdom and guidance.

29. You can read about God and His Son, Jesus, in the Bible or in a Bible storybook. You begin to have personal Bible reading and time with God.

AGES 5–6

something, but at other times you can take them to God for wisdom. They need to know what to do when you're not around. So take the time to walk them through a process of thinking and praying that they can use when you're not there.

Topic No. 29

You Can Read About God and His Son, Jesus, in the Bible or a Bible Storybook; You Begin to Have Personal Bible Reading and Time with God.

It's time to take Bible reading to another level. Let your children know that God can teach them things as they read. Begin to get into the habit of quickly asking God, with your child, to help you learn from and understand His Word before you read it. (See also Topic No. 31, "The Bible Tells You the Kind of Person God Wants You to Be.")

❖ *"These are the scriptures that testify about me"* (John 5:39).
❖ See Psalm 119:97–105.

Hints and Helps

♦ From time to time, mention to your children that eventually they'll read the Bible on their own. Help them look forward to this as part of being a "big kid"—and part of spending time with God daily and getting to know Him better. At this point you probably will read with them, but let them take some initiative. For instance, they can get their Bible storybook and put it away, place the bookmark when you're done, and help to decide whether you read one, two, or three stories at a time.

♦ As you read, you may be amazed at how often something in a Bible story coincides with your children's current struggles or even with what happened that day. Talk to your children about the parallel. Show them how what happened in the story compares with what happened in their day. This helps them see how relevant the Bible is and how God uses it to speak to them.

♦ Look for opportunities to work a Bible story's truths into your child's prayer time. For example, you might pray, "God, please help Jeannie trust You like David trusted You with Goliath." This affirms that Bible lessons are for applying, and that we can trust God to help us change as we learn from His Word.

You Can Be All God Wants You to Be

Topic No. 30

God Has a Plan for You.

God cares not only what your children are like now but also about the people they're going to be. He cares about what they're going to do with their lives. Assure them that they're special to God, and that He has a plan for their lives that suits them perfectly.

> ❖ *"I praise you because I am fearfully and wonderfully made; your works are wonderful, I know that full well. My frame was not hidden from you when I was made in the secret place. When I was woven together in the depths of the earth, your eyes saw my unformed body. All the days ordained for me were written in your book before one of them came to be"* (Psalm 139:14–16).
>
> ❖ *"We are God's workmanship, created in Christ Jesus to do good works, which God prepared in advance for us to do"* (Ephesians 2:10).

Hints and Helps

- Most children love to hear stories about what it was like when they were born and what they did when they were babies. When you speak of events surrounding your children's births, include God's involvement in the story. He was not an absentee Father; He was there, involved in their creation and eagerly awaiting their entry into His world.

- Take time to dream about the future with your children. Ask, "What would you like to be when you grow up? How could you help other people in a way that maybe no one else could?" Plant the idea that God has a plan for them. Remind them that God wants them to be all they can be, and He will help them do that.

- Children need to feel wanted. It's a good foundation for building a sense of purpose, too. You can help children know that both you and God want them, that you're excited they're in the world. You can remind them of this anytime, but birthdays are an especially good time to do so. When you say, "I'm so glad you were born," mention that God is glad too.

Topic No. 31

The Bible Tells You the Kind of Person God Wants You to Be.

Even young children can understand that the Bible is the most important book they'll ever read—because it explains how life works, what

---

LIVING

**D.
You Can Be All
God Wants You
to Be**

30. God has a plan for you.

31. The Bible tells you the kind of person God wants you to be.

32. God's way works best. You can be all God wants you to be by following Jesus.

33. God wants you to put only good things into your heart.

34. When you sin, you should ask God to forgive you—and He will.

AGES 5–6

LIVING

D.
You Can Be All God Wants You to Be

AGES 5-6

30. God has a plan for you.

31. The Bible tells you the kind of person God wants you to be.

32. God's way works best. You can be all God wants you to be by following Jesus.

33. God wants you to put only good things into your heart.

34. When you sin, you should ask God to forgive you—and He will.

God is like, and how He wants them to be (see Topic Nos. 7, 21, 47–50, and 74–76 for more on the Bible). Explain that the Bible stories and verses help them learn how to please God.

❖ *"All scripture is God-breathed and is useful for teaching, rebuking, correcting and training in righteousness, so that the man of God may be thoroughly equipped for every good work"* (2 Timothy 3:16–17).

Hints and Helps

◆ Is your child afraid of a bully at school? Read and discuss the story of Daniel in the lions' den (Daniel 6). Is your child refusing to forgive someone? Talk about the parable of the unmerciful servant (Matthew 18:21–35). When your children struggle with stress or character issues, remind them of Bible stories that can help them understand how God wants them to be and behave in those situations. This reinforces how relevant God's Word is and that God cares how they feel and act.

◆ Let your children know about an issue with which *you* struggle—controlling your temper, being generous, trusting God, etc. Show them how you can look in the Bible (starting with a concordance) to find verses that will help you in that area. Let them see you write a few of the verses on index cards; post these where you'll encounter them often. Give children a report every week or so on how God's Word is enabling you to make progress with your problem. At the end of a month, help your children go through a similar process with difficulties they face.

Topic No. 32

God's Way Works Best. You Can Be All God Wants You to Be by Following Jesus.

God must have known kids would need a practical, concrete motivation to follow His way, so He had Paul put it into words. He told children to obey their parents so that it would go well with them and they would *enjoy* long life (Ephesians 6:1–3). If they know and trust God and learn to do things His way, they'll have what they need to get through life instead of being plowed under by it.

God also knew they needed an example. So Jesus lived God's way, and His story in the Bible shows your children how God wants them to act.

❖ *"I have told you these things, so that in me you may have peace. In this world you will have trouble. But take heart! I have overcome the world"* (John 16:33).

❖ *"Children, obey your parents in the Lord, for this is right. 'Honor your father and mother'—which is the first commandment with a promise—'that it may go well with you and that you may enjoy long life on the earth'"* (Ephesians 6:1–3).

Hints and Helps

◆ When using Bible stories to show how to live God's way, help your children make the connection between the Bible characters' acts and the results. For example, Joseph was faithful to God. He suffered for a time in prison, but later God rewarded his faithfulness, making Joseph the second most important man in Egypt. Jonah illustrates the negative consequences of doing things your own way. Other stories that show consequences clearly are those of King Saul, Gideon, and Pharaoh and the plagues. The stories of Jesus, meanwhile, show the right way to live.

◆ It's easy when you're tense or hurried to answer your children's questions with "Because I said so." But this reasoning doesn't help them understand that your instructions are for their own good; it doesn't help them trust you. In the same way, "Because God says so" is inadequate. God doesn't just tell us what to do in the Bible; He often tells us why. If you don't know the *why* behind a command, look it up— or ask someone who knows his or her Bible better.

Topic No. 33

God Wants You to Put Only Good Things into Your Heart.

Children at this age are starting to watch more TV shows and videos. It's important to teach them early the concept of guarding their hearts. You might say something like "Guarding your heart means being careful about what goes into it. God wants you to choose good things to put into your heart so that you'll be happy." Remind them that, as God is good and kind and loving, we want to be that way, too. As a result we want to watch things that are good and kind and loving.

❖ *"The good man brings good things out of the good stored up in his heart, and the evil man brings evil things out of the evil stored up in his heart.*

LIVING

D.
You Can Be All God Wants You to Be

30. God has a plan for you.

31. The Bible tells you the kind of person God wants you to be.

32. God's way works best. You can be all God wants you to be by following Jesus.

33. God wants you to put only good things into your heart.

34. When you sin, you should ask God to forgive you—and He will.

AGES 5–6

311

30. God has a plan for you.

31. The Bible tells you the kind of person God wants you to be.

32. God's way works best. You can be all God wants you to be by following Jesus.

33. God wants you to put only good things into your heart.

34. When you sin, you should ask God to forgive you—and He will.

For out of the overflow of his heart his mouth speaks" (Luke 6:45).

❖ "Finally, brothers, whatever is true, whatever is noble, whatever is right, whatever is pure, whatever is lovely, whatever is admirable—if anything is excellent or praiseworthy—think about such things" (Philippians 4:8).

Hints and Helps

◆ Wondering how TV, books, and other media are influencing your kids? Children's "pretend" play is an excellent window into their hearts. Watch what they pretend and you'll see what has gone into their hearts. Do they pick up action figures and "battle" to the death? Do they make dolls "talk" harshly to each other, or about inappropriately "adult" themes? If you can trace these behaviors back to specific shows or other sources, decide whether you need to make those sources off-limits—and explain why.

◆ Children this age can be fearful and have nightmares, especially if they're getting the wrong input. Explain to your children that when they have bad dreams, it may be the result of watching things that bother them. Comfort and pray for them first, then try to help them identify the source of their fears. Let them know that if they want good dreams, they need to put good things into their hearts.

◆ Are your children bothered by "minor" violence, scariness, or "bad words" in TV shows or movies? Instead of implying that they're weak, praise them for being sensitive. Help them make the decision to walk away from such sights and sounds.

◆ Be careful not to set a double standard in your home, saying, in effect, "You can't watch certain things, but I can watch anything because I'm an adult." Show your children that you also put limits on what you watch in order to guard your heart and please God.

Topic No. 34

When You Sin, You Should Ask God to Forgive You—and He Will.
It's important to teach children, when they willfully disobey you and do something wrong, that they need to ask God to forgive them. They also need to ask whoever else was involved to forgive them. This helps them learn the difference between right and wrong and reinforces their choice to do what is right.

Often children (and adults) can get caught up in making similar mistakes repeatedly. They need to come to a point of conscious choice where they say, "I will not be that way or do that any more!" Repentance helps them do this. When they stop for a time-out after bad behavior, talk to them about forgiveness, telling them the following two points. First, when they repent and ask for forgiveness, they are making a decision to leave that behavior behind and asking God for help to do it right from now on. Second, God wants them to learn to do right because He wants them to have a good life. So when they ask for forgiveness, God instantly forgives them. They start again with a clean slate.

> ❖ *"If we confess our sins, he is faithful and just and will forgive us our sins and purify us from all unrighteousness"* (1 John 1:9).

Hints and Helps

♦ After correcting your children, show them what they could have done instead. For example, if your child breaks something then denies it or lies about it, explain that you are more upset with the lie than with the fact that the object is broken. Gently tell them what the proper response would have been—they should have come to that you and simply explained what happened. Then you would have had only the accident to deal with, not the issue of the lie.

♦ Make sure, once you've talked about the sin and prayed about it, that you don't harp on it any more. Represent God to them: hug them, tell them how much you love them, how pleased you are generally with their behavior and how pleased you are with how they responded.

♦ When your children are asking for forgiveness from God, they might be uncomfortable because they feel so bad. In this case it's a good idea for you to pray for them. Keep it short and simple: ask God to forgive them and teach them, thank Him for some good things about your children that you enjoy, and end the prayer.

You Can Do All God Wants You to Do

Topic No. 35

God Wants You to Spend Time with Other Christians.

If you and your children are involved with peers at church, keep it up! If not, start now. Relational development is very important in this stage. Teach your children the difference between, on one hand, loving and being friendly with everyone, and on the other hand, finding good friends that you will want to spend a lot of time with. The Bible teaches that we become like the people we spend time with and get close to.

LIVING

E.
You Can Do All
God Wants You
to Do

AGES 5–6

35. God wants you to spend time with other Christians, both at church and in the community.

36. God wants you to help others and be nice to them.

37. God wants you to obey Him and follow Jesus in everything.

38. God wants you to share and take good care of everything He gives you: Stewardship.

39. God wants you to understand and memorize Bible verses.

LIVING

E.
You Can Do All
God Wants You
to Do

AGES 5-6

35. God wants you to spend time with other Christians, both at church and in the community.

36. God wants you to help others and be nice to them.

37. God wants you to obey Him and follow Jesus in everything.

38. God wants you to share and take good care of everything He gives you: Stewardship.

39. God wants you to understand and memorize Bible verses.

Your children should be involved in a Sunday school class, children's church, or group where they learn about God, Jesus, and the Bible, have a good time, and meet people who can become good friends. Help them meet other adult Christians who can be mentors to them too.

❖ *"Do not be misled: 'Bad company corrupts good character'"* (1 Corinthians 15:33).

❖ *"Let us consider how we may spur one another on toward love and good deeds. Let us not give up meeting together, as some are in the habit of doing, but let us encourage one another—and all the more as you see the Day approaching"* (Hebrews 10:24–25).

Hints and Helps

◆ You can't choose your children's friends; after all, they may not click with the same personality types you do. But you can choose the environment from which they take their friends. Make it easy for them to spend time with Christian children. Drive them to church events, have Christian children over, encourage return visits.

◆ Follow up on the time your children spend at church. Discuss what they learned and sang and what their favorite parts were. Many Sunday schools send home papers and memory verses; if yours does, go over these with your children, making sure they understand the story and lesson. You might even read the same Bible story together during the week. Hanging the Sunday school material and memory verses on the refrigerator or bulletin board may help you remember to review it. This involvement quietly but powerfully demonstrates to your children that church and what they do there is important.

Topic No. 36

God Wants You to Help Others and Be Nice to Them— Learning to Get Along with Others.

At this age, your children are forming habits of relating and communicating that will be with them the rest of their lives. Now's the time for them to learn to respect other people's bodies, property, space, rights, and feelings. You can teach them to . . .

❖ *Respect others' ownership of their own person.* A person's body is his or her own, and he or she sets the limits on whether and how he or she wishes to be touched.

❖ *Respect others' property.* When something belongs to someone else, your children cannot use it without permission.

❖ ***Respect others' personal space.*** Some people like to get really close, but others need more space. This also applies to sound levels and going into rooms or looking into cupboards if children haven't been invited.

❖ ***Respect others' feelings.*** Children need to be caring and compassionate toward others.

❖ ***Respect with words.*** Yelling, being mean, saying cruel things, and name-calling are unacceptable. Children need to be gentle, kind, and loving with their words.

> ❖ *"This is his [God's] command: to believe in the name of his Son, Jesus Christ, and to love one another as he commanded us"* (1 John 3:23).

> ❖ *"If anyone says, 'I love God,' yet hates his brother, he is a liar. For anyone who does not love his brother, whom he has seen, cannot love God, whom he has not seen"* (1 John 4:20).

Hints and Helps

◆ How can you teach children about respectful touching? Let's say, Michelle is in the way, so brother Sean pushes her roughly. Tell Sean that Michelle's body is hers, and he doesn't have the right to touch her unless she wants him to. Explain that he mustn't push, punch, or pinch. He shouldn't even tickle if she doesn't want it. If she asks him to stop, he must stop. Tell Sean to ask Michelle to please move because he would like to get through. That way Michelle is able to please him without having him touch her without respect.

◆ Show your children how to respond compassionately to someone—brother, sister, friend—who is hurt or upset. If someone gets hurt during play, blame is usually the first issue. Help children make concern for the hurt or upset person the first issue. As you insist that feelings are dealt with first and apologies are given, blame tends to become a nonissue.

◆ Explain the long-term benefits of treating others well: growing relationships that are strong and precious because of trust and love; being trusted, loved, and sought after; getting along well at school, on the playing field, with friends, at church, and (later) at work.

35. God wants you to spend time with other Christians, both at church and in the community.

36. God wants you to help others and be nice to them.

37. God wants you to obey Him and follow Jesus in everything.

38. God wants you to share and take good care of everything He gives you: Stewardship.

39. God wants you to understand and memorize Bible verses.

AGES 5–6

Topic No. 37

God Wants You to Obey Him and Follow Jesus in Everything.

Your children won't always understand why God says to do something. But if you're teaching them who God is and what His character is like, they'll be more likely to trust that His way is best. Children also need to know that, whether they understand the reason or not, it's vital to obey. Their obedience does not depend on their understanding; He is, after all, God.

❖ *"Jesus replied, 'If anyone loves me, he will obey my teaching. My Father will love him, and we will come to him and make our home with him. He who does not love me will not obey my teaching. These words you hear are not my own; they belong to the Father who sent me'"* (John 14:23–24).

❖ *"Dear friends, if our hearts do not condemn us, we have confidence before God and receive from him anything we ask, because we obey his commands and do what pleases him"* (1 John 3:21–22).

Hints and Helps

◆ Many children in this stage are fascinated by the human body and how it works. Using age-appropriate books, explore with your children the amazingly intricate way in which God has created us—from our infection-fighting blood cells to our self-mending skin. Point out that God knows everything about us because He made us; we need to respect Him and obey Him simply because He's our Creator.

◆ Talk with your children about how they need to obey you right away, even if they don't understand. They can ask questions *after* they've obeyed. If they're walking into the street and don't see a car coming, they must obey you immediately when you tell them to stop and come back. That's not the time to debate reasons. They need to trust that you have their best in mind, even if they can't see how obeying will benefit them. It's the same with God.

Topic No. 38

God Wants You to Share and Take Care of Everything He Gives You: Stewardship.

God owns absolutely everything. He made it all! But He gives it to you and your children to use and manage for Him. That's the job of a steward. When you tell your children that everything they have belongs to God and that they're just stewards of it, get specific: toys, clothes, games, videos, books, money, the natural world around them. They're also stewards of their abilities, time, energy, minds, hearts, relationships with God and people, and hopes for the future. All of these are gifts from God. How should they use these gifts? The way God has shown them to through His example: generously, selflessly, wisely.

❖ *"The earth is the LORD's, and everything in it, the world, and all who live in it"* (Psalm 24:1).

❖ *"Who makes you different from anyone else? What do you have that you did not receive? And if you did receive it, why do you boast as though you did not?"* (1 Corinthians 4:7).

Hints and Helps

◆ Children may resist sharing if they're worried about not having enough left for themselves. Explain that when they obey God by sharing, they don't have to worry about running out. It's God's job to take care of them. Their faith and trust in His care are shown by their willingness to give back to God and to help others.

◆ Are you starting to give your children an allowance? If so, it's a good time to teach them why you give to the church. Explain that you give some of your money back to God as a thank-you for all the wonderful things He's given you. Giving to the church is also a way to show God that you trust Him to look after your needs—and it helps to get God's work done.

◆ Most children in this stage can easily understand what it means to be "stewards" of God's creation—taking care of the environment, not wasting water or other resources, keeping the world clean by not littering, etc. Explain that this applies to all the things God has given us.

◆ Teaching children to be good stewards teaches them other spiritual truths, too. For example, tithing teaches them to be thankful for God's care and to value God's church and the Christian community. Giving to missions teaches them their responsibility to reach those who don't know Jesus.

35. God wants you to spend time with other Christians, both at church and in the community.

36. God wants you to help others and be nice to them.

37. God wants you to obey Him and follow Jesus in everything.

38. God wants you to share and take good care of everything He gives you: Stewardship.

39. God wants you to understand and memorize Bible verses.

LIVING

E.
You Can Do All
God Wants You
to Do

35. God wants you to spend time with other Christians, both at church and in the community.

36. God wants you to help others and be nice to them.

37. God wants you to obey Him and follow Jesus in everything.

38. God wants you to share and take good care of everything He gives you: Stewardship.

39. God wants you to understand and memorize Bible verses.

AGES 5–6

Topic No. 39

God Wants You to Understand and Memorize Bible Verses.

Why does the Bible encourage memorizing scripture? So that God's Word, hidden in children's minds and hearts, can guide them. Prizes and rewards can help to motivate memorizing—but if the purpose doesn't go beyond that, kids might as well memorize Shakespeare. It's also more important for children to *understand* the verses than to have them letter-perfect.

The best verses to memorize are ones you've quoted or looked up together when you helped your children understand one of life's principles. In so doing, you've given them a context that helps make their meaning clear.

❖ *"Your word is a lamp to my feet and a light for my path"* (Psalm 119:105).

❖ *"Anyone who listens to the word but does not do what it says is like a man who looks at his face in a mirror and, after looking at himself, goes away and immediately forgets what he looks like. But the man who looks intently into the perfect law that gives freedom, and continues to do this, not forgetting what he has heard, but doing it—he will be blessed in what he does"* (James 1:23–25).

Hints and Helps

♦ To help your children memorize a verse with meaning, read it and guide them to think about it. Talk about what it means. Read it again and ask, "When might this verse help you?" Remind children that they want to get the verse's meaning inside, in their thoughts and hearts. Read the verse a few more times, then close the Bible and say it out loud with them. Repeat it with them until they have it. Repetition, not memory concentration, is the key to memorizing at this age. For variety, try using rhythms or songs that make the words stick.

♦ Don't overdo it by giving children too many verses to memorize. And avoid picking verses randomly. Choose a few that reinforce what you've been teaching them lately.

♦ Here are some simple memory verses to try: Genesis 1:1; Proverbs 3:5; 17:17; Luke 6:31; John 3:16; Galatians 5:22–23; Ephesians 4:2; Philippians 4:6; 2 Timothy 1:7. See also Appendix III.

CHAPTER 31

From Bikes to Bibles: What Your 7–9-Year-Old Can Learn

Who God Is

Topic No. 40

You Can Be Sure That God Is Real.

How do you know God is real? Children in this stage often want to know. The apostle Paul pointed out that the world God created makes it obvious He exists. You can help your children understand that our beautiful, incredibly complicated, amazingly intertwined universe clearly shows the hand of a Creator.

❖ *"What may be known about God is plain to them, because God made it plain to them. For since the creation of the world God's invisible qualities—his eternal power and divine nature—have been clearly seen, being understood from what has been made, so that men are without excuse"* (Romans 1:19–20).

Hints and Helps

◆ Start with the assumption that your children already think God is real. Build on their belief. When they ask questions, assume they ask out of curiosity and a desire to know rather than out of skepticism. They want to have their faith bolstered. Make these truths a matter-of-fact, comforting addition to their faith.

◆ Give your children good reasons to believe. Share with them the following aspects of creation, including some things found in ourselves,

---

KNOWING

A. Who God Is

40. You can be sure that God is real.

41. There is only one God.

42. God exists in three Persons: Father, Son, and Holy Spirit. This is called the "Trinity."

43. God (Father, Son, and Holy Spirit) is eternal.

44. Jesus is both God and Man.

45. Nothing exists apart from God.

46. God's character is true, honest, loving, compassionate, generous, selfless, forgiving, merciful, trustworthy, faithful, just, impartial, and holy.

AGES 7–9

319

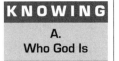

**A.
Who God Is**

40. You can be sure that God is real.

41. There is only one God.

42. God exists in three Persons: Father, Son, and Holy Spirit. This is called the "Trinity."

43. God (Father, Son, and Holy Spirit) is eternal.

44. Jesus is both God and Man.

45. Nothing exists apart from God.

46. God's character is true, honest, loving, compassionate, generous, selfless, forgiving, merciful, trustworthy, faithful, just, impartial, and holy.

AGES 7–9

that show God's hand:

❖ *Orderliness.* Things fall down, never up. Water boils when you add heat. Wood burns. Every day the sun rises and sets. The world is so predictable and orderly that scientists can make rules about it. This could not happen by chance. It makes sense to believe that God designed it all!

❖ *Beauty.* From newborns to nasturtiums, the world is full of beauty. Why? There's no reason for beauty except to give pleasure. Why "evolve" something with no function? Only God would make something purely for enjoyment.

❖ *The God Idea.* As long as there have been people, they have believed in God or gods. Where did that idea come from? God put it into people. He made humans to know that He's real. Even people who say they don't believe in God often turn to Him in trouble. We're made to need something or Someone other than ourselves—God.

❖ *Right and Wrong.* Listen to people argue and you'll hear, "But you promised!" "It's not fair." People think promises should be kept, and that fairness is important. How does everyone know this? Because there's a law or rule built into everyone that says so. Your conscience tells you when you break this "rule." Where did this law come from? From God, who made right and wrong and people.

Topic Nos. 41, 42, 43, 44, 45

There Is Only One God; God Exists in Three Persons: Father, Son, and Holy Spirit; God Is Eternal; Jesus Is Both God and Man; Nothing Exists Apart from God.

In Stage Two (ages 5–6) under Topic No. 19 are some simple ways to show your children how people are different from God. Here are additional truths about God for which your child is now ready.

There Is Only One God. (No. 41)

Hearing that there's only one God can be welcome news to children. It gives them the security of knowing that the "rules" won't change and the hope that they can relate directly to Him.

❖ *"Before me no god was formed, nor will there be one after me"* (Isaiah 43:10).

❖ *"I am the first and I am the last; apart from me there is no God"* (Isaiah 44:6).

God Exists in Three Persons: Father, Son, and Holy Spirit. (No. 42)

This is called the "Trinity" or "Three in One." God is a whole—One. That means you can't divide Him into parts. At the same time He is three Persons. Jesus' baptism gives a clear picture of this: Jesus was in the water, the Father spoke from heaven, and the Spirit came down like a dove (Matthew 3:16–17). The three Persons have different jobs:

- ❖ *The Father* is the source of everything. He sent His Son. (See John 5:37; 1 Corinthians 8:6.)
- ❖ *The Son, Jesus,* when He was on earth, showed who God is and what He's like. He's your role model and example. He died to save you from your sins. He will judge everyone in the end. (See John 5:22; Romans 5:8; 8:34; Hebrews 1:30.)
- ❖ *The Holy Spirit* helps you get to know God and grow as His child. He guides you into the life God has planned for you. He's with you, teaches you, and gives you gifts to help you do what God wants. (See John 14:16–17, 26; 1 Corinthians 12:4; 2 Thessalonians 2:13).

God (Father, Son, and Holy Spirit) Is Eternal. (No. 43)

God created time along with everything else, so it can't have any effect on Him. What does that mean? God is never rushed! Your children never need to worry about Him running out of time—or disappearing. He is always around—always was, always will be.

- ❖ *"[The heavens] will perish, but you remain"* (Hebrews 1:11).
- ❖ *"'I am the Alpha and the Omega,' says the Lord God, 'who is, and who was, and who is to come, the Almighty'"* (Revelation 1:8).

Jesus Is Both God and Man. (No. 44)

Jesus is God—and human, too. He lived on earth, showing people what God the Father is like. It's a mystery how someone can be divine and human, but with God everything's possible. Because Jesus is God, He could live perfectly and pay for our sins; because He is human, He knows from experience what it's like to walk in your children's shoes.

AGES 7–9

321

KNOWING

A.
Who God Is

40. You can be sure that God is real.

41. There is only one God.

42. God exists in three Persons: Father, Son, and Holy Spirit. This is called the "Trinity."

43. God (Father, Son, and Holy Spirit) is eternal.

44. Jesus is both God and Man.

45. Nothing exists apart from God.

46. God's character is true, honest, loving, compassionate, generous, selfless, forgiving, merciful, trustworthy, faithful, just, impartial, and holy.

AGES 7-9

❖ *"[Jesus], being in very nature God, did not consider equality with God something to be grasped, but made himself nothing, taking the very nature of a servant, being made in human likeness"* (Philippians 2:6–7).

Nothing Exists Apart from God. (No. 45)

Not only did God make everything; He keeps it going. God is the ultimate source of everything.

❖ *"For in him we live and move and have our being"* (Acts 17:28).

❖ *"God, for whom and through whom everything exists"* (Hebrews 2:10).

Hints and Helps

◆ Point out to your children that God's qualities all fit together. For example, if God is the only God but not eternal, then something could exist when He's not around—possibly other gods. Or if God did not *know* everything, how could He *do* everything? There would be things He wouldn't know how to do! God is either all of these things or none of them.

◆ Pray that your children will want to know God and what He's like. Fuel their desire to discover more about Him by admitting that *you* don't know all there is to know about Him, and that you're learning more all the time.

◆ Sometimes we try to put God in a box—to make Him small, safe, and completely understandable. But we need to take all the limits off God; there are none! You can get this point across to your children by having them go through your home and collect a variety of boxes—shoeboxes, large cartons, lunch boxes, tiny jewelry boxes. Put all the boxes on the floor and ask, "Which of these boxes would God fit into? Do you think He'd like to live in a box? Why might somebody try to keep Him in a box?" Explain that even though God wants to be our Friend, we can't "tame" Him, turn Him into a "pet," or control Him. He's always bigger and more powerful than our words can describe. We can expect life with Him to be full of surprises, to blow us away!

Topic No. 46

God's Character Is . . .

Here are seven of God's character qualities that your children can begin to grasp at this stage.

1. **God is true and honest.** When God makes a promise, He fulfills it. You can count on Him to do what He says and be who He says. His Son, Jesus, showed us how to live a completely honest life.

   ❖ *"Into your hands I commit my spirit; redeem me, O LORD, the God of truth"* (Psalm 31:5).

2. **God is loving and compassionate.** God does not just feel loving or do loving things; He is love. This can give your children great confidence in approaching and trusting Him.

   ❖ *"God is love"* (1 John 4:8).

3. **God is generous and selfless.** God gives good gifts, even when He doesn't have to. He loved us even when we didn't love back.

   ❖ *"'Test me in this,' says the LORD Almighty, 'and see if I will not throw open the floodgates of heaven and pour out so much blessing that you will not have room enough for it'"* (Malachi 3:10).

4. **God is forgiving and merciful.** Thankfully, God doesn't give us what we deserve. He forgives. While He was here, Jesus forgave sins and mercifully healed people.

   ❖ *"The Lord our God is merciful and forgiving, even though we have rebelled against him"* (Daniel 9:9).

5. **God is trustworthy and faithful.** Your children can put their lives in God's hands, knowing that He will take care of them and guide them. He never goes back on His word or plays tricks on us.

   ❖ *"Know therefore that the LORD your God is God; he is the faithful God, keeping his covenant of love to a thousand generations of those who love him and keep his commands"* (Deuteronomy 7:9).

6. **God is just and impartial.** God can't be bribed or manipulated. He'll always be as loving and involved in your children's lives as in anyone else's.

   ❖ *"He is the Rock, his works are perfect, and all his ways are just. A faithful God who does no wrong, upright and just is he"* (Deuteronomy 32:4).

AGES 7–9

323

KNOWING

B.
What God Has
Done

47. The Bible is true.
It is God's Word, and
you can trust it.

48. God made sure
all stories in the Bible
together tell the One
Big Story.

49. The Bible you
have is exactly what
God wanted to give
you.

50. God wants you to
learn and study the
Bible.

51. The world is full
of sin. There is an
enemy in the world
(Satan). Not everyone
obeys God.

52. Jesus died to
save you from the
penalty for sin.

53. Jesus defeated
sin and Satan.

54. Jesus is the only
way to God.

AGES 7–9

7. *God is holy.* There's nothing wrong, impure, dirty, sly, or underhanded in God. He's perfect. His Son, Jesus, lived a sinless life, showing people what holy living is.

❖ *"You are to be holy to me because I, the LORD, am holy"* (Leviticus 20:26).

Hints and Helps

◆ To help children remember God's character traits, encourage them to come up with a visual symbol for each one; for example, a judge's gavel for justice and impartiality, and a bar of soap for holiness (purity). Have them draw these on a poster. Or use them in a guessing game, to see whether family members can figure out what the symbols represent.

◆ As you teach your children what God is like, help them to see small ways in which they can develop some of the same character traits. For instance, a child might reflect God's generosity by letting a sibling read a favorite magazine first when it comes in the mail. Encourage children to commit to a specific action to be carried out on a specific day.

What God Has Done

Topic No. 47

The Bible Is True. It Is God's Word and You Can Trust It.

Your children may ask how you know the Bible is true and trustworthy. What will you tell them? The simple answer is that it can be trusted because it's God's book. You can know it's God's book because of how it came to be.

❖ *"All scripture is God-breathed"* (2 Timothy 3:16).

❖ *"Above all, you must understand that no prophecy of scripture came about by the prophet's own interpretation. For prophecy never had its origin in the will of man, but men spoke from God as they were carried along by the Holy Spirit"* (2 Peter 1:20–21).

Hints and Helps

◆ As you approach this topic, assume that your children believe the Bible is God's Word. Offering evidence simply preempts doubts and prepares them for the next stage.

◆ Want evidence to back up your claim that the Bible is God's book?

Try sharing the following with your children:

> God used more than 40 people to help Him write the Bible's 66 books. He used their personalities, ways of speaking, cultures, and experiences to write down exactly what He wanted us to have.
>
> Some of the people God used were rich; others were poor. They were kings, poets, prophets, generals, priests, farmers, shepherds, fishermen, prisoners—even a doctor and a politician. They lived over a period of 1,500 years, on three continents, and spoke different languages. Yet they all agreed about life, God, and right and wrong! Without God overseeing this process it would have been impossible.
>
> Over the years, many have doubted the Bible. Since they had no other sources that talked about some of the things in the Bible, they said the Bible was wrong. Then archaeologists began studying old things to learn about the past. They found evidence that confirmed what the Bible said. Here are just a few of things people doubted and what they found:

God Is Awesome

"Who has measured the waters in the hollow of his hand . . . Who has held the dust of the earth in a basket, or weighed the mountains on the scales . . . Who has understood the mind of the LORD . . . Whom did the LORD consult to enlighten him . . .

"'To whom will you compare me? Or who is my equal?' says the Holy One.

"Do you not know? Have you not heard? The LORD is the everlasting God, the Creator of the ends of the earth. He will not grow tired or weary, and his understanding no one can fathom. He gives strength to the weary and increases the power of the weak" (Isaiah 40:12–14, 25, 28–29).

What They Thought	*What They Found*
Moses couldn't have written the first Bible books (Deuteronomy 31:24) because when he lived, no one knew how to write yet.	A carved rock from 300 years before Moses with laws written on it, known as the "Black Stele"; tablets from the excavated city of Ebla, written a thousand years before Moses; many other ancient writings.
Pontius Pilate wasn't a real person. If he was, he wouldn't have been called "Prefect," as the New Testament calls him.	A large stone in Caesarea, saying, "Pontius Pilate, Prefect of Judea."

KNOWING

**B.
What God Has
Done**

47. The Bible is true. It is God's Word, and you can trust it.

48. God made sure all stories in the Bible together tell the One Big Story.

49. The Bible you have is exactly what God wanted to give you.

50. God wants you to learn and study the Bible.

51. The world is full of sin. There is an enemy in the world (Satan). Not everyone obeys God.

(See also *The New Evidence That Demands a Verdict* by Josh McDowell; *801 Questions Kids Ask About God* by Dave Veerman et al; the *I Want to Know About . . .* series by Rick Osborne with K. Christie Bowler; and the Resource List in Appendix II.)

Topic No. 48

God Made Sure All Stories in the Bible Together Tell "The One Big Story."

It's important to know how Bible stories fit together. Without this, your children will have difficulty keeping Bible events and characters straight or understanding how scripture as a whole points to Christ. If you haven't already read them "The One Big Story" summarizing the Bible (see Topic No. 21, page 297), this would be a good time to do so.

❖ *"In the past God spoke to our forefathers through the prophets at many times and in various ways, but in these last days he has spoken to us by his Son, whom he appointed heir of all things, and through whom he made the universe"* (Hebrews 1:1–2).

❖ *"Concerning this salvation, the prophets, who spoke of the grace that was to come to you, searched intently and with the greatest care, trying to find out the time and circumstances to which the Spirit of Christ in them was pointing . . . It was revealed to them that they were not serving themselves but you"* (1 Peter 1:10–12).

Hints and Helps

◆ Help children learn the order of Bible events with the following game. Write at least 10 of the major events (Creation, the Flood, David's reign, Jesus' birth, Paul's ministry, etc.) on index cards, mix them up, and have kids line them up in the proper order. When children have learned the order of the biggest events, do the same with other events (high points of Jesus' ministry, for example) and characters.

◆ Try a "sword drill" using a children's Bible or Bible storybook. Call out the name of a story ("Moses and the Burning Bush," for instance) and see whether your children can find it. Do this with several stories, helping as needed. After playing the game several times, children will have improved their grasp of how the stories fit into the Bible's chronology.

Topic No. 49

The Bible You Have Is Exactly What God Wanted to Give You.

God has guarded the Bible over the centuries so that what Christians have is what He wants them to have. For many hundreds of years before the first printing press, scripture was copied by hand—carefully. We can be sure it is God's Word to us.

❖ *"We did not follow cleverly invented stories when we told you about the power and coming of our Lord Jesus Christ, but we were eyewitnesses of his majesty"* (2 Peter 1:16).

Hints and Helps

◆ If your children want evidence for the Bible's accuracy, share the following with them:

The older the copy we have of something is, the more accurate it probably is—since it was copied from things that were closer to the original and so there were fewer chances for mistakes to be made. There are over 5,000 old, handwritten copies or parts of copies of the New Testament. The oldest is part of the Gospel of John, copied only 20 to 70 years after John wrote it. Imagine, if John had children or grandchildren, they could have seen or touched it! There are also tens of thousands of pieces of copies of the Old Testament. And scholars have the whole New Testament from only 300 years after the last book in it was written! Comparing these manuscripts to today's Bibles shows that it hasn't changed in any way that affects what we believe.

When manuscripts from different places and times say the same things, it shows they were copied accurately. Until 1947, the oldest piece of the Old Testament was from 800 years after Jesus. But the Dead Sea Scrolls were discovered that year; they included a copy of Isaiah from about 200 years before Jesus—a thousand years older than the oldest copy we had—and the two are almost exactly the same!

The stories about Jesus, the Gospels, were written down less than 50 years after the events happened. Many people who had been there at the time, or their children (who had probably

KNOWING

**B.
What God Has
Done**

47. The Bible is true. It is God's Word, and you can trust it.

48. God made sure all stories in the Bible together tell the One Big Story.

49. The Bible you have is exactly what God wanted to give you.

50. God wants you to learn and study the Bible.

51. The world is full of sin. There is an enemy in the world (Satan). Not everyone obeys God.

52. Jesus died to save you from the penalty for sin.

53. Jesus defeated sin and Satan.

54. Jesus is the only way to God.

AGES 7–9

KNOWING
**B.
What God Has
Done**

47. The Bible is true. It is God's Word, and you can trust it.

48. God made sure all stories in the Bible together tell the One Big Story.

49. The Bible you have is exactly what God wanted to give you.

50. God wants you to learn and study the Bible.

51. The world is full of sin. There is an enemy in the world (Satan). Not everyone obeys God.

52. Jesus died to save you from the penalty for sin.

AGES 7–9

heard the stories umpteen times), would still have been alive. If the stories were wrong, they would have said so!

♦ To bring home how amazing the Bible's accuracy is, get your children to copy several verses by hand. They're bound to make a mistake or two—and that's only in one small section!

Topic No. 50

God Wants You to Learn and Study the Bible.

When it comes to maps, the Bible is the most valuable one you can find—if you want to arrive at the goal of a fulfilling life that serves God. Help your children learn to refer to it for direction.

❖ *"Oh, how I love your law! I meditate on it all day long. Your commands make me wiser than my enemies, for they are ever with me. I have more insight than all my teachers, for I meditate on your statutes. I have more understanding than the elders, for I obey your precepts. . . . I gain understanding from your precepts; therefore I hate every wrong path. Your word is a lamp to my feet, and a light to my path"* (Psalm 119:97–100, 104–105).

❖ *"You diligently study the scriptures because you think that by them you possess eternal life. These are the scriptures that testify about me"* (John 5:39–40).

Hints and Helps

♦ Children won't study the Bible unless they know it's the authority for all of life's decisions. Reinforce that truth by letting your children see *you* go to God's Word for answers.

♦ When your children face challenges—a test, surgery, the death of a grandparent—go to the Bible with them to find its advice on the subject. Make a habit of asking, "What does the Bible say about this?" Discuss what you find. Show older children in this age group how to locate relevant passages in a concordance. Some Bibles also list verses to read when facing specific struggles—

everything from money problems to grief. Call children's attention to helps like these.

◆ Keep at least one easy-to-read Bible accessible, especially in a well-traveled area, so children can see it's ready to use as life's instruction manual.

◆ Help children begin to see the difference between reading and studying the Bible. Explain that we read to help us grow in our relationship with God; after all, spending time with His book is spending time with Him. Studying the Bible is about finding out what to do in specific situations and learning to do things God's way. It's like mining for gold.

Topic No. 51

The World Is Full of Sin. There Is an Enemy in the World. Not Everyone Obeys God.

Evil can be an uncomfortable subject. But your children are growing up in a world that's disfigured by the results of sin, and they need to know why. They need to know that Satan is real, that he has power on earth—and that Jesus has ultimately defeated him. They need to know that bad things happen because of sin's side effects, and that Satan has blinded many people to the truth of God's Word.

❖ *"How you have fallen from heaven, O morning star, son of the dawn! You have been cast down to the earth, . . . You said in your heart, 'I will . . . make myself like the Most High.' But you are brought down to the grave, to the depths of the pit"* (Isaiah 14:12–15). Note: The Latin translation, called the Vulgate, translates "morning star" as "Lucifer."

❖ *"Submit yourselves, then, to God. Resist the devil, and he will flee from you. Come near to God and he will come near to you"* (James 4:7–8).

❖ *"The creation waits in eager expectation for the sons of God to be revealed. For the creation was subjected to frustration . . . in hope that the creation itself will be liberated from its bondage . . . We know that the whole of creation has been groaning as in the pains of childbirth right up to the present time"* (Romans 8:19–22).

❖ *"The god of this age has blinded the minds of unbelievers, so that they cannot see the light of the gospel of the glory of Christ, who is the image of God"* (2 Corinthians 4:4).

KNOWING

B. What God Has Done

47. The Bible is true. It is God's Word, and you can trust it.

48. God made sure all stories in the Bible together tell the One Big Story.

49. The Bible you have is exactly what God wanted to give you.

50. God wants you to learn and study the Bible.

51. The world is full of sin. There is an enemy in the world (Satan). Not everyone obeys God.

52. Jesus died to save you from the penalty for sin.

53. Jesus defeated sin and Satan.

54. Jesus is the only way to God.

AGES 7–9

Hints and Helps

♦ To help your children understand who Satan is, you may want to share the following:

> A very long time ago an angel named Lucifer rebelled against God. He wanted all the power, to be like God, and to replace God. His sin led to his being thrown out of heaven and sent to earth. Other angels—now demons—chose to follow him. On earth he told the first lie and tricked Adam and Eve into disobeying God too. That was just the beginning.
>
> Satan is powerful. But he was created—so he's far, far less powerful than God. He can't create. The Bible calls him a liar and the Father of Lies because he started out with lying and he's still at it. He hates God and anyone who follows God, so he tries to keep people away from Him. He loves evil.
>
> But don't be afraid. When Jesus died and rose again, Satan's power was broken. For help against him, all a Christian has to do is go to God and ask. Satan hates that!

♦ Why do bad things happen? Help children understand by sharing thoughts like these:

> Satan is part of the reason bad things happen in the world. But people do bad things, too, when they decide their way is better than God's. And every time it leads to trouble!
>
> God wants people to be free to choose to love Him. So He gave everyone a free will—the ability to make choices. Because people are sinful, they often choose wrong things. Every wrong choice has consequences. Some bad things happen because people make evil or bad choices. God could stop it, but that would mean taking away people's free will. He lets people have what they choose, but He can turn the bad into good to help us grow.
>
> Other bad things, like death and disease, are a result of sin, too. This doesn't mean that people who get sick are being punished for their sins. It means that when Adam and Eve sinned, it affected every created thing. Because we live in a world where Satan still has power, there is pain and suffering. But the end of the story is clear: Jesus wins!

♦ Your children will meet people who don't believe in God, who believe wrong things about Him, or who follow different religions. You can

AGES 7–9

help them understand why with an explanation like the following:

> Some people don't want to believe in God. Some have seen "Christians" who didn't act like followers of Jesus. They think, *If that's what believing in God does to you, I don't want it.* Others don't want to believe because they don't like being told what they can or can't do. They like sinning and don't want to hear that what they're doing is wrong. Still others simply don't know about Jesus. Or their families have taught them to believe in other religions. We can pray for them—and let them know why we believe as we do.

♦ When you're talking about the Devil and his demons, keep the focus on God. Emphasize that God is in control and has His plan on track. Yes, there's a roaring lion wanting your children to do wrong and to destroy their lives, but Jesus overcame the Devil. Your children can overcome too. If they're afraid of Satan or demons, remind them that Jesus is with them all the time—and He's much stronger than Satan. All they have to do is pray for help. Jesus will keep them safe as they follow Him.

Topic Nos. 52, 53, 54

Jesus Died to Save You from the Penalty for Sin; Jesus Defeated Sin and Satan; Jesus Is the Only Way to God.

If your children don't yet know why and how to accept Jesus as their Savior, you can tell them. For help, turn to Topic No. 22 for a summary of the salvation story and "The Gospel in a Nutshell."

❖ *"For all have sinned and fall short of the glory of God, and are justified freely by his grace through the redemption that came by Christ Jesus. God presented him as a sacrifice of atonement, through faith in his blood. He did this to demonstrate his justice, because in his forbearance he had left the sins committed beforehand unpunished—he did it to demonstrate his justice at the present time, so as to be just and the one who justifies those who have faith in Jesus"* (Romans 3:23–26).

Hints and Helps

♦ As one child in this stage asked, "Why did Jesus have to die? It isn't fair." Younger children may simply accept without questioning that Jesus died for them. In this stage, questions are more likely. If your

---

KNOWING

**B.
What God Has Done**

47. The Bible is true. It is God's Word, and you can trust it.

48. God made sure all stories in the Bible together tell the One Big Story.

49. The Bible you have is exactly what God wanted to give you.

50. God wants you to learn and study the Bible.

51. The world is full of sin. There is an enemy in the world (Satan). Not everyone obeys God.

52. Jesus died to save you from the penalty for sin.

53. Jesus defeated sin and Satan.

54. Jesus is the only way to God.

AGES 7–9

LOVING

C.
**You Can Have
a Relationship
with God**

55. You read the Bible to learn about who God is (Father, Son, and Holy Spirit) and what He has done and is doing.

56. You can pray your own prayers with your parents.

57. Prayer benefits you in many ways.

58. Keep praying: persistence, tests, and trials.

59. You can trust God and turn your life over to Him.

60. You should learn to seek God.

61. Jesus gives you peace.

children wonder why the sacrifice of Jesus was necessary, you may want to share the following with them:

Why did Jesus have to die? Well, He didn't *have to*. He *chose* to, out of love.

God loves the world. He wants to have with everyone the kind of close relationship He had with Adam and Eve in the very beginning. The only way to do that was to take care of the sin problem.

God made people and chose to be their Father. He chose to be responsible for them. Parents pay for what their children break. If parents don't pay, who will? The child usually can't. In a similar way, God made Himself responsible to pay for the thing His children "broke"—their relationship with Him. He did this knowing what it would cost, because He was a loving Father. If He didn't pay for it, who could? No one.

The punishment for sin is death. Since everyone sins, everyone would have to pay the death penalty. Only someone who was not born sinful (which excludes everyone since Adam and Eve) could die for others. Everyone else could die only for himself or herself. The only perfect Person is Jesus. He defeated Satan and sin when He died and rose again. This is why Jesus is the only way to God.

You Can Have a Relationship with God

Topic No. 55

You Read the Bible to Learn Who God Is (Father, Son, and Holy Spirit) and What He Has Done and Is Doing.

As they move through this stage, your children may want more and more to know why it's so important to read the Bible. Their questions usually will flow from curiosity, not doubt, as they look for information to back up their faith and for

AGES 7-9

a reason to keep reading the Bible.

Let them know that the Bible is a living book. The Holy Spirit uses it to teach them to deal with whatever they're facing. It applies to their lives. (See Topic Nos. 21 and 47–50 for more about what the Bible is, what it says, and how you can know it's true.)

- ❖ *"These are the commands, decrees and laws the* LORD *your God directed me to teach you to observe . . . so that . . . your children . . . may fear the* LORD *your God as long as you live by keeping all his decrees and commands . . . and so that you may enjoy long life"* (Deuteronomy 6:1–2).

- ❖ *"I seek you with all my heart; do not let me stray from your commands. I have hidden your word in my heart that I might not sin against you"* (Psalm 119:10–11).

Hints and Helps

- ◆ Your children's personal Bible storybook needs to grow with them. As their ability to read increases, they'll need a new book that contains more of the Bible stories and tells them in more detail. They'll begin to want to read some of a story on their own and some with you. Encourage them to read stories to you, too.

- ◆ Continue to reinforce the idea of a regular time in the Bible. Pray with your children before reading scripture; help them expect God to teach them from it. Expect this for yourself, too. If you're learning from Bible stories alongside your children, they'll see this as "the way it is" and look forward to it.

- ◆ Encourage personal Bible reading time by placing a children's Bible, Bible storybook, or children's devotional book next to your child's bed. Some children at this stage find it comforting to read Bible stories or other faith-oriented books at bedtime, especially if they struggle with fears of the dark or bad dreams.

- ◆ Toward the end of this stage, most children will be able to begin reading their Bible storybook and talking to God on their own. Encourage them to pick up their Bible storybook and read it even when you're not there. God can speak to them through it. They're ready to begin to see that their relationship with God is their very own—and they can experience it with no one else around.

AGES 7–9

LOVING

**C.
You Can Have
a Relationship
with God**

55. You read the
Bible to learn about
who God is (Father,
Son, and Holy Spirit)
and what He has
done and is doing.

56. You can pray
your own prayers
with your parents.

57. Prayer benefits
you in many ways.

58. Keep praying:
persistence, tests,
and trials.

59. You can trust
God and turn your life
over to Him.

60. You should learn
to seek God.

61. Jesus gives you
peace.

AGES 7–9

Topic No. 56

You Can Pray Your Own Prayers with Your Parents.

It's time to take prayer to the next level! Children may still pray with you, but most of the prayers are now theirs. Step back and let them take more initiative. Encourage them to pray conversational prayers anytime during the day, as well as "business" prayers at set times that cover more fully the topics God wants us to talk to Him about.

❖ *"In the same way, the Spirit helps us in our weakness. We do not know what we ought to pray for, but the Spirit himself intercedes for us with groans that words cannot express. And he who searches our hearts knows the mind of the Spirit, because the Spirit intercedes for the saints in accordance with God's will"* (Romans 8:26–27).

❖ For the Lord's Prayer, see Matthew 6:9–13; Luke 11:2–4.

Hints and Helps

◆ "What should I pray about?" Whether or not children ask this question, they often need help thinking of topics to bring before their heavenly Father. You can lift them out of the "God bless everybody" rut by sharing the following list with them:

1. **Thank-you prayers.** Show appreciation for who God is and what He's done.

2. **Prayers about God's kingdom.** Pray that you—and everyone, everywhere—will do what God wants. Ask that other people will come to know Jesus and that Jesus' church will grow strong so it can do its job.

3. **Leader prayers.** Pray that leaders and those in authority (even teachers and babysitters) will obey God.

4. **Personal requests.** Pray about your own needs and concerns—for health, protection, friendship, etc.

5. **Growing prayers.** Confess wrongs and ask for forgiveness; pray about becoming a stronger Christian.

6. **Prayer for others.** Ask God to help friends, family, and anyone else with needs.

7. **Guidance prayers.** Pray for God to lead you, to help you

make the best choices.

8. *Praise prayers.* "Cheer" for God because He's your Creator, and because He has the power to answer all your other prayers!

♦ Sometimes children don't know how to express their fears, sadness, or even joy in their prayers. Assure them that God can help them know what to say. And because God understands what's in their hearts, He knows how they feel even if all they can do is sigh or cry.

♦ As your children become more independent, you can still help them develop a prayer list—written or unwritten—by discussing the day's events and helping them choose concerns and blessings to pray about.

♦ After prayer, instead of rushing straight to good-night kisses or some other activity, try having a short period of quiet. This reinforces the fact that God is there and that we need to listen in case He wants to give us wisdom on how to deal with an issue we've prayed about. Avoid implying that children should expect audible answers, but assure them that God responds in His way and time.

Topic No. 57

Prayer Benefits You in Many Ways.

Just as children ask why they should read the Bible, they'll ask why they should pray. The main benefit is a relationship with the Creator of the universe, who loves them very much. Out of this relationship, built by prayer, come several other benefits:

❖ Joy and peace (John 16:24; Philippians 4:6–7)
❖ Wisdom and understanding (Proverbs 2:3, 5–6; Jeremiah 33:3)
❖ Strength and courage (Psalm 138:3)
❖ Protection and rescue from harm and evil (Psalm 22:4)
❖ Purpose and guidance (Psalm 57:2)
❖ Meeting of our needs (Romans 8:32)
❖ Fulfillment of our desires (Psalm 37:4)
❖ Help and encouragement (Psalm 10:17)

Hints and Helps

♦ Use comparisons to help your children understand prayer. For example, prayer is like a telephone (it keeps you in touch with your Friend—God); a map (it helps you find landmarks, danger spots, and the best way to get places); clothes (it protects you); a party (it's a time of thanksgiving and celebration with your best

---

LOVING

C.
You Can Have
a Relationship
with God

55. You read the Bible to learn about who God is (Father, Son, and Holy Spirit) and what He has done and is doing.

56. You can pray your own prayers with your parents.

57. Prayer benefits you in many ways.

58. Keep praying: persistence, tests, and trials.

59. You can trust God and turn your life over to Him.

60. You should learn to seek God.

61. Jesus gives you peace.

AGES 7-9

Friend); and a tree house (it's a private place for you to spend time with your good Friend and share your thoughts with no fear of them getting spread around).

◆ Do your children wonder why they don't always get what they ask for in prayer? You may want to offer an explanation like the following:

If you ask me at your age, "Can I borrow the car?" you'll get an automatic no. If you ask, "Can I do my homework?" you'll probably get an automatic yes. If you ask, "Can I play with my friend?" the answer will depend on what's best at the time.

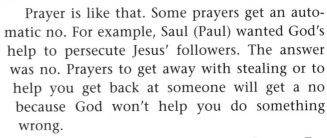

Prayer is like that. Some prayers get an automatic no. For example, Saul (Paul) wanted God's help to persecute Jesus' followers. The answer was no. Prayers to get away with stealing or to help you get back at someone will get a no because God won't help you do something wrong.

Other prayers get an automatic yes. For example, a prayer for forgiveness, to understand the Bible, to become more like Jesus, to find a way to help someone else, for courage to tell someone about Jesus—all these get a yes. After all, God tells us to pray for these things!

Then there are the less clear prayers, the ones the Bible isn't specific about. These might get a yes, a no, or a "wait." For example, you might pray, "Help me make the team," or "Please give me a bike for my birthday," or "Please make Jenny want to be my friend." The best thing to do when we pray about these things is to ask that God will work them out in the way that pleases Him most. That's what people mean when they pray for God's will. Then, whatever the answer is, you'll know it's what's best for you.

Sometimes God says no to a request because we're disobeying Him or fighting or not forgiving. He may put our request "on hold" until we deal with that issue. In any case, God hears every prayer, and He answers according to what's best for us.

Topic No. 58

Keep Praying: Persistence, Tests, and Trials.

A best friend is moving away; a beloved pet is dying; a bully continues to rule the playground. Your children have prayed about these things, but God hasn't granted their requests. How can you help them deal with the disappointment?

Even at this age, your children's faith will be tested. Bring them back to the fact of God's love. God cares about their feelings, but He also knows what's best. He wants us to keep praying and not give up. Timing is in His hands.

So are the answers. We may not like or understand them. The hard truth is that God wants our faith to grow strong and to be focused on the right things—His love and care—and not on getting what we want or having a smooth life. It's not easy to help our children or ourselves move from "Why don't You . . .?" to "I trust You, God, even if I don't understand." But you can begin this process together, starting with your example as you learn to accept what God sends and allows.

❖ *"We also rejoice in our sufferings, because we know that suffering produces perseverance; perseverance, character; and character, hope. And hope does not disappoint us, because God has poured out his love into our hearts by the Holy Spirit, whom he has given us"* (Romans 5:3–5).

❖ *"These have come so that your faith—of greater worth than gold, which perishes even though refined by fire—may be proved genuine and may result in praise, glory and honor when Jesus Christ is revealed"* (1 Peter 1:7).

Hints and Helps

◆ Try the following one day at lunch or dinner. Bring out a pathetic-looking meal, perhaps a couple of crackers on a plate. Say, "I'm going to give you a choice. You can eat this now, or you can wait 20 minutes. If you wait, I have something better planned—but I won't tell you what it is." Let kids decide whether to wait. For those who do, serve a favorite food 20 minutes later. Use this as an object lesson to reinforce the truth that sometimes God makes us wait because He has something far better planned.

◆ As you learn to trust God during tests and trials, be honest with Him and with your children. Show them in the psalms how David swung

---

LOVING

**C.
You Can Have
a Relationship
with God**

55. You read the Bible to learn about who God is (Father, Son, and Holy Spirit) and what He has done and is doing.

56. You can pray your own prayers with your parents.

57. Prayer benefits you in many ways.

58. Keep praying: persistence, tests, and trials.

59. You can trust God and turn your life over to Him.

60. You should learn to seek God.

61. Jesus gives you peace.

AGES 7–9

LOVING

C.
**You Can Have
a Relationship
with God**

55. You read the Bible to learn about who God is (Father, Son, and Holy Spirit) and what He has done and is doing.

56. You can pray your own prayers with your parents.

57. Prayer benefits you in many ways.

58. Keep praying: persistence, tests, and trials.

59. You can trust God and turn your life over to Him.

60. You should learn to seek God.

61. Jesus gives you peace.

AGES 7–9

back and forth between frustration and praise, reinforcing the truth that it's okay to express your real feelings to God. It's also important to come back to trusting Him, as David did.

♦ Ask your children to list all the junk food they think they could eat in a single day. Then ask them whether it would really be a good idea. Explain that even though eating a lot of junk food might feel good, it would hurt them in the long run. In the same way, God knows that some of our requests might make us happy for a while but would end up hurting us. Assure your children that God cares about how they feel, but He knows the big picture, too.

Topic No. 59

You Can Trust God and Turn Your Life over to Him.

Who knows the best way to use a computer, mountain bike, or video camera? The person who designed and made it! The designer can tell you how everything was meant to work, how to get the most out of that thing, and what not to do with it. As the designer of life, God knows better than anyone else how life works. It only makes sense to abide by His guidelines (see Topic No. 70, "God Has Taught You Right from Wrong").

For your children, turning their lives over to God means agreeing that He knows what's best for them, and that He has a great plan for their lives. It means entrusting their dreams and ambitions to His care.

❖ *"Trust in the LORD with all your heart and lean not on your own understanding; in all your ways acknowledge him, and he will make your paths straight"* (Proverbs 3:5–6).

❖ *"If anyone would come after me, he must deny himself and take up his cross and follow me. For whoever wants to save his life will lose it, but whoever loses his life for me and for the gospel will save it"* (Mark 8:34–35).

Hints and Helps

♦ Facing a change in your family? Use your next time of uncertainty—looking for a new job, moving, or having financial difficulties—to teach your children what trust looks like. Gather your family together and entrust your situation to God, telling Him that you want His will even if it's different from yours.

♦ If it's hard for you to trust God with your future, don't hide this fact from your children. Share your difficulty with them, though without going into more detail than is appropriate for your children. Be honest as you make an effort to grow in this area. They'll see that this "trusting God" stuff is practical, down-to-earth.

◆ Your eight-year-old son, Taylor, is new at school. He's trying to trust God to lead him to some new friends, but you don't see it happening. Should you step in? Before you do, consider that God may have something planned that you can't foresee, and that Taylor may learn a valuable lesson by waiting and trusting. It's hard not to "answer" your children's prayers yourself when you see them becoming disappointed, and sometimes parents *are* meant to be God's vehicle to answer their children's prayers. But be careful not to rescue your children when you don't think God is answering. He may want to teach *both* of you something!

Topic No. 60

You Should Learn to Seek God.

The way to find God is to look for Him. This is one of the most important things you can teach your children. Seeking God isn't so much a matter of how much time your child spends praying and meditating on His Word (though it does take time); it's more a matter of wanting to follow God with all their hearts. The better they know God, the more they'll love Him and the more of Him they'll want.

> ❖ *"As the deer pants for streams of water, so my soul pants for you, O God. My soul thirsts for God, for the living God. When can I go and meet with God?"* (Psalm 42:1–2).

> ❖ *"But seek first his [God's] kingdom and his righteousness, and all these things will be given to you as well"* (Matthew 6:33).

Hints and Helps

◆ Do *you* seek God? Or do you feel more like you're running from Him? If the latter is the case, consider talking with your pastor, a Christian counselor, or an experienced Christian friend about the guilt, anger, or other feelings that may be keeping you from drawing closer to the Lord. If your children are to know what it looks like to seek God, it's best if they can see and hear

LOVING

**C.
You Can Have
a Relationship
with God**

55. You read the Bible to learn about who God is (Father, Son, and Holy Spirit) and what He has done and is doing.

56. You can pray your own prayers with your parents.

57. Prayer benefits you in many ways.

58. Keep praying: persistence, tests, and trials.

59. You can trust God and turn your life over to Him.

60. You should learn to seek God.

61. Jesus gives you peace.

AGES 7–9

LOVING

C.
You Can Have
a Relationship
with God

55. You read the
Bible to learn about
who God is (Father,
Son, and Holy Spirit)
and what He has
done and is doing.

56. You can pray
your own prayers
with your parents.

57. Prayer benefits
you in many ways.

58. Keep praying:
persistence, tests,
and trials.

59. You can trust
God and turn your life
over to Him.

60. You should learn
to seek God.

61. Jesus gives you
peace.

AGES 7-9

you trying to know Him better.

◆ Suggest ways in which your children can pray as they seek God. For example: "Dear God, please help me understand how You feel about me." Or "God, I'd really like to know why You seem angry in the Old Testament and loving in the New Testament." Don't make this something they "must do." Rather, tell them that praying these prayers sincerely and regularly is a way to become closer to their heavenly Father.

Topic No. 61

Jesus Gives You Peace.

Why call Jesus the "Prince of Peace"? Because He can give us peace with God and peace in the middle of trying circumstances. Your children need to know they can go to Him when they're frustrated, confused, angry, or worried. Jesus is bigger than anything that upsets them; His peace can calm them in any situation.

❖ *"You will keep in perfect peace him whose mind is steadfast, because he trusts in you"* (Isaiah 26:3).

❖ *"Peace I leave with you; my peace I give you. I do not give to you as the world gives. Do not let your hearts be troubled and do not be afraid"* (John 14:27).

Hints and Helps

◆ Point out to your children when they're lacking peace, so that they can begin to identify what its lack and its presence feel like. Examples: when your children panic because they forgot a page of homework; when they express doubt that they'll have enough money when they grow up; when they feel guilty over hitting a sibling; when they're angry over being treated unfairly by a teacher; when they're nervous about having to sing in a concert.

◆ Conversely, make sure your children know what peace is. Tell them it's a quiet, settled, relaxed feeling. Point out peaceful times—a moment when family members are eating at the table without bickering, or a day when a child has made a confident speech in class. When they recognize its presence, they'll be able to ask God for peace more easily when it's absent.

◆ Model going to God for peace when you need it. Does tension start you thinking about God's promises? Or do you find yourself heading for that half gallon of ice cream in the freezer? Let children see you taking time to calm down and to pray or read a Bible passage that offers comfort.

You Can Be All God Wants You to Be

Topic No. 62

God Wants You to Learn and Grow and Become Like Jesus.

Talk about role models! Jesus is the perfect example for your children. He showed by His life and teachings how God wants them to live.

"Being like Jesus" could be confusing to your children. Explain that this doesn't mean wearing long robes, walking everywhere, and speaking in parables. They're to pattern themselves after Jesus' *character.*

❖ *"When he saw the crowds, he had compassion on them, because they were harassed and helpless, like sheep without a shepherd"* (Matthew 9:36).

❖ *"Jesus said to them, 'The kings of the Gentiles lord it over them; and those who exercise authority over them call themselves Benefactors. But you are not to be like that. Instead, the greatest among you should be like the youngest, and the one who rules like the one who serves. For who is greater, the one who is at the table or the one who serves?'"* (Luke 22:25–27).

❖ *"I have set you an example that you should do as I have done for you"* (John 13:15).

Hints and Helps

◆ Use stories from the life of Jesus to show children how they need to be like Him. Here are just a few:

❖ *Jesus stands up to the devil* (Matthew 4:1–11). Jesus refused to do things Satan's way. He trusted God to take care of Him and chose God's way. He quoted the Bible when He was in trouble.

❖ *Jesus touches the leper* (Mark 1:40–44). Most people avoided lepers. But Jesus touched this man and healed him. Jesus loved unpopular people and helped those whom others avoided.

LIVING

D.
You Can Be All God Wants You to Be

62. God wants you to learn and grow and become like Jesus.

63. Growth is a learning process.

64. Your character should match God's character.

65. God wants you to develop your talents.

66. God wants you to develop the Fruit of the Spirit.

67. God wants you to mature and develop your personality.

AGES 7-9

LIVING

**D.
You Can Be All
God Wants You
to Be**

62. God wants you to learn and grow and become like Jesus.

63. Growth is a learning process.

64. Your character should match God's character.

65. God wants you to develop your talents.

66. God wants you to develop the Fruit of the Spirit.

67. God wants you to mature and develop your personality.

❖ *Jesus tells it like it is* (Matthew 5:21–48; 11:20–24). Because He loved people, Jesus warned them when they were wrong. He was not afraid to call sin what it really is. He was straightforward and just.

❖ *Jesus forgives rejection* (Luke 22:56–62; John 21:15–19). Jesus didn't hate Peter, who had denied Him. He forgave Peter and was his friend again. Jesus understood His friend and loved him no matter what.

❖ *Jesus feels people's sadness* (John 11:1–44). Jesus felt His friends' grief and cried with them. He let them see that He understood their pain.

❖ *Jesus serves others* (John 13:1–17). He did the most lowly task—foot washing—for His friends. He served them willingly and selflessly.

◆ What would Jesus do? Have children come up with real-life dilemmas they might encounter. For instance, at a friend's house the friend wants to watch a violent video your child knows is off-limits; at school, your child knows who stole trading cards from backpacks at recess. Ask, "What do you think Jesus would do in this situation? How do you know?" Point out that the answer to the question starts with who Jesus is as a Person—His character—and then is expressed in His actions.

Topic No. 63

Growth Is a Learning Process.

Like physical growth, spiritual growth doesn't happen overnight. It occurs little by little as your children regularly spend time with God and internalize what they learn. It happens as they make right choices—and as they make mistakes and learn from them.

Your children need the comfort of knowing that growth involves mistakes and second tries. Instead of expecting instant perfection, God knows that becoming like Jesus is a process, just as are discovering how to write letters, memorizing multiplication tables, or painting pictures.

❖ *"Continue to work out your salvation with fear and trembling, for it is God who works in you to will and to act according to his good purpose"* (Philippians 2:12–13).

❖ *"His divine power has given us everything we need for life and godli-*

ness through our knowledge of him who called us by his own glory and goodness. . . . For this very reason, make every effort to add to your faith goodness; and to goodness, knowledge; and to knowledge, self-control; and to self-control, perseverance; and to perseverance, godliness; and to godliness, brotherly kindness; and to brotherly kindness, love. For if you possess these qualities in increasing measure, they will keep you from being ineffective and unproductive in your knowledge of our Lord Jesus Christ" (2 Peter 1:3, 5–8).

Hints and Helps

♦ Let your children know that you're growing too—as a person, a parent, and a follower of Jesus. Admit that you make mistakes and that you're learning from them. Treat mistakes—yours, theirs, and other people's—gently. Try to see errors as rungs on the ladder of growth rather than as failures.

♦ Remember that appearances are not the most important thing. Focus on your children's hearts. Avoid pressuring them to act a certain way when their hearts are far from that; they must take ownership of the right attitude before their actions will mean anything. Pushing children's faith experience past their understanding and beyond their hearts can reduce their Christianity to a matter of performance—which implies that if they blow it, they're failures. Actions are important, but good actions mean the most when they flow from the heart.

♦ Introduce "stretching" experiences in small steps. For example, instead of trying to teach your children to be good servants by making them sing solos at a nursing home, start by having them help you hand out birthday cards or treats at the facility. Work your way up to having the kids do more as they become comfortable in the unfamiliar environment. Give them small "success experiences" that build their confidence about doing the right thing. Embarrassing failures can cause children to fear trying again.

Topic No. 64

Your Character Should Match God's Character.

Does building godly character produce clones? Hardly! Character isn't the same as personality. Each child's personality is unique. Character, on the other hand, should be a reflection of who God is and what He's like (see Topic No. 46, "God's Character Is . . ."). It's the same for all people,

---

LIVING

**D.
You Can Be All
God Wants You
to Be**

62. God wants you to learn and grow and become like Jesus.

63. Growth is a learning process.

64. Your character should match God's character.

65. God wants you to develop your talents.

66. God wants you to develop the Fruit of the Spirit.

67. God wants you to mature and develop your personality.

AGES 7–9

but it's expressed in different ways through different personalities.

Why is character so important? Because good character will protect your children from evil. Doing things God's way builds a strong tower of protection around them.

❖ *"The Son is the radiance of God's glory and the exact representation [character] of his being"* (Hebrews 1:3).

Hints and Helps

◆ Here are seven key character traits of God that your children need to incorporate into their lives. A motto is included with each trait—a phrase with which children can affirm to themselves that they're growing in that area. Encourage kids to use the mottoes or come up with their own—and to make the phrases part of their identity by copying the words onto posters, jewelry, calendars, or other personal items they'll see frequently.

1. *Truth and honesty* (Ephesians 4:15): "God doesn't lie, and neither do I!"
2. *Love and compassion* (John 15:17; Colossians 3:12): "My heart's in the right place."
3. *Generosity and selflessness* (1 Timothy 6:18): "Something's got to give: me!"
4. *Forgiveness and mercy* (Colossians 3:13): "I 4give U."
5. *Trustworthiness and faithfulness* (Galatians 5:22–23): "Count on me!"
6. *Justice and impartiality* (Matthew 23:23): "Life's not fair, but I try to be."
7. *Holiness* (Romans 12:1): "Caution: Set apart."

◆ Point out character traits at work in everyday life. For example, when your child's best friend decides to hang out with someone else, talk about faithfulness; when a child gets too much change at the store, talk about honesty.

◆ Spell out the benefits of godly character. For instance, honesty works—it's as simple as that. A

Ten Godly Qualities (Psalm 15)

A godly person walks blamelessly, acts righteously, speaks truthfully, does his neighbor no wrong, casts no slur on others, despises the vile, honors those who fear God, keeps oaths even when it hurts, lends money without usury, and doesn't accept bribes.

person who tells the truth consistently will be trusted; others will want him or her as a friend. In contrast, a dishonest person gets a bad reputation; others stop trusting that person with belongings, secrets, and responsibility. When your children understand the benefits of character, they'll be more likely to choose the right direction because they'll know it works best.

Topic No. 65

God Wants You to Develop Your Talents.

Saxophone playing, somersaulting, storytelling, sewing—talents are God-given abilities. Your children's talents are an important part of God's plan for them.

Talents might come easy, but it takes work to develop them through music lessons, baseball practice, art classes, and so on. You can help your children reach the potential God has in mind for them by identifying and cultivating their talents.

❖ *"Do you see a man skilled in his work? He will serve before kings; he will not serve before obscure men"* (Proverbs 22:29).

❖ See also Exodus 35:25–26, 30–36:1; Proverbs 22:6; Daniel 1:17, 20.

Hints and Helps

◆ As your schedule and budget allow, encourage your children to try a variety of activities and lessons to help them discover their talents. Let them explore. When your children show an aptitude for something or enjoy a particular activity, affirm them in that and try to make it possible for them to grow in it.

◆ Point out examples of people using their talents to serve God. Obvious ones might include those who sing songs about Jesus and those who preach, but don't overlook the rest—the photographer who stirs compassion by taking pictures of famine victims, the cook who prepares meals for visiting missionaries, the attorney who defends the poor, etc.

◆ God needs people with talents—and willing hearts. Help your children make the most of their talents,

LIVING

D.
You Can Be All God Wants You to Be

62. God wants you to learn and grow and become like Jesus.

63. Growth is a learning process.

64. Your character should match God's character.

65. God wants you to develop your talents.

66. God wants you to develop the Fruit of the Spirit.

67. God wants you to mature and develop your personality.

AGES 7–9

LIVING

D.
You Can Be All
God Wants You
to Be

62. God wants you to learn and grow and become like Jesus.

63. Growth is a learning process.

64. Your character should match God's character.

65. God wants you to develop your talents.

66. God wants you to develop the Fruit of the Spirit.

67. God wants you to mature and develop your personality.

AGES 7-9

but discourage them from bragging about their abilities or substituting talent for godly character. Encourage them to see how their abilities might be used to call people's attention to Jesus, not just to themselves.

Topic No. 66

God Wants You to Develop the Fruit of the Spirit.

The fruit of the Spirit is so much more than just being nice. This group of qualities comes from inside, in your children's hearts, and can be developed only in cooperation with the Spirit of God. God's fruit makes relationships work and helps us to become more like Him.

❖ *"But the fruit of the Spirit is love, joy, peace, patience, kindness, goodness, faithfulness, gentleness and self-control. Against such things there is no law"* (Galatians 5:22–23).

Hints and Helps

◆ Words like *love*, *joy*, and *peace* can sound admirable—but vague. What does the fruit of the Spirit look like in real life? Here are some thoughts to help you prepare to teach your children about this subject.

1. *Love* is a commitment to unselfish thoughts, acts, and emotions. To give love, your children need to have their "love tanks" filled up by God's love—and yours. Love works by giving, listening, hugging, defending, and more. To help children "grow" love, remind them that other people are important because they're eternal and made in God's image, that God has made everyone different (and that's good), and that we need to think of others' concerns first. (See Ephesians 2:4–5; 1 John 4:16, 19.)

2. *Joy* is a deep, cheerful contentment. It comes from understanding God's love and what Jesus did for us. It comes from accepting God's constant care and knowing that He'll never let us down. Joy is contagious. Help children grow joy by reviewing their "thankful list," reminding them of how big God is, encouraging them to value each moment God gives them, and reminding them of heaven. (See Romans 14:17; 1 Thessalonians 5:16; 1 Peter 1:8.)

3. *Peace* is assurance that all is well because we serve a loving, wonderful God. Peaceful people tend to be relaxed, full of trust, confident. Peace with and from God becomes peace between them

and others, too. Help your children grow peace by reminding them to focus on the fact that God is in charge, to tell God about every aspect of their lives, and to trust God to take care of all their concerns. (See Isaiah 26:3; Ephesians 2:14.)

4. *Patience* is showing God's grace to others despite what they "deserve." God is patient with us because He knows we're still growing. We need to remember that no one else is finished growing yet, either. Help your children grow patience by suggesting that they imagine everyone is wearing a button that says, "Please be patient, God isn't finished with me yet." When they're tempted to be impatient, kids can try "rewinding" and taking a deep breath until they can respond patiently. (See Ephesians 4:2; Hebrews 12:3.)

5. *Kindness* is being considerate of others' feelings. It includes being polite, going out of our way to encourage others, and never giving up on people. Children can grow kindness as they think about how others want to be treated, as they look for ways to help people, and as they watch their words. (See Luke 6:35–36; Colossians 3:12.)

6. *Goodness* is choosing right over wrong. God is completely good—always perfect, always right. Goodness isn't just a matter of not doing bad things; it's doing the right thing. Children can begin to grow goodness by listening to their consciences and to God's Spirit, and by learning from the Bible what God says is right. (See Nahum 1:7; Galatians 6:10.)

7. *Faithfulness* is a constant commitment to God and people, and a constant expression of that commitment. It's doing what we say we'll do, taking care of what we're responsible for, obeying God no matter how others act. The Holy Spirit may use difficult times to teach your children faithfulness. They also can grow faithfulness by remembering that God doesn't change no matter how people treat Him, and by vowing to be the same way: "God never gives up, so neither do I!" (See Deuteronomy 7:9; Galatians 6:10.)

8. *Gentleness* is an inner strength that lets us serve others without feeling threatened or inferior. It never hurts another person's feelings or dreams. It's a strong, selfless caring. You can help children grow gentleness by assuring them that they're loved; when

LIVING

D.
You Can Be All
God Wants You
to Be

62. God wants you to learn and grow and become like Jesus.

63. Growth is a learning process.

64. Your character should match God's character.

65. God wants you to develop your talents.

66. God wants you to develop the Fruit of the Spirit.

67. God wants you to mature and develop your personality.

AGES 7-9

they know that, they can put aside the need to be important and to fight for respect, and they can begin to treat others gently. Children also can grow gentleness by reminding themselves that God loves others as much as He loves them, and that the other person is always more important than winning. (See Matthew 11:29; Romans 12:3; Philippians 4:5.)

9. *Self-control* is doing what's right no matter how we feel. The "self" in *self-control* means we are required to work at it. Self-control involves choosing God's way—with the Holy Spirit's help. Aid children in growing self-control by encouraging them to memorize Bible verses that will fortify them when they're tempted to choose wrong; instead of trying to control their behavior yourself, let them know that you expect them to learn to control themselves. (See Proverbs 25:28; Romans 8:8–9.)

◆ Pray regularly that God will help your children to grow His fruit. Encourage them to pray this for themselves, and point out when they're making progress. Explain that God doesn't expect us to grow the Spirit's fruit on our own; He is eager to help.

Topic No. 67

God Wants You to Mature and Develop Your Personality.

Maturing is the processing of growing up, of becoming all we're meant to be. We're all meant to reflect God's character, but in unique ways that are colored by our personalities. Encourage your children's uniqueness, but at the same time guide them to express their individuality in ways that are more and more Christlike.

Personality is no excuse for immature or wrong behavior. For example, a child who has strong leadership traits does not have an excuse for disobedience; an imaginative child does not have an excuse for lying. You can help your children find godly, mature expressions of the personalities God has given them.

❖ *"Therefore, as God's chosen people, holy and dearly loved, clothe yourselves with compassion, kindness, humility, gentleness and patience. . . . And over all these virtues put on love, which binds them all together in perfect unity. . . . And whatever you do, whether in word or deed, do it all in the name of the Lord Jesus, giving thanks to God the Father through him"* (Colossians 3:12, 14, 17).

Hints and Helps

◆ If your child has a Lion personality type (see page 91), explain that this doesn't give him or her permission to always take charge and tell people what to do. Others need opportunities to cultivate their leadership skills too. Help your Lion develop in his or her weaker areas, such as sensitivity to others.

◆ If your child is an Otter (see page 92), explain that he or she can't always be the life of the party. Much as they might like to, Otters must not invade others' space and make a joke of everything. They need to learn to deal with details and to be sensitive to those who prefer things quiet rather than loud and crazy.

◆ Is your child a Golden Retriever (pages 92–93)? He or she may want to take care of everyone. Let your child know, however, that he or she can't make everyone happy. Golden Retrievers need to learn to let people be themselves emotionally. They also need to develop their leadership skills, which they tend to avoid in case their decisions might upset someone.

◆ If your child is a Beaver (see pages 93–94), point out that Beavers are great at organization and details. But they aren't allowed to force others to be organized and to insist that everything be done in a certain way. Beavers need to learn how to relax, even when they don't know how things will turn out, and let others do things in new ways. They also need to develop their sense of fun and begin to see the big picture.

You Can Do All God Wants You to Do

Topic No. 68

Church Is God's Idea. Jesus Is the Head of the Church. At Church You Learn About God and Encourage Each Other to Follow Jesus.

Church is people. It's a community of Christians who meet together to learn about God, encourage one another, grow, and worship. God knew you and your children wouldn't be able to follow

---

LIVING

E.
You Can Do All God Wants You to Do

68. Church is God's idea. Jesus is the head of the church. At church you learn about God and encourage each other to follow Jesus.

69. God wants you to understand what a blessing people and good relationships are.

70. God has taught you right from wrong. He did this to keep you safe and to give you a good life.

71. The Ten Commandments are a good guide for life.

72. God wants you to share your faith.

AGES 7–9

Him alone, so He gave you the church.

Jesus is the head of the Church. It's His "bride." That means He's responsible for it. He loves His church and watches over it to make sure it benefits His children—including yours.

- ❖ *"God placed all things under his feet and appointed him to be head over everything for the church, which is his body, the fullness of him who fills everything in every way"* (Ephesians 1:22–23).
- ❖ *"Consequently, you are no longer foreigners and aliens, but fellow citizens with God's people and members of God's household, built on the foundation of the apostles and prophets, with Christ Jesus himself as the chief cornerstone. In him the whole building is joined together and rises to become a holy temple in the Lord. And in him you too are being built together to become a dwelling in which God lives by his Spirit"* (Ephesians 2:19–22).

Hints and Helps

- ◆ "But *why* do I have to go to church?" Your children need to understand why you're asking them to go and how church benefits them. Explain that there they learn about God, are part of a supportive group, and find good friends. It's not just *your* church; it's *their* church, *their* community. They'll need help to truly connect with others there. Make it as easy as you can for them to get involved, to meet and spend time with people from church.
- ◆ To help children see how church relates to their lives as a whole, make a point of mentioning church during the week. For example, recall something you heard during a sermon and explain how it might help you resolve a problem you're facing. Get together with another church family. Pray together about concerns listed in the church bulletin. Have a family meeting to decide how much to donate to a special church offering and how each family member might get involved.
- ◆ Avoid simply going to church and leaving as quickly as you can. Stick around to talk with other adults and to meet the children in your kids' classes. Use this time to make connections for yourself and for your children.
- ◆ On the way to church, pray together as a family that God will help you learn about Him and develop relationships in which you can both provide and receive support. On the way home, discuss what you learned. Rather than simply asking, "What did you do in

Sunday school?" try to be specific. Ask whether your children had fun, what songs they sang, whether they learned anything surprising, what the Bible story was, and how the lesson might help them during the coming week.

Topic No. 69

God Wants You to Understand What a Blessing People and Good Relationships Are.

The second greatest commandment (Mark 12:31) brings with it the second greatest blessing—good relationships with people of all ages. Being able to get along with all kinds of people—even those who are "different"—will benefit your children throughout their lives. If they really learn how to love others as they love themselves, nothing will hold them back.

❖ *"For if you forgive men when they sin against you, your heavenly Father will also forgive you. But if you do not forgive men their sins, your Father will not forgive your sins"* (Matthew 6:14–15).

❖ *"Bear with each other and forgive whatever grievances you may have against one another. Forgive as the Lord forgave you"* (Colossians 3:13).

Hints and Helps

◆ Read together what the Bible says about relationships. For examples, see Proverbs 12:18; 15:1–2; 17:27; 20:3; 21:23; 29:8; Matthew 5:9; 7:12; James 3:3–13.

◆ Teach your children how to forgive and to ask for forgiveness. If Ben hits Ryan, begin by dealing with Ben. Explain why hitting is wrong and have him ask for forgiveness. Then ask Ryan to forgive Ben. If Ryan refuses to forgive, explain that we always need to forgive as God has forgiven us. Avoid giving the impression, however, that we have to deny our hurt feelings in order to forgive. Feelings are valid and important; they need to be acknowledged and comforted. Still, God tells us to forgive.

◆ Conflicts happen in all relationships. Help your children realize that what they do with conflict can be bad or good. To help them deal with disagreements in a way that enables everyone to feel cared for, try sharing the following conflict resolution skills.

1. *Be an active listener.* Let others finish talking before you start. If you're planning your next words while the other person is talk-

LIVING

E.
You Can Do All
God Wants You
to Do

68. Church is God's idea. Jesus is the head of the church. At church you learn about God and encourage each other to follow Jesus.

69. God wants you to understand what a blessing people and good relationships are.

70. God has taught you right from wrong. He did this to keep you safe and to give you a good life.

71. The Ten Commandments are a good guide for life.

72. God wants you to share your faith.

AGES 7–9

LIVING

E.
You Can Do All
God Wants You
to Do

68. Church is God's idea. Jesus is the head of the church. At church you learn about God and encourage each other to follow Jesus.

69. God wants you to understand what a blessing people and good relationships are.

70. God has taught you right from wrong. He did this to keep you safe and to give you a good life.

71. The Ten Commandments are a good guide for life.

72. God wants you to share your faith.

AGES 7-9

ing, you're not listening. Look at the other person when he or she is speaking; try not to fidget or make disbelieving faces. Make sure you clearly understand the other person's point of view before you share your own. Tell the other person what you think he or she is saying. If you get it wrong, the other person can clear up the misunderstanding.

2. **Remember that your way isn't the only way.** The other person may be right!

3. **Stick to the issue.** Don't attack the other person personally or drag in past mistakes or disagreements.

4. **Use "I" statements instead of "you" statements.** Talk about how you feel ("I feel irritated when I hear knuckles cracking") instead of blaming the other person ("You make me mad when you crack your knuckles").

5. **Avoid "always" and "never" statements.** For example, saying, "Sometimes I feel you aren't listening to me" is less likely to cause problems than saying, "You never listen!"

6. **Choose your battles.** Some things aren't worth fighting over! And the person is always more important than the issue.

7. **Look for a win/win solution.** There doesn't *have* to be a winner and a loser. If you're creative, you can come up with a solution where everyone benefits.

Topic No. 70

God Has Taught You Right from Wrong. He Did This to Keep You Safe and to Give You a Good Life.

In a world that tends to reject the idea of absolute truth, it can be tough to teach your children that some things are right or wrong in all places for all people. Fortunately, your job is made easier by the fact that right and wrong actions often have obvious consequences. Lying, for example, frequently leads to betrayal and broken relationships. Bragging can stir up jealousy. Living God's way, on the other hand, leads to trust, respect, generosity, kindness, love, and a great relationship with God. Choosing the right way pays off.

God didn't tell us to do things a certain way in order to be controlling or make us sad. He did it because He knows how life works best. Living God's way gives the greatest chance for a satisfying life.

❖ *"Be careful to obey all these regulations I am giving you, so that it may always go well with you and your children after you, because you will be doing what is good and right in the eyes of the LORD your God"* (Deuteronomy 12:28).

❖ *"'For I know the plans I have for you,' declares the LORD, 'plans to prosper you and not to harm you, plans to give you hope and a future'"* (Jeremiah 29:11).

Hints and Helps

◆ Help your children to see the *why* and the *who* behind the rules. Just *knowing* the rules gives no real motivation to keep them. Let's say, for example, that your daughter cries, "But I don't want to clean my room!" Tell her that we clean our rooms because it's important to take care of our possessions, which then last longer.

Once your children understand the reason behind a rule, take them to the Ruler behind the reason: God. Behind every rule and reason in the Bible stands God and His character. In the case of room cleaning, you could point out that God owns all our possessions and entrusts them to our care. He also created the universe to operate in an orderly way; a clean room reflects that.

◆ While following God's instructions does lead to the best kind of life, that kind of life isn't necessarily the easiest kind. Doing the right thing can get us in trouble here on earth. People have, after all, been killed for obeying God. Point out to your children that real success in this life is pleasing God—and we may not see the rewards until we're in heaven.

Topic No. 71

The Ten Commandments Are a Good Guide for Life.

The Ten Commandments (Exodus 20:1–17; Deuteronomy 5:6–21) are God's basic laws for life. You'll want to help your children memorize them and, more importantly, understand and follow them.

1. **No other gods:** This is the foundation of all the other commandments. Before anything else, your children need the right relationship with God *in their hearts.*

2. **Don't make or worship idols:** If God is first in your children's hearts, they won't have idols—anything that's more important to them than God is, anything to which they look for ultimate happiness.

3. **Don't misuse God's name:** God's name is to be used only with respect, because of who He is.

LIVING

E.
You Can Do All God Wants You to Do

68. Church is God's idea. Jesus is the head of the church. At church you learn about God and encourage each other to follow Jesus.

69. God wants you to understand what a blessing people and good relationships are.

70. God has taught you right from wrong. He did this to keep you safe and to give you a good life.

71. The Ten Commandments are a good guide for life.

72. God wants you to share your faith.

AGES 7–9

4. *Keep the Sabbath:* Genesis tells us that God created the world and everything in it in six days, and on the seventh (Sabbath) day He rested. He tells us to set apart a day of rest, too.

5. *Honor your parents:* One way in which your children learn to know God and get along with people is by obeying you. This is the first step in God's growth process.

6. *Don't murder:* The heart of this commandment is to love one another. When we respect life as precious, we treat people as God wants them to be treated—instead of "murdering" them in our thoughts or actions (see Matthew 22:37–39).

7. *Don't commit adultery:* Some relationships are more important than others. In the family, the closest is between husbands and wives. Marriage is a picture of the relationship between people and God—one not to be cheapened or betrayed.

8. *Don't steal:* Stealing puts your own wants above the rights of others. It also shows that you aren't trusting God to meet your needs. Helping children not to steal flows from helping them trust God and respect others.

9. *Don't lie:* God is truth, so lying is wrong. If your children love people, they'll respect them by telling the truth to and about them.

10. *Don't covet:* Coveting isn't just wanting what we don't have; it's wanting what we have no right to—someone else's stuff. Coveting puts things before people and God.

Hints and Helps

◆ To help your children memorize the commandments, try these ideas:

   ❖ Choose a Bible version they understand.

   ❖ Work with your kids to put the commandments to music or in the form of a rap.

   ❖ Have your children copy the commandments (without numbers) onto index cards. Then mix the cards up. See whether the children can put them back in order.

   ❖ Put up a large sheet of paper in your child's room. Write the first commandment on the sheet and challenge your child to memorize it. Continue the process one commandment at a time until all are memorized. You may want to offer a small prize for learning all 10.

◆ Once your children have learned the commandments, have family members help each other to notice situations in which the commandments apply. When a family member sees such a situation, he or she can call out the number of the related commandment. For instance, if sister grabs brother's cassette player because she feels entitled to it, one of you can say, "Number 10!"

◆ Explain to your children that people can't keep all the commandments on their own. These rules were given by God to show people that they are sinners and need His forgiveness. But the commandments are a standard to strive for, and God can help your children keep them. Jesus made it possible for the commandments to be written on their hearts (Jeremiah 31:33; see also 1 Thessalonians 5:23–24).

Topic No. 72

God Wants You to Share Your Faith.

Sharing our faith is simply telling others what God has done for us— from giving us eternal life to answering our prayers to changing our habits. Your children are "witnessing" whether they're talking about God or not. Their lives speak loudly about who they are and what God means to them.

Jesus left His disciples the job of telling everyone about Him and what He did. That's an assignment for you and your children, too.

❖ *"Therefore go and make disciples of all nations, baptizing them in the name of the Father and of the Son and of the Holy Spirit, and teaching them to obey everything I have commanded you"* (Matthew 28:19–20).

❖ *"But in your hearts set apart Christ as Lord. Always be prepared to give an answer to everyone who asks you to give the reason for the hope that you have. But do this with gentleness and respect"* (1 Peter 3:15).

Hints and Helps

◆ To help children get used to the idea of talking about something they believe in, ask them to tell you about a favorite TV show, sport, hobby, or best friend. Note their enthusiasm and lack of self-consciousness. Then explain that sharing our faith is telling what we believe about Jesus and why. We don't need to be experts. We just need a personal, living relationship with God that's worth talking about.

LIVING

E.
You Can Do All God Wants You to Do

68. Church is God's idea. Jesus is the head of the church. At church you learn about God and encourage each other to follow Jesus.

69. God wants you to understand what a blessing people and good relationships are.

70. God has taught you right from wrong. He did this to keep you safe and to give you a good life.

71. The Ten Commandments are a good guide for life.

72. God wants you to share your faith.

AGES 7–9

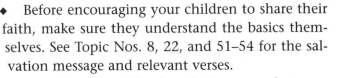

♦ Before encouraging your children to share their faith, make sure they understand the basics themselves. See Topic Nos. 8, 22, and 51–54 for the salvation message and relevant verses.

♦ Speak respectfully of nonbelievers so that your children will understand that they need to tell people about Jesus in a loving way. Explain that we need to respect other people's God-given right to decide for themselves, and not be pushy. Praying for others is a great idea, but the choice to accept or reject Jesus is theirs alone.

♦ If children fear "witnessing" because they might not know the answer to a friend's question, assure them that they don't have to know all the answers. If a puzzling question comes up, they can feel free to say, "I don't know, but I can find out," and get help later from you, a book, or a teacher. Many people aren't convinced by "proofs" or arguments anyway. They want to see Christians who show real love, as Jesus did.

CHAPTER 32

From Wrestling to Worship: What Your 10–12-Year-Old Can Learn

Who God Is

Topic No. 73

Not Everyone Believes the Truth About God . . . ; Handling Contrary Opinions About God.
At this stage, your children are internalizing what you've taught them about God, making it part of their own personal belief system. They've also noticed, however, that not everyone believes the same things. Friends, teachers, media—all will challenge your children's relationship with God and their understanding of who He is. You can help prepare them for these assaults so they won't be taken by surprise or be confused, or deceived (see also Topic Nos. 20, 44).

❖ *"The fool says in his heart, 'There is no God'"* (Psalm 14:1).

❖ *"In the beginning God created the heavens and the earth"* (Genesis 1:1).

❖ *"Now faith is being sure of what we hope for and certain of what we do not see. . . . And without faith it is impossible to please God, because anyone who comes to him must believe that he exists and that he rewards those who earnestly seek him"* (Hebrews 11:1, 6).

Hints and Helps

◆ To help your children sort out views of God, you may want to share the following definitions with them:

❖ ***Monotheism:*** Belief in one God. Christianity, Judaism, and

---

KNOWING

**A.
Who God Is**

73. Not everyone believes the truth about God, but there are ways you can respond to their objections. (Handling contrary opinions about God; basic apologetics; other religions)

AGES 10–12

357

Islam share this, but the latter two don't accept the idea that Jesus is God.

❖ *Polytheism:* Belief that there are many gods, or at least more than one.

❖ *Universalism:* Belief that all faiths lead to God. Many people with this view are offended by the Bible's position that Jesus is the only way to God.

❖ *Atheism:* Belief that there is no God. Many with this view would say that the universe and everything in it came to be by accident.

❖ *Pantheism:* Belief that the universe *is* God. Many with this view would say that God is not a Person, but the sum of all the forces of nature.

❖ *Agnosticism:* Belief that you can't know for sure whether God is real. Some with this view would say that faith—believing without absolute proof—is foolish.

◆ Kids may find it easy to reject ideas like atheism or pantheism, but they may fall prey to more subtle distortions of who God is. For example, they may get the impression that God is the "Eye in the sky," watching and waiting for them to mess up—rather than Someone who is on their side, enjoying them and helping them to try again when they fail. Or they may fall prey to the opposite notion—that God doesn't care about sin and just wants everyone to be happy. To help children form a balanced, biblical view of God, keep bringing them back to what the Bible says about Him in verses like Romans 6:23; 2 Thessalonians 1:6; 1 John 4:8.

◆ Explain *why* it's important to believe what the Bible says about God. For example, if Jesus isn't God, He couldn't have been perfect or died to pay for our sins; He would have had to pay for His own. The result: no forgiveness or life in heaven with God after we die.

◆ One of the challenges your children will face is the theory of evolution. They need to know that believing in a biblical view of creation is reasonable and based on evidence. Here are just a few faith-building facts you can share with them:

1. Evolutionists generally assume that single-cell creatures evolved into fish that crawled onto land and eventually evolved into

humans. But even if the earth is four billion years old, as evolutionists say, many scientists realize this is not nearly long enough for even single-cell creatures to develop. Even with enough time, the odds of all the parts of a single-cell creature coming together by themselves in the right way to form life are from 1 in 1,060 to 1 in 1,040,000. And what about a human being, made of millions of cells and many interconnecting systems? The odds are impossible to calculate!

2. There's still no solid evidence of transitional creatures between reptiles and birds and between apelike animals and humans. "Missing link" discoveries have proven false. Some consider Heidelberg man, reconstructed from a jawbone, to be a missing link—but fully human natives of New Caledonia have the same jawbone.

3. Some people think that if God cannot be proven scientifically to exist, then He does not exist and there must be some other explanation for the universe. But even science assumes the existence of unseen subatomic particles simply because of their effects on their surroundings. Isn't it reasonable to believe God exists when His effects can be seen all around us?

4. Evolution or creation? Since none of us were present at the beginning, it's a matter of faith either way. Everyone believes "unprovable" things—some more reasonable than others. Based on the evidence, faith in God seems at least as reasonable as the alternative.

◆ As you seek to counter false ideas about God, keep in mind three tips that can make your job easier:

1. Unless they indicate otherwise, assume your children are with you, believing what you've taught them.

2. Avoid force-feeding. Instead, watch for times when children are curious. Give them what they can handle and come back later when they're ready for more.

3. Help children find books, videos, and other resources that offer evidence for the biblical view. Not all the answers have to come directly from you. If children have trouble understanding the resources alone, explore them together.

KNOWING

B.
What God Has
Done

74. God wants you to explore the One Big Story.

75. God put the Bible together in a fascinating way.

76. You need to learn how to study the Bible.

77. God lets His people serve Him and express their worship of Him in different ways.

78. God gave us an accurate record of His Son, Jesus.

79. God wants you to tell others about what Jesus has done.

80. Jesus will return as Judge and there will be a new heaven and a new earth.

What God Has Done

Topic Nos. 74, 75

God Wants You to Explore the One Big Story; God Put the Bible Together in a Fascinating Way.

By this time your children may understand what Jesus has done for them and may have received Him as Savior. If not, you'll want to review Topic Nos. 21–24, 52–54 and share needed information with them.

Once children grasp and accept the basics, remind them that receiving Jesus is the beginning—the first step on the road to a fulfilling life and a wonderful relationship with God. Your goal now is for them to choose to be part of God's big story. They need to understand that story on a deeper level than they have before. You can help them do that by easing them into reading a full-text, age-appropriate Bible of their own.

- ❖ *"Everything must be fulfilled that is written about me in the Law of Moses, the Prophets and the Psalms"* (Luke 24:44).
- ❖ See also Matthew 22:40; Luke 16:31.

Hints and Helps

- ◆ Since the Bible can be overwhelming, especially if we aren't sure how to approach it, you can make things easier by telling your children how the Bible is structured. You may even want to read the following to them:

    The Bible is a whole library of books. Like a library, it's organized into sections. First, it's divided into two main parts—the Old Testament and the New Testament.

The Old Testament contains 39 books:

- ❖ *Five books of the **Law*** (Genesis to Deuteronomy)—Creation, Adam and Eve and the first sin, Noah, the patriarchs (Abraham to Jacob), Joseph, Moses and the Exodus, the Israelites' wandering in the desert, and the rules God gave them.
- ❖ *Twelve books of **history*** (Joshua to Esther)—the conquering and settling of Canaan, the judges, the kings of Israel and Judah, what happened when the kingdoms were conquered and taken captive by Assyria and Babylon, how the Jews came back to the land God promised them, and how Esther saved them all.
- ❖ *Five books of **poetry*** (Job to Song of Songs)—instructions for life and wisdom about relationships with God.

❖ *Five **major prophets*** (Isaiah to Daniel) and *12 **minor prophets*** (Hosea to Malachi)—the words and actions of some of the prophets God sent to Israel and Judah during the time of the kings, during the exile in Babylon, and during the first century after the Jews returned to their land. They're called "major" and "minor" because of the lengths of the books, not their importance.

The New Testament contains 37 books:

❖ *Four **Gospels*** or "good news" books (Matthew, Mark, Luke, and John)—separate accounts of Jesus, each with a different emphasis.

❖ *One book of **history*** (Acts)—what happened after Jesus returned to heaven, how the news about Him spread through the Roman world, and how the church began.

❖ *Fourteen **letters or epistles*** (Romans to Hebrews)—explanations of the Christian faith and instructions on how to follow Jesus, most of which were written by the apostle Paul.

❖ *Seven **general letters or epistles*** (James to Jude)—guidance on Christian living written by other early church leaders. These letters are "general" because they weren't addressed to any particular person or church.

❖ *One book of **prophecy*** (Revelation)—a vision the apostle John had while a prisoner on the island of Patmos; it talks about what will happen in the end, including the return of Jesus.

◆ To help your children remember the library layout of the Bible, tell them that the Old Testament books are "5–12–5–5–12": 5 books of law, 12 books of history, 5 books of poetry, 5 major prophets, and 12 minor prophets. The New Testament books are "4–1–14–7–1": 4 Gospels, 1 book of history, 14 epistles to specific churches, 7 general epistles, and 1 book of prophecy.

Topic No. 76

You Need to Learn How to Study the Bible.

As your children begin to read full-text Bibles, you can introduce them to the idea of studying God's Word. You don't need to turn them into Bible scholars. The important thing is that they discover that the Bible really contains answers to their questions, and that digging into it will help them live the most satisfying lives.

❖ *"Now the Bereans were of more noble character than the Thessalonians,*

KNOWING

**B.
What God Has
Done**

74. God wants you to explore the One Big Story.

75. God put the Bible together in a fascinating way.

76. You need to learn how to study the Bible.

77. God lets His people serve Him and express their worship of Him in different ways.

78. God gave us an accurate record of His Son, Jesus.

79. God wants you to tell others about what Jesus has done.

80. Jesus will return as Judge and there will be a new heaven and a new earth.

AGES 10–12

for they received the message with great eagerness and examined the scriptures every day to see if what Paul said was true" (Acts 17:11).

Hints and Helps

◆ There's more than one way to study the Bible. Tell your children about the following methods. In fact, why not try them yourself and let your children watch and learn?

❖ *Topical studies* help you discover what the Bible says on a certain subject, such as love or forgiveness.

❖ *Word studies* involve looking up verses in which a certain word, such as "grace" or "worship" is used, so that you can get a clearer picture of what it means.

❖ *Character studies* help you find out all you can about a Bible character like David or Deborah.

❖ *Book studies* focus on one book in the Bible, such as Ruth or Galatians, and explore what it means and how it applies to today.

◆ Show your children tools like the following that can help with Bible study. If you don't have these, try borrowing some from the church library or a friend.

❖ *Concordance:* This is an index of most words used in the Bible and where to find them. Many Bibles have a simplified one in the back. This tool is especially useful when you know part of a verse but not where to find it, or when you're doing a word study.

❖ *Topical index:* This reference lists verses by subject—even those that don't use a particular word. For example, if you're studying forgiveness, a topical index will take you to the story of the Prodigal Son, which is about forgiveness but doesn't use the word.

❖ *Cross-references:* These are the numbers and notes found in the margins or center column in many Bibles. They help you to find related verses.

❖ *Bible dictionary:* This gives you the meanings of words used in the Bible, plus background material on biblical people and places.

❖ **Bible commentary:** This tool comments on verses and sections, helping you understand the context of the passage, the author's original meaning, and how it might apply today. Some Bibles have brief commentaries at the bottom of the pages; other commentaries are in separate volumes.

❖ **Book introductions:** Many Bibles introduce each Bible book with background information (such as who wrote it, when, and why) and an overview or outline of the book.

❖ **Bible atlas or maps:** In the back of many Bibles—and in separate books—are maps that help you see where the Bible's events took place.

◆ To encourage kids to start searching the scriptures for themselves, challenge them to find out on their own what the Bible says about a situation they're facing—a rocky friendship, for instance, or a decision about how to spend some money. If they get stuck, help them out. When they're done, ask them to share with you what they found.

◆ The ancient names of the Bible's countries and cities, even when shown on maps, may seem like imaginary places to your children. Using a contemporary atlas, point out these places on modern maps. Babylon, for example, seems far, far away; Iraq seems much more immediate.

Topic No. 77

God Lets His People Serve Him and Express Their Worship of Him in Different Ways.

Christians generally agree on the basic doctrines of the Apostles' Creed. But your children will encounter many differences among churches, and they may wonder why. You can help clear up the confusion and guide children to appreciate the freedom God gives us to honor Him in a variety of ways.

KNOWING
B. **What God Has Done**

74. God wants you to explore the One Big Story.

75. God put the Bible together in a fascinating way.

76. You need to learn how to study the Bible.

77. God lets His people serve Him and express their worship of Him in different ways.

78. God gave us an accurate record of His Son, Jesus.

The Apostles' Creed

I believe in God, the Father almighty, creator of heaven and earth.

    I believe in Jesus Christ, His only Son, our Lord. He was conceived by the power of the Holy Spirit and born of the Virgin Mary. He suffered under Pontius Pilate, was crucified, died, and was buried. He descended into hell. On the third day He rose again. He ascended into heaven and is seated at the right hand of the Father. He will come again to judge the living and the dead.

    I believe in the Holy Spirit, the holy Christian church, the communion of saints, the forgiveness of sins, the resurrection of the body, and life everlasting.

AGES 10-12

KNOWING

B.
What God Has
Done

74. God wants you to explore the One Big Story.

75. God put the Bible together in a fascinating way.

76. You need to learn how to study the Bible.

77. God lets His people serve Him and express their worship of Him in different ways.

78. God gave us an accurate record of His Son, Jesus.

79. God wants you to tell others about what Jesus has done.

80. Jesus will return as Judge and there will be a new heaven and a new earth.

❖ *"Make every effort to keep the unity of the Spirit through the bond of peace. There is one body and one Spirit—just as you were called to one hope when you were called—one Lord, one faith, one baptism; one God and Father of all, who is over all and through all and in all"* (Ephesians 4:3–6).

Hints and Helps

◆ You can help your children distinguish the *essentials* of the Christian faith from the way Christians *express* and *celebrate* that faith. Explain that God made people with a great variety of personalities and tastes. Naturally, this comes through in how Christians serve and worship Him. Some churches emphasize certain parts of the Christian life—sharing one's faith, studying the Bible, helping the poor, etc. Churches also tend to emphasize certain forms of worship, based on tradition and preference—choosing one kind of music over another, dressing in a particular way, moving or not moving to show their feelings, etc.

◆ Try taking a family field trip to a church unlike your own, so that your children can experience another form of worship. Then ask, "How might the things they did be expressions of their love for God? How is that church like ours?"

◆ It's important to focus on the things Christians have in common. But feel free to teach your children about the things that make your church unique too, so that they can fully participate in your worship service and the rest of your church's program.

Topic No. 78

God Gave Us an Accurate Record of His Son, Jesus.

We shouldn't be surprised when those who want to undermine Christianity attack Jesus. After all, He's the cornerstone of the Christian faith! Your children will face those who say that Jesus never really lived or that He wasn't really God. You can help prepare them for this by making sure their faith in Him is solidly grounded.

❖ *"Men of Israel, listen to this: Jesus of Nazareth was a man accredited by God to you by miracles, wonders and signs, which God did among you through him, as you yourselves know"* (Acts 2:22).

❖ *"We did not follow cleverly invented stories when we told you about the power and coming of our Lord Jesus Christ, but we were eyewitnesses of his majesty"* (2 Peter 1:16; see also John 21:24–25).

❖ *"But God raised him from the dead, freeing him from the agony of death, because it was impossible for death to keep its hold on him. . . . God has raised this Jesus to life, and we are all witnesses of the fact. . . . God has made this Jesus, whom you crucified, both Lord and Christ"* (Acts 2:24, 32, 36).

Hints and Helps

◆ Can you "prove" to your children that Jesus really lived? Perhaps not. But you can offer some convincing evidence. If you like, read the following to them or share it in your own words.

1. *Eyewitness accounts:* The Bible is our main source for information about Jesus. Is the Bible accurate? It's been shown to tell the truth about so much else that you can be confident it tells the truth about Jesus (see Topic No. 47, "The Bible Is True"). Those who wrote the Gospels were convinced that what they'd seen and heard was real. Their books were written when others who'd been there were still alive. If the Gospel writers had been telling lies, these others would certainly have exposed them—but they didn't.

2. *Extra-biblical sources:* The Bible isn't the only book that mentions Jesus. Others who wrote not long after He lived show that He was a real, historical person. Flavius Josephus, a Jewish historian who lived around A.D. 70, mentioned Jesus, saying that He was condemned to death by Pilate and then appeared alive again on the third day. Josephus also mentioned Jesus when he told how James, Jesus' brother, was killed. Then there's a letter from a leading Roman, Tacitus (around A.D. 112), mentioning that Jesus was put to death under Pilate. And some Jewish teachers of the time referred to Jesus or *Yeshua*.

◆ At this stage, many children want evidence to back up the claim that Jesus is God—especially if they've encountered peers who disagree. Here are some thoughts you may want to offer:

1. *Jesus claimed He was God.* As C. S. Lewis wrote, there are only three things you can believe about Jesus' claim: He is who He says He is (God and Lord); He was a liar who knew He was lying; or He just thought He was telling the truth when He wasn't—in other words, He was a lunatic.

   Lots of people would agree that Jesus was a great teacher of right and wrong. If He was, He couldn't be a liar. Was He crazy?

None of His other words or actions suggest that He was. The only possibility left is that He's who He claims to be—Lord.

2. *Jesus rose from the dead.* Jesus died, yet three days later He was alive again. What happened? The Romans made sure Jesus was dead. His body was wrapped in cloths with spices, which made the grave clothes stick to the body—very difficult to remove. He was placed in a burial chamber cut into solid rock, its one exit covered by a huge stone that took several people to move. Soldiers guarded the tomb; they knew that sleeping on the job brought a death penalty.

Yet three days later, the tomb was empty. The huge stone had been moved away from the tomb; the grave clothes were empty as if Jesus' body had passed right through them. The soldiers were bribed to say they'd fallen asleep, yet they were not punished for it. Nor were the disciples punished for stealing Jesus' body. More than 500 people saw Jesus alive after His death. And the disciples were never the same, changing from scared people hiding from the authorities to bold people who were willing to suffer beatings and even death. Knowing Jesus rose from the dead helped them to be bold.

◆ How do we know Jesus is the Messiah? One way is through the predictions that Jesus fulfilled—60 major Old Testament prophecies about the Messiah! Here are some you may want to point out to your children:

Prophecy	OT Reference	NT Fulfillment
The Messiah would be or have:		
The Son of God	Psalm 2:7; Proverbs 30:4	Matthew 3:17; Luke 1:32
Born of virgin	Isaiah 7:14	Matthew 1:18–25; Luke 1:26–35
Born in Bethlehem	Micah 5:2	Matthew 2:1; Luke 2:4–6
From tribe of Judah	Genesis 49:10	Matthew 1:2; Luke 3:33–34
Betrayed	Psalm 41:9	John 13:18, 21, 26–27
Beaten	Isaiah 50:6	Matthew 26:67; 27:26, 30
Crucified	Psalm 22:1, 6–18; 69:21	Matthew 27:34–50; John 19:28–30
Bones unbroken	Psalm 34:20	John 19:31–37
Pierced	Psalm 22:16; Zechariah 12:10	John 19:34, 36
Raised from dead	Psalm 16:10	Luke 24:1–12; Acts 13:35–37

Topic No. 79

God Wants You to Tell Others About What Jesus Has Done.

Many Christians are intimidated by the idea of witnessing. But when Jesus is an important part of your children's lives, talking about Him will be as natural and easy as talking about a best friend. Rather than treating sharing their faith as a separate "job" Christians are supposed to do, encourage kids to see it as a way of letting their good feelings about God overflow into other people's lives.

The best way to help your children tell others about Jesus is to help them fall in love with Him. Few have an urge to share *knowledge* that's strong enough to overcome shyness or fear. But most who are in *love* find it easy to talk about the object of their affection.

❖ *"Therefore go and make disciples of all nations, baptizing them in the name of the Father and of the Son and of the Holy Spirit, and teaching them to obey everything I have commanded you. And surely I am*

KNOWING

**B.
What God Has
Done**

74. God wants you to explore the One Big Story.

75. God put the Bible together in a fascinating way.

76. You need to learn how to study the Bible.

77. God lets His people serve Him and express their worship of Him in different ways.

78. God gave us an accurate record of His Son, Jesus.

79. God wants you to tell others about what Jesus has done.

80. Jesus will return as Judge and there will be a new heaven and a new earth.

with you always, to the very end of the age" (Matthew 28:19–20).

❖ *"But in your hearts set apart Christ as Lord. Always be prepared to give an answer to everyone who asks you to give the reason for the hope that you have. But do this with gentleness and respect"* (1 Peter 3:15).

Hints and Helps

◆ "I can't tell people about Jesus," your children might say. "They'll get mad if I say Jesus is the only way and their religion is wrong." How can you reply?

Help your children to understand that Christianity isn't exclusive and narrow-minded—it's inclusive and welcoming. "Membership" in most religions is available to a select few—those who perform certain tasks to earn God's favor, who are born into a certain culture, or who otherwise fit a certain profile. Christianity is the only faith that says you can do nothing to earn heaven—yet your entrance can be guaranteed! Jesus clearly stated the way: *"I am the way and the truth and the life. No one comes to the Father except through me"* (John 14:6).

This does not *exclude* people; it *includes* everyone. No matter where you're from, what you look like, how smart or hardworking or lazy you are, you're welcome. All you have to do is accept God's free gift of forgiveness, delivered to you through Jesus' death. Make sure your children understand that He is the wide-open door to heaven through which *anyone* can enter and through which *everyone* must enter. We don't need to "fight" other religions; we just need to tell people the truth and give them the chance to meet Jesus.

◆ Some children, feeling anxious about whether their friends will go to heaven, may try to pressure those friends into becoming Christians. Encourage your children to be gentle in the way they talk about Jesus. They need to be ready, respectful, humble, and caring. No matter what the other's person's response is, he or she deserves to be treated with respect. Each person has a God-given right to choose to follow Jesus or not. Arguments, demands, and pressure don't bring people into God's kingdom; loving them, respecting them, and answering their questions can. Urge your children to trust God to help them tell others about Him, and to leave the results in His hands.

◆ Even the most enthusiastic child needs knowledge and answers to back up his or her zeal. Show your children where to find Bible verses explaining how to accept Jesus (see Topic No. 22 for "The Gospel in a Nutshell"). There are many ways to explain the gospel; encourage kids to tell the story of their journey with Jesus in their own words.

Topic No. 80

Jesus Will Return as Judge and There Will Be a New Heaven and a New Earth.

Children are often drawn to—and confused by—the prophetic parts of the Bible. As they read their Bibles or listen in Sunday school, your children will encounter Ezekiel, Daniel, Revelation, and other sections that are difficult to understand. They may be even more confused when they learn that Christians interpret these writings in different ways. You can help reduce the confusion—and assure your children that the most important thing to know about the future is that God has a wonderful plan for us, a plan that includes the return of Jesus.

❖ *"For the Lord himself will come down from heaven, with a loud command, with the voice of the archangel and with the trumpet call of God, and the dead in Christ will rise first. After that, we who are still alive and are left will be caught up together with them in the clouds to meet the Lord in the air. And so we will be with the Lord forever. Therefore encourage each other with these words"* (1 Thessalonians 4:16–18).

❖ *"Now, brothers, about times and dates we do not need to write to you, for you know very well that the day of the Lord will come like a thief in the night"* (1 Thessalonians 5:1–2).

Hints and Helps

◆ When children ask what prophetic passages mean, use the opportunity to explain a couple of basic guidelines for interpreting the Bible:

❖ *Start with the straightforward.* God presented clearly what He really wants us to know. Things about the future that are less urgent to know He presents symbolically. It's better to first read "basic" scriptures that deal with the end times (like Matthew 24:1–5 and 1 Thessalonians 4:13–5:11) and *then* move to more

KNOWING

**B.
What God Has
Done**

74. God wants you to explore the One Big Story.

75. God put the Bible together in a fascinating way.

76. You need to learn how to study the Bible.

77. God lets His people serve Him and express their worship of Him in different ways.

78. God gave us an accurate record of His Son, Jesus.

79. God wants you to tell others about what Jesus has done.

80. Jesus will return as Judge and there will be a new heaven and a new earth.

AGES 10–12

81. You can pray on
your own.

82. You can read the
Bible on your own.

83. You can learn to
worship God and
Jesus on your own or
in a group.

symbolic passages (such as Revelation and Daniel 7–12), rather than the other way around.

❖ *Look for the big idea.* The question to ask about tough passages is "What's the main point?" The main point of Revelation, for instance, is "Jesus is coming back. Be ready!"

◆ How can you deal with differing views of the end times? Let children know that Christians have various opinions about the meaning of certain scriptures, especially those that contain symbolic language or that don't go into great detail about an issue. Let them know your viewpoint. Help them understand that the principles are more important than the details, and that God's Spirit will help them understand what they need to know. As for prophecy, explain that none of us will completely understand it—until it happens!

You Can Have a Relationship with God

Topic No. 81

You Can Pray on Your Own.

At this stage most children are able to pray their own prayers, though you'll probably want to be on the scene in the early years of this age range to help them be consistent and to offer input when necessary. Eventually children may want to pray silently. This usually shows they're getting personal with God and can talk to Him about things they're uncomfortable talking with anyone else about. It's a good sign. In time they'll want you to let them pray entirely on their own.

As needed, you can review with your children information from Topic Nos. 9, 10, 26, 56–58. Tell them some things you've learned in your own prayer life too.

❖ *"Pray continually; give thanks in all circumstances, for this is God's will for you in Christ Jesus"* (1 Thessalonians 5:17–18).

❖ *"Is any one of you in trouble? He should pray. Is anyone happy? Let him sing songs of praise. Is any one of you sick? He should call the elders of the church to pray over him and anoint him with oil in the name of the Lord. And the prayer offered in faith will make the sick person well; the Lord will raise him up. If he has sinned, he will be forgiven. Therefore confess your sins to each other and pray for each other so that you may be healed. The prayer of a righteous man is powerful and effective"* (James 5:13–16).

Hints and Helps

◆ Keep praying and reading the Bible with your children as long as they want you to. There's no need to rush them into doing these things alone. These times together can be important to parents *and* children—and forcing children to go solo before they're ready could cause them to flounder and give up.

◆ Encourage children to pause after each topic of prayer. This helps them slow down and think about what they're doing, and it reminds them that God is interested and involved in the conversation. Pausing at the end of a prayer gives them a chance to add anything else that comes to mind.

◆ It's helpful to make prayer itself the first topic of a prayer. Encourage your children to begin by thanking God for hearing them and asking Him to help them pray as He wants them to. This "meeting to plan the meeting" prepares the heart.

Topic No. 82

You Can Read the Bible on Your Own.

It's time for a rite of passage! If your children don't have full-text Bibles of their own, take them to a Christian bookstore and let them help choose one. Their involvement will increase their sense of ownership and, ultimately, their willingness to read. If possible, steer them toward Bibles designed for preteens or teenagers, appropriate for their reading level, containing simple notes and reference tools.

Remind your children that reading their Bible regularly and thinking about what it says is God's idea. He came up with that idea because He knows so well what they need.

❖ *"Do not let this Book of the Law depart from your mouth; meditate on it day and night, so that you may be careful to do everything written in it. Then you will be prosperous and successful"* (Joshua 1:8).

❖ *"Your word is a lamp to my feet and a light for my path"* (Psalm 119:105).

LOVING

**C.
You Can Have
a Relationship
with God**

81. You can pray on your own.

82. You can read the Bible on your own.

83. You can learn to worship God and Jesus on your own or in a group.

AGES 10–12

Hints and Helps

◆ Approaching your first full-text Bible can be a daunting task. Help your children decide how they'd like to start (see Topic Nos. 74, 75 for information on the Bible and how it's organized). Here's one way to do it—the "First Find Plan," which gives kids a good overview of the Big Story of scripture:

1. Beginnings: Genesis
2. Forming a Nation: Exodus
3. Jesus' Story: Luke
4. The Church Begins: Acts
5. Practical Living: James

◆ Once your children have completed the "First Find Plan" or a similar introduction to Bible reading, try having them move on to the "Treasure Trove Plan." You may want to photocopy this list, have your children keep it in their Bibles, and encourage them to check off the passages as they read.

Old Testament

Beginnings: Genesis 1–50 (also in the "First Find Plan")
Forming a Nation: Exodus 1–40 (also in the "First Find Plan")
Israel in the Desert: Numbers 8–27
Following God and Taking Over: Deuteronomy 6–7; 34
Conquest of the Promised Land: Joshua 1–10; 24
Unusual Judges: Judges 1–7; 13–16
Loyalty and Reward—Ruth
Saul's Fall; David, Fugitive Hero: 1 Samuel 1–21; 23–31
David Gets the Kingdom: 2 Samuel 5–7
Praise and Dedication: Psalm 23; 32; 100; 103; 130; 139
Solomon's Wisdom, Riches, and Wives: 1 Kings 3–5; 8–12
Prophets, Kings, and Other Things: 2 Kings 2–5; 7; 12; 18–20; 22–24
Messiah's Astonishing Mission: Isaiah 53
Fatal Fall of Jerusalem: Jeremiah 52:1–16
Daniel, Courageous Captive: Daniel 1–6
King Cyrus Lets Jews Return: 2 Chronicles 36:22–23
Rebuilding Altar and Temple: Ezra 1; 3; 6

Rebuilding Jerusalem's Walls: Nehemiah 1–8
Queen Saves the Day: Esther 1–10

New Testament
Jesus' Story: Luke 1–24 (also in the "First Find Plan")
Jesus, God's Son: John 1–21
Witness to the World: Acts 1–28
Sins and a Savior: Romans 1–8; 12–14
Life in the Body: 1 Corinthians 12–14
Earth and Heaven: 2 Corinthians 4–5
Giving: 2 Corinthians 9
Real Freedom: Galatians 5–6
Unity, Goodness, Obedience, and Armor: Ephesians 4–6
Follow the Leader: Philippians 2–4
Pleasing God: 1 Thessalonians 3–4
Love God, Not Money: 1 Timothy 6
God's Prisoner Gives Advice: 2 Timothy 2; 4
Do What's Good: Titus 3
The Faith Hall of Fame: Hebrews 11
Holiness and Hard Times: 1 Peter 1–3
The Day of the Lord: 2 Peter 3
Practical Living: James 1–5 (also in the "First Find Plan")
Love God and Others: 1 John 1–5
Warnings and Rewards: Revelation 1–3; 20–22

◆ If children express confusion about what they're reading, look together for answers in a Bible commentary or Bible dictionary (see Topic No. 76, "You Need to Learn How to Study the Bible"). Make sure their Bible translation is easy to read. Remind them to pray before they read the Bible that God will give them understanding and wisdom and continue to teach them from it.

Topic No. 83

You Can Learn to Worship God and Jesus on Your Own or in a Group.

What's worship? Children need to know that it takes many forms but boils down to one thing: giving of yourself to God in response to who He is. In worship we praise God honestly from our hearts, with our whole lives. Worship may happen in a group setting or when we're alone—anytime, anyplace. Getting together with other Christians to

---

LOVING

**C.
You Can Have
a Relationship
with God**

81. You can pray on your own.

82. You can read the Bible on your own.

83. You can learn to worship God and Jesus on your own or in a group.

AGES 10-12

worship, however, can encourage us to give more of ourselves to God—and it makes a visible statement to the rest of the world that God is truly worth praising.

❖ *"God is spirit, and his worshipers must worship in spirit and in truth"* (John 4:24).

❖ *"Therefore, I urge you, brothers, in view of God's mercy, to offer your bodies as living sacrifices, holy and pleasing to God—this is your spiritual act of worship"* (Romans 12:1).

Hints and Helps

◆ To help kids understand how worship works, tell them about the "Worship Loop":

Worship is like a loop, a circle. It starts with God. We learn about God and realize we can trust Him: He keeps His promises, knows everything, can do anything, is everywhere, and always loves us. That makes us feel like praising and thanking Him and trusting Him with more of our lives. When we let Him take charge of more of our lives, He changes us, making us more like Jesus. When that happens, our praise comes from even deeper inside. We get together with others and tell how wonderful God is. This helps our trust in Him get even stronger, which leads us to greater worship. And on it goes; we get closer to God and worship Him more, which brings us even closer.

◆ Your children may wonder why people worship God in different ways using various styles of music, postures, phrases, etc. Explain that each person is different and has a different relationship with God, so it makes sense that people would express that relationship in ways that fit who they are. Churches have different personalities and traditions too. What worship looks like is not as important as what's going on inside each person—something only God can know for sure.

◆ When your children join you in your adult worship service, try to emphasize attitude over outward conformity. For example, if your church has a long worship service, kids might not be able to concentrate and participate the whole time. If their concentration is dwindling, suggest that they ask for God's help to focus; then they can sit quietly and wait, without distracting others. It's far better for them to worship from their hearts for five minutes than to just go through the motions for an hour. In addition, encourage them to worship along with the songs that are meaningful to them. If some lyrics are over their heads, tell kids that they may sit or stand quietly during those songs and talk to God in their hearts. After the service, explain the lyrics so that children can join in next time.

♦ Show your children how God can be worshiped outside of a church service. Give them a tape or CD featuring praise music, and encourage them to listen to it on their own with a worshipful attitude. Take on a service project as a family—cleaning up a local park, serving food at a rescue mission, washing a disabled person's car—and explain how our work can fit the worship definition of "giving of yourself to God in response to who He is."

You Can Be All God Wants You to Be

Topic No. 84

God Wants You to Choose to Grow, Learn, and Seek His Wisdom.

Can you *make* your children grow spiritually? Not really. Even God doesn't force anyone to seek Him or obey Him. It's a choice He's left to each person.

Still, you *can* guide your children toward *choosing* to be what God wants them to be—and allowing God to work in them to change them. You can do this by pointing out the benefits of spiritual growth, noting real-life examples of people who are growing, and showing your children how to get started. Assure them that growth is a lifelong process— a journey toward getting closer to God and becoming more like Jesus.

❖ *"Therefore I urge you, brothers, in view of God's mercy, to offer your bodies as living sacrifices, holy and pleasing to God—this is your spiritual act of worship. Do not conform any longer to the pattern of this world, but be transformed by the renewing of your mind. Then you will be able to test and approve what God's will is—his good, pleasing and perfect will"* (Romans 12:1–2).

LIVING

**D.
You Can Be All
God Wants You
to Be**

84. God wants you to choose to grow, learn, and seek His wisdom.

85. God's grace: You don't have to do it on our own. God is working in you by His Holy Spirit.

86. God wants you to find and follow His will for your life.

AGES 10–12

84. God wants you to choose to grow, learn, and seek His wisdom.

85. God's grace: You don't have to do it on our own. God is working in you by His Holy Spirit.

86. God wants you to find and follow His will for your life.

❖ *"Do you not know that in a race all the runners run, but only one gets the prize? Run in such a way as to get the prize. Everyone who competes in the games goes into strict training. They do it to get a crown that will not last; but we do it to get a crown that will last forever. Therefore I do not run like a man running aimlessly; I do not fight like a man beating the air. No, I beat my body and make it my slave so that after I have preached to others, I myself will not be disqualified for the prize"* (1 Corinthians 9:24–27).

Hints and Helps

◆ Point out people in your church whose lives show the benefits of living for God. For example, a business owner may have prospered by earning a reputation for honesty. A retired missionary may have the satisfaction of knowing that he or she helped people find the way to heaven. A teenager may have enjoyed a summer trip to build houses in Central America. Give your children biblical examples of people who pursued God too, such as David and Paul.

◆ Come alongside your children and grow *with* them. Let them see you in the process of becoming more of the person God wants you to be. Apologize to your children when you make mistakes with them; it's a powerful lesson! When you apologize, try saying something like "I'm learning too. I'm asking God to change me and make me a better parent so I'll do better next time. I know I'm not perfect; I'm on the road to becoming a little more like Jesus. That's what God wants for all of us."

◆ The Bible contains a wealth of verses about growing spiritually, seeking God, and not giving up. Here are some passages you may want to urge your children to memorize and meditate on: Psalm 25:4–5; 42:1–2; Philippians 2:12–13; 3:7–11, 13–14; Colossians 3:1–4, 5–17; 2 Timothy 2:15; Hebrews 6:1; 12:1.

Topic No. 85

God's Grace: You Don't Have to Do It on Your Own. God Is Working in You by His Holy Spirit.

"Being a Christian is just too hard!" If your children feel that way, they'll appreciate the truth that we don't have to live the Christian life under our own power. Let them know that their part is mainly to cooperate with what God wants to do in their lives. He's right there, ready to help them become more like His Son.

Point out to children that if they've received Jesus as Savior, God is with them continuously through His Spirit who teaches them from His Word, reminds them of His way, and gives them strength to make the right choices when they ask for it. God is *for* them, cheering them on, helping them grow to the next step.

❖ *"No temptation has seized you except what is common to man. And God is faithful; he will not let you be tempted beyond what you can bear. But when you are tempted, he will also provide a way out so that you can stand up under it"* (1 Corinthians 10:13; see also 15:10).

❖ *"Being confident of this, that he who began a good work in you will carry it on to completion until the day of Christ Jesus"* (Philippians 1:6).

Hints and Helps

◆ When children do the wrong thing and feel guilty about it, they may wonder whether trying to follow Jesus is a lost cause. Assure them that God is never surprised by our mistakes or sins. If anything, He works to bring these into the open so that we know about them and can deal with them. God is there when we blow it; the best Person to talk to right then is God Himself, as we ask Him to forgive us and to help us obey Him more completely.

◆ Does teaching your children seem like an overwhelming task? Just as they're not alone, neither are you! The responsibility for training your children spiritually is not solely on your shoulders. You teach them truths about God, modeling those truths as well as you can, and God works them into your children's hearts and lives. It's a cooperative process. Remember that God loves your children, and He knows exactly how to guide them.

◆ Children may be confused over how much of the Christian life is up to them and how much is up to God. Explain that God doesn't do it all, moving us around and talking through us as if we were ventriloquist's dummies. God is more like a coach, ready to help us learn how to be and what to do. We can choose to cooperate with Him or not. God helps us love, for instance, but doesn't do it for us. That has to come from our hearts.

Topic No. 86

God Wants You to Find and Follow His Will for Your Life.

God has a plan for each of your children—a perfect match for the tal-

---

LIVING

**D.
You Can Be All
God Wants You
to Be**

84. God wants you to choose to grow, learn, and seek His wisdom.

85. God's grace: You don't have to do it on our own. God is working in you by His Holy Spirit.

86. God wants you to find and follow His will for your life.

AGES 10–12

ents, gifts, and personality He's given each child.

How do your children discover that plan? A little at a time! Knowing God's will starts with making right choices day by day. Each day we need to ask God what He has for us to do, then follow Him in that direction. If we're seeking a close relationship with God and are obeying Him, He'll lead us into what we're best suited for—what we'll enjoy and find fulfilling.

❖ *"Delight yourself in the LORD and he will give you the desires of your heart. Commit your way to the LORD; trust in him and he will do this"* (Psalm 37:4–5).

❖ *"The LORD will fulfill his purpose for me"* (Psalm 138:8).

Hints and Helps

◆ What does it mean to be a success? Do your children think that fame or money should be their goal? Help them see that real success comes from doing what God has designed us to do, even if our specific tasks change from time to time. Point out examples of Christians in your church who are serving God as homemakers, attorneys, artists, janitors—paid or unpaid, well-known or not. If possible, arrange for your children to spend time with a few of these people, finding out how they found their niches and how they continue to seek God's direction for their futures.

◆ Ask your children, "What do you want to be when you grow up?" You'll probably get job-oriented answers; these are fine, but encourage kids to think "outside the box," too. What do they want to *be*? What *qualities* do they hope to have when they're adults? Use this activity to remind children that God has a plan for the *kind* of people He wants us to be—not just for the things He wants us to do.

◆ How can you help point your children toward the occupation, career, or ministry that's right for them? Encourage them to write down a list of "seeds" they think God may have planted in them— their personality type, talents and gifts, likes and wants. These seeds may give clues to what your children will be most fulfilled by doing one day. In the meantime, let them explore a variety of activities so they can find out what they enjoy and are good at. Urge them to pray for help to make the right choices. Remind them that God promises to give wisdom to those who ask (James 1:5).

You Can Do All God Wants You to Do

Topic No. 87

God Wants You to Choose to Commit Your Entire Life and Everything You Have to Him.

More than once Jesus said it was better to lose your life for His sake than to gain the world. Purposely "losing your life"—putting aside your own wants in favor of God's agenda—is hardly something that comes naturally to most of us, no matter how old we are.

But Jesus said doing this is *better* than gaining the whole world! You can help your children see why. Explain that turning their lives over to God is more rewarding than running things on their own, because they can trust Him to take better care of them than they can themselves.

Help them know *how* to do this, too—by surrendering their lives to God every day, even minute by minute when necessary. They can learn to let Him be Lord in reality, not just in name.

* ❖ *"Whoever finds his life will lose it, and whoever loses his life for my sake will find it"* (Matthew 10:39).
* ❖ See also Matthew 16:25; Mark 8:35; Luke 9:24; 17:33; John 12:25.

Hints and Helps

* ◆ "Losing your life" for the sake of Jesus doesn't always lead to obvious rewards on earth. Be honest about this with your kids. Admit that obeying God can lead to being laughed at, making less money, being misunderstood—even being killed. Balance this with a look at the rewards heaven offers (see Topic No. 23, "God Has Prepared a Place for You in Heaven").
* ◆ Affirm your children's choices to obey God in the small things—when they choose to forgive a bully instead of getting revenge, when they take homework to a sick friend, when they turn down the chance to watch a forbidden movie. As they learn to surrender to God in the "minor" matters of daily life, they'll find it easier to surrender to Him in the bigger things.
* ◆ Some children (and adults) fear that giving God control of their lives will lead to misery. For example, asking God to teach them patience will result in having to endure an itchy rash or a loud-mouthed

---

LIVING

**E.
You Can Do All God Wants You to Do**

87. God wants you to choose to commit your entire life and everything you have to Him.

88. God wants you to choose His way because you love Him and want to be like Jesus.

89. God wants you to learn to seek and follow His Spirit's leading.

90. You need to learn how to resist Satan and temptation.

91. You need to get involved in church and find your place in the body of Christ.

AGES 10-12

LIVING

**E.
You Can Do All
God Wants You
to Do**

87. God wants you to choose to commit your entire life and everything you have to Him.

88. God wants you to choose His way because you love Him and want to be like Jesus.

89. God wants you to learn to seek and follow His Spirit's leading.

90. You need to learn how to resist Satan and temptation.

classmate. Or surrendering to His plan will mean having to go to a land that features rainy weather, slimy food, and a language no one can learn. Assure your children that God is loving and kind. If they need to learn patience, they can trust God to teach them in the best possible way. If God wants to send them somewhere, He'll prepare them. God's goal isn't to ask them to do what they hate the most. He has an awesome plan for them.

Topic No. 88

God Wants You to Choose His Way Because You Love Him and Want to Be Like Jesus.

At this age, your children are making their own choices—including some you may not know about. How can you help them make the right ones?

Walk them through the decision-making process, using a real-life choice they face. Help them weigh the pros and cons, see what God says about it, then choose the wisest course. Just as importantly, tell them *why* we need to choose right over wrong—out of love for God and a desire to be like Jesus. No mere list of dos and don'ts will provide the motivation for your children to obey God over the long run. As you help them develop a closer relationship with God, that love and desire will grow as well.

❖ *"Train a child in the way he should go, and when he is old he will not turn from it"* (Proverbs 22:6).

❖ *"We know that in all things God works for the good of those who love him, who have been called according to his purpose"* (Romans 8:28).

Hints and Helps

◆ Tempting as it might be to make all your children's decisions for them, it won't prepare them for the future. They need to learn how to tell right from wrong for themselves and how to make godly choices. You can begin this process by giving them "safe" arenas in which to choose. For example, let them decide whether to go to a particular church activity; then discuss their choice. Let them decide whether to study for a test; then discuss the results. To help you determine which choices are "safe" for them to make, take their maturity level and track record into account. Let them know that as they earn your trust, you'll trust them with more and more choices.

♦ Discuss *ahead of time* the decisions children may face and how they'll handle them. For example, when your children are going over to a friend's house to watch a video, help them decide in advance what kind of movie they'll watch or what they'll do if their friend wants to view something inappropriate. If they enjoy acting, do role-plays in which they act out various scenarios with different results.

♦ When children have made a wrong choice, discuss what happened. Ask, "What other choices could you have made in this situation? How might you have done better?" Ask them to list the reasons for the decision they made. Then ask them to list reasons for a better choice they could have made, so that they can apply those reasons to other situations.

Topic No. 89

God Wants You to Learn to Seek and Follow His Spirit's Leading.

To whom are your children listening? They probably hear plenty of advice from you, from peers, from teachers, from screens and CD players. But do they hear God's voice?

It's usually a still, small voice rather than an audible one. It takes practice to hear, a willingness to obey, and a turning away from distractions. But God's Spirit wants to guide your children into truth and remind them of Jesus' teaching. You can help your children become more sensitive to His leading as you teach them to listen for His influence on their thoughts as they pray, read the Bible, and hear the counsel of other Christians.

❖ *"The Counselor, the Holy Spirit, whom the Father will send in my name, will teach you all things and will remind you of everything I have said to you"* (John 14:26).

❖ *"It is because of him that you are in Christ Jesus, who has become for us wisdom from God—that is, our righteousness, holiness and redemption"* (1 Corinthians 1:30).

Hints and Helps

♦ Have you ever felt God was telling you something through an event, something you read, a sermon you heard, or the words of a friend?

LIVING

E.
You Can Do All God Wants You to Do

87. God wants you to choose to commit your entire life and everything you have to Him.

88. God wants you to choose His way because you love Him and want to be like Jesus.

89. God wants you to learn to seek and follow His Spirit's leading.

90. You need to learn how to resist Satan and temptation.

91. You need to get involved in church and find your place in the body of Christ.

AGES 10–12

87. God wants you to choose to commit your entire life and everything you have to Him.

88. God wants you to choose His way because you love Him and want to be like Jesus.

89. God wants you to learn to seek and follow His Spirit's leading.

90. You need to learn how to resist Satan and temptation.

91. You need to get involved in church and find your place in the body of Christ.

AGES 10–12

If so, tell your children the story. What did you do about the "message"? What was the result?

♦ Encourage your children to start the day by asking God to guide them. If they expect to face specific problems that day, it's a good idea to ask for specific direction. God may not hand them solutions right away, but they can trust Him to give them wisdom when the time comes.

♦ To help children understand what it means to "hear God's voice," explain that God can communicate with us in any way He likes. Since His Spirit lives in those who belong to Him, He may sometimes help us to know things in our hearts without our having to hear them through our ears. Since our own thoughts and feelings may confuse us, it can be helpful to talk with a more experienced Christian before acting on the things we believe God has "told" us. One guideline to remember: God doesn't tell people things that disagree with what He's already said in the Bible. If we think God is telling us something, we should compare it with His Word to make sure there's no contradiction.

Topic No. 90

You Need to Learn How to Resist Satan and Temptation.

Your children need to know that they have an enemy: the Devil, or Satan (see Topic 51, "The World Is Full of Sin . . ."). It isn't necessary to talk about Satan and his demons a lot, but your children need the basic facts. The key fact is that when Jesus died and rose again, He defeated Satan. Still, when people do things Satan's way by disobeying God, they give the Devil a foothold in their lives and let him accomplish some of his goals through them.

When your children resist Satan by doing things God's way—making right decisions, asking for forgiveness when they sin—it's a victory for the winning side.

❖ "'In your anger do not sin': Do not let the sun go down while you are still angry, and do not give the devil a foothold" (Ephesians 4:26–27).

❖ "Submit yourselves, then, to God. Resist the devil, and he will flee from you" (James 4:7).

❖ *"Be self-controlled and alert. Your enemy the devil prowls around like a roaring lion looking for someone to devour"* (1 Peter 5:8).

Hints and Helps

◆ Tell your children that when they face temptation it's a good idea to turn to the Bible. When He was tempted, Jesus dealt with the Devil's attacks by quoting scripture. Your children can do what Jesus did—counter the Devil's lies with verses they know (or can find) in the Bible, and choose God's way. Encourage them to pray when they're tempted, too—even if they're in the middle of making a mistake. When they ask for help, God will answer.

◆ Reassure your children that even when they've blown it and given Satan a foothold, they can go to God for strength and forgiveness. You can model God's unconditional love by maintaining an open door policy for your children when they've done wrong. Let them know that you're available for help and forgiveness, not just punishment.

◆ Avoid giving your children the impression that the Devil is scary. He's a master deceiver, a master liar. Seeking the truth and following God makes him powerless in our lives. Rather than railing against him (see Jude 9), however, let God judge him. Satan's fate is sealed. He's just trying to cause as much damage as he can before he's thrown into the lake of fire forever.

Topic No. 91

You Need to Get Involved in Church and Find Your Place in the Body of Christ.

Your children aren't just the church of tomorrow. They're the church of today! You can help them see your church as *their* church and find a place to be involved. Kids don't have to wait until they grow up to be supportive of pastors and other leaders, or to give time, money, and energy to God's work.

Finding friends at church is a key to feeling part of it all. As your children get to know others at church, they'll feel an increasing sense of belonging and a desire to be there.

❖ *"They devoted themselves to the apostles' teaching and to the fellowship, to the breaking of bread and to prayer. . . . All the believers were together and had everything in common. . . . Every day they continued to meet together in the temple courts. They broke bread in their homes and ate together with glad and sincere hearts"* (Acts 2:42, 44, 46).

LIVING

**E.
You Can Do All
God Wants You
to Do**

87. God wants you to choose to commit your entire life and everything you have to Him.

88. God wants you to choose His way because you love Him and want to be like Jesus.

89. God wants you to learn to seek and follow His Spirit's leading.

90. You need to learn how to resist Satan and temptation.

91. You need to get involved in church and find your place in the body of Christ.

AGES 10–12

❖ *"And let us consider how we may spur one another on toward love and good deeds. Let us not give up meeting together, as some are in the habit of doing, but let us encourage one another—and all the more as you see the Day approaching"* (Hebrews 10:24–25).

Hints and Helps

◆ If you can find places for your children to help at church—places that fit their abilities and interests—they'll blossom. If they're outgoing, they might become greeters or join those who visit new families. Are they musical? Perhaps they can play or sing at meetings or join a youth choir. Do they like cooking? Let them help in the church kitchen or make goodies for a bake sale. Kids who like computers might help in the church office; budding artists could paint a mural in a Sunday school room; actors could put on skits or use puppets in children's church. If your children are starting to baby-sit or just like playing with younger kids, they might assist in the church nursery or with vacation Bible school.

◆ How can you help your children find friends at church? If your kids are having trouble fitting in, talk with their Sunday school teacher or the person in charge of children's ministry at your church. Ask whether there are opportunities in the church's program for kids to get to know each other, perhaps in a club program, summer camp, or service project. Meet parents in your church whose children are in your kids' age range; invite these families over for dinner or another activity.

◆ Are *you* enthused about church? Do *you* have a sense of belonging? Chances are that your children can tell whether church is a labor of love for you—or just labor. Expecting them to get fired up about something that leaves you cold is unrealistic. If that's the case with you, take the same steps for yourself that you'd take with your children. Find a spot to serve that taps into your gifts and passions. Join a small group that contains potential friends for you. As you gain a sense of belonging, your children will be more likely to think the same is possible for them.

PART IV

Practical Questions and Resources

Appendix I: Topical Questions and Answers

Appendix II: Resource List

Appendix III: Memory Verses

Topical Questions and Answers

Apologetics

1. How can I teach my children to be bold in their faith when they face rejection about their beliefs in Jesus Christ?

There are two important things that you need to help your children understand when they experience rejection for their faith—things that will help them put their experience in context.

First, explain to your children that it isn't them that is being rejected, it's Christianity or Jesus. It wouldn't matter who they were; the rejection would be the same. Jesus said that if people rejected Him, they will also reject us.

Second, many children who grow up in a Christian family and church setting start to assume that everyone is a Christian. Explain to them that many people are not Christians and that some are even hostile toward people who believe.

Knowing these two things will help your children separate someone rejecting the faith from the bad feelings attached to being personally rejected.

There are also three simple guidelines to sharing their faith that you can teach your children which will help them avoid unnecessary persecution:

1. Don't hide or push. Help your children

understand that they should not hide what they believe by never mentioning it or refusing to talk about it. This approach would cause them to miss opportunities where some of their friends are curious or interested. But they should also not push, or in other words, tell others what they should or should not do or believe. Nor should they talk about the faith when others don't want to hear it.

2. Respect others' choices. Help your children understand that, just like they don't want to be put down for what they believe, neither does anyone else. Treat non-Christians with respect and don't make fun of them for what they think, do, or believe. Respecting also means keeping their ideas and information about what they believe to themselves if someone doesn't want to hear it.

3. Let your life talk. Teach your children that the most important part of telling others about Jesus is following Him themselves. Being kind, considerate, loving, forgiving, and respectful of others will cause people to want to know why they are different.

All of these simple truths can be taught to your children in a one-on-one conversation with them or in the context of a special Family Night. It may help to role-play some situations, taking turns at who plays which parts. Talk to

387

your children about experiences you've had sharing your faith. The more you talk to them about this topic, the more at ease and bold they'll become when confronted with rejection or an opportunity.

2. How do I explain to my child that everyone's "truth" is not equally relevant?

These days, when you share the gospel with a non-Christian, it's common to hear them say something like "That may be true for you, but I live by my own truth." This sort of talk can confuse children.

"How can there be more than one version of the truth?" they may ask. The obvious answer is, there can't be. Something is either true for everyone or it isn't true at all.

The next time your children hear someone say there is more than one truth or more than one way to God, use this explanation to help them understand why there can only be one version of the truth, and that truth can only be found in Jesus.

Here's an example: Because of gravity, everything on earth falls down. No one in his or her right mind would deny this fact. And gravity doesn't suddenly reverse its properties for people who believe that things should operate the opposite way. Gravity simply exists, regardless of our views on it.

The same can be said of God. Either He is who the Bible says He is or He is something else. He can't be both, and we can't just remake Him the way we want Him to be because we don't want to face up to the truth. The Bible tells us that there is only one God (Isaiah 43:10; 44:6; 46:9) and that Jesus Christ is the only way to reach Him (John 14:6; Acts 17:16–34). Either this is true for everyone or it is true for no one. It can't be true for some people and not for others because Jesus' words do not allow for this option. For more information, see "Who God Is," Topic No. 73.

The Bible

3. How should I teach my children to respond to people, especially Christians, who don't take the Bible literally?

Unfortunately, the trend among many people today, particularly some academics, is to write off the Bible as nothing more than a collection of myths and fables. They believe these stories contain many valuable moral and life lessons, but they do not regard the Bible as an authentic, reliable historical record.

Your children may encounter this belief at school or among their friends and be unsure of how to respond. The best thing you can do is equip them with evidence of the Bible's historicity and validity so they can be confident that the Bible is the true, accurate, inspired Word of God.

One example of this evidence is recent archaeological discoveries, including ancient manuscripts that have come to light, which confirm that the Bible rests on historic fact rather than fantasy. Over the years, one archaeological discovery after another has brought forth evidence confirming the historicity of characters and events mentioned in the Bible, of nations such as the Hittites, of cities such as Nineveh and Ur, and of various kings of Israel and Judah.

One specific example of a discovery was reported in the December 18, 1995 issue of TIME magazine in an article entitled "Is the Bible Fact or Fiction?"

A team of archaeologists uncovered a ninth century B.C. inscription at an ancient mound called Tel Dan, in the north of Israel in 1993. Words carved into a chunk of basalt referred to the "House of David" and the "King of Israel." It is the first time the Jewish monarch's name has been found outside the Bible, and appears to prove he was more than a legend.

There are many, many more such examples of evidence that support the historicity of the Bible. When your children are interested in more information on the accuracy and preservation of the Bible, consult the Resource List in Appendix II. Get some useful age-appropriate material and work through it with your children. Your whole family's faith will be strengthened. For more information, see "Who God Is," Topic No. 73.

4. How can I get my children interested in reading the Bible?

Your attitude toward the Bible is contagious; it will likely become your children's attitude. With this in mind, respect God's Word as a practical guide to life rather than treating it as an obscure religious handbook that sits quietly on the shelf gathering dust. When you're making decisions as a family, helping your children make their own decisions, or feeling curious about what God has to say about various life topics, pull down the Bible and see what it says on the subject. When you're teaching your children life principles, such as honesty and kindness, anchor your teachings with actual verses from the Bible.

But be careful not to refer to the Bible only when things are serious. Allow it to become a normal part of your everyday life. By giving your children daily access to God's Word, His wisdom will be constantly working in their hearts and minds, and they will be excited about how the Bible can change their lives.

In the Bible, God provided us with a book full of marvelous stories about kings and peasants, battles and miracles, fish that swallow people, and donkeys that talk. Remember this during your children's Bible time so you don't fall into the same rut day after day.

Children love adventure and variety. Consider buying or renting some animated Bible story videos and using them as a special once-a-week replacement for the regular Bible story or reading. Consider using a different Bible or Bible storybook from time to time, or do the reading in a special location. If at any time your children get bored with Bible time, examine your presentation and change what you're doing until the excitement level builds up again. For more information, see "You Can Have a Relationship with God," Topic Nos. 9, 10, 24–29, 55–61, 81–83.

5. What are some ways to incorporate scripture into daily activities?

One of the most effective ways to teach your children about the Bible is right in the middle of life. Since the Bible's teachings are instructions for life, everyday life is the ideal classroom. When you're teaching your children about the principles that govern life, attitudes, behavior, or relationships, refer them to what the Bible teaches, emphasizing that the Bible is life's instruction manual. For example, if you realize that the grocery clerk gave you too much change, return the money. Use the opportunity to explain what the Bible says as the reason for what you did. This may feel a little forced at first, but you need to be intentional about explaining to your children why you behave the way you do.

Another idea is if you are approaching the checkout stand with a huge cartload of groceries and you see someone who has a cabbage and a jug of milk, let that person go first. Later, tell your children what Jesus said about loving others as you love yourself (Matthew 22:39). Also, when you are teaching your children about honesty, getting along, patience, sharing, or any number of the everyday things we teach to our children, use what the Bible says as the foundation of truth and the explanation for what you are teaching them. Getting into this habit will help your children realize that their faith is expressed through their life and behavior.

6. How should I explain scary stories in the Bible, such as the Crucifixion, to my toddlers?

Eventually, your children need to know that the Bible tells true stories about real people who actually lived and died. Sometimes these stories can seem scary to us. However, they weren't put there to scare us but to depict a real event, to serve as a warning of what to avoid, and to help us learn how to live. Your toddler needs to learn primarily about God's love and character. Some of the violent events told about in the Bible might scare them and confuse them. When you are reading a Bible storybook to your very young children, read ahead, and if you think a particular story will be too much for them, skip it or don't read certain parts of it. Don't avoid the fact that Jesus died on the cross for us, but it's okay to leave out the gruesome details until they are old enough to understand.

Christian Walk

7. How can I teach my children to express their anger or disappointment without sinning?

Before the "how," we need to establish a foundation. Jesus called loving others the second greatest commandment. But the Bible doesn't just tell us to love others; it's full of practical advice on *how* to love and relate to them—advice on how we speak, express our feelings, listen, care, put others first, are kind, are patient, and much, much more.

As parents we can't just tell our children to love or get along with each other and expect them to do it. They need to be shown and taught how to do it; for example, expressing anger or disappointment in an appropriate way. Explain to your children that the Bible tells us that when we are angry we should be extra careful not to sin. In other words, explain that anger is not an excuse for yelling, saying unkind words, or any other unacceptable behavior.

When your children are angry, it will be hard at first for them to get this. Stay patient yourself, take them by the hand and guide them through the process. First show them how to stop and think. Then have them explain, as gently as they can, what they are thinking to the person they are angry with. Then teach them to listen to the other person and look for a way to work it out or compromise.

Think. Talk. Listen. Work it out. Your children won't just get it the first time and do it from then on. You need to be consistent with them and continue to patiently walk them through it. Point out how things worked out much, much better by doing it this way, and your children will eventually handle their anger or feelings of injustice this way on their own.

8. How can I help my children make responsible decisions about which movies, TV shows, Web sites, and video games they view?

Many television shows, movies, video games, and Web sites are not at all good for children, even if children are their target market. According to a recent study, by the time the average child reaches 14 years of age, he or she will have witnessed 18,000 murders on TV alone, never mind the countless hours of related violence and mayhem on video games and movies and the harmful images imbibed through unsupervised access to the Internet.

On the flip side, television, with its unparalleled capacity for teaching and edifying, often demonstrates its potential for good. Many science and nature programs, sports events, and even a few morally sound family dramatic series or comedies dot the television landscape. In addition, many movies contain profound teachings about God and life. Some video games may be somewhat addictive, but they are not intrinsically harmful to children. And we are just beginning to discover the incredible capacity of the Internet to enhance our lives as it helps us communicate and puts us in touch with untold amounts of information.

With this in mind, it's obvious that the key solution to helping your children make responsible decisions about what they view is not to simply destroy the TV or sell the computer or video game system. You need to show your children why they should make responsible decisions—why viewing things like violence and sex can harm them—and how they can use the Bible to help them decide what they should and shouldn't take in.

One way to do this is to use the analogy of junk food. Junk entertainment is like junk food—it tastes good even though it's bad for us. Many people watch garbage on TV, in the movies, or on the Internet because they like it, even though it is bad for them.

However, God wants you to be discerning. He wants you to recognize the junk entertainment for what it is and avoid it, even if it seems fun or harmless. The following Bible verse is a good one to keep in mind when you are making decisions about what you should or shouldn't take in. "Whatever is true, whatever is noble, whatever is right, whatever is pure, whatever is lovely, whatever is admirable—if anything is excellent or praiseworthy—think about such things" (Philippians 4:8).

Remember: You need to be careful about what you watch because once you've watched something, you can't "un-watch" it. You will always stand the chance of it coming back and replaying itself on the "movie screen" in your mind. Also remember a double standard won't work. What you watch is what your children will want to watch. You may allow yourself a little more latitude than your young children because you are more able to discern, but even that will need to be explained to your children. For more information, "You Can Be All God Wants You to Be," Topic Nos. 12, 13, 30–34, 62–67, 84–86.

9. How can I keep my children from resenting God and church when they are used as a reason for saying no to certain music, movies, and activities?

It's easy for children to resent God and church if they are constantly being used as reasons to restrict what they can see or do. But this is a problem of perception. You need to explain to them that God doesn't want to stop them from doing everything that's fun; He only wants to restrict them from a few harmful things for their own good. Once your children understand this, you will get them on your side because they will see how living according to God's principles helps them live better lives. Use the following analogy to help them understand how rules can benefit them.

The rules of soccer define the length and width of the playing field, the size of the net and ball, how many players on each team, and the types of behavior that are acceptable. If you take away the rules from soccer, all you have is a group of people chasing a ball around a field. There is no purpose to the game, no penalties for rough play, and no way to decide who wins or loses. In short, the game has no point, and it's no longer any fun. Explain that in the same way that we need rules to make sports fun and safe, we need rules and guidelines for life that will keep us safe and give us the best life possible.

391

10. How can I help my children choose their heroes wisely?

Every child looks up to somebody. If it's not a parent, it's an older brother or sister, or perhaps another family member or someone else in the community. God made us this way so we could learn from our mentors and grow into people who love and obey Him. But more and more, the people whom children are turning to for examples of how to live are rock stars or characters from TV or the movies. While this trend is not intrinsically harmful, the simple fact is that most of these characters live very unbiblical lifestyles that can confuse and mislead young children. This presents a challenge to parents who want their children to emulate Jesus or people who strive to live their lives according to God's will. The following suggestions will help you guide your children as they choose role models for their lives.

One of the first things you can do is limit your children's access to media that will present them with examples of behavior that are harmful and unbiblical. You can't totally control what your children see and do, but you can help them by showing them the qualities of real heroes. Take a proactive approach by substituting "regularly scheduled programming" with positive books and videos about people, past or present, who use their lives to serve others. This includes Christians who helped spread the gospel or meet the physical needs of others through mission work, or people who simply used their gifts, talents, and abilities to serve society through science, art, or exploration. Explain to your children that these people are heroes because they made the most of what God gave them. They didn't use their talents to hurt others or to simply gain wealth or fame for themselves. Many of these people may be wealthy and famous, but those things are merely a by-product of people reaching their full potential.

Another idea is when your children are excited about someone they saw on TV or in a movie, talk to them about why they admire this person and what qualities they want to emulate. It's important that you be aware of the people, either real or fictional, who are exerting an influence on your children. By dialoguing with your children about their heroes, you will be able to stay on top of what they are watching or listening to. But even more important, you will be able to openly and honestly share what the Bible has to say about the kind of people we should be and who we should follow so your children can develop a solid, biblical framework for how they choose their heroes. For more information, see "You Can Be All God Wants You to Be," Topic Nos. 12, 13, 30–34, 62–67, 84–86.

11. How do I help my children understand that all of their actions are either right or wrong before God?

In Matthew 12:36, Jesus says that on the day of judgement, people will have to give an account for every careless word they've spoken. God is concerned with everything, even little details that don't seem to matter to us. To God, everything we think, say, or do is important. It's important that you communicate this fact to your children.

At the same time, you need to teach them that not every choice we make is either right or wrong. You can explain that sometimes we just like certain things more than others, such as ice cream flavors. If you like strawberry better than chocolate, it isn't right or wrong; it's just a preference you may have. Or you might have two toys to play with and you choose one over the other. Both would be all right, but you choose one.

We live in a world, however, that seems to promote the idea that every decision should be made with only ourselves and what is best for us as the focus. A good way to help your children understand that there should be three points of focus, not one, in all our decisions is to sit down with them and write out three things that need to be decided on. For example: (1) Should we go to church? (2) My little brother or sister needs my help but I don't want to help. What should I do? (3) What flavor of ice cream cone do I want from the store?

Show them how with question number one, despite how we feel about it, church is God's idea and we need to go because He wants us to and He knows what's best. With number two, God wants us to think of others and take care of their needs, so the child's decision should be to help his or her sibling. With question number three, it's totally up to your children—whatever makes them happy.

Our decision focus is God, others, and ourselves. Come up with some other choices and help your child figure out the answers. For more information, see "You Can Do All God Wants You to Do," Topic Nos. 14–16, 35–39, 68–72, 87–91.

Church

12. Should I force my children to attend church functions or give them a choice?

Ideally, you will never have to force your children to attend church functions because you have been able to successfully communicate the importance of church to them. Make it a positive experience and model a great attitude about it.

One of the most important things we can teach our children about church is why we go and why it is important. It's easy to get stuck in a habit of going to church and never understand the practical, beneficial reasons why God wants us to go. Then, when it gets boring, we have nothing to keep us going or to help us reexamine our experiences and priorities in regard to church attendance. Take time to look up Topic Nos. 68 and 91 in this book, check out some of the tools that will help you teach these to your children, then set an evening aside and talk about church with your kids.

Next, ask some open questions (for example, "How do you like church?" "How do you like your Sunday school class?" "What friends do you have there?"). This dialogue will help you see and understand problems your children may be having with church and may help you make church a more positive experience for your family.

Also, remember that your children will adopt your attitude toward getting up on Sunday morning and attending church. Spend some time alone examining your own attitudes and church experience. What could you do to make it more beneficial and enjoyable for yourself?

After the middle adolescent years (13 to 16), some children resent being told exactly what to believe. They don't want religion "forced down their throats," and rightly so. They should be given more and more autonomy in deciding what they believe. But if the early exposure to church has been positive and properly conducted, they will have an inner conviction and belief in the importance of church that will sustain them. This early teaching, then, is the key to the spiritual attitudes they will carry into adulthood.

Despite this need to take more of a come-along-beside approach to spiritual training as your child moves through adolescence, it is still appropriate for you to establish and enforce a Christian standard of behavior in your home. Therefore, you should require your children and teens to attend church with the family. For more information, see "You Can Do All God Wants You to Do," Topic Nos. 14–16, 35–39, 68–72, 87–91.

13. How can I reintroduce my family to church after an extended absence?

If you're just beginning to introduce or reintroduce your children to church, start small and build slowly. A good first step is to sit down and talk to your children about what church is and why we should go. Tell them who God is, why He created church, and how it is relevant to their lives. Talk about your own personal reasons for wanting the family to go.

The next step may be attending a church service or perhaps a church barbecue or sports event (if you want to make the experience as enjoyable and nonthreatening as possible). A good idea is to link up with another family in the church that has children the same ages as yours. This will help your kids feel more comfortable in this new setting. You may even want to try out more than one church until you find one that your entire family feels comfortable with.

Once the importance of church has been established and your children have had some firsthand experience of what church is all about, start to establish a regular pattern of attendance. At first, you might go only once a month or once every two weeks. That's okay. Move at a pace that the entire family is comfortable with. God is not in a hurry, and you shouldn't be either. If your children have events or practices that conflict with church times, announcing that church now takes precedence might backfire. Instead, find a different service that is later or earlier on Sunday or perhaps on a Saturday night. Or go when you can. Then, next time you sign your child up for such an event, look for a club that doesn't conflict with

church attendance times. The worst thing you could do is try to force church on your children without them understanding what it is or why they should go. That kind of approach will only breed resistance and rebellion. Instead, start slowly and build up to regular weekly attendance.

14. Is there a right and a wrong way for a church to teach? How do I approach this topic with my children without degrading churches that are different than ours?

When answering this question, it's critical that you separate for your children the *essentials* of your faith from the way you *express* and celebrate your faith. All genuine Christian churches agree on the basics of the faith as outlined in the Apostles' Creed (see Topic No. 77), a statement of the essentials of the faith dating to the first three centuries of the church. It includes key beliefs about God, salvation, and the Trinity (see "Who God Is," 1–4, 17–20, 40–46, 73 and "What God Has Done," Topic No. 22). A church that does not hold to these essentials is teaching wrong doctrine.

The things that vary among genuine Christian churches fall into three broad categories: First, the way we express our faith, which is affected by culture and the history and traditions of each particular church or denomination. Second, the emphasis or flavor of the message. This is also shaped by the history of each church and the needs of the community or culture the church is in. Third, the way in which secondary issues and doctrines are viewed. Some churches, for example, emphasize divine healing. This isn't a core doctrine of the historic church or a prerequisite to faith in God. In fact, other churches take the stand that healing isn't something we should teach at all. While it's interesting to discuss and debate these issues, they shouldn't divide us as long as we all agree on the basics.

If your children want to attend a different Christian church with a friend, encourage them to do so. Maybe your family can even purposely go to a church that is quite different from yours as a family outing. Discuss the differences together. Seeing how others express their faith can serve to strengthen our sense of unity and diversity.

If you explain these things to your children—what's essential to our faith and what's more a matter of taste, expression, emphasis, and history—you can help them avoid some basic problems later on.

Divorce

15. I've just gone through a divorce and I'm worried about how this will impact my children's spiritual training. How do I help them grow in their faith under these circumstances?

There is no reason why your divorce should have any fundamental impact on your children's spiritual training *per se*. Biblical truths remain the same, regardless of the family setting. So do the basic moral and spiritual principles you want your youngsters to absorb and live by. Teaching and modeling these precepts can be more difficult for single mothers and fathers since they have to walk that road alone. But this only emphasizes the need for persistence and consistency. Despite the special obstacles you're facing, it's critical that you stay faithful to whatever plan or program of Christian teaching you have chosen for your children, both at home and in the church.

Having said this, it's important to add that your family situation may very well have an impact on your children's spiritual growth. Divorce affects children deeply at *every* level of their existence—mental, emotional, physical, social, *and* spiritual. Your kids are going to need time and space to process the implications of the

breakup of their family. They may have to ask some very hard questions like "If God loves us, why did He allow this happen to us?" The good news is that, with prayer and sensitive handling, even *this* can be turned into an opportunity for deepening their understanding of God's grace and love. Stay open and honest in the way you respond to their expressions of hurt and doubt. Show them how to carry every burden to the Lord in prayer. If you can do this, you will be providing your children with a powerful demonstration of practical faith in action.

Friends and School

16. How can I explain the importance of associating with godly children and families?

When your children are choosing their friends, help them understand the difference between close friendships and other relationships. Tell them that God wants them to be loving and kind to everyone, but that doesn't mean they have to be close friends with everyone. Some people can be bad influences on them. If they spend too much time with these people, they can find themselves acting in ways they wouldn't have otherwise.

A practical way of illustrating this with your children is to watch them closely after they have spent some time with someone. If you know that the friend speaks harshly to his or her siblings or has an attitude problem, point out the residual effects of the friend's visit to your children when they snap at their siblings or whine at you. Do it gently and explain how we need to choose our friends carefully, how they affect us, and how we are going to affect them. Next, let your children know that if they are to spend time with that friend, these changes must not take place in their behavior.

It is good to want to be a good influence on others. So your children should try to be friendly to all kids. It is okay to have non-Christian friends, but their closest friends should be Christians who share their faith and values. This is because Christian friends will encourage your children to grow in their faith. This growth will help your children become a positive influence on their non-Christian friends. For more information, see "You Can Do All God Wants You to Do," Topic Nos. 14–16, 35–39, 68–72, 87–91.

17. How can I help my children understand that love, not violence, is the proper way to resolve conflicts?

Conflict, especially physical conflict, is one of the most difficult things for Christians to deal with effectively. When someone does something bad to your children, such as hit them or tease them, it seems natural for them to want to do something bad in return. But you need to teach your children that it is never right to do something bad to another person just because that person did something bad to them. The Bible calls that "evil for evil" (Romans 12:17), and Jesus says it is wrong. The Bible also says that we shouldn't try to get back at people who hurt us. We do not have the right to punish people for the things they do wrong. Instead, we should talk about the situation with God and leave it up to Him. It's all right to protect ourselves, but it's not okay to get even.

If we're confronted with someone who is pushy or who wants to fight, or even just yell and argue, we should stay calm and kind and refuse to be drawn in. We should explain how we feel, that we don't want to fight. The Bible says that a gentle answer will help calm any situation (Proverbs 15:1). Staying cool, saying a quick prayer, and being as nice as we can is our best chance for a good outcome. Sometimes this won't work out that well for them at first and your children will be tempted to fight. But

encourage them not to do it; they should either walk away or go and tell a teacher or other adult what is going on.

This may seem difficult and unfair, but only God knows how to judge fairly; we don't. By refusing to return evil for evil, we let God take care of making things right. And God is perfect in all His judgments.

Just because someone else is sinning doesn't give us the excuse to sin. We should always try to obey God and do what is right. God's way is always best and works out better for our lives and friendships in the long run. Getting back at others usually doesn't solve the problem; it just makes things worse.

Two effective and practical ways that will help your children understand this better are telling them some stories about your own experiences and role-playing some situations with them. When telling your stories, emphasize how things didn't work out when you didn't follow God's directions, and did work out when you did follow them.

Remember to comfort your children first and try to understand how they feel. If we are too quick to teach before comforting, we can give our children the idea that it's their fault that someone is bullying them. For more information, see "You Can Do All God Wants You to Do," Topic Nos. 14–16, 35–39, 68–72, 87–91.

18. How can I best respond to my child when he or she wants to dress in a way I don't think is appropriate?

Let your children know that it's all right to wear nice clothes that are in style or even different as long as they aren't so extreme that they contradict your children's faith. For example, they shouldn't be too revealing and they shouldn't be covered in offensive slogans or symbols. Explain that the way we dress should reflect who we are on the inside.

Sometimes our children want to dress a certain way just because others are. Helping them understand that they should make clothing choices based not only on the current style but also on who they are and what they like will help them build a balanced and proper sense of style.

Be careful not to inflict your sense of style on your children—this can really backfire. Your children aren't you—and styles change. Also, before making a judgment on your children's choices of clothing or style, ask yourself, *Do I not like it because it's an extreme style and not what I like, or because it truly reflects something contrary to my faith?*

19. How can I help my children respond to science teachers and textbooks that deny creation?

The best thing you can do for your children is arm them with the truth so they are prepared to deal with these situations as they come up. There are two tasks in arming them with the truth: First, they need to know what the Bible says, and second, they need to know what evolution teaches and why it doesn't make sense. Arming your children with both will help them think through the issues and be strong in their views as opposed to just parroting what you say is true while still having doubts. Take the time to explore this topic with your children. Read some resources yourself, like Philip Johnson's *Defeating Darwinism by Opening Minds.* (Intervarsity Press, 1997). Take notes, then sit down and have a discussion with your children.

Perhaps a good way to get started is to read the Genesis account of Creation together. Then briefly explain the theory of evolution. Tell them this story: A man was walking along in the woods and saw a beautiful pocket watch with intricate carvings and a detailed chain. He picked it up and exclaimed, "Wow! What a wonderful coincidence. This watch came together all by itself over billions of years." When your children tell you how silly the story is, you can explain how intricate and detailed God's creation is and how the watch coming together all by itself is way more probable than the world coming together by itself.

Explain that people believe the theory of evolution for three main reasons: First they prefer not to believe in God. Second, many scientists tell us that the theory of evolution explains the fossil record. (It doesn't. It is only one possible and improbable way of explaining it.) Third, so many people believe the theory of evolution that others assume it must be true.

But evolution is merely a theory, just one improbable way of explaining the past. Many textbooks and teachers today present it as fact, but it is not. For more information on this topic, see the Resource List in Appendix II. See also "Who God Is," Topic No. 73.

Grief and Loss

20. How do I talk to my children about the death of a loved one?

The best way to approach this topic with your children is from an eternal perspective. Explain it like this: People die because of humanity's sin. When God created the first human beings, they weren't supposed to die. Their bodies would never grow old or wear out. But then they disobeyed God and sin and death entered the world. From that point on, every person has been born a sinner into a sinful world. With sin came death, and so plants, animals, and people started to die. Every person has to die.

But people can live eternally in heaven with God if they trust in Christ and ask God to forgive their sins. In heaven we won't be broken anymore; there is no sickness or pain or dying there.

The body you have here on earth is a physical, imperfect, short-term holding place for your soul. It's not made to last. When it's dead, it will decay. The real you is your soul, not your body. But in heaven you will be given a new body that will last forever. The physical body will die, but the spiritual body will last forever. Therefore, if you are a Christian, you have no reason to fear death because when you die you will go to heaven and be with God forever. If your loved one was a Christian, he or she is with God right now.

If you are not sure whether the loved one who died knew Christ, be open but gentle with your children about it. Say that you're not sure but that God is the only One who can judge and know for sure. Read the story about the thief on the cross beside Jesus (Luke 23:39–43) to your kids. Explain that God is merciful and will try to reach us right up until our last breath. Also remember not to just tell your children to be happy because their loved one is somewhere better. That's part of it, but grieving the fact that that special person won't be part of your life until you see him or her in heaven is natural and good. Let your children cry if they need to; comfort them and talk about how you'll miss the person too. For more information, see "What God Has Done," Topic Nos. 5–8, 21–23, 47–54, 74–80.

Parenting and Parent/ Child Relationships

21. Where is the line between sheltering my children and trusting God to take care of them and what they're exposed to?

Many parents have asked if it is possible to love their children too much. This shouldn't be a problem as long as the love is mature and unconditional. However, much that is called "love" is not healthy for a child. Some parents invest all of their hopes, dreams, desires, and ambitions in their children. The natural outcome of this way of thinking is overprotection.

Childhood illness and accidents are always difficult for loving parents to tolerate. But when the slightest threat produces intolerable anxiety for you, it's likely that you're being overprotective. If this is the case, not only will you suffer but so will your children. An unhealthy dependent relationship develops between children and their overprotective parents. These children are prone to falling behind the normal social and emotional timetable for children their age because Mommy and Daddy do everything for them. They have no opportunity to mature and take responsibility for themselves or their assigned duties. As a result, they grow up into self-centered, helpless adolescents and adults with no idea of how to take care of themselves or how to have healthy relationships with others.

If you feel yourself slipping into overprotectiveness, remember this: the best preparation for responsible adulthood is training in responsibility during childhood. When your children are born, they are completely helpless and utterly dependent on you. But shortly after birth you begin transferring responsibilities from your shoulders to your children's. This includes things like holding their own bottle, sleeping through the night, and going to the potty. Each year your children should make more decisions than in the prior year. Gradually, the routine responsibilities of living will become part of their lives as they grow into adulthood.

Don't abdicate your parental responsibility altogether during this process. Rather, give conscious thought to the reasonable, orderly transfer of freedom and responsibility so that you are preparing your children each year for the moment of full independence that must come. For more information, see "You Can Be All God Wants You to Be," Topic Nos. 12, 13, 30–34, 62–67, 84–86.

22. What scripture promises do I have as a parent?

God has given you the privilege and responsibility of helping to form your children into wonderful adults. He has also given you a choice as to how you will go about it. You can do it on your own or you can raise your children in partnership with Him and ask for His help and wisdom. This latter course is called "grace parenting," and it is the best news a parent will ever hear.

You don't have to do things on your own. God promised that He would always be with you, helping and guiding you and showing you what's right. *"For it is God who works in you to will and to act according to his good purpose"* (Philippians 2:13). The writer of Hebrews echoes this passage: *"[May God] equip you with everything good for doing his will, and may he work in us what is pleasing to him, through Jesus Christ, to whom be glory for ever and ever. Amen"* (Hebrews 13:21). When you raise your children in harmony with God's principles and how He created everything to work, you have the greatest possibility of success.

Remember, God loves you. He also loves your children—even more than you do, if you can imagine that. He wants to help and serve you even more than you want Him to. So don't beat yourself up or try to do things on your own. The next time you feel overwhelmed with your parental responsibilities, take a moment to thank God for His help and invite Him to make more of His wisdom and guidance available to you. For more information, see "grace parenting," pages 39–40.

23. How can I encourage my children to develop their unique strengths and to mature in areas of weaknesses without being too critical?

As a parent, you should celebrate your children's uniqueness and individuality. This is easier to do when your children are behaving properly and getting good grades than when they're constantly getting into trouble or disobeying you. Personality is wonderful, and although you mustn't squelch your children's personalities or attempt to force them into an "ideal" mold, you still need to train them in how to express themselves appropriately.

Personality should never be used as an excuse for bad character. A child who misbehaves is displaying bad character, not a unique personality trait. For example, if your child is constantly getting angry at people, you can't just say, "That's just who he is. He gets impatient and shouts at people." You need to be clear with your children that character is "God likeness." It shouldn't change, no matter what their personalities are. Your children's personalities, however, will express this "God likeness" in their own unique ways.

Children must be trained in the correct expression of who they are. For example, if they show leadership potential, you need to spend time teaching them the qualities of good leadership, such as servanthood, obedience, and cooperation. The same goes for any other type of gifting or personality strength. But regardless of their personality, the fruit of the Spirit must be evident in their lives (see Galatians 5:22–23). If it isn't, this needs to be addressed and corrected.

It's your job as a parent to train your children's personalities and how they express their uniqueness. You need to help them learn to express their wonderful individuality in ways that go along with having good character, respecting others, and moving their relationships forward. If you find yourself always correcting and being critical of your children, you need to reassess this aspect of your parenting. It's easy to get into the habit of criticizing and correcting on the go and praising only on special occasions. Make a conscious choice to reverse the habit. Praise as you go, every chance you get. If your children need correction, wait a minute; they may recover on their own. If not, and if it's a smaller thing, wait until later when you can talk to them privately and teach and build as opposed to being critical. For more information, see "You Can Be All God Wants You to Be," Topic Nos. 12, 13, 30–34, 62–67, 84–86.

24. How can I be a Christian example for my children, and why is this critical?

Children love and look up to their parents. God designed it that way. They watch what you do in both good and bad situations. Don't think you can teach something only if you've mastered it. Watching you learn is a great training tool. Children listen to how you talk about work, other people, and problems. They notice your responses to temptation, frustration, windfalls, and shortages. They know more about your honesty, diligence, and money handling than you realize. Do they see you keep that extra change or gossip about a colleague? Or do they see you return the change and pray for that colleague? Whatever you're doing, they're learning.

The key is to make sure they're seeing you do what you want them to do. You're the one they pattern themselves after. Your fears and small dishonesties will become theirs. In the

same way, your good money management, positive attitudes, trust, and diligence will also become theirs. Use their attentiveness to your life for their benefit. And remember: You don't have to be perfect. God's grace is bigger than your failures. When you blow it, simply admit your mistake and let them see you ask God and others to forgive you—and then try to make it right and grow from it. That shows it's okay for *them* to make mistakes and learn. In fact, growing together in God's grace is the most effective way to learn. You can say, "I'm trusting God to teach me. Let's trust Him together." It's an excellent opportunity to pray together, asking for wisdom and help. For more information, see "Teachable Moments," pages 181–184.

Resource List

Apologetics/Archaeology
Books 401
Children
General
Books 402
Videos 404
Audiocassettes/CDs 405
Board Games 406
Magazines 406
Adventures in Odyssey
Books 407
Videos 407
Audiocassettes/CDs 407
Stewardship for Kids
Books 408

Board Games 408
Heritage Builders
Books 409
Audiocassettes 411
Holiday Resources
Books 411
Learning Styles/Personalities
Books 411
Audiocassettes 412
Morality/Values
Books 413
Audiocassettes 414
Parenting
Books 414

Audiocassettes 418
Spiritual Training
Books 419
Audiocassettes 421
Teens
Books 421
Magazines 424

At the time of printing these resources were available.

Please note that the Focus on the Family Booklets and Broadcast cassettes are available only through Focus on the Family.

APOLOGETICS/ ARCHAEOLOGY

BOOKS

Baker Encyclopedia of Christian Apologetics by Norman L. Geisler (Baker).

This book provides a comprehensive coverage of every key issue, person, and concept related to Christian apologetics. It includes articles on important people, philosophies, biblical controversies, contemporary issues, and ongoing apologetic discussions. It also offers valuable information and advice for a wide audience including pastors, Christian leaders, and students.

It Couldn't Just Happen by Lawrence O. Richards (Word).

Fascinating facts about God's world that gives us thousands of pieces of evidence to prove that He created and sustains the universe.

Mere Christianity by C. S. Lewis (Fountain).

This classic apologetic work brings together what C. S. Lewis considered to be the fundamental truths of the Christian faith. It contemplates life, religion, God, the Resurrection, and humankind's place in the universe. In the process, this book gives solid philosophical and theological arguments for why Christianity is the only viable answer to the mysteries and perplexities of life.

The New Evidence That Demands a Verdict by Josh McDowell (Thomas Nelson).

This book is an authorative defense of Christianity, containing scholarly, practical arguments from one of the finest Christian apologists of our times. McDowell's conclusions are backed by solid evidence that will satisfy those who are willing to honestly consider the Bible's claims.

RESOURCES

CHILDREN
General

BOOKS

Adventure Bible Handbook by Ed M. Van der Maas (Zondervan).

A group of kids scan themselves into their dad's supercomputer and embark on a high-tech, zany holographic trip through the entire Bible.

The Amazing Treasure Bible Storybook by K. Christie Bowler (Zondervan).

This gorgeously illustrated book, full of hilarious cartoons, records a family's archaeological adventure through the entire story of the Bible.

The Black and White Rainbow by John Trent, Ph.D. (Waterbrook).

Could your children use a lesson in the incredible importance of forgiving others? This latest of John's children's books tells the story of a group of mice who wake up to a "black and white world"—and can only get all the color back when they learn to forgive.

Genesis for Kids by Doug Lambier and Robert Stevenson (Tommy Nelson).

A book of science experiments that show the wonder and power of God's creation. A favorite with Christian schools and home schoolers!

Growing with Jesus: 100 Daily Devotionals by Andy Holmes (Tommy Nelson).

Each devotion provides a scripture verse, a fun thought to grow on, and a fascinating "factoid" about our amazing, ever-growing body and the world around us—from the uniqueness of our fingerprints to a shark that goes through 24,000 teeth to how our body grows at night and then shrinks back during the day. This is the one book that will help kids grow as much on the inside as they're growing on the outside!

Holy Spirit in Me by Carolyn Nystrom (Moody).

This book will help Christian children understand the purpose of the Holy Spirit in their lives. Questions are answered simply and directly, and beautiful illustrations aid comprehension.

I'd Choose You! by John Trent, Ph.D. (Tommy Nelson).

This book tells the story of the lovable elephant Norbert and how his mother wisely gives him all five elements of the Blessing: meaningful touch, a spoken word, attachment of high value, picturing a special future, and genuine commitment. As in John's other books, Judy Love's wonderful illustrations add just the right touch. It's bedtime reading at its best!

The I Want to Know . . . **series** by Rick Osborne and K. Christie Bowler (Zondervan).

Each of these beautiful books gives a colorful, relevant, theologically sound presentation of a major Bible topic.

- ***I Want to Know About the Bible.***
- ***I Want to Know About God.***
- ***I Want to Know About Jesus.***
- ***I Want to Know About Prayer.***
- ***I Want to Know About the Church.***
- ***I Want to Know About the Holy Spirit.***
- ***I Want to Know About the Ten Commandments.***
- ***I Want to Know About the Fruit of the Spirit.***

Just the Way You Are by Max Lucado
(Crossway).

Just the Way You Are bears an unforgettable message: God doesn't want His children to spend time trying to impress Him; He longs instead for them to simply spend time with Him. Previously titled *Children of the King*, this re-released best-seller has new illustrations. Max Lucado and illustrator Sergio Martinez have joined their creative gifts to bring families a book they'll treasure.

Kidcordance by Rick Osborne with Ed Strauss and Kevin Miller (Zonderkidz).

Aimed at kids 8 to 12, this illustrated concordance gives a clear, foundational understanding of the people, places, things, and events of the Bible.

The NIrV Kids' Quest Study Bible by Lightwave and Livingstone (Zonderkidz).

A study Bible especially designed for kids! Lots of fun illustrations, mixed with questions and answers, bring theology down to children's level.

Parables for Kids by Danae Dobson and Dr. James Dobson (Tyndale).

This book retells eight parables, such as the Prodigal Son, the persistent widow, and the Good Samaritan, in terms of modern situations. It includes the biblical version and interpretive text.

Someday Heaven by Larry Libby (Zondervan).

Young and old alike wonder about this place God has prepared for us. This thoughtful and sensitive book addresses your children's questions about heaven, such as "Where is heaven?" and "Will my pets go there?" Readers of all ages will find this book to truly be a little bit of heaven on earth!

Someone Awesome by Larry Libby (Zondervan).

Many truths about God can be too big for kids (and grown-ups!) to comprehend. Tackling difficult questions like "If God made everything, who made God?" this collection of delightful stories and captivating illustrations will help children of all ages develop a deeper understanding and love for "Someone Awesome."

Someone with You by Larry Libby (Zondervan).

God is always with us, even when it's hard to feel His presence. In this comforting book, Libby reminds you that no problem is too big for prayer and faith. Great for families to read together!

Somewhere Angels by Larry Libby (Zondervan).

Is there really such a thing as a heavenly Secret Service? Children of all ages ask questions like "Do I have a guardian angel?" and "Do angels look like people?" This collection of warm, sensitive stories about angels and the people they protect will satisfy everyone's natural curiosity. You'll learn what angels can teach us about obeying, worshiping, and rejoicing in God.

There's a Duck In My Closet! by John Trent, Ph.D. (Tommy Nelson).

Best-selling author John Trent helps kids and parents laugh their way through this problem with a delightful story that turns a closet filled with "monsters" into a child's own personal zoo! Trent's charming verse and Judy Love's whimsical illustrations provide cheer and comfort for boys and girls, as well as for their concerned mommies and daddies.

The Treasure Tree by John and Cindy Trent and Gary and Norma Smalley (Word).

This award-winning book explores the world of children's personalities and helps them realize God has created each of us with unique strengths. It's a fun way for parents and children to discover how they've been created, how to get along, and how to enjoy each other.

The Two Trails by John Trent, Ph.D. (Tommy Nelson).

This book is the long-awaited sequel to *The Treasure Tree*. When your kids have different personality types, it's like asking a lion, otter, beaver, and golden retriever to get along. This fun adventure was created to help your kids learn to get along and enjoy each other.

What Happens When We Die? by Carolyn Nystrom (Moody).

The thought of dying can make any child sad and scared. Will it hurt? Does God want me to die? Where is heaven? Will Mom and Dad be there? How do I get there if I'm buried in the ground? In this simple yet profound book your children will see for themselves the reasons people die . . . and what God has in store for them in heaven.

What Is a Christian? by Carolyn Nystrom (Moody).

What is a Christian? An important question, especially for your children. How do they belong to Christ and He to them? Why are they called Christians when they receive Jesus into their hearts? This carefully worded book offers simple but direct answers. Your children will learn what forgiveness and being a Christian really mean.

Who Is God? by Carolyn Nystrom (Moody).

Children naturally have many questions about God. In simple language they can understand, Carolyn Nystrom answers many of their basic questions. Brightly colored pictures complement the text and make this a perfect book to help children better understand who God is.

VIDEOS

Jay Jay the Jet Plane (Focus on the Family published by Tommy Nelson).

This state-of-the-art animated 6-video series will have your little ones ages 2 to 7 laughing and learning lessons about the Christian faith. Jay Jay's inquisitive nature leads him on exciting adventures with his pals in the picturesque valley of Tarrytown. Each episode is 11-minutes long—a perfect length for preschool attention span!

- *You Are Special*
- *Fantastic Faith*
- *Forever Friends*
- *Sharing & Giving*
- *Bright 'N Beautiful*
- *Caring & Loving*

Last-Chance Detectives (Focus on the Family published by Tyndale).

Four friends form a junior detective agency and set up shop in an old B-17 bomber—and the adventures begin! The fast-paced live action of this series will have the whole family gripped with excitement from beginning to end. From a reminder of the importance of forgiveness and doing what's right to trusting in God through all circumstances, each video delivers an unforgettable faith lesson to kids ages 8 and up.

1. *Mystery Lights of Navajo Mesa*
2. *Legend of the Desert Big Foot*
3. *Escape from Fire Lake*

McGee & Me (Focus on the Family published by Tyndale).

This popular 12-video series combines high-adventure, live action and innovative animation for ages 8 and up. Young viewers are sure to be captivated by Nicholas and his cartoon pal McGee, who always seem to learn valuable lessons from their wild adventures.

1. *The Big Lie*
2. *A Star in the Breaking*
3. *The Not-So-Great Escape*
4. *Skate Expectations*
5. *Twister and Shout*
6. *Back to the Drawing Board*
7. *Do the Bright Thing*
8. *Take Me Out of the Ball Game*
9. *'Twas the Fight Before Christmas*
10. *In the Nick of Time*
11. *The Blunder Years*
12. *Beauty in the Least*

The StoryKeepers (Zondervan).

These action-packed adventures will captivate your young viewers as they dodge Roman soldiers and fight for what's right. Set in the dramatic time of Jesus' days on earth, each fully-animated video is full of lessons about faith, trust, and God's love in tough times. Ages 6 and up.

1. *The Breakout!*
2. *Raging Waters*
3. *Catacomb Rescue*
4. *Ready, Aim, FIRE!*
5. *Sink or Swim*
6. *Starlight Escape*
7. *Roar in the Night*
8. *Captured!*
9. *Trapped!*

- *The Christmas StoryKeepers*
- *The Easter StoryKeepers*

Veggie Tales (Big Idea Productions).

Veggie Tales is a kids' video series that teaches timeless values like honesty, kindness, and forgiveness in a delightfully wacky way. Hosted by Bob the Tomato and Larry the Cucumber, each video in the series teaches a life lesson—without ever being preachy. These hilarious stories feature top-quality computer animation, infectious songs, and lovable characters. Ages 4 and up.

- *Madame Blueberry*
- *Josh and the Big Wall!*
- *Larry-Boy & the Fib from Outer Space!*
- *Dave and the Giant Pickle*
- *The Toy That Saved Christmas*
- *Rack, Shack, & Benny*
- *Are You My Neighbor?*
- *Where's God When I'm S-Scared?*
- *God Wants Me to Forgive Them?!?*
- *Larry-Boy and the Rumor Weed*
- A *Very Silly Sing-Along!*
- *Silly Sing-Along 2: The End of Silliness?*
- *King George and the Ducky*

AUDIOCASSETTES/CDS

Focus on the Family's Radio Theatre (Focus on the Family published by Tyndale).

Focus on the Family Radio Theatre provides extraordinary entertainment in the form of the highest possible, quality radio drama. Designed specifically for family listening, Radio Theatre offers families a chance to hear a variety of "morally safe" adaptations of some of the world's best known and loved contemporary, historical, or classical stories—rooted in biblical values. Available in CD or cassette versions. These Radio Theatre dramas feature internationally acclaimed casts and film-quality sound and music. They're a family night waiting to happen!

- *Dietrich Bonhoeffer: The Cost of Freedom* (Peabody Award Winner)
- *The Legend of Squanto: Pilgrim of the Heart* by Paul McCusker
- *A Christmas Carol* by Charles Dickens
- *The Lion, the Witch, and the Wardrobe* by C. S. Lewis
- *The Magician's Nephew* by C. S. Lewis
- *The Horse and His Boy* by C. S. Lewis
- *Ben-Hur*
- *The Secret Garden*

The Singing Bible (Focus on the Family cassettes published by Tyndale).
    Children ages 2 to 7 will love *The Singing Bible*, which sets Bible stories and facts to music with over 50 sing-along songs! New from Heritage Builders, a ministry of Focus on the Family, it introduces your kids to people like Jonah and the whale and Daniel in the lion's den, making *The Singing Bible* a fun, fast-paced journey kids will remember.

BOARD GAMES

Book Game, The (Tyndale).
    Children will build character while they brush up on Bible trivia when playing *The Book Game*.

House Rules Game (Focus on the Family published by Tyndale).
    House Rules is a fast-paced team game full of spills, upsets, and unexpected twists. Teams race against the clock to answer family-related questions and head up through the house.

Sticky Situations (Focus on the Family published by Tyndale).
    Sticky Situations, with McGee & Me, is a fast-paced game that reinforces positive values and good decisions through surprise, laughter, and exciting board game play.

WWJD? Game, The (Tyndale).
    In this board game, children constantly face situations where they must decide what Jesus would do. To win, they must make the right choices and gain Christian virtue.

MAGAZINES

Clubhouse (Focus on the Family).
    Intriguing and entertaining, this magazine for kids ages 8 to 12 reinforces traditional values and promotes family closeness with hands-on activities, challenging puzzles and exciting stories.

Clubhouse Jr. (Focus on the Family).
    Children ages 4 to 8 love to learn with the fun stories, games and puzzles in *Clubhouse Jr.*, the activity-filled magazine that emphasizes family values while teaching character.

Adventures in Odyssey

Adventures in Odyssey began as a radio series in 1987 and is today heard on over 1600 stations. Since its beginning, the series has expanded to include over 35 audio packages, 14 video episodes and 2 book series. Also included in the series are the Adventures in Odyssey Bible, Activity Packs and various toys and games—all created to instill values and practical life lessons in kids of all ages!

BOOKS

This series of books by Paul McCusker is based on the Adventures in Odyssey radio series. These unique stories take place in the familiar setting of Odyssey with many of your favorite characters—and some new ones. Geared toward kids ages 8 to 12 (Focus on the Family books published by Tommy Nelson).

1. *Strange Journey Back*
2. *High Flyer With a Flat Tire*
3. *The Secret Cave of Robinwood*
4. *Behind the locked Door*
5. *Lights Out at Camp What-a-Nut*
6. *The King's Quest*
7. *Danger Lies Ahead*
8. *Point of No Return*
9. *Dark Passage*
10. *Freedom Run*
11. *The Stranger's Message*
12. *A Carnival of Secrets*

The Adventures in Odyssey Bible (NKJV) (Focus on the Family book published by Tommy Nelson)

The Passages Series (Focus on the Family published by Tommy Nelson).

The passages book series takes the readers to another world on adventures that parallel Biblical stories.

1. *Darien's Rise*
2. *Arin's Judgement*
3. *Annison's Risk*
4. *Glennall's Betrayal*
5. *Draven's Defiance*
6. *Fendar's Legacy*

Welcome to Odyssey: The Start of Something Big! (Focus on the Family published by Tommy Nelson).

Picture book for kids ages 3 to 8.

VIDEOS

This video series follows the adventures of Dylan Taylor and his spunky basset hound Sherman as they learn lessons about friendship and trust. Recommended for kids ages 6 and up (Focus on the Family published by Tommy Nelson).

1. *The Knight Travelers*
2. *A Flight to the Finish*
3. *A Fine Feathered Frenzy*
4. *Shadow of a Doubt*
5. *Star Quest*
6. *Once upon an Avalanche*
7. *Electric Christmas*
8. *Go West, Young Man*
9. *Someone to Watch over Me*
10. *In Harm's Way*
11. *A Twist in Time*
12. *A Stranger Among Us*
13. *Baby Daze*

AUDIO-CASSETTES/CDS

These audio packages are filled with action-packed episodes where Whit and the kids from Odyssey make valuable discoveries about faith, obedience, and commitment.

Each of the following packs consist of six double-sided audiocassettes (or four CDs starting with #16). They are recommended for fans ages 8 and up. (Focus on the Family published by Tommy Nelson).

1. *The Early Classics*
2. *Grins, Grabbers, and Great Getaways*
3. *Secrets, Surprises, and Sensational Stories*
4. *Puns, Parables, and Perilous Predicaments*
5. *Daring Deeds, Sinister Schemes*
6. *Terrific Tales, Mysterious Missions*
7. *Courageous Characters, Fabulous Friends*

8. *Cunning Capers, Exciting Escapades*

9. *Amazing Antics, Dynamic Discoveries*

10. *Other Times, Other Places*

11. *It's Another Fine Day*

12. *It All Started When . . .*

13. *At Home and Abroad*

14. *Meanwhile in Another Part of Town*

15. *A Place of Wonder*

16. *Flights of Imagination*

17. *On Earth As It Is in Heaven*

18. *A Time of Discovery*

19. *Passport to Adventure*

20. *A Journey of Choices*

21. *Wish You Were Here*

22. *The Changing Times*

23. *Twists and Turns*

24. *Risks and Rewards*

25. *Darkness Before Dawn*

26. *Back on the Air*

27. *The Search for Whit*

28. *Welcome Home!*

29. *Signed, Sealed, and Committed*

30. *Through Thick and Thin*

31. *Days to Remember*

32. *Hidden Treasures*

33. *Virtual Realities*

34. *In Your Wildest Dreams*

Classics Series (Focus on the Family published by Tommy Nelson).

Compiled from the most well-loved original Adventures in Odyssey radio Broadcasts, these special editions will send your kids on fun, faith-filled adventures!

1. *Welcome to Odyssey*

2. *A Maze of Mysteries*

3. *Bible Eyewitness—Old Testament*

4. *Bible Eyewitness—New Testament*

5. *Comic Belief*

6. *Star-Spangled Stories*

Stewardship for Kids

BOOKS

50 Money-Making Ideas for Kids by Lauree and L. Allen Burkett (Tommy Nelson).

A book of home business ventures for kids. Each project teaches biblical financial principles, such as stewardship, goal setting, integrity, and much more!

Money Matters for Teens Workbook by Larry Burkett with Todd Temple (Moody).

These workbooks (ages 11–14 edition and ages 15–18 edition) help teens apply biblical financial principles to their lives in a very hands-on, practical way.

What If I Owned Everything? by Larry Burkett with Lauree Burkett (Tommy Nelson).

Twins Jeremy and Jenny embark on a fantastic adventure of the imagination as they learn the principles of stewardship.

BOARD GAMES

Money Matters Board Game (Rainfall).

A realistic family finance game that will help you communicate basic biblical financial principles to your kids in a fun format.

Money Matters for Kids Board Game (Rainfall).

This fun, imaginative board game teaches children biblical principles of financial stewardship by stressing the importance of tithing, saving, and spending.

HERITAGE BUILDERS RESOURCES

BOOKS

Bedtime Blessings (Focus on the Family book published by Tyndale).

Strengthen the precious bond between you, your child, and God by making *Bedtime Blessings* a special part of your evenings together. From best-selling author John Trent, Ph.D., and Heritage Builders, this book is filled with stories, activities, and blessing prayers to help you practice the biblical model of "blessing." Designed for use with children ages 7 and under, *Bedtime Blessings* will help affirm the great love and value you and God have for your child, and will help each of your evenings together be filled with cherished moments in loving company.

Extending Your Heritage by J. Otis Ledbetter and Randy Scott (Focus on the Family book published by Cook Communications).

The latest release in the Framework Series extends Heritage Builders principles beyond the immediate family. *Extending Your Heritage* provides tools that grandparents, extended family, and any caring adult can use to help the kids in their lives enjoy a godly heritage.

The Family Compass by Kurt and Olivia Bruner (Focus on the Family book published by Cook Communications).

Discover how wrestling with your son or playing a game with your daughter can become the perfect opportunity to point your child's spiritual compass toward God. This important book offers plenty of practical ideas for passing along your faith to your children regardless of their age.

Family Fragrance by J. Otis and Gail Ledbetter (Focus on the Family book published by Cook Communications).

This book explains how to create an environment of love in the home. Parents will learn how five key qualities—affection, respect, order, merriment, and affirmation—contribute to a sweet family aroma creating an awesome memory-recalling legacy.

Family Nights Tool Chest by Jim Weidmann et al. (Focus on the Family books published by Cook Communications).

This series brings fun and spiritual growth together on a regular basis. The ideas and activities in them have been tried and tested by families like yours. They are designed to make lasting impressions on children of all ages and help your children learn about their Christian faith, God, Jesus, resisting temptation, taming the tongue, obedience, and much, much more. If you want to build a spiritually strong family these tools can help make your task easy and fun.

Each book contains a dozen or more complete biblical object lessons, including a list of items that will be needed, the main teaching point(s) to get across during each session, and detailed explanations and tips to help parents lead each session. Here is a list of current Family Nights activity books:

- ***An Introduction to Family Nights***
- ***Family Nights Tool Chest: Basic Christian Beliefs***
- ***Family Nights Tool Chest: Christian Character Qualities***
- ***Family Nights Tool Chest: Holidays***
- ***Family Nights Tool Chest: Money Matters***

- *Family Nights Tool Chest: Proverbs*
- *Family Nights Tool Chest: Simple Science*
- *Family Nights Tool Chest: The Ten Commandments*
- *Family Nights Tool Chest: Wisdom Life Skills*
- *New Testament Bible Stories for Preschoolers*
- *Old Testament Bible Stories for Preschoolers*

Family Traditions
by J. Otis Ledbetter
and Tim Smith
(Focus on the Family
book published by
Cook Communi-
cations).

Healthy traditions
are a key component
of a godly heritage
because they strengthen
the family. This book
will help you renew
your sense of apprecia-
tion for the fun of traditions in family life by
introducing fresh, mean-
ingful impressions to
undergird traditions you
may already celebrate.

Joy Ride! (Focus on the Family book published by Tyndale).

Use your drive time to teach your kids how faith can be part of everyday life with *Joy Ride!* A wonderful resource for parents, this book from Heritage Builders, a ministry of Focus on the Family, features activities, puz-zles, games, and discussion starters to help get your kids thinking about—and living out—what they believe.

Mealtime Moments (Focus on the Family book published by Tyndale).

Make your family's time around the din-ner table meaningful with *Mealtime Moments*. New from Heritage Builders, a ministry of Focus on the Family, this book brings you great discussion starters and activities for

teaching your children about your faith. Kids will have fun getting involved with games, trivia questions, and theme nights, all based on spiritually sound ideas. Perfect for the whole family! Spiralbound.

My Time With God (Focus on the Family book published by Tyndale).

Send your child on an amazing adven-ture—a self-guided tour through God's Word! *My Time With God*, a Heritage Builders resource from Focus on the Family, shows your 8 to 12-year-old how to get to know God regularly in fun ways. Through 150 days' worth of fun facts and mind-boggling trivia, prayer starters, and interesting questions, your child will discov-er how awesome God really is!

Teaching Your Child How to Pray by Rick Osborne (Focus on the Family book published by Moody).

In a step-by-step approach, this book lays out a plan for teaching children how to pray, from the time they're toddlers until they leave home.

Your Heritage by Kurt Bruner and J. Otis Ledbetter (Focus on the Family book pub-lished by Cook Communications).

Rooted in biblical guidance, this book explores the importance of family heritage, God's design for passing on beliefs from par-ent to child, and how family traits are handed down through generations. Also provided is a "tool chest" of ideas and suggestions to help ensure that future generations receive the best possible heritage.

AUDIOCASSETTES

The Singing Bible (Focus on the Family cassettes published by Tyndale).

Children ages 2 to 7 will love *The Singing Bible*, which sets Bible stories and facts to music with over 50 sing-along songs! New from Heritage Builders, a ministry of Focus on the Family, it introduces your kids to people like Jonah and the whale and Daniel in the lion's den, making *The Singing Bible* a fun, fast-paced journey kids will remember.

HOLIDAY RESOURCES
BOOKS

50 Great Ideas for a Joyous Christmas by Dean and Grace Merrill and Emilie Barnes.

Very specific and practical activities and traditions fill this booklet—from Advent ideas to ways for keeping the holidays free from stress.

Family Nights Tool Chest: Holidays by Jim Weidmann et al. (Focus on the Family book published by Cook Communications).

Enjoy holidays even more when they become a legacy-passing opportunity. This book contains thirteen fun-filled sessions designed around the major holidays.

The Legend of the Candy Cane by Lori Walburg (Zonderkidz).

One dark November night, a stranger rides into a small prairie town. But who is he? And what is he doing? The townspeople wish he were a doctor, a dressmaker, or a trader. But the children have the greatest wish of all! Will their wish come true? In the tradition of the best-selling *One Wintry Night* and *Tale of Three Trees*, this sensitive and imaginative story introduces children to the Christian symbolism of their favorite Christmas candy—the candy cane.

The Legend of the Easter Egg by Lori Walburg (Zonderkidz).

Featuring the beloved setting and characters from *The Legend of the Candy Cane*, this moving new story takes us deeper into the mystery of Christianity. From the darkness of Good Friday to the light and life of Easter, this story reminds Christians that because of Christ's sacrifice and resurrection, we too will conquer death and receive the glorious gift of eternal life.

LEARNING STYLES/PERSONALITIES
BOOKS

Boys! Shaping Ordinary Boys into Extraordinary Men by William Beausay II (Thomas Nelson).

Based on the assertion that boys and girls have different developmental needs, this book offers practical advice for parents of boys. Guidance is given for expressing love, participating in his activities, fueling his thoughts and ideas, helping him develop healthy attitudes, and building his self-esteem.

Bringing Out the Best in Your Child: 80 Ways to Focus on Every Kid's Strengths by Cynthia Ulrich Tobias and Carol Funk (Vine).

This book is designed to help parents identify and understand their child's individual learning style and then create strategies that build on those strengths and lead to social and academic success. Eighty practical suggestions for identifying traits based on real-life topics are given.

Girls! Helping Your Little Girl Become an Extraordinary Woman by William and Kathryn Beausay (Revell).

Based on the assertion that boys and girls have different developmental needs, this book offers practical advice for parents of girls. Guidance is given for helping her organize her personal life, influence people through leadership, learn discipline habits, develop intelligence, and build a strong spiritual foundation.

Raising a Modern-Day Knight: A Father's Role in Guiding His Son to Authentic Manhood by Robert Lewis (Focus on the Family book published by Tyndale).

This book offers practical, step-by-step guidance for fathers desiring to lead their sons to biblical masculinity. It illustrates the need for "modern knighthood" and the necessity for affirmation from father to son.

She Calls Me Daddy: Seven Things Every Man Needs to Know About Building a Complete Daughter by Robert Wolgemuth (Focus on the Family book published by Tyndale).

Though primarily directed at men who have young girls, this book offers advice applicable to fathers with daughters at any age. Robert Wolgemuth, a father of two grown daughters, cites seven foundational principles for raising healthy girls and addresses a variety of parenting topics.

Understanding Your Child's Personality by Dr. James Dobson (Focus on the Family booklet).

Dr. James Dobson's perceptive assessment of the causes of inferiority in children closes with a summation of the six most common ways children deal with inferiority.

The Way They Learn by Cynthia Tobias (Focus on the Family book published by Tyndale).

Specific strategies are given to parents and teachers for understanding the unique learning styles of children and helping them stay on task and finish homework.

Your Child Wonderfully Made by Larry Burkett and Rick Osborne (Moody).

This book is designed to help you understand your child's personality type and help prepare him or her for a career and wise adult choices.

AUDIOCASSETTES

Motivating Your Child to Learn I–II by Cheri Fuller and Dr. James Dobson (Focus on the Family Broadcast cassette).

Cheri Fuller gives suggestions to parents on how they can enhance their children's curiosity and make learning fun. She discusses motivation, grades, pressure, and positive role modeling by parents.

No Two Alike I–II by Cynthia Tobias and Dr. James Dobson (Focus on the Family Broadcast cassette).

In a humorous presentation, Cynthia Tobias helps parents understand that each of their children is unique and must be dealt with according to his or her individual style in matters of discipline and learning. Tobias also explains four learning styles based on organizational preferences and personality temperaments.

Raising a Handicapped Child I–II by Derek, Nancy, and Michael Lewis; H. Norman Wright; Dr. James Dobson (Focus on the Family Broadcast cassette).

Derek and Nancy Lewis share the emotions

and blessings they've experienced in raising their 21-year-old son, Michael, who has severe cerebral palsy. They discuss the effect of Michael's illness on their marriage and provide encouragement for parents of children with special needs. Special emphasis is given on the spiritual needs and capabilities of the handicapped.

MORALITY/ VALUES

BOOKS

10 Secrets for a Successful Family by Dr. Adrian Rogers (Crossway).

In this book, Dr. Adrian Rogers looks at each of the Ten Commandments and uses them as a springboard for discussing the life values that God expects parents to pass on to their children. He also demonstrates how to effectively model and teach those truths daily, encouraging children to develop into mature Christians.

Children at Risk (revised) by Dr. James Dobson and Gary L. Bauer (Thomas Nelson/Word).

Since this book's original release in 1990, Dobson and Bauer's warnings have proven prophetic. They've now expanded their message with new chapters and new insights for today's families. Updated "What You Can Do" sections in every chapter show you how to seize the opportunity to reinforce godly values in your children.

Faithful Parents, Faithful Kids by Greg Johnson and Mike Yorkey (Tyndale).

Topics on disciplining children, teaching kids spiritual values, dealing with rebellion, sex talks, popularity, teaching discernment, making memories, communication, and shaping values.

Point Man by Steve Farrar (Multnomah).

Lead your family safely through the "enemy-occupied territory" of the world! In this challenging book, Farrar helps you become an active leader, not an absentee landlord, by encouraging you to take your marriage and family seriously, study the Word voraciously, and much more. Includes a study guide.

Raising Kids on Purpose for the Fun of It by Gwen Weising (Revell).

This book gives fun ideas for family recreation and spending time together, and using these instances to instill values in a child. The author also tells parents how to foster a child's curiosity and interest in reading, and then talk about their discoveries and questions.

Right from Wrong by Josh McDowell (Word).

This book summarizes the findings of a survey conducted by the Barna Research Group, which discusses the alarming evidence that Christian, as well as unchurched, youth have lost the ability to determine right from wrong. Parents are advised to model godly behavior, maintain good communication, and convey biblical truth as the basis for all morality. Lists of other resources are given that address specific issues covered in the book.

The Seduction of Our Children by Neil T. Anderson and Steve Russo (Harvest House).

Are your children being asked to "center down" before class, or use "guided imagery" to resolve conflict? Anderson and Russo document how the New Age Movement is entering school curriculum in many subtle ways. They offer direction for parenting in a spiritually deceptive age, discerning occult involvement, and building lasting foundations for good communication with your children.

Values in the Home by Dr. James Dobson (Focus on the Family Booklet).

This booklet contains a specific plan by which values can be transmitted to children, as well as a list of 40 values Dr. Dobson used with his children.

What Really Matters at Home?: Eight Crucial Elements for Character in Your Family by John and Susan Yates (Thomas Nelson/Word).

You can't hide your flaws at home. It's the perfect place for refining character in kids—and in parents, too! With fun stories (and a few embarrassing ones!), John and Susan Yates describe how they and their five kids cooperate in building up each other's characters. They include focus questions for each chapter and an appendix listing great character-building books for kids.

AUDIOCASSETTES

Building Your Child's Conscience I–II by Dr. James Dobson (Focus on the Family Broadcast cassette).

Dr. James Dobson explores ways parents can help their children develop the God-given capacity to understand right from wrong. He includes a checklist for spiritual training.

PARENTING

BOOKS

10 Things Every Parent Should Know by Dr. James Dobson (Focus on the Family Booklet).

Dr. Dobson offers advice to parents on discipline, communication (especially with teens), homework, manners, defiance, boundaries, and discipline in divorce situations.

A Comprehensive Guide to Parenting on Your Own by Dr. Lynda Hunter (Zondervan).

Dr. Lynda Hunter combines her personal insights with hundreds of single parents across the country to offer this definitive handbook for single parenting.

Dobson 2-in-1: Love Must Be Tough/ Straight Talk by Dr. James Dobson (Word).

This two-in-one volume contains the classic best-sellers *Love Must Be Tough* and *Straight Talk*—each loaded with practical, straightforward advice for relationship building. In *Love Must Be Tough*, Dr. Dobson attacks the root problem of most marital crises—a lack of respect—offering practical help for rekindling mutual respect and mature love. *Straight Talk* stakes a clear path through the confusion of men's roles, teaching men how to build stable, loving, and satisfying relationships with their wives and children.

Family Walk: Love, Anger, Courage, and 49 Other Weekly Readings for Your Family by Bruce H. Wilkinson (Zondervan).

This family devotional is a compilation of daily Bible studies from Walk Thru the Bible Ministries' *Family Walk* monthly devotional guide. It is carefully designed to help parents train children to apply biblical truths to everyday situations. The book tackles 52 weekly topics. They are ideal for families with children from ages 6–12.

Family Walk Again: Family, Friends, Self-Esteem, and 49 Other Weekly Readings for Your Family by Bruce H. Wilkinson (Zondervan).

This family devotional is a compilation of daily Bible studies from Walk Thru the Bible Ministries' *Family Walk* monthly devotional guide. It is carefully designed to help parents train children to apply biblical truths to everyday situations. The book tackles 52 weekly topics. They are ideal for families with children from ages 6–12.

The Family Walk Devotional Bible by Bruce H. Wilkinson (editor), et al. (Zondervan).

This Bible combines the full NIV Bible text and the best of the *Family Walk* devotional series. If you've struggled to have devotions as a family, this Bible will bring that special time to life.

Financial Parenting by Larry Burkett and Rick Osborne (Moody Press).

This handy book teaches parents how to effectively communicate biblical tried-and-proven financial principles to their children.

The Five Key Habits of Smart Dads by Paul Lewis (Zondervan).

Paul Lewis offers a model for fathering that will help dads forge a stronger connection with their children, ultimately improving their family life in general.

The Focus on the Family Complete Book of Baby and Child Care: From Pre-birth Through the Teen Years by the Focus on the Family Physicians Resource Council (Tyndale).

This fully illustrated comprehensive resource offers advice to parents of children

from the pre-birth stage to the teen years. Sections include emergency care, medical reference, photos of skin conditions, musculoskeletal problems, immunization schedule, atlas of the body, baby product information, food guide pyramid, growth charts, and recommended resources.

The Gift of the Blessing by Gary Smalley and John Trent, Ph.D. (Thomas Nelson).

In this book Gary Smalley and John Trent detail the five elements of the parental blessing, the greatest gift a mother or father can give a beloved child: meaningful touch, the spoken word, the expression of high value, the description of a special future, the application of genuine commitment.

Helping Children Survive Divorce by Archibald Hart (Thomas Nelson/Word).

This book will help you build a healthier postdivorce life for your children so that they can be counted among those who not only survived divorce but became the better for it. You will find specific ways to help, including minimizing damage to your child, common mistakes, how to handle guilt, essential steps to help your child cope with depression and anger, ensuring your child's healthy postdivorce development, four issues that must be dealt with when you remarry, and dos and don'ts for successfully building a blended family.

Hide or Seek by Dr. James Dobson (Revell).

Dr. James Dobson presents 10 comprehensive strategies that parents and teachers may use to cultivate self-esteem in every child and combat the epidemic of inferiority in our society. He asserts that only Christian values free people from the tyranny of "self" and offer dignity and respect to every human being.

How to Be a Hero to Your Kids by Josh McDowell (Thomas Nelson/Word).

All it takes is love, motivation, and a workable plan. Discover how Josh McDowell and Dick Day's six-point biblically based recipe for positive parenting can transform you into a real hero to your kids. You will learn how to demonstrate the kind of compassion, character, and consistency that all adds up to being a positive role model. You will find that being a hero is practical, fulfilling, and even fun. But most of all, it will build up the kind of relationship with your kids that will equip them to live fulfilled and abundant lives, even in a dangerous and hostile world. What else could any superparent want?

How to Parent Your "Tweenager": Understanding the In-Between Years of Your 8- to 12-Year-Old by Dr. Mary Manz Simon (Thomas Nelson).

This book offers support for the parent of a child in the gray area between childhood and the teen years, ages 8 to 12. Part I addresses how the preadolescent develops physically, socially, and spiritually. Part II looks at practical issues, such as raising a "latchkey" child, using organization, setting boundaries, and much more.

The Key to Your Child's Heart by Gary Smalley (Thomas Nelson).

Did you know there are four types of parents—but only one is successful? In this eye-opening book, Smalley helps you succeed by giving you ways to motivate your child, steps to reopen your child's spirit, and much more. You'll also learn how to avoid unhealable rifts and weave strong family ties instead.

Leaving the Light On by Gary Smalley and John Trent, Ph.D. (Multnomah).

Fifteen proven relational principles offer parents the chance to build solid, memory-filled family relationships today that will encourage their children tomorrow to return to where love is freely given—home.

Let's Hide the Word by Gloria Gaither with Shirley Dobson (Word).

Gloria Gaither and Shirley Dobson believe that the home needs to be the place where Christian values are both caught and taught. Their book shows how parents can create a home climate saturated with biblical practices and principles.

Let's Make a Memory (revised) by Gloria Gaither and Shirley Dobson (Word).

The authors share a wealth of ideas on how to make family traditions reinforce lasting values in your home. The suggestions include holiday activities, vacation ideas, and relationship builders.

The Mommy Book by Karen Hull (Zondervan).

Karen Hull uncovers some mysteries of motherhood: potty training, teething, handling housework, and teaching children about Jesus, to name a few. The book is filled with creative ideas and practical tips for raising happy, healthy, well-adjusted, and self-confident children.

The New Dare to Discipline by Dr. James Dobson (Tyndale).

This revised and updated version of Dr. James Dobson's classic *Dare to Discipline* offers not only advice about raising children but also an entire philosophy on child rearing. It details foundations to commonsense parenting, principles to maximize the law of reinforcement, categories of children who do poorly in school, and numerous suggestions for helping mothers make it through the day.

Parenting Isn't for Cowards by Dr. James Dobson (Thomas Nelson/Word).

This classic confidence builder for parents is designed to help even parents of "difficult children" find the joy and fulfillment parenthood was intended to bring. Speaking both as a therapist and a parent—and drawing on a landmark study of 35,000 parents—Dr. Dobson offers guilt-banishing insight on why some children really are harder to raise than others . . . along with sound guidance for doing it! There are trouble-proofing strategies for parents of young children and sanity-protecting tactics for weathering adolescence. An energy-restoring plan for overcoming parental burnout is included as well as relationship-enhancing guidance for letting go of your children at the right time. It also includes a chapter-by-chapter study guide to enrich your reading and facilitate group study!

Parenting Passages by David Veerman (Tyndale).

Practical advice is given for navigating the parenting passages—those critical times of transition parents face. David Veerman identifies 11 passages from pregnancy and infancy through the empty nest, and offers help for coping.

Pictures the Heart Remembers by John Trent, Ph.D. (Waterbrook).

We are called to be a blessing. But being a blessing is not merely our calling. It's a choice we need to make daily with regard to our past and with regard to each person who comes across our path. But how do we choose to bless, when the events of our past evoke emotions of failure, shame, or deep disappointment? How can we bless the people around us today when their actions make us want to respond not with a blessing, but with a curse? In this book, John Trent shows us how we can face the painful pictures of our past and choose to live—and give—God's blessing.

Preparing for Adolescence by Dr. James Dobson (Vision House/Gospel Light).

Dr. Dobson recommends that parents prepare their preteen-ager (10–12 years old) for the adolescent experience. This book will be helpful with topics of greatest concern: inferiority, conformity, puberty, the meaning of love, and the search for identity.

Preparing for Adolescence Group Guide by Dr. James Dobson (Living Word).

This Preparing for Adolescence workbook is a 10-session course for youth leaders to use in a group situation. Each unit contains leader's preparation materials, lesson plans, reproducible worksheets, and ideas on how to decorate the environment to motivate students for learning.

Ready for Kindergarten by Sharon Wilkins (Gold 'n' Honey).

This book offers 156 activities—games, cooking, crafts, a visit to the library—that are designed to help children, ages four to six, prepare for kindergarten. Each activity is clearly explained and is accompanied by a verse of scripture.

Scrapbook Storytelling: Journaling and Your Own Creativity, Save Family Stories and Memories with Photos by Joanna Campbell Slan (Writer's Digest).

This inspiring, visual book offers crafters, family historians, and proud parents dozens of great ideas for documenting family stories and events with "scrapbooking." Following easy-to-understand steps, readers will learn new ways to discover and recover favorite stories and combine these stories with cherished photos, collages, fabric art, mosiacs, and illustrations.

Single Parenting: A Wilderness Journey by Robert Barnes (Tyndale).

With biblical insight, Robert Barnes examines such topics as communication, finances, discipline, visitation, self-esteem, sex education, and value building. Each chapter ends with a review and questions.

Solid Answers by Dr. James Dobson (Tyndale).

This text was written as a reference book that answers many often-asked questions on such topics as marital relationships, infants, discipline of young children, spiritual training, home management, physical problems, adolescence, and a host of other subjects.

Straight Talk to Men and Their Wives by Dr. James Dobson (Thomas Nelson/Word).

Be strong. Be sensitive. Make your mark. Make more money. What's a husband and father supposed to do? Dobson gives clear guidance on issues such as marriage, fatherhood, work, money, and more to help you become an effective family leader and enjoy a satisfying relationship with your wife and children.

Successful Single Parenting by Gary Richmond (Harvest House).

Packed with advice, this complete guide covers how to set financial priorities, help children handle change, explain the other parent's absence, deal with discipline, handle visitations, and more.

You and Your Child by Charles R. Swindoll (Thomas Nelson/Word).

This is a book for moms and dads engaged in the exacting task of raising children—moms and dads who are weary of theories and seminars and opinions that sound good but prove unrealistic. This is a book full of practical information, sound advice, and solid principles from one of America's most beloved writers and teachers, Charles Swindoll. He writes with clarity, humor, and passion about effective, practical parenting—a topic he's learned from extensive biblical study and from surviving life "in the trenches."

AUDIOCAS-SETTES

Children and Financial Discipline I–II by Larry Burkett and Dr. James Dobson (Focus on the Family Broadcast cassette).

A financial counselor discusses the biblical perspective on allowances, spoiling children, tithing, earning money, and other vital topics concerning teaching children from preschool to 18 years old about financial management.

Preparing for Adolescence by Dr. James Dobson (Gospel Light).

This package includes two leadership tapes as well as six tapes in which Dr. Dobson talks directly to the preteen-ager about the years immediately ahead. His casual, conversational approach to these sessions provides an informative and entertaining discussion of the adolescent experience. It is suggested that the tapes be heard by parent and child together (or perhaps by groups of preteen-agers), providing the basis for further discussion and interaction.

SPIRITUAL TRAINING

BOOKS

801 Questions Kids Ask About God by David Veerman, et al. (Focus on the Family book published by Tyndale). Available November 2000.

This is a compilation of questions from the best-selling *101 Questions Children Ask* series. It is a very practical resource that will help you answer your children's questions about God, the Bible, the church, and Christian living.

FaithTraining by Joe White (Focus on the Family book published by Tyndale).

This book is designed to help parents train children of all ages to love the Lord. One section features 365 ways to tell your child "I love you" without saying the words.

Family Times by Jerry and Patti MacGregor (Harvest House).

When home-schooling lessons are done, it's time for some fun! Best-selling authors, the MacGregors now offer hundreds of activities everybody in your family can enjoy together—indoor and outdoor games to play, Bible stories to act out, recipes to make, great movies to watch, excellent books to read—take your pick! Each activity helps to build a firm foundation of communication, teamwork, and Christian values.

Gentle Art of Mentoring by Donna Otto (Harvest House).

Offering week-by-week topics, preparation steps, discussion questions, and encouraging "mentoring moments," this handbook will help you provide the tools and resources a young woman needs to build a solid marriage, raise well-adjusted children, and develop a stronger, more vibrant relationship with the Lord.

The Gift of the Blessing by Gary Smalley and John Trent, Ph.D. (Thomas Nelson).

A powerful, award-winning book no family should be without. In their warm and unique way, Gary and John blend insightful teaching with powerful stories to detail the five elements of the blessing: meaningful touch, the spoken word, the expression of high value, picturing a special future, and giving genuine commitment. It's an important resource to have for anyone wanting to know how to show unconditional love and acceptance to the people you love.

Growing Little Women by Linda Holland and Donna Miller (Moody).

To combat constant peer and media pressure, Linda Holland and Donna Miller offer you and your special young lady teachable moments from His Word. Invest an hour a week and establish a bond that will smooth her passage to womanhood.

The "Learning for Life" series.

Each book shows you how to teach your child about Jesus, the Bible, and the Christian faith in the middle of a busy life.

- ***Your Child and Jesus*** by Rick Osborne with Kevin Miller (Moody).
- ***Your Child and the Bible*** by Rick Osborne with Kevin Miller (Moody).
- ***Your Child and the Christian Life*** by Rick Osborne with K. Christie Bowler (Moody).

LifeTraining by Joe White (Focus on the Family book published by Tyndale).

This devotional is designed primarily for parents and teens. However, younger children that have teen siblings will also benefit. Volume one covers Matthew, Luke, John, Acts, James, and Revelation. Volume two covers the rest of the New Testament. Each volume also contains 100 scripture memory verses.

Making God's Word Stick by Emmett Cooper and Steve Wamberg (Thomas Nelson/Word).

Even the most experienced teachers find it a challenge to make God's Word accessible to young students. That's why Pastor Cooper and curriculum author Wamberg have put together this resource that helps you make the Bible understandable and memorable for your elementary-age kids. It's packed with how-to tips, real-life anecdotes, and lots of encouragement.

Pictures Your Heart Remembers by John Trent, Ph.D. (Waterbrook).

The daily choice to "bless" or "curse" is enormously important. Through gripping stories and careful explanation of scripture, you learn how choosing light over darkness, life over death, and blessing over cursing can change your life, and your family's, forever.

The Power of a Praying Parent by Stormie Omartian (Harvest House).

Stormie Omartian, drawing on her own experience as a parent and prayer warrior, offers 30 short, easy-to-read chapters full of advice on how to pray through every age and stage of a child's life.

Raising Kids God's Way by Kathi Hudson (Good News/Crossway).

This book gives parents the clear princi-

ples and practical tips they need, rooted in the purity of God's Word. This book pinpoints the difference between teaching and training, offers an array of biblical methods of parenting, and shows how you can use all of life as a classroom. Practical, biblical discussion on such topics as decision making, determining God's will, and reading and study skills will help you bring up your children so they will walk with God for a lifetime.

Raising Kids Who Turn Out Right by Tim Kimmel (Questar).

Tim Kimmel talks about developing your child's character and ways to build children's faith, integrity, poise, and discipline. He shows parents how to be an example and protect the values they instill in their children.

Talking to Your Children About God by Rick Osborne (HarperSanFrancisco).

A parent's practical guide to God, Bible stories, children and church, prayers, virtues, and other spiritual stuff.

The Two Sides of Love by Gary Smalley and John Trent, Ph.D. (Focus on the Family book published by Tyndale).

If you've ever wondered how to balance the tough and tender sides of love, this is a must read. Gary and John first explore the uniqueness of our strengths and weaknesses, then show how we can strike that Christlike balance between love's hard and soft sides. Affection, closeness, and lasting commitment are the result.

Woman of Influence: How to Pray for Your Children by Jean Fleming (NavPress).

The author suggests how to use each sliver of available time to transform the rushed prayer into more meaningful intercession. Jean explains how a Christian mother can most strongly influence the lives of her children.

AUDIOCASSETTES

Blessing Others by Gary Smalley, John Trent, Ph.D., and Dr. James Dobson (Focus on the Family Broadcast cassette).

Gary Smalley and John Trent discuss their book *The Blessing*, which captures five elements from the Old Testament practice of blessing children.

A Checklist for Spiritual Training by Dr. James Dobson (Focus on the Family Broadcast cassette).

Parents concerned about their children's moral development are given a set of six concepts to use in evaluating where children are in their spiritual understanding.

Keys to the Human Heart I–II by Dr. Gary Smalley and Dr. James Dobson (Focus on the Family Broadcast cassette).

Gary Smalley explores the concept of a child's closed spirit and the key to keeping an open relationship.

The Spiritual Training of Children by Dr. James Dobson (Focus on the Family Broadcast cassette).

This discussion is a challenge to parents to remember the privilege and responsibility they have in leading their children to a personal faith in God. Dr. James Dobson also challenges parents to answer their children's major questions in life about identity, purpose, and values.

TEENS

BOOKS

13 Things You Gotta Know by Josh McDowell and Bob Hostetler (Thomas Nelson/Word).

Being a Christian is great—but *living* as a Christian can be tricky. Old habits, new temptations, and everyday confusions can drain you, discourage you, and take the zing out of your attempts to reach others for Christ. That's where this book, a PowerLink Student Devotional, can help. Over the course of 13 weeks, it will plug you deeply into God's Word and show you how to stay plugged in to His power and light.

Bondage Breaker, **Youth Edition** by Neil Anderson and David Park (Harvest House). This book is specifically written for youth and addresses issues many young people are struggling with, such as sexual temptation, peer pressure, insecurity, and doubt. The authors explain how Satan tries to control people and involve them in spiritual conflict. Anderson and Park also relate practical and effective means that can be used to fight back and experience the freedom God wants all of us to have in our everyday life.

Can I Be a Christian Without Being Weird? by Kevin Johnson (Bethany House).

A teen devotional for junior highers on getting to know God and being a follower of Jesus Christ.

Catch the Wave by Kevin Johnson (Bethany House).

This book helps teens find their place in God's worldwide plan by exposing them to His work in the world—showing them how to develop a "catching" faith through prayer and ministry at church, school, and across cultures.

Don't Check Your Brains at the Door: Know What You Believe and Why by Josh McDowell and Bob Hostetler (Thomas Nelson/Word).

All too often, Christian students trip blithely off to secular colleges or jobs—and return with their faith shattered. Why? Many teens don't know what or why they believe. This entertaining course enables teens to firmly secure their faith. Then, when questions and doubts come, they'll have a ready defense. Ideal for junior and senior high students.

Extreme Teen Bible, NKJV: No Fear, No Regrets, Just a Future with a Promise (Thomas Nelson).

This Bible equips teens to take their faith to new heights with a well-grounded sense of who they are, what they believe, and what God promises for their future! Innovative study helps are geared to the teen culture—guaranteed to address the issues young people deal with every day. Book introductions and relevant study notes bring the message of the Bible into focus and help teens target God's plan for their lives. Profiles tell the stories of amazing young people in the scripture who allowed God to work through them to make an impact on their world. The New King James text doesn't talk down to teens. Instead, this Bible gives them the "straight truth" they want to hear—and helps them find that truth!

If the Pasta Wiggles, Don't Eat It by Martha Bolton (Servant).

In this devotional book, Martha Bolton relies on her understanding of teens and her great sense of humor to teach young people

how to grow closer to God and live wholesome lives. This collection of 90 devotions entertains and instructs youths in practical spiritual living.

Jesus Freaks by dc Talk and the Voice of the Martyrs (Albury).

The first book ever released by Toby McKeehan, Michael Tait, and Kevin Max—the award-winning trio known as dc Talk! They challenge you to examine your own faith and dedication with compelling real-life stories of believers who refused to deny Jesus—even in the face of death. The book includes eye-opening information about persecution in the world today.

Josh McDowell's Handbook on Counseling Youth by Josh McDowell and Bob Hostetler (Thomas Nelson/Word).

This easy-to-use handbook will equip parents, teachers, pastors, and youth workers to help youth cope with the major issues they face, from simple challenges to major crises. Some of the major issues dealt with include: emotional issues, relational issues, family issues, sexual issues, abuse, disorders, addictions, educational and vocational issues.

Life Happens: Help Your Teenager Get Ready by Barry St. Clair (Broadman/Holman).

One idea, two points of view. One book talks to teens about how they can find their calling in God's world; the second tells parents how they can help.

Life on the Edge by Dr. James Dobson (Thomas Nelson/Word).

Money, relationships, power—these are just some of the many pressures and choices your high schoolers face. In this wisdom-filled collection, Dr. Dobson helps armor teens for the tough battles they face as they edge toward adulthood.

Never Ask Delilah for a Trim by Martha Bolton (Servant).

This teen devotional is fresh, engaging, and thought-provoking. It features Bolton's trademark zany humor, speaking straight to 12- to 15-year-olds about forgiving friends, holding grudges, using their talents, and much more. Each devotion includes a scripture passage from Matthew's gospel, a prayer, and a "bumper sticker" thought to ponder.

Old Enough to Know by Michael W. Smith with Fritz Ridenour (Thomas Nelson/Word).

Christian recording artist Michael W. Smith gives straight, biblical answers to hot questions on sex, drugs, alcohol, parental conflicts, empty religion, materialism, and more. It features Smith's songs and personal experiences, insight from scripture, and real letters from teens.

Parenting Today's Adolescent by Dennis and Barbara Rainey (Thomas Nelson/Word).

Normally confident moms and dads grow weak-kneed when their children enter—gasp!—puberty. Barbara and Dennis Rainey map out the unfamiliar, demanding landscape of both preadolescence (ages 10–12) as well as the teen years that follow. The Raineys deliver a proactive, tested approach to help children and parents build a satisfying relationship while forging a vision for a productive, God-honoring life—before, during, and after adolescence.

Reality 101 by Wayne Rice and David R. Veerman (Tyndale).

This book provides answers to 101 real-life questions that Christian teens have asked about faith, friendship, family, finances, and other issues.

Start Where You Are by Charles R. Swindoll (Thomas Nelson/Word).

Swindoll shares wisdom, thoughts, and encouragement for life's passages using four key themes: leadership, success, compassion, and life's trials.

The Teenage Q & A Book by Josh McDowell and Bill Jones (Thomas Nelson/Word).

Adolescence can be both exciting and terrifying! This question-and-answer handbook for teens covers the two extremes and everything in between in a practical and biblical way.

Understanding Your Teenager by Wayne Rice and David Veerman (Thomas Nelson/Word).

This book explores the changing world of today's youth, providing invaluable insight into adolescent development and our contemporary culture's influence on teens. The information is supplemented with parenting principles and practical approaches to raising healthy, spiritually developed teens.

Why Is God Looking for Friends? by Kevin Johnson (Bethany House).

A teen devotional for junior highers on the all-consuming ache for real friendships—with God and others. Same format as *Can I Be a Christian Without Being Weird?*

Your Place in This World by Michael W. Smith (Thomas Nelson).

What am I supposed to do with my life? It's a question often asked by both teenagers and young adults. In this uplifting yet practical book, best-selling Christian artist Michael W. Smith takes readers on a journey for answers based on God's Word. Along the way, Michael provides a biblical definition of successful living and relates personal stories that illustrate that God truly does have a place for all who follow Him.

The Youth Builder by Jim Burns (Harvest House).

A comprehensive resource on relational youth ministry by one of the nation's leading authorities. The book contains proven, effective methods, specific recommendations, and hands-on solutions for handling scores of problems and challenges. You may not be a dynamic speaker, know the latest rock bands, or dress in the hottest fashions, but if you love young people and desire to invest in their lives, your influence can change lives.

MAGAZINES

Brio (Focus on the Family).

The inside scoop for teen girls with hot tips on everything from fashion and food to fitness and faith.

Breakaway (Focus on the Family).

Teen guys get the lowdown on sports, celebrities . . . even girls! Also, advice, humor and spiritual guidance.

Memory Verses

Anger

An angry man stirs up dissension, and a hot-tempered one commits many sins. (Proverbs 29:22)

Everyone should be quick to listen, slow to speak and slow to become angry. (James 1:19)

Arguments

Don't have anything to do with foolish and stupid arguments, because you know they produce quarrels. (2 Timothy 2:23)

The Bible

It is written: "Man does not live on bread alone, but on every word that comes from the mouth of God." (Matthew 4:4)

Heaven and earth will pass away, but my words will never pass away. (Matthew 24:35)

If anyone teaches false doctrines and does not agree to the sound instruction of our Lord Jesus Christ and to godly teaching, he is conceited and understands nothing. (1 Timothy 6:3–4)

All scripture is God-breathed and is useful for teaching, rebuking, correcting and training in righteousness. (2 Timothy 3:16)

Church

Now you are the body of Christ, and each one of you is a part of it. (1 Corinthians 12:27)

Let us not give up meeting together, as some are in the habit of doing, but let us encourage one another—and all the more as you see the Day approaching. (Hebrews 10:25)

Contentment and Desires

Delight yourself in the Lord and he will give you the desires of your heart. (Psalm 37:4)

Look at the birds of the air; they do not sow or reap or store away in barns, and yet your heavenly Father feeds them. Are you not much more valuable than they? (Matthew 6:26)

I have learned the secret of being content in any and every situation, whether well fed or hungry, whether living in plenty or in want. (Philippians 4:12)

Be joyful always; pray continually; give thanks in all circumstances, for this is God's will for you in Christ Jesus. (1 Thessalonians 5:16–18)

Discipline

My son, do not make light of the Lord's discipline, and do not lose heart when he rebukes you, because the Lord disciplines those he loves. (Hebrews 12:5–6)

No discipline seems pleasant at the time, but painful. Later on, however, it produces a harvest of righteousness and peace for those who have been trained by it. (Hebrews 12:11)

Don't Be Disorderly

For God is not a God of disorder but of peace. (1 Corinthians 14:33)

Everything should be done in a fitting and orderly way. (1 Corinthians 14:40)

Don't Worry or Fear

I will lie down and sleep in peace, for you alone, O LORD, make me dwell in safety. (Psalm 4:8)

Cast your cares on the LORD and he will sustain you; he will never let the righteous fall. (Psalm 55:22)

And the peace of God, which transcends all understanding, will guard your hearts and your minds in Christ Jesus. (Philippians 4:7)

Cast all your anxiety on him because he cares for you. (1 Peter 5:7)

Enemies

But I tell you: Love your enemies and pray for those who persecute you, that you may be sons of your Father in heaven. (Matthew 5:44–45)

If you are insulted because of the name of Christ, you are blessed, for the Spirit of glory and of God rests on you. (1 Peter 4:14)

Forgiveness

For if you forgive men when they sin against you, your heavenly Father will also forgive you. But if you do not forgive men their sins, your Father will not forgive your sins. (Matthew 6:14–15)

Be kind and compassionate to one another, forgiving each other, just as in Christ God forgave you. (Ephesians 4:32)

Getting Along

Do nothing out of selfish ambition or vain conceit, but in humility consider others better than yourselves. Each of you should look not only to your own interests, but also to the interests of others. (Philippians 2:3–4)

Live in peace with each other. (1 Thessalonians 5:13)

Remind the people . . . to slander no one, to be peaceable and considerate, and to show true humility toward all men. (Titus 3:1–2)

Giving and Sharing

Give to the one who asks you, and do not turn away from the one who wants to borrow from you. (Matthew 5:42)

Watch out! Be on your guard against all kinds of greed; a man's life does not consist in the abundance of his possessions. (Luke 12:15)

Jesus himself said: "It is more blessed to give than to receive." (Acts 20:35)

Each man should give what he has decided in his heart to give, not reluctantly or under compulsion, for God loves a cheerful giver. (2 Corinthians 9:7)

God

In the beginning God created the heavens and the earth. (Genesis 1:1)

Hear, O Israel: The LORD our God, the LORD is one. (Deuteronomy 6:4)

I am the first and I am the last; apart from me there is no God. (Isaiah 44:6)

I the LORD do not change. (Malachi 3:6)

For since the creation of the world God's invisible qualities— his eternal power and divine nature—have been clearly seen, being understood from what has been made, so that men are without excuse. (Romans 1:20)

God, the blessed and only Ruler, the King of kings and Lord of lords, who alone is immortal and who lives in unapproachable light, whom no one has seen or can see. To him be honor and might forever. (1 Timothy 6:15–16)

"I am the Alpha and Omega," says the Lord God, "who is, and who was, and who is to come, the Almighty." (Revelation 1:8)

You are worthy, our Lord and God, to receive glory and honor and power, for you created all things, and by your will they were created and have their being. (Revelation 4:11)

God's Attributes

He is the Rock, his works are perfect, and all his ways are just. A faithful God who does no wrong, upright and just is he. (Deuteronomy 32:4)

Great is our Lord and mighty in power; his understanding has no limit. (Psalm 147:5)

As the heavens are higher than the earth, so are my ways higher than your ways and my thoughts than your thoughts. (Isaiah 55:9)

"Can anyone hide in secret places so that I cannot see him?" declares the LORD. "Do not I fill heaven and earth?" (Jeremiah 23:24)

Ah, Sovereign LORD, you have made the heavens and the earth by your great power and outstretched arm. Nothing is too hard for you. (Jeremiah 32:17)

With God all things are possible. (Matthew 19:26)

God is spirit, and his worshipers must worship in spirit and in truth. (John 4:24)

God is love. Whoever lives in love lives in God, and God in him. (1 John 4:16)

God's Leading

Trust in the LORD with all your heart and lean not on your own understanding; in all your ways acknowledge him, and he will make your paths straight. (Proverbs 3:5–6)

If any of you lacks wisdom, he should ask God, who gives generously to all without finding fault, and it will be given to him. (James 1:5)

Godly Life

You are to be holy to me because I, the LORD, am holy. (Leviticus 20:26)

Be imitators of God, therefore, as dearly loved children and live a life of love, just as Christ loved us. (Ephesians 5:1–2)

Whoever claims to live in him must walk as Jesus did. (1 John 2:6)

Good Attitudes

Blessed are the poor in spirit, for theirs is the kingdom of heaven. Blessed are those who mourn, for they will be comforted. Blessed are the meek, for they will inherit the earth. Blessed are those who hunger and thirst for righteousness, for they will be filled. Blessed are the merciful, for they will be shown mercy. Blessed are the pure in heart, for they will see God. Blessed are the peacemakers, for they will be called sons of God. Blessed are those who are persecuted because of righteousness, for theirs is the kingdom of heaven. (Matthew 5:3–10)

Do not judge, or you too will be judged. For in the same way you judge others, you will be judged. (Matthew 7:1–2)

But the fruit of the Spirit is love, joy, peace, patience, kindness, goodness, faithfulness, gentleness and self-control. Against such things there is no law. (Galatians 5:22–23)

Do everything without complaining or arguing, so that you may become blameless and pure children of God. (Philippians 2:14–15)

Finally, brothers, whatever is true, whatever is noble, whatever is right, whatever is pure, whatever is lovely, whatever is admirable—if anything is excellent or praiseworthy—think about such things. (Philippians 4:8)

Anyone who claims to be in the light but hates his brother is still in the darkness. Whoever loves his brother lives in the light, and there is nothing in him to make him stumble. (1 John 2:9–10)

Good Speech

There is a time for everything, . . . a time to be silent and a time to speak. (Ecclesiastes 3:1, 7)

But I tell you that men will have to give account on the day of judgment for every careless word they have spoken. (Matthew 12:36)

Do not let any unwholesome talk come out of your mouths, but only what is helpful for building others up according to their needs, that it may benefit those who listen. (Ephesians 4:29)

Make it your ambition to lead a quiet life, to mind your own business and to work with your hands. (1 Thessalonians 4:11)

Helping Others

If someone forces you to go one mile, go with him two miles. (Matthew 5:41)

Therefore, as we have opportunity, let us do good to all people, especially to those who belong to the family of believers. (Galatians 6:10)

Anyone, then, who knows the good he ought to do and doesn't do it, sins. (James 4:17)

Honesty

You shall not steal. (Exodus 20:15)

Do not steal. Do not lie. Do not deceive one another. (Leviticus 19:11)

Therefore each of you must put off falsehood and speak truthfully to his neighbor, for we are all members of one body. (Ephesians 4:25)

Jealousy

You shall not covet . . . anything that belongs to your neighbor. (Exodus 20:17)

Jesus

In the beginning was the Word, and the Word was with God, and the Word was God. He was with God in the beginning. Through him all things were made; without him nothing was made that has been made. (John 1:1–3)

I am the light of the world. Whoever follows me will never walk in darkness, but will have the light of life. (John 8:12)

I am the gate; whoever enters through me will be saved. (John 10:9)

I am the good shepherd. The good shepherd lays down his life for the sheep. (John 10:11)

I am the vine; you are the branches. If a man remains in me and I in him, he will bear much fruit; apart from me you can do nothing. (John 15:5)

For what I received I passed on to you as of first importance: that Christ died for our sins according to the scriptures, that he was buried, that he was raised on the third day according to the scriptures, and that he

appeared to Peter, and then to the Twelve. (1 Corinthians 15:3–5)

For we do not have a high priest who is unable to sympathize with our weaknesses, but we have one who has been tempted in every way, just as we are—yet was without sin. (Hebrews 4:15)

Jesus Christ is the same yesterday and today and forever. (Hebrews 13:8)

I am the First and the Last. I am the Living One; I was dead, and behold I am alive for ever and ever! (Revelation 1:17–18)

Jesus' Return and Heaven

In my Father's house are many rooms; if it were not so, I would have told you. I am going there to prepare a place for you. And if I go and prepare a place for you, I will come back and take you to be with me that you also may be where I am. (John 14:2–3)

No eye has seen, no ear has heard, no mind has conceived what God has prepared for those who love him. (1 Corinthians 2:9)

For the Lord himself will come down from heaven, with a loud command, with the voice of the archangel and with the trumpet call of God, and the dead in Christ will rise first. After that, we who are still alive and are left will be caught up together with them in the clouds to meet the Lord in the air. And so we will be with the Lord forever. (1 Thessalonians 4:16–17)

Loving God

But seek first his kingdom and his righteousness, and all these things will be given to you as well. (Matthew 6:33)

"Love the Lord your God with all your heart and with all your soul and with all your mind." This is the first and greatest commandment. And the second is like it: "Love your neighbor as yourself." (Matthew 22:37–39)

Loving People

Do to others as you would have them do to you. (Luke 6:31)

By this all men will know that you are my disciples, if you love one another. (John 13:35)

Love is patient, love is kind. It does not envy, it does not boast, it is not proud. It is not rude, it is not self-seeking, it is not easily angered, it keeps no record of wrongs. Love does not delight in evil but rejoices with the truth. It always protects, always trusts, always hopes, always perseveres. Love never fails. (1 Corinthians 13:4–8)

The entire law is summed up in a single command: "Love your neighbor as yourself." (Galatians 5:14)

Above all, love each other deeply, because love covers over a multitude of sins. (1 Peter 4:8)

Dear children, let us not love with words or tongue but with actions and in truth. (1 John 3:18)

And this is his command: to believe in the name of his Son, Jesus Christ, and to love one another as he commanded us. (1 John 3:23)

We love because he first loved us. (1 John 4:19)

Obedience to Parents

Honor your father and your mother. (Exodus 20:12)

Listen, my son, to your father's instruction and do not forsake your mother's teaching. (Proverbs 1:8)

Children, obey your parents in the Lord, for this is right. (Ephesians 6:1)

Obey your leaders and submit to their authority. (Hebrews 13:17)

Obedience to the Word

Do not let this Book of the Law depart from your mouth; meditate on it day and night, so that you may be careful to do everything written in it. Then you will be prosperous and successful. (Joshua 1:8)

The law of his God is in his heart; his feet do not slip. (Psalm 37:31)

I have hidden your word in my heart that I might not sin against you. (Psalm 119:11)

Therefore everyone who hears these words of mine and puts them into practice is like a wise man who built his house on the rock. The rain came down, the streams rose, and the winds blew and beat against that house; yet it did not fall, because it had its foundation on the rock. (Matthew 7:24–25)

If you love me, you will obey what I command. (John 14:15)

Do not merely listen to the word, and so deceive yourselves. Do what it says. (James 1:22)

Power

Stand firm then, with the belt of truth buckled around your waist, with the breastplate of righteousness in place, and with your feet fitted with the readiness that comes from the gospel of peace. In addition to all this, take up the shield of faith, with which you can extinguish all the flaming arrows of the evil one. Take the helmet of salvation and the sword of the Spirit, which is the word of God. (Ephesians 6:14–17)

I can do everything through him who gives me strength. (Philippians 4:13)

Prayer

The righteous cry out, and the LORD hears them; he delivers them from all their troubles. (Psalm 34:17)

Then you will call upon me and come and pray to me, and I will listen to you. You will seek me and find me when you seek me with all your heart. (Jeremiah 29:12–13)

Call to me and I will answer you and tell you great and unsearchable things you do not know. (Jeremiah 33:3)

This is how you should pray: "Our Father in heaven, hallowed be your name, your kingdom come, your will be done on earth as it is in heaven. Give us today our daily bread. Forgive us our debts, as we also have forgiven our debtors. And lead us not into temptation, but deliver us from the evil one. (Matthew 6:9–13)

Ask and it will be given to you; seek and you will find; knock and the door will be opened to you. For everyone who asks receives; he who seeks finds; and to him who knocks, the door will be opened. (Matthew 7:7–8)

Come to me, all you who are weary and burdened, and I will give you rest. Take my yoke upon you and learn from me, for I am gentle and humble in heart, and you will find rest for your souls. For my yoke is easy and my burden is light. (Matthew 11:28–30)

He who did not spare his own Son, but gave him up for us all—how will he not also, along with him, graciously give us all things? (Romans 8:32)

Do not be anxious about anything, but in everything, by prayer and petition, with thanksgiving, present your requests to God. (Philippians 4:6)

Protection

The LORD is my shepherd, I shall not be in want. He makes me lie down in green pastures, he leads me beside quiet waters, he restores my soul. He guides me in paths of righteousness for his name's sake. Even though I walk through the valley of the shadow of death, I will fear no evil, for you are with me; your rod and your staff, they comfort me. You prepare a table before me in the presence of my enemies. You anoint my head with oil; my cup overflows. Surely goodness and love will follow me all the days of my life, and I will dwell in the house of the LORD forever. (Psalm 23:1–6)

The righteous cry out, and the LORD hears them; he delivers them from all their troubles. (Psalm 34:17)

Submit yourselves, then, to God. Resist the devil, and he will flee from you. Come near

to God and he will come near to you.
(James 4:7–8)

Salvation: How to Be Saved

Jesus declared, "I tell you the truth, no one can see the kingdom of God unless he is born again." (John 3:3)

For God so loved the world that he gave his one and only Son, that whoever believes in him shall not perish but have eternal life. (John 3:16)

If you confess with your mouth, "Jesus is Lord," and believe in your heart that God raised him from the dead, you will be saved. For it is with your heart that you believe and are justified, and it is with your mouth that you confess and are saved. (Romans 10:9–10)

For it is by grace you have been saved, through faith—and this not from yourselves, it is the gift of God—not by works, so that no one can boast. (Ephesians 2:8–9)

Salvation: The Need for It

For all have sinned and fall short of the glory of God. (Romans 3:23)

For the wages of sin is death, but the gift of God is eternal life in Christ Jesus our Lord. (Romans 6:23)

Salvation: Only in Jesus

Jesus answered, "I am the way and the truth and the life. No one comes to the Father except through me." (John 14:6)

Salvation is found in no one else, for there is no other name under heaven given to men by which we must be saved. (Acts 4:12)

For there is one God and one mediator between God and men, the man Christ Jesus. (1 Timothy 2:5)

Sin and Repentance

Do not be deceived: God cannot be mocked. A man reaps what he sows. The one who sows to please his sinful nature, from that nature will reap destruction; the one who sows to please the Spirit, from the Spirit will reap eternal life. (Galatians 6:7–8)

Let us throw off everything that hinders and the sin that so easily entangles, and let us run with perseverance the race marked out for us. Let us fix our eyes on Jesus, the author and perfecter of our faith. (Hebrews 12:1–2)

If we confess our sins, he is faithful and just and will forgive us our sins and purify us from all unrighteousness. (1 John 1:9)

Sons and Daughters of God

The LORD is compassionate and gracious, slow to anger, abounding in love. . . . For as high as the heavens are above the earth, so great is his love for those who fear him; as far as the east is from the west, so far has he removed our transgressions from us. (Psalm 103:8, 11–12)

For I am convinced that neither death nor life, neither angels nor demons, neither the present nor the future, nor any powers, nei-

ther height nor depth, nor anything else in all creation, will be able to separate us from the love of God that is in Christ Jesus our Lord. (Romans 8:38–39)

Therefore, if anyone is in Christ, he is a new creation; the old has gone, the new has come! (2 Corinthians 5:17)

How great is the love the Father has lavished on us, that we should be called children of God! And that is what we are! (1 John 3:1)

Temptation

No temptation has seized you except what is common to man. And God is faithful; he will not let you be tempted beyond what you can bear. But when you are tempted, he will also provide a way out so that you can stand up under it. (1 Corinthians 10:13)

Victory in Jesus

Because he himself suffered when he was tempted, he is able to help those who are being tempted. (Hebrews 2:18)

Be self-controlled and alert. Your enemy the devil prowls around like a roaring lion looking for someone to devour. Resist him, standing firm in the faith. (1 Peter 5:8–9)

The reason the Son of God appeared was to destroy the devil's work. (1 John 3:8)

The one who is in you is greater than the one who is in the world. (1 John 4:4)

Witnessing

Therefore go and make disciples of all nations, baptizing them in the name of the Father and of the Son and of the Holy Spirit,

and teaching them to obey everything I have commanded you. (Matthew 28:19–20)

Go into all the world and preach the good news to all creation. (Mark 16:15)

Always be prepared to give an answer to everyone who asks you to give the reason for the hope that you have. But do this with gentleness and respect. (1 Peter 3:15)

Index

A

Abraham, *297, 298*
Absolute truth, *352*
Accountability, *29*
Action steps, *248,*
262–263
  form, *248, 263*
Actions, *284–285, 343*
Active listening, *351–352*
Activity
  sample, *12–13, 153,*
158–159, 165,
171–172, 181–183,
199–200, 207–211,
220
Adam and Eve, *297, 299,*
330, 332, 360
Adultery, *354*
Adventures in Odyssey,
57, 164, 170, 406–408
Ages 0–4, *107–113,*
277–289
  chart, *113, 273*
  church, *110–111*
  common reflections of
  faith, *111*
  consistency, *109*
  developmental distinc-
  tives, *107–108*
  foundation, *107*
  love, *107*
  memory marker: dedica-
  tion, *112*
  nurture, *107*
  obedience, *110*

physical and mental
  development, *107–108*
prayer, *108, 279*
spiritual development,
  108
Ages 5–6, *115–120,*
291–318
  chart, *120, 274*
  common reflections of
  faith, *118*
  developmental distinc-
  tives, *115–117*
  growing autonomy, *117*
  Jesus, *119*
  memory marker: intro-
  ducing the gospel, *119*
  obedience, *118*
  physical and mental
  development, *115–116*
  prayer, *118*
  relationships, *115,*
117–118
  spiritual development,
  115, 116–117
Ages 7–9, *121–127,*
319–356
  age of reason, *122*
  Bible examples, *124*
  Bible stories, *124*
  chart, *127, 275*
  common reflections of
  faith, *125*
  concerns, *124*
  developmental distinc-
  tives, *121–123*

encouragement,
  123–124
"eraser-age," *121*
growing autonomy, *124*
memory marker: explo-
  ration and expres-
  sions, *125–126*
physical and mental
  development, *121–122*
prayer, *123, 334–335*
questions, *122, 124*
reasons, *122–123*
self-esteem, *122*
spiritual development,
  122–123
trust, *121*
values, *121*
Ages 10–12, *129–134,*
357–384
  Bible reading, *132*
  chart, *134, 276*
  choices, *129, 130,*
131–132, 133
  church, *132*
  common reflections of
  faith, *133*
  developmental distinc-
  tives, *129–131*
  disciplines, *131, 133*
  grow together, *132*
  growing autonomy, *129*
  independence, *129, 130*
  memory marker: com-
  mitment, *133–134*
  physical and mental
  development, *129–130*

Ages 10–12 *(continued)*
prayer, *131, 370–371*
quiet time, *132*
responsibility, *131, 133*
spiritual development,
130–131
taking ownership,
131–132
transition, *131, 135*
Ages and stages, *42,*
101–135
Agnosticism, *358*
Allowance, *317*
Angels, *303, 330*
Anger, *390, 425*
Apologetics, *387–388, 397*
Bible, *324–326, 327–328*
evolution, *358–359, 397*
God, *319–320, 357–359*
Jesus, *364–367, 387*
tools, *401*
Apostle's Creed, *363, 394*
Application, *50, 174*
Approach points
"beavers," *94*
"golden retrievers," *93*
"lions," *91*
"otters," *92*
Archaeology, *325,*
388–389
tools, *401*
Arguments, *425*
Ark, *297*
Artists, *81–82*
Arts Network, *81–82,*
84–85
Atheism, *358*
Athletes, *81*
Athletes in Action, *81*
Attitude, *343, 428*
Audiocassettes
tools, *405–406, 407–408,*
411, 412–413, 414,
418, 421
Autonomy, *117, 124, 129*

B
Balance, *175–176*

Basic Plan, *233, 234,*
237–238, 239, 241,
245, 249, 250,
252–253, 256, 257,
263
Beauty, *320*
"Beavers," *93–94, 239,*
240, 349
Bedtime, *161–166, 241,*
252, 260, 278
Bible, *166*
Bible reading, *162, 164*
Bible stories, *162*
children's needs,
163–164
demonstrating love,
162–163
developing relation-
ships, *162, 163*
individual times, *163*
keys to success, *163–164*
maintaining interest,
163
overcoming obstacles,
164
prayer, *56–57, 162, 164,*
165
relevant, *164*
routine, *161–163, 306*
sample activities, *165*
sample blessing, *12*
time with God, *162*
tools, *164–165*
variety, *163*
Behavior, *284–285*
Being, *284*
Beliefs, *177, 178, 387*
challenged, *357–359*
different, *387*
false/wrong, *330–331,*
357–359
reason for, *319*
Bible, *30, 295–300, 353,*
364–366, 371–373,
388–390, 425
accuracy, *325, 327–328,*
388–389
answers, *361*

archaeology and, *325,*
388–389
attitude toward, *389*
authority, *328*
authors, *325*
autobiography, *222, 296*
believing, *358*
choosing, *166, 280*
chronology, *326–327*
confirmation of, *325,*
388–389
epistles, *361*
extra-biblical sources,
365
foundation, *31*
from God, *280, 325,*
327–328
God's book, *280,*
295–296, 324
God's plan, *222,*
295–296
God's Word, *31, 324,*
328
Gospels, *361*
guide, *30, 310, 318, 353,*
382, 389
handbook, *29–30, 223,*
389
history, *296, 360, 361,*
388–389
history of, *325*
inspired, *388*
interpreting, *369–370*
law, *360, 361*
library, *360–361*
life's instruction manu-
al, *29–30, 223,*
295–296, 309–310,
329, 389
living, *333*
love letter, *222, 295–296*
memorize, *318, 376*
one big story, *297–300,*
326
poetry, *360, 361*
practical, *389–390*
promises, *399*
prophecy, *361, 369–370*
prophets, *361*

protects, *382–383*
reading, *241, 258, 260, 283, 308, 329, 332–333, 371–373, 389*
  fun, *284*
  personal, *296, 308, 333, 371–373*
  plans, *372–373*
  prayer, *284*
  purpose, *283–284*
  regular, *283, 333, 371*
  relevant, *310, 328–329, 388, 389*
  reveals God, *284, 332–333*
  scary stories, *390*
  stories, *81, 124, 252, 280, 283, 326, 333, 390*
  storybook, *241, 280, 283, 296, 308, 333, 390*
  structure, *360–361*
  study, *31, 223, 227–228, 328, 329, 361–363*
  tools, *362–363*
  types, *362*
  teaching children, *30, 308*
  tools, *362–363*
  true, *280, 296, 308, 324, 325, 388–389*
  trustworthy, *324*
  view of God, *358*
Bible atlas, *363*
Bible commentary, *363, 373*
Bible concordance, *362*
Bible dictionary, *362, 373*
Biographies, *82*
Biography Network, *82, 84–85*
Blended families, *37, 43*
Blessing ceremonies, *197–201*
  affirmation, *198*
  commitment, *199*
  elements, *197, 198–199*

  frequency, *200*
  gift, *198*
  keys to success, *200*
  meaningful touch, *198*
  overcoming obstacles, *200–201*
  sample, *165, 199–200*
  tools, *201*
  transition events, *200*
  value, *198*
  words, *198*
Board games, *77, 79, 80, 95, 170, 406, 408*
Boundaries, *20*

C

Career, *378*
"Carriage family," *74, 251*
Character, *178, 343–344, 399–400*
  benefits, *344–345*
  godly, *16, 20, 285, 322–324*
  Jesus', *341, 342*
  matching God's, *343–345*
  modeling, *162*
  protects, *344–345*
  studies, *362*
  traits, *16, 17, 323–324, 344*
Charts/Forms
  Action Steps, *248, 263*
  Ages 0–4, *113, 273*
  Ages 5–6, *120, 274*
  Ages 7–9, *127, 275*
  Ages 10–12, *134, 276*
  Child's Personality Survey, *90*
  Family Activities, *244, 256*
  Family Commitment Card, *262*
  Family Pace, *78*
  Family Portrait Summary, *98–99*
  Family Profile, *243, 255*

  Family Spiritual Growth Plan, *245, 257*
  Individual Spiritual Growth Plan, *246–247, 259, 261*
  Parent's Commitment Card, *53*
  Passions (network), *84–85*
  Personal Strengths, *89, 90, 96*
  Specific Resource Checklist, *264–265*
  Spiritual Growth Plan sample, *243–248, 255–263*
  Spiritual Heritage Plan, *55*
  Spiritual History, *72*
  Spiritual Training Assessment, *105*
  Sunday School Learning Log, *148*
  Sunday School Teacher Interview, *147*
Cheating, *271*
Children
  of God, *432–433*
  tools, *402–408*
Children's strengths, *94*
Child's personality survey, *90*
Choices, *44, 125, 129, 312–313, 330, 342, 368–369, 375–376, 377–379, 380–381, 392–393*
  godly, *380*
  right, *312, 378*
  wrong, *312, 377–378, 381*
Christian
  athletes, *81*
  bubble, *132*
  faith, *387*
  foundation, *108*
  maturity, *70*
  new, *45*
  relationship, *302*

Christian *(continued)*
  teen beliefs
    statistics, *10*
  walk, *390–393*
Christmas (see Holidays)
Church, *25, 28, 48,*
    143–149, 251, 376,
    393–395, 425
  attendance, *21, 57, 143,*
    393–394
  attitude toward, *384,*
    393
  background, *48*
  benefits, *48, 286, 350,*
    393
  body of Christ, *383–384*
  boring, *25, 393*
  community, *48,*
    313–314, 349–350,
    376, 383–384, 395
  differences, *48, 363–364,*
    374–375, 394–395
  enjoyable, *110–111*
  fellowship, *313–314*
  finding/choosing, *48,*
    286, 393–394
  follow-up, *144*
  friends, *143, 313–314,*
    383–384, 394–395
  giving, *316–317*
  God's idea, *286,*
    313–314, 349–350
  involvement, *9, 57, 145,*
    286, 287, 314, 350,
    383–384, 393–394
  keys to success, *144–145*
  parent's ally, *144*
  parent's involvement,
    145
  prayer, *144*
  programs, *143, 144, 384*
  purpose, *286, 350, 394*
  responsibility of, *9*
  sample activities,
    146–148
  Sunday school, *144–148,*
    350, 384
  teaching, *394–395*
  tools, *145*

  worship, *143, 374–375*
Clothing (see also
  Fashion), *396–397*
Commandments (see also
  Ten Commandments)
  learning, *355*
  standard, *355*
Commitment, *133, 234,*
  260, 349
  card, *52–53, 234, 249,*
    260, 262
  level required, *52*
  of children to God, *112*
  to God, *379–380*
  to spiritual parenting,
    112
Compassion, *315, 323,*
  344
Confession, *208*
Conflict, *351–352, 396*
Conflict resolution,
  351–352, 396
Connectedness, *236, 350*
Consistency, *57, 109, 266*
Content
  of training, *269–384*
Contentment, *306, 346,*
  425
Coveting, *354*
Creation, *81, 279,*
  293–294, 319–320,
  358–359, 397
  people, *28, 292, 309*
Creativity, *235*

D

Daniel, *310*
David, *17, 44, 298–299,*
  308, 337, 338, 376,
  388
Dead Sea Scrolls, *327*
Death, *330, 397–398*
Decision-making, *52,*
  380–381, 389,
  390–391, 392–393
Dedication, *112*
Demons (see also Satan),
  330–331, 382–383

Desires, *425*
Development
  physical and mental,
    107–108, 115–117,
    121–123, 129–131
  spiritual, *108, 116, 122,*
    130
Developmental distinc-
  tives
  ages 0–4, *107*
  ages 5–6, *115–117*
  ages 7–9, *121*
  ages 10–12, *129*
Developmentally chal-
  lenged, *105*
Devil (see also Satan),
  331, 341, 382–383
Devotions, *241*
  family, *7, 42, 57, 61,*
    139, 185–188
  traditional, *26, 139–140*
Disabilities (see also
  Learning disabilities)
  developmental, *105*
Discovery Network,
  80–81, 84
Disobedience, *297, 312,*
  329–330, 382–383
Divorce, *395*
Doctrine, *49*
Doubts, *44, 45, 222*
Downs Syndrome, *47*
Drive time, *57, 76,*
  155–160, 240, 252
  Bible, *158*
  fun, *156, 157*
  keys to success, *156–157*
  learning, *156*
  overcoming obstacles,
    157–158
  relevant, *156*
  sample activities/games,
    158–159
  simple, *157*
  tools, *158–160*

E

Earth
  new, *369–370*

Easter (see Holidays)
Easter resurrection eggs, *210–211*
Eden, *297*
Egypt, *298*
Eli, *69*
End times, *370*
Enemies, *41, 329, 382, 426, 433*
Epistles, *361*
Esther, *360*
Eternal life, *18, 355*
Evil, *329, 330, 344*
Evolution, *358–359, 397*
Exodus, *298*
Exploration time, *221–228*
  application, *224*
  Bible, *222–223*
  interesting, *225*
  keys to success, *224–225*
  need for, *222*
  ongoing, *226*
  opportunity, *225*
  overcoming obstacles, *226*
  process, *220–224*
  regular, *223–224*
  relevant, *225*
  rewarding, *224*
  sample study, *227–228*
  teachable, *225*
  tools, *226–227*

F
"F-16 family," *76–77, 238, 251, 254*
Faith, *32, 33, 39, 41, 44, 45, 70, 192, 358, 359*
  emphasis, *395*
  essentials of, *364, 394–395*
  expression, *364, 394–395*
  foundation, *222*
  history of, *67–72, 254*
  real, *122*
  reasonable, *122*
  reasons for, *121, 122*
  sharing (see Share faith and Witnessing)
  tested, *337*
  understanding, *222*
Faith stories, *126, 189–191*
  documenting, *190–191*
  effectiveness, *190*
  journal, *126*
  keys to success, *190–191*
  opportunities, *191*
  overcoming obstacles, *191*
  snapshots, *190, 191*
  strengthen faith, *190*
Faithfulness, *41, 323, 344, 347*
Family (see also Ages and Stages)
  activities, *56, 244*
  blended, *37, 43*
  inventory, *63*
  pace, *73–74, 76–77, 179–180, 251, 254*
  passions, *254*
  personalities, *254*
  profile, *243, 254, 255*
  uniqueness, *62*
Family Commitment Card, *260, 262*
Family devotions, *185–188*
  basic activities, *186–187*
  discussion, *187–188*
  flexible, *141*
  keys to success, *187–188*
  leadership style, *187*
  overcoming obstacles, *188*
  prayer, *186*
  time limit, *187*
  tools, *188*
  traditional, *139–140*
  transition, *187*
  variety, *140*
Family interests, *79–85*
Family meeting, *234, 240, 241, 260–262, 266*
Family missions trip, *57*
Family Night, *8, 26, 39, 56, 177–183, 250, 252, 253*
  flexible, *179*
  frequency, *179*
  fun, *26, 178, 179*
  intentional, *178*
  keys to success, *179*
  leadership style, *179*
  overcoming obstacles, *179–180*
  sample activity, *178, 181–183*
  simple, *179*
  tools, *180, 409–410*
  variety, *179*
Family Pace Sheet, *78*
Family portrait, *65–99*
Family Portrait Summary Sheet, *98–99*
Family profile, *243, 254–255*
Family Spiritual Growth Plan, *234, 236, 237–242, 250, 252–253, 254–257, 266*
  form, *245*
Fashion (see Clothing)
Fear, *12–13, 312, 333, 426*
Feelings, *285, 338, 351, 367, 382, 390*
First Generation Christians, *44, 67–68, 72*
Flood, the, *297*
Focus on the Family, *2, 57*
Follow God, *339, 343, 349–350, 378*
Forgiveness, *44, 208, 281, 301, 302, 304, 312–313, 342, 344, 351, 355, 358, 368, 377, 426*
Forgiving, *323*
Foundation, *49, 107, 108, 122*

Foundation (continued)
  Bible, *31*
  Christian, *108*
  unshakable, *16–17, 22*
Free will, *330*
Friends, *236, 313–314,
    342, 345, 357, 368,
    381, 383–384,
    395–397*
  godly, *395–396*
  impact of, *395–396*
Fruit of the Spirit,
    346–348
Fun, *33, 35, 163, 169, 240*
Fun time, *167–172, 256*
  active, *168*
  children's needs, *168*
  creativity, *169*
  develop relationships,
    168
  events, *168*
  fun, *169*
  games, *168, 169, 170*
  keys to success, *168–169*
  media, *167, 168*
  music, *168*
  overcoming obstacles,
    169–170
  sample activities,
    171–172
  simple, *169*
  spiritual training, *35,
    168, 169*
  spontaneous, *33, 34*
  tools, *170*
  variety, *168*
  videos, *168, 169, 170*

G

Gabriel, *303*
Games, *168, 169, 170,
    253*
Generation, *67–72*
  First, *67–68*
  Second, *68–70*
  Third, *70–71*
Generosity, *344*
  and selflessness, *323*

Gentleness, *347–348, 368*
Getting along (see also
    Relationships), *426*
Gideon, *311*
Giving, *317, 426–427, 428*
Goals, *43, 50*
God, *427*
  all-encompassing, *320,
    322*
  all-knowing, *293, 374*
  all-powerful, *159, 293,
    374*
  awesome, *325*
  be like Him, *285*
  cares, *108, 277–278, 282,
    317, 323, 337, 338*
  character, *121, 277, 294,
    316, 319, 322–324,
    348, 353, 390, 425,
    427*
  coach, *377*
  creator, *279, 293, 316,
    322*
  desire for you, *285,
    341–342, 375–376,
    379–380*
  different from us,
    293–294
  eternal, *320, 321*
  everywhere, *293*
  existence, *10–11, 277,
    278, 359*
  Father, *321*
  forgives, *313*
  gives gifts, *323*
  grace, *40, 52, 376–377,
    400*
  guidance, *18, 307–308,
    313*
  help, *220, 313*
  holy, *324, 344*
  Holy Spirit, *321*
  idea of, *320*
  in His image, *292–293,
    346*
  invisible, *305*
  is love, *45, 323*
  knows best, *337, 338,
    352*

  leading, *427*
  loving Father, *277–278,
    291–292, 309, 332*
  meets needs, *108*
  merciful, *323*
  one, *320, 388*
  plan, *207–208, 296, 300,
    303, 309, 377*
  pleasing, *312, 353*
  power, *293, 294,
    300–301*
  "proofs" for reality of,
    320
  protection, *12–13,
    431–432*
  qualities, *320–322*
  real, *10–11*
  reality, *319, 358*
  relationship, *49, 282,
    291, 305, 340*
  seek Him, *339–340,
    375–376, 381–382*
  Son, *321*
  trinity, *320, 321*
  trust in, *294, 337, 338,
    347, 374*
  trustworthy, *275, 323,
    338, 344*
  understands, *292*
  views of, *49, 357–359*
    biblical, *358*
    false, *357–359*
  wants the best, *286, 313*
  will, *377–379*
    finding, *378–379*
  wisdom, *307–308, 335*
Godly, *427–428*
God's
  children, *297, 299–300,
    432–433*
  kingdom, *299, 300, 334*
  love, *47, 277–278, 286,
    293, 299, 332, 337,
    346, 348, 374, 383,
    390*
  name, *353*
  promises, *340*
  Spirit, *347, 370, 377*

way
  always works best,
    310–311, 344, 352
Gods
  false, *353, 358*
"Golden retrievers,"
  92–93, 238, 239, 349
Goliath, *298, 308*
Goodness, *284–285, 347*
Gospel, the, *302, 369*
Gospels, *278, 327, 361,*
  365
Grace, *52, 95, 347,*
  376–377, 400
Grace parenting, *39–40,*
  103–104, 377, 399
Grandparents, *70*
Grief, *342, 397*
Growth, *45, 109, 334,*
  342–343, 347, 348,
  375–376
  process, *342–343,*
    375–376
Guidance, *307–308,*
  334–335, 382
Guidelines, *19, 338, 391*

H

Hannah, *69, 112*
Healing, *43–44, 299, 341*
Hearts, *285, 311–312,*
  343, 346, 373, 375,
  382
  guarding, *285–286,*
    311–312, 390–391
Heaven, *159, 303, 330,*
  368, 379, 397–398,
  429
  New, *300, 369*
Helping others, *314–315,*
  428
Heritage, *54*
  family, *67*
Heritage Builders, *2–3,*
  12, 56
  tools, *409–411*
  web site, *56, 57*
Heroes, *392*

History, *360, 361*
Holidays, *203–211*
  Christmas, *203, 204–205*
  Christmas origins, *204,*
    205
  church programs, *205*
  Easter, *203, 204–205*
  Easter bunny, *204, 205*
  gifts, *206, 207*
  involvement, *205*
  Jesus, *204*
  keys to success, *205–206*
  leadership style, *205*
  overcoming obstacles,
    206–207
  sample activities,
    207–211
  Santa Claus, *204, 205*
  spiritual training, *203*
  Thanksgiving, *203, 206*
  tools, *207, 211, 411*
  traditions, *204, 206*
  videos, *206*
Holiness, *344*
Holy, *324, 427*
Holy Spirit, *299, 321,*
  333, 346–349, 370,
  376–377, 381–382
  draws people, *119*
  leading, *381–382*
Honesty, *174, 175, 323,*
  337, 339, 344, 429
Honor parents, *354*
Humor, *236*
Hurts, *43–44*
Hypocrisy, *32–33*

I

"I" statements, *352*
Idols, *353*
Image of God, *292, 293,*
  346
Impartial, *323, 344*
Impression points, *11*
Independence, *129, 130*
Individual Spiritual
  Growth Plan, *234,*
  237, 258–260, 266

  form, *246–247, 259, 261*
Individuality (see
  Uniqueness)
Intentional, *3, 12, 16, 28,*
  51–54, 57, 169, 178,
  234, 236, 251
Interests (see Passions)
Internal line, *17–21, 22*
Isaac, *297–298*
Islam, *358*
Israel, *298*
Israelites, *298*

J

Jacob, *298*
Jealousy, *429*
Jesus, *112, 119, 204, 210,*
  300–305, 310–311,
  355, 429
  accepting, *119, 302,*
    368–369
  arrest, *299, 301*
  baptized, *299, 321*
  be like Him, *341–342,*
    375–377, 380–381
  birth, *299*
  character, *341–342*
  cornerstone, *364*
  creator, *294–295*
  death, *119, 207, 281,*
    282, 299, 300–303,
    321–322, 366
  defeated Satan, *330,*
    331–332
  died, *299*
  died for you/your sins,
    281, 299, 300–301,
    331–332, 358
  eternal, *294–295*
  example, *278, 284,*
    310–311, 341
  follow, *339, 343,*
    349–350, 377
  forgives, *299*
  foundation, *17, 364*
  fulfilled prophecy, *367*
  God, *294–295, 320, 358,*
    364–366

Jesus *(continued)*
God and man, *275,
321–322*
God's Son, *273, 281,
295, 299, 300, 321*
head of church, *275,
349–350*
judge, *276, 369*
knows best, *294*
loves, *273, 277*
man, *275, 294–295*
ministry, *299*
modeled God, *300*
paid for our sins, *299,
300–301, 331–332*
peace, *275*
perfect, *301*
perfect model, *284, 341*
Prince of peace, *340*
really lived, *364–366*
resurrection, *299, 301,
366*
return, *274, 301, 303,
369–370, 429*
sacrifice, *301*
saves us, *275, 281, 299,
302, 331, 360, 377, 429*
way to God, *331–332,
358, 368, 388, 432*
Job, *360*
John, *300, 327, 361*
Jonah, *311*
Joseph
Jacob's son, *298, 311,
360*
Jesus' father, *299, 303*
Josephus, *365*
Joshua, *69, 111–112, 360*
Joy, *346*
Judas, *299, 300–301*
Just, *323, 342, 344*

K

Kindness, *284–285, 347*
"Knowing," *49, 113, 221,
222, 223, 259, 273*
Knowledge, *49, 221, 222,
369*

L

Law, *298, 360, 361*
Leader
prayer for, *334*
Learning
exciting, *110*
interest based, *109–110*
ongoing, *46*
styles, *95, 411–413*
together, *46, 68*
Learning disabilities,
47–48
Left-brain, *82*
Life
choices, *44*
classroom, *27, 31, 389*
context of training, *32,
141, 174, 389*
godly, *427–428*
"Lions," *91, 95, 239, 240,
251, 349*
"Living," *50, 113, 174,
273*
Losing your life, *379–380*
Love, *107, 227–228, 344,
346, 367–368,
398–399, 430*
God's, *277, 278*
modeling, *162*
parent's, *278*
"Loving," *50, 113, 214,
273*
Loving
God, *430*
others, *284–285, 430*
"Low-bar," *231–233, 237*
Lucifer, *330*
Lying, *313, 330, 352, 354*

M

Magazines, *170–171, 406,
424*
Mary, *112, 299, 303*
Maturity, *348–349*
Christian, *70*
Mealtime, *149–153, 249*
devotions, *139–140*
effectiveness, *151–152*
keys to success, *151–152*
length, *151–152*
personalize, *151*
prayer, *150*
relevant, *152*
sample activity, *153*
spiritual conversation,
149, 152
timing, *151*
tools, *152*
Meaningful memories,
189–195
Media, *312, 357, 392*
Memorize
Bible, *318, 348*
commandment,
354–355
how to, *318*
meaning, *318*
understand, *318*
Memory Marker, *111,
192–195, 260, 267*
commitment ceremony,
133–134
dedication, *112, 193*
exploration and expres-
sion, *125–126*
faith journal, *126, 194*
Joshua, *111–112, 192*
keys to success, *194*
overcoming obstacles,
194
salvation, *119, 302–303*
snapshot, *192*
spiritual training,
192–193
tools, *194–195*
Memory verses, *105, 274,
318, 425–433*
Mentoring, *42, 70*
Mercy, *323, 344*
Messiah, *297, 299,
366–367*
Methods, *139–228, 254*
match child, *34–35,
94–95*
match family, *235, 254*
Missions, *57, 317*

Mistakes, *312–313, 342–343, 376, 377, 400*

Model
God, *108–109*
relationship, *109*

Modeling, *68, 109, 162, 174–175, 215, 285, 287, 304, 307, 313, 340, 377, 383, 400*
prayer, *282, 313*

Monotheism, *357–358*

Morality
tools, *413–414*

Moses, *22, 69, 111, 192, 298, 325, 360*

Movies/videos (see also Videos), *19, 56, 79, 311–312, 379, 381, 390–391*
Christian, *110, 404–405, 407*

Murder, *354*

Music tapes
Christian, *105, 110, 411*

N

Nazareth, *299*

Needs, *163*
met, *108*

Network, *80–83*
arts, *81–82, 84–85*
biography, *82, 85*
discovery, *80–81, 84*
sports, *81, 84*

New Testament
contents, *360–361*

Nightmares, *312*

Noah, *297, 360*

Nurture, *107*

O

Obedience, *41, 110, 287, 316, 353, 377–379, 430*
benefits of, *310*
reasons for, *110, 118, 288, 310–311*

Old Testament
contents, *360–361*

One Big Story, *297–300, 326*

Order, *320, 426*

"Otters," *92, 239, 240, 349*

Ownership
of toys, *288–289*
of faith, *343, 371, 383–384*

P

Pace, *73–78*
assessment, *77*
"carriage," *73–75, 78*
"F-16," *73, 76–77, 179, 238, 251*
family, *73, 74, 77*
family sheet, *78*
of learning, *104, 272*
"steam engine," *73, 75–76, 249*

Pain, *330, 342*

Pantheism, *358*

Parenting, *398–400*
by example, *32, 33, 400*
commitment card, *53*
fellow learners, *33, 45*
imperfections, *32*
inadequacy, *37, 39–40, 44–45*
process, *123*
responsibility, *399*
spiritual trainers, *9–13, 21, 123*
tools, *414–418*
with Spirit, *236*

Parent's
commitment card, *53*
responsibility, *10, 399*

Parents
honor, *354*

Passion
assessment, *83–85*
(networks) chart, *84–85*

Passions (see also Network), *79–85*

family, *79*
understand, *79–80*

Passover, *298*

Patience, *105, 145, 337, 339, 347, 379–380*

Paul, *21, 22, 34, 222, 299–300, 310, 361, 376*

Peace, *306, 340, 346–347*

Perseverance, *20, 50*

Persistence (see Perseverance)

Personal Strengths Chart, *96*

Personal Strengths Survey, *87–90*

Personality, *87–96, 258, 275, 343–344, 348–349, 378, 399–400*
"beavers," *93–94, 95, 251, 349*
developing your, *348–349*
"golden retrievers," *92–93, 95, 238, 249, 349*
"lions," *91, 93, 95, 251, 349*
"otters," *92, 95, 249, 251, 349*
strengths, *87, 94–95*
tools, *411–413*
types, *95*

Petition, *334*

Pharaoh, *298, 311*

Philistines, *298*

Photo album, *108, 303*

Pictures/snapshots, *13, 15, 40, 43, 46, 108, 123, 131, 139, 140, 141, 190, 303*

Plagues, *298, 311*

Plan (see also God)
for individual, *309, 338, 369, 377–378, 380*

Plautus, *38*

Poetry, *360, 361*

Polytheism, *358*

Power, *431*
Praise, *335, 338, 373–375*
Prayer, *241, 252, 258, 276, 279, 300, 337, 350, 356, 370, 371, 431*
  analogies of, *335–336*
  answers, *22, 123, 283, 293–294, 306–307, 336, 337, 339, 383*
  bedtime, *56–57, 306*
  benefits, *275, 335–336*
  consistent, *108, 370*
  family life, *56*
  forgiveness, *313*
  from heart, *335*
  fun, *282–283*
  how to, *282–283, 334–335*
  in Jesus' name, *282*
  mealtime, *57, 150–151*
  modeling, *282–283*
  normal, *283*
  ownership, *283, 305–306, 334*
  persistence, *337*
  personal, *118, 305, 370–371*
  priority, *55*
  quiet, *335, 371*
  regular, *282, 340, 348, 370*
  relationship, *282*
  relevant, *34, 283, 306*
  respect, *306*
  sample, *12–13, 283*
  talking to God, *282, 305*
  teaching, *55*
  topics, *283, 294, 334, 335*
  transition, *286, 305, 306, 335*
  trust, *294*
  types, *305, 334–335, 336*
  variety, *153, 306*
Pretend, *312*
Promised Land, *69, 298*
Prophecy, *361, 369–370*
  fulfilled, *366–367*

interpreting, *369–370*
Prophets
  major, *361*
  minor, *361*
Protection
  God's, *12–13, 431–432*

Q

Quiet time, *213–220, 252*
  application, *217*
  Bible, *214, 218*
  consistent, *217*
  demonstrate, *215, 216*
  growth, *214–216*
  habit, *214*
  keys to success, *215–217*
  openness, *216*
  overcoming obstacles, *217–219*
  ownership, *216*
  prayer, *214*
  regular, *215*
  relational, *123*
  relationship, *214*
  sample, *220*
  schedule, *215*
  tools, *219*
  transition, *217–218*

R

Realistic, *234*
Relationships, *115, 275, 289, 304–306, 346, 351–352, 395–397, 398–400, 426*
  and church, *350–351*
  blessing of, *251–252*
  developing, *115, 117, 305, 315*
  importance of, *116*
  learning about, *116, 117*
  ownership of, *333*
  parent/child, *26, 27–28, 33–34, 398–400*
  trust in, *315*
  with God, *49, 115, 117, 133, 272, 282, 299, 355*

with parent, *282, 398–400*
Religions
  other, *330–331*
Repentance, *312–313, 432*
Respect, *314–315, 348, 356, 368*
Reward, *17, 20*
Right and wrong, *10, 18, 21, 124, 275, 285, 312, 320, 347, 352–354, 380–381, 393–394*
  consequences, *352*
Right-brain, *82*
Righteousness, *19, 20*
Ruler, *353*
Rules, *353*
  reason for, *353*

S

Sabbath, *354*
Safe, *13, 108, 352, 380*
Salvation, *119, 207–208, 281, 299, 300–303, 360, 432*
  a beginning, *304, 360*
  age at, *302*
  "beavers," *94*
  "golden retrievers," *93*
  "lions," *91*
  "otters," *92*
  prayer, *45, 301–302*
Samuel, *69, 112*
Santa Claus, *204, 205*
Sarah, *297*
Satan, *45, 275, 276, 297, 299, 329–331, 341, 382–383*
  blinds, *329*
  created, *330*
  deceives, *383*
  defeated, *329, 330, 331, 382–383, 433*
  liar, *330, 383*
  resisting, *382–383*
Saul, *298, 311*
Savior, *297, 299, 360, 377*

School, *395–397*
Science, *79, 80, 397*
Second Generation
    Christians, *68–70*
Seek
    God, *339–340, 375–376*
    truth, *383*
Self-control, *348*
Selfishness, *289*
Selflessness, *323, 342,*
    344, 347
Separation from God, *297*
Serve God, *363–364*
    variety of ways to, *363*
Service, *342, 375, 428*
Share faith (see also
    Witnessing), *275,*
    276, 355–356,
    367–369, 387, 433
Sharing, *273, 288–289,*
    316–317, 426–427
Sheltering, *398–399,*
    431–432
Sickness, *330, 398*
Sin, *30, 81, 208–209,*
    275, 281, 297, 299,
    302, 312–313,
    329–331, 332, 342,
    358, 377, 390, 396,
    432
    payment for, *299, 301,*
        302, 332
    results of, *297, 302,*
        329, 330, 332
Single parents, *40–41,*
    164, 249–250
Situational ethics, *20*
Skepticism, *319*
Snapshots/pictures, *13,*
    15, 40, 43, 46, 117,
    123, 131, 139, 140,
    190, 303
Songs, *33, 105*
Specific Resource
    Checklist, *264–265*
Speech, *178, 428*
Spirit (see Holy Spirit)
Spiritual Background
    Sheet, *71–72*

Spiritual development, *51*
Spiritual growth, *9,*
    342–343, 375–376
    benefits, *376*
    responsibility, *266*
Spiritual Growth Plan,
    13, 43, 50, 63, 68, 70,
    74, 77, 79, 83, 97, 144,
    231–267
    action steps, *262–263*
    basic plan, *233, 234,*
        237–238, 239, 241,
        249, 250, 252–253
    commitment, *234*
    connected, *236–237*
    creative, *235–236*
    family, *234, 236, 237,*
        241, 242, 252, 253,
        254–257, 262, 266
    family meeting, *234,*
        241, 260, 263, 266
    forms, *255–257, 259,*
        261
    sample, *243–248*
    gather information, *253*
    individual, *237, 240,*
        241, 252, 258–260,
        262, 266
    "low–bar," *231–233,*
        237, 258
    realistic, *234*
    reminders, *234–237*
    samples, *237–253*
    seven steps, *233, 237,*
        253–267
    share it, *237*
    specific, *234–235*
    support plan, *233, 235,*
        238, 240, 242, 250,
        253, 256
Spiritual heritage, *54*
Spiritual Heritage Plan,
    55
Spiritual legacy, *28, 62,*
    63, 272
Spiritual training, *9,*
    21–22, 23–24, 38–39,
    50, 73, 74, 75, 77,
    399–400

appropriate methods,
    34, 141
"beavers," *95*
benefits, *18*
boredom, *7, 8*
church's role, *9*
commitment to, *52, 234*
content, *269–384*
core of being and life,
    21–22
creative, *235–236*
development, *108*
effective, *74, 87*
examples, *10–13*
expectations, *232*
failure, *28, 232*
flexible, *141*
foundation, *21, 49*
fun, *8, 35, 251*
"golden retrievers,"
    92–93
growth, *108*
growth together, *45, 46*
importance, *52*
intentional, *12, 16, 26,*
    28, 169, 234, 236
"lions," *91, 95*
match family/individ-
    ual, *141*
obstacles, *41*
"otters," *92*
pace, *272*
parent's fears, *7, 10*
parent's role, *8, 10*
persistence, *50*
practical, *22*
preparation for life, *21,*
    24
process, *52*
realistic, *234*
relevant, *109–110*
responsibility, *377*
schedule, *139*
time, *38–39*
tools, *419–421*
truth, *69*
variety, *140*
Spiritual Training
    Assessment, *105*

"Spiritually single," *41*
Sports, *81*
Sports Network, *81, 84*
Standards, *17–20, 312,
    355*
Statistics
    Christian teen beliefs, *10*
Stealing, *271, 342, 354*
"Steam engine family,"
    75, 249
Stewardship, *274,
    316–317*
    tools, *408*
Strengths, *399–400*
Success, *378–379*
Suffering, *330*
Sunday school, *21, 27,
    105, 143, 144, 236,
    314, 384*
    follow–up, *144*
    helps, *146–148*
    interview form, *147*
    involvement, *145*
    learning log, *146, 148*
    memory verses, *144,
        425–433*
    prayer, *144*
    thankfulness, *145*
Support, *236, 251, 258*
    plan, *233, 235, 238, 242,
        245, 250, 253, 256,
        257, 263*
Swearing, *353*
Sword drill, *326*

T

Talents, *232, 236,
    345–346, 377–378,
    384*
    developing, *345–346*
Teachable moments,
    173–176, 236, 389
    God's help, *174*
    keys to success, *175*
    modeling, *174–175*
    overcoming obstacles,
        175–176
    proactive, *175*

recognize moments,
    174, 236
short and simple, *175*
spiritual training, *173*
tools, *176*
Teenagers, *42–43, 133,
    135*
    tools, *421–424*
Television, *20, 50, 80,
    215, 311–312, 355,
    390–391*
Temptation, *348,
    382–383, 433*
Ten Commandments, *21,
    150, 275, 287, 298,
    353–355*
Tests, *337*
Thankfulness, *306–307,
    334, 346, 371, 374*
    modeling, *307*
Thanksgiving (see
    Holidays)
Theology, *46*
Third Generation
    Christians, *70–71*
Thoughts, *285, 382*
Time, *38*
    optimize, *39*
Tools, *77, 94–95, 141,
    145, 152, 157,
    158–160, 164–165,
    170, 176, 180, 188,
    194–195, 201, 207,
    211, 218, 219,
    226–227, 235,
    264–265, 401–424*
Topical index, *362*
Topical studies, *362*
Touch, *285, 315*
Training (see also
    Spiritual Training), *9,
    22, 23–24*
    in life, *31*
    match child, *124*
    relevant, *109–110*
    with God, *104*
Trials, *220, 337*
Trust, *40, 121, 288,
    338–339, 345, 346,*

347, 374, 381
God (see also God,
    trust), *347, 369,
    379–380, 382,
    398–399*
Trustworthiness, *323, 344*
Truth, *280, 344, 352, 365,
    381, 388*
    about God, *357–359*
    absolute, *388*

U

Uniqueness, *62, 87–88,
    348, 399–400*
    family, *62, 87*
    individual, *62, 87–88,
        259, 304, 343*
Universalism, *358*
Unselfish, *289, 346*

V

Vacation Bible School
    (VBS), *105, 143, 144*
Values, *28, 121, 130, 177,
    178*
    tools, *413–414*
Variety, *163, 168*
Video games, *80, 390–391*
Videos/movies (see also
    Movies/videos), *56,
    79, 206, 235, 240, 253,
    301, 359, 389,
    390–392*
    Christian, *105, 404–405,
        407*
    tools, *404–405, 407*
Violence, *396*

W

Web sites, *235, 390–391*
Win/win solution, *352*
Wisdom, *40, 43, 307–308,
    335, 375, 382*
Witnessing (see also Share
    faith), *355–356,
    367–369, 433*
Word studies, *362*

Worry, *165, 426*
Worship, *143, 276, 349,*
364, 373–375
  forms, *364*
  "loop," *374*
  variety, *374*

Scripture Index

Genesis
1:1, *277, 279, 318, 357, 427*
1:2–31, *279*
1:26–27, *292*
49:10, *367*

Exodus
14:1–15:20, *220*
14:9–31, *220*
20:1–17, *353*
20:12, *183, 287, 430*
20:15, *429*
20:17, *429*
31, 35–37, *82*
35:25–26, 30–36:1 *345*

Leviticus
19:11, *429*
20:26, *324, 427*

Deuteronomy
4:9, *8*
5:6–21, *353*
6:1–2, *333*
6:4, *427*
6:4–9, *69*
6:5–7, 9–10, *22*
6:6–7, *53*
6:6–9, 32, *174*
6:7, *155*
6:20–24, *190*
7:9, *323, 347*
11:19, *8*
12:28, *353*
30:19, *44*
31:24, *325*
32:4, *323, 427*

Joshua
1:8, *371, 430*
4:20–24, *111, 192*

Judges
2:10, *69*

1 Samuel
1, *112*
1:1–2:11, 18–26, *69*
2:12, 22–25, *69*
2–3, *69*
3:1–21, *69*

2 Samuel
12:23b, *48*

Psalms
2:7, *367*
4:8, *426*
8:2, *119*
10:17, *335*
14:1, *357*
15, 16–17, *344*
16:10, *367*
16:11, *11*
22:1, 6–18, *367*
22:1–2, *44*
22:3–4, *44*
22:4, *335*
22:16, *367*
23:1–6, *431*
23:4a, *13*
24:1, *317*
25:4–5, *376*
31:5, *323*
33:4, *280*
34:17, *431*

34:20, *367*
37:4, *335, 425*
37:4–5, *378*
37:31, *430*
41:9, *367*
42:1–2, *339, 376*
55:22, *426*
57:2, *335*
69:21, *367*
78:4–8, *53*
91:14, *220*
103, *294*
103:8, 11–12, *432*
104:4, *303*
119:10–11, *333*
119:11, *430*
119:97–100, *328*
119:97–105, *308*
119:105, *296, 318, 371*
119:130–131, *284*
119:160, *280*
138:3, *335*
138:8, *378*
139, *28*
139:13–16, *47, 279, 309*
147:5, *293, 427*
148, *11*

Proverbs
1:8, *430*
2:3–5, *307*
2:3, 5–6, *335*
3:5, *318*
3:5–6, *338, 427*
12:18, *351*
15:1, *396*
15:1–2, *351*

17:17, *318*
17:27, *351*
20:3, *351*
21:23, *351*
22:6, *9, 15, 345, 380*
22:29, *345*
25:28, *348*
29:8, *351*
29:22, *425*
30:4, *367*

Ecclesiastes
3:1, *7, 428*

Isaiah
7:14, *367*
14:12–15, *329*
26:3, *340, 347*
35:10, *303*
40:12–14, *325*
40:25, 28–29, *325*
43:10, *320, 388*
44:6, *320, 388, 427*
46:9, *388*
50:6, *367*
55:9, *427*

Jeremiah
23:24, *293, 427*
29:11, *353*
29:12–13, *431*
31:33, *355*
32:17, *293, 427*
33:3, *335, 431*

Daniel
1:17, 20, *345*
6, *310*
9:9, *323*
7–12, *370*

Micah
5:2, *367*

Nahum
1:7, *347*

Zechariah
12:10, *367*

Malachi
3:6, *427*
3:10, *323*

Matthew
1:2, *367*
1:18–25, *367*
2:1, *367*
3:16–17, *321*
3:17, *367*
4:1–11, *341*
4:4, *425*
5:3–10, *428*
5:9, *351*
5:21–48, *342*
5:41, *428*
5:42, *426*
5:44–45, *426*
6:6, *305*
6:9–13, *334, 431*
6:14–15, *351, 426*
6:26, *425*
6:26, 28, 30, *278*
6:28–30, *165*
6:33, *339, 430*
7:1–2, *428*
7:7–8, *431*
7:12, *351*
7:24–25, *430*
9:36, *341*
10:30, *293*
10:39, *379*
11:20–24, *342*
11:28–30, *431*
11:29, *348*
12:36, *392, 428*
16:25, *379*
18:21–35, *310*
19:14, *119*
19:26, *293, 427*
21:16, *119*
22:37–39, *354, 430*
22:39, *389*
22:40, *360*
23:23, *344*
24:1–5, *369*
24:35, *425*
25:14–30, *232*
26:14–15, *210*
26:26–28, *210*
26:67, *367*
27:26, 30, *367*
27:34–50, *367*

27:37, *211*
28:19–20, *355, 367–368, 433*

Mark
1:40–44, *341*
8:34–35, *338*
8:35, *379*
10:14, 16, *34*
10:16, *34–35, 198*
12:31, *351*
15:15, *210*
15:17, *210*
16:15, *433*

Luke
1:26–35, *367*
1:32, *367*
2:4–6, *367*
2:21–38, *112*
3:11, *289*
3:33–34, *367*
6:31, *318, 430*
6:35–36, *347*
6:45, *285, 312*
9:24, *379*
11:2–4, *334*
12:1b–3, *32*
12:15, *426*
14:28–29, *51*
15:10, *303*
16:31, *360*
17:33, *379*
22:25–27, *341*
22:56–62, *342*
23:39–43, *398*
24:1–12, *367*
24:2, *211*
24:6, *211*
24:44, *360*

John
1:1–3, *295, 429*
1:14, *295*
3:3, *432*
3:16, *45, 208, 227, 281, 302, 303, 318, 432*
4:24, *374, 427*
5:22, *321*
5:37, *321*

S C R I P T U R E I N D E X

John *(continued)*
5:39, *280, 308*
5:39–40, *328*
8:12, *429*
10:9, *429*
10:10, *11, 141*
10:11, *429*
11:1–12:19, *292*
11:1–44, *342*
12:25, *379*
13:1–17, *342*
13:15, *341*
13:18, 21, 26–27, *367*
13:35, *430*
14:2–3, *303, 429*
14:6, *368, 388, 432*
14:6–7, *304*
14:14, *220*
14:15, *430*
14:16–17, 26, *321*
14:17, *294*
14:23, *304*
14:23–24, *316*
14:26, *381*
14:27, *340*
15:5, *429*
15:12, *284*
15:17, *344*
16:24, *335*
16:33, *311*
19:17, *211*
19:28–30, *367*
19:29–30, *211*
19:31–37, *367*
19:34, *211*
19:34, 36, *367*
20:25, *211*
21:15–19, *342*
21:24–25, *364*

Acts
2:22, *364*
2:24, 32, 36, *365*
2:42, 44, 46, *383*
4:12, *432*
13:35–37, *367*
17:11, *362*
17:16–34, *388*
17:28, *322*

20:35, *426*

Romans
1:19–20, *319*
1:20, *277, 427*
3:21–26, *302*
3:23, *208, 281, 302, 432*
3:23–26, *331*
5:3–5, *337*
5:8, *321*
6:23, *208, 281, 302, 358, 432*
8:8–9, *348*
8:19–22, *329*
8:26–27, *334*
8:28, *380*
8:31, *294*
8:32, *335, 431*
8:34, *321*
8:38–39, *433*
10:9–10, *45, 302, 432*
10:17, *49*
12:1, *344, 374*
12:1–2, *375*
12:3, *348*
12:17, *396*
14:17, *346*

1 Corinthians
1:30, *381*
2:9, *303, 429*
3:10–11, *17*
4:7, *317*
8:6, *321*
9:20–22, *34*
9:24–27, *376*
10:1–2, *220*
10:13, *377, 433*
12:4, *321*
12:5, *153*
12:27, *425*
13:4–8, *430*
14:33, *426*
14:40, *426*
15:3–5, *429*
15:10, *377*
15:33, *314*

2 Corinthians
4:4, *329*

5:17, *433*
9:7, *427*
12:9, *40*
12:10, *40*

Galatians
5:14, *430*
5:22–23, *318, 344, 346, 399, 428*
6:7–8, *432*
6:10, *347, 428*

Ephesians
1:22–23, *350*
2:4–5, *346*
2:8–9, *432*
2:10, *309*
2:14, *347*
2:19–22, *350*
4:2, *318, 347*
4:3–6, *364*
4:15, *344*
4:25, *429*
4:26–27, *382*
4:29, *428*
4:32, *426*
5:1–2, *428*
6:1, *430*
6:1–3, *287, 310, 311*
6:4, *21, 22*
6:14–17, *431*

Philippians
1:6, *41, 377*
2:3–4, *426*
2:6–7, *322*
2:12–13, *342, 376*
2:13, *399*
2:14–15, *428*
3:7–11, 13–14, *376*
4:5, *348*
4:6, *306, 318, 431*
4:6–7, *282, 335*
4:7, *426*
4:8, *312, 391, 428*
4:12, *306, 425*
4:13, *39, 431*

Colossians
2:13–14, *208*
2:13–15, *302*

3:1–4, 5–17, *376*
3:12, *344, 347*
3:12, 14, 17, *348*
3:13, *344, 351*
3:20, *287*

1 Thessalonians
2:13, *280*
4:11, *428*
4:13–5:11, *369*
4:16–17, *429*
4:16–18, *369*
5:1–2, *369*
5:13, *426*
5:16, *346*
5:16–18, *425*
5:17, *282*
5:17–18, *370*
5:23–24, *355*

2 Thessalonians
1:6, *358*
2:13, *321*

1 Timothy
2:5, *432*
6:3–4, *425*
6:15–16, *427*
6:18, *289, 344*
6:19, *17*

2 Timothy
1:7, *318*
2:15, *222, 376*
2:23, *425*
3:15, *284*
3:16, *30, 280, 324, 425*
3:16–17, *296, 310*

Titus
3:1–2, *426*

Hebrews
1:1–2, *326*
1:3, *344*
1:11, *321*
1:14, *303*
1:30, *321*
2:10, *322*
2:14, *292*
2:18, *292, 433*
4:15, *429*

6:1, *376*
9:22, *302*
9:23–28, *302*
10:24–25, *314, 384*
10:25, *425*
11:1, 6, *357*
12:1, *209, 376*
12:1–2, *432*
12:3, *347*
12:5–6, *426*
12:11, *426*
13:8, *429*
13:17, *430*
13:21, *399*

James
1:5, *40, 307, 379, 427*
1:17, *291*
1:19, *425*
1:22, *430*
1:23–25, *318*
3:3–13, *351*
3:15–17, *307*
4:7, *382*
4:7–8, *329, 432*
4:17, *428*
5:13–16, *371*

1 Peter
1:7, *337*
1:8, *346*
1:10–12, *326*
3:15, *355, 368, 433*
4:8, *430*
4:14, *426*
5:7, *305, 426*
5:8, *383*
5:8–9, *433*

2 Peter
1:3, 5–8, *342–343*
1:5, *49*
1:16, *327, 364*
1:20–21, *324*

1 John
1:9, *209, 432*
2:6, *428*
2:9–10, *428*
3:1, *291, 433*
3:8, *433*

3:18, *430*
3:21–22, *316*
3:23, *315, 430*
4:4, *433*
4:8, *323, 358*
4:16, *346, 427*
4:19, *277, 346, 430*
4:20, *315*

Jude
9, *383*

Revelation
1:8, *321, 427*
1:17–18, *429*
4:11, *427*
21:3–4, *303*

Welcome to the Family!

We hope you've enjoyed this book. Heritage Builders was founded in 1995 by three fathers with a passion for the next generation. As a new ministry of Focus on the Family, Heritage Builders strives to equip, train, and motivate parents to become intentional about building a strong spiritual heritage.

It's quite a challenge for busy parents to find ways to build a spiritual foundation for their families—especially in a way they enjoy and understand. Through activities and participation, children can learn biblical truth in a way they can understand, enjoy—and *remember.*

Passing along a heritage of Christian faith to your family is a parent's highest calling. Heritage Builders' goal is to encourage and empower you in this great mission with practical resources and inspiring ideas that really work— and help your children develop a lasting love for God.

***

How To Reach Us

For more information, visit our Heritage Builders Web site! Log on to **www.heritagebuilders.com** to discover new resources, sample activities, and ideas to help you pass on a spiritual heritage. To request any of these resources, simply call Focus on the Family at 1-800-A-FAMILY (1-800-232-6459) or in Canada, call 1-800-661-9800. Or send your request to Focus on the Family, Colorado Springs, CO 80995. In Canada, write Focus on the Family, P.O. Box 9800, Stn. Terminal, Vancouver, B.C. V6B 4G3

To learn more about Focus on the Family or to find out if there is an associate office in your country, please visit www. family.org

We'd love to hear from you!

Try These Heritage Builders Resources!

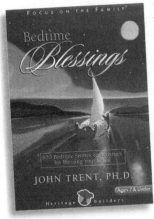

Bedtime Blessings

Strengthen the precious bond between you, your child, and God by making **Bedtime Blessings** a special part of your evenings together. From best-selling author John Trent, Ph.D., and Heritage Builders, this book is filled with stories, activities, and blessing prayers to help you practice the biblical model of "blessing." Designed for use with children ages 7 and under, *Bedtime Blessings* will help affirm the great love and value you and God have for your child, and will help each of your evenings together be filled with cherished moments in loving company.

My Time With God

Send your child on an amazing adventure—a self-guided tour through God's Word! **My Time With God** shows your 8 to 12-year-old how to get to know God regularly in exciting ways. Through 150 days' worth of fun facts and mind-boggling trivia, prayer starters, and interesting questions, your child will discover how awesome God really is!

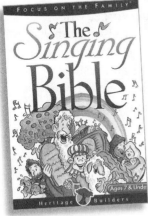

The Singing Bible

Children ages 2 to 7 will love **The Singing Bible**, which sets the Bible to music with over 50 original, sing-along songs! New from Heritage Builders, *The Singing Bible* walks your child through the Old and New Testament Scripture. Introduce Adam and Eve in the Garden, the Ten Commandments, Jonah and the Whale, the Lord's Prayer, and many other biblical characters and facts in this four-cassette collection of songs that will have kids singing along! Memorable lyrics, tongue twisters, and an energetic narrator to guide them makes understanding the Bible an exciting journey. Fun and fast-paced, *The Singing Bible* is perfect for listening and learning!

Heritage
Builders

Helping You Build a Family of Faith

Mealtime Moments

Make your family's time around the dinner table meaningful with *Mealtime Moments*, a book that brings you great discussion starters and activities for teaching your children about your faith. Kids will have fun getting involved with games, trivia questions, and theme nights, all based on spiritually sound ideas. Perfect for the whole family!

Joy Ride!

When you think of all the time kids spend in the car, it makes sense to use the time to teach lasting spiritual lessons along the way. *Joy Ride!* is a fun and challenging activity book that helps parents blend biblical principles into everyday life. Games, puzzles, Bible-quiz questions, and discussion starters give parents fun ways to get the whole family involved in talking and thinking about their faith. Make the most of your time together on the road with this fun, inspiring guide. Small enough to fit into a glove compartment, it's great for vacations *and* local trips!

An Introduction to Family Nights

Make devotions something your children will *never* forget when you involve them in "family nights"—an ideal way to bring fun and spiritual growth together on a weekly basis. *An Introduction to Family Nights* delivers 12 weeks' worth of tried-and-tested ideas, object lessons, and activities for helping kids learn how to tame the tongue, resist temptation, be obedient, and much more!

Heritage Builders™

Helping You Build a Family of Faith

Every family has a heritage—a spiritual, emotional, and social legacy passed from one generation to the next. There are four main areas we at Heritage Builders recommend parents consider as they plan to pass their faith to their children:

Family Fragrance

Every family's home has a fragrance. Heritage Builders encourages parents to create a home environment that fosters a sweet, Christ-centered AROMA of love through Affection, Respect, Order, Merriment, and Affirmation.

Family Traditions

Whether you pass down stories, beliefs, and/or customs, traditions can help you establish a special identity for your family. Heritage Builders encourages parents to set special "milestones" for their children to help guide them and move them through their spiritual development.

Family Compass

Parents have the unique task of setting standards for normal, healthy living through their attitudes, actions, and beliefs. Heritage Builders encourages parents to give their children the moral navigation tools they need to succeed on the roads of life.

Family Moments

Creating special, teachable moments with their children is one of a parent's most precious and sometimes, most difficult responsibilities. Heritage Builders encourages parents to capture little moments throughout the day to teach and impress values, beliefs, and biblical principles onto their children.

We look forward to standing alongside you as you seek to impart the Lord's care and wisdom onto the next generation—onto your children.

Heritage Builders™

Helping You Build a Family of Faith

General Editors

John Trent, Ph.D.

Dr. Trent is President of Encouraging Words; a ministry committed to strengthening marriage and family relationships worldwide. Over the past five years, John has spoken to more than 400,000 people at his seminars and special events.

He has authored and co-authored more than a dozen award winning and best-selling books including *The Blessing, The Gift of Honor, The Language of Love, Love is a Decision, The Two Sides of Love, LifeMapping, Love for All Seasons, Choosing to Live the Blessing, The Treasure Tree, The Two Trails, "I'd Choose You!"* and *The Black and White Rainbow.* There are more than 2,100,000 copies of his books in print, in nine different languages!

John received a Master's Degree in New Testament Greek from Dallas Theological Seminary, and his Doctoral Degree in Marriage and Family Counseling. For ten years he worked with Gary Smalley in ministering to couples and families. When Gary moved to Branson, Missouri, in 1994, John started Encouraging Words and teaches relationship seminars across the country. John and his wife, Cindy, have been married for twenty years, and have two precious daughters, Kari and Laura.

Visit Encouraging Words' Internet site at www.encouragingwords.com

Rick Osborne

Rick Osborne, author and speaker, encourages and teaches parents to pass on their Christian faith to their children. He is the author of the award-winning books *Teaching Your Child How to Pray* and *Talking to Your Children About God.* He co-wrote the books *Financial Parenting* and *Your Child Wonderfully Made* with Larry Burkett. He also co-authored the best-selling *101 Questions Children Ask* series and the *Learning for Life* books.

For the past 15 years, Rick and his wife Elaine have been producing high quality books, music, and games that help parents teach their children about God and the Bible. Among the more than 50 books and resources that they have developed are *Proverbs for Kids from The Book, The Singing Bible, The Kids Quest Study Bible,* the *I Want to Know* series, *Kidcordance, JoyRide!, Mealtime Moments,* and *My Time With God.*

Rick lives with his family in British Columbia, Canada.

Visit Lightwave's Internet site at www.lightwavepublishing.com.

Kurt Bruner, M.A.

Kurt Bruner, a graduate of Talbot School of Theology, serves as Vice President of the Focus on the Family Resource Group. He directs the creation of film, book, magazine, and radio drama resources—including the popular *Adventures in Odyssey* program. Kurt and his wife, Olivia, have been married since 1985 and have three sons—Kyle, Shaun, and Troy. In 1996, Kurt co-founded the Heritage Builders Association, a network of parents and churches committed to passing on a strong spiritual heritage to the next generation. The author of several books, Kurt co-wrote *Your Heritage, The Family Compass,* and the best selling *Family Nights Tool Chest* series.

Visit Heritage Builders' Internet site at www.heritagebuilders.com